Agile Development in the Real World

Alan Cline

Apress®

Agile Development in the Real World

ISBN-13 (pbk): 978-1-4842-1678-1

ISBN-13 (electronic): 978-1-4842-1679-8

Managing Director: Welmoed Spahr
Lead Editor: James DeWolf
Development Editor: Douglas Pundick
Technical Reviewers: Harlan Bridges and Terry Wiegmann
Editorial Board: Steve Anglin, Pramila Balin, Louise Corrigan, James DeWolf, Jonathan Gennick, Robert Hutchinson, Celestin Suresh John, Michelle Lowman, James Markham, Susan McDermott, Matthew Moodie, Jeffrey Pepper, Douglas Pundick, Ben Renow-Clarke, Gwenan Spearing
Coordinating Editor: Melissa Maldonado
Copy Editor: Mary Behr and Kim Burton
Compositor: SPi Global
Indexer: SPi Global
Artist: SPi Global

Distributed to the book trade worldwide by Springer Science+Business Media New York, 233 Spring Street, 6th Floor, New York, NY 10013. Phone 1-800-SPRINGER, fax (201) 348-4505, e-mail orders-ny@springer-sbm.com, or visit www.springer.com. Apress Media, LLC is a California LLC and the sole member (owner) is Springer Science + Business Media Finance Inc (SSBM Finance Inc). SSBM Finance Inc is a Delaware corporation.

For information on translations, please e-mail rights@apress.com, or visit www.apress.com.

Apress and friends of ED books may be purchased in bulk for academic, corporate, or promotional use. eBook versions and licenses are also available for most titles. For more information, reference our Special Bulk Sales–eBook Licensing web page at www.apress.com/bulk-sales.

Any source code or other supplementary material referenced by the author in this text is available to readers at www.apress.com. For detailed information about how to locate your book's source code, go to www.apress.com/source-code/.

Contents at a Glance

Contents

About the Author

Alan Cline has been a project manager for over 30 years, and a consultant for 20. He has run projects in a variety of domains: aerospace, telecommunications, finance, insurance, and software development. Cline also worked in various organization cultures from single personality-driven shops to large government shops.

Cline began doing concurrent engineering, incremental development, and Kaizen (a precursor to agile development) in the early 1990s. He was at the conference in Sunbird, Utah, in 2001 when the manifesto for *Agile Software Development* (more commonly known as *The Agile Manifesto*) was signed and agile was officially unveiled. (Read more about the history and principles at www.agilemanifesto.org.) This book tries to pass the torch of successful projects to those entering the industry.

As a consultant, Cline has measured his projects' success rate for marketing purposes: 68% of the projects he has completed were released with zero defects and maintained that value well into their life spans. About 98% of his projects have completed on time and, when cost was under his control, within 5% of the budget. (Back in the mid-1990s, that kind of result invited mockery and disbelief: "Zero-defect projects are simply not possible" was the complaint.) Today, these kinds of statistics are routine for agilists.

Cline earned his M.S. in Physics and B.S. in Mathematics, both contributing to his passionate zeal for rigor in software development and project management.

About the Technical Reviewers

Harlan Bridges has worked as an independent consultant and contractor developing or managing the development of web based applications and software projects, including managing projects and teams. Since 2004, Bridges has worked as a contractor at multiple corporations, including USAA, an insurance and financial services company, and Foremost Insurance Corporation. He has significant expertise in the areas of project management, web development, virtual team leadership and training development. His projects included many different technologies such as ASP, PHP, mySQL, Access, Windows 2000, Linux, Internet Information Server and Apache. Mr. Bridges holds a B.S. in Interdisciplinary Studies from the New York Institute of Technology. He is a Project Management Professional (Project Management Institute certification).

Terry Wiegmann: Curious, resourceful, accomplished, well-read problem solver, change agent, presenter and author; a long-time practitioner in technology, including commercial and back-office software product development in a variety of domains, methodologies, and roles. She is a frequently invited presenter throughout the Midwest on topics such as agility, business analysis, quality assurance, organizational change management, and project management. Her articles have appeared in *Agile Connection*, *Sticky Minds*, and *Best Practices for Better Business Analysis*. Her current focus is benefits planning and realization.

Wiegmann's certifications include

- International Institute of Business Analysis Certified Business Analysis Professional

- American Society for Quality Certified Software Quality Engineer

- Scrum.org Professional Scrum Product Owner

- Toastmasters International Advanced Communicator Gold

- Ambassador, Lewis & Clark Trail Heritage Foundation

Acknowledgments

I would like to thank all the people involved in this work. Dr. Martha Lindeman, a user interface expert and professional reviewer whose advice helped reshape and guide the book; Mary Lynn Monge, a PM and professional reviewer who kept me honest; Tim Armstrong, a practicing software developer agilist who helped keep me on track, challenged me with new agile ideas, and wrote the Emergent Design section in Chapter 10; and Dave Campbell, who added the humorous artwork found in Chapter 1. I also thank the kind folks at Apress, whose guidance and diligence kept the book readable: James DeWolfe, Melissa Maldonado, Douglas Pundick, Mary Behr, and Kim Burton. Of course, I thank my wife for supporting and tolerating the many long hours I spent downstairs away from the family in my man cave.

—Alan Cline, PMP, PMI-ACP, ICAgile
November 2015

Introduction

Why Yet Another Agile Book?

Software development has undergone a sea change in the last 15 years, as the industry evolved from the traditional "heavy-weight" project processes to the "lighter" development processes. The development pendulum has swung from formal practices to extremely informal practices, from Big Up-Front Design (BUFD) to the No-Up-Front-Anything of emergent design. The agilists' argument was that because the product cannot be fully known until the project was completed, don't waste time on discovery and documenting: learn as you go, learn from conversations as you write code, and don't waste time learning up front.

Fortunately, project studies show that we, as a software development industry, need to move back to more upfront learning. There is a balance between doing some initial analysis and design and none at all; a balance between writing code on day one, and then paying the price in long durations of rework. The middle ground involves some upfront design and rigor, particularly in the areas of requirements analysis, high-level design, and business value.

I noticed that some recent conference speakers and technical blogs are moving back to more upfront learning before coding. I gathered my courage and put together what you are now reading. I don't expect the reader to take my word for many of the ideas enclosed, so I cite studies and evidence, from formal academic papers to anecdotes to support the ideas proposed as to why one practice may be better than another. The bibliography is lengthy.

There are many good books on agile principles and practices, but there are also common omissions in those books. The biggest omission is the lack of skills sets that are needed by the technical team members. Many times the work is given to "the team" or "developers" and miracle happens there.

Also, most agile books have omitted the project aspects that must occur before the technical team takes over. Agile was developed by developers for developers, and the actions needed before developers get involved in the project are frequently missing, such as project selection and chartering, sponsor scoping, initial requirements, defining stakeholders, and establishing a working business-technical partnership. These things need to be done, but often are needed before the technical team starts their work, or before the technical team is even acquired in most cases.

We need an agile book that is good on hand-holding those who are trying agile for the first time. Most agile books recommend an agile coach to help the technical and business team with their first agile project. What if an agile coach is not available? And if a coach is available who is guided by the agile books alone, the coach may have the same omissions in their "coaching" as the agile books.

Another aspect that concerns us more for this book, is that the traditional (predictive) approach did not incorporate the sciences of psychology, sociology, anthropology, and team dynamics that now show up in modern project management as clear factors of stakeholder management, cultural and organizational influences, politics, and self-empowered and self-organizing project teams. While the predictive process recognized that people were important to project success, none of this knowledge was explicitly factored into the theory or practices.

Why Did I Write this Book?

Agile is one of those things that is easier to do than to explain, like riding a bicycle; but on the other hand, it is much more complex and can benefit from an instructions manuals to provide specific practical guidance, and indicate where variations may be chosen. It is paradoxical that the more one prescribes a particular method, the less agile that method will be—but I had to try.

Originally, I was afraid to write this book. I feared that I would receive massive criticisms for not adhering to the agile think of any one particular method. Then Bertrand Myer (2014) wrote his courageous and inspiring book Agile! The Good, the Hype, and the Ugly in which he classified the various agile practices: brilliant ideas, good ideas, ideas of hype (practices that don't affect the project success but "feel good"), down to practices that he calls "ridiculous."

There are many myths about agile practices, partly fed by the fact that there is no one canonical agile process, and partly because there are conflicting and varying flavors of agile. Even professional organizations do not agree on a single agile approach: there at least seven professional certifications for agile practitioners.

There is a lot of emotional energy and dogma about which agile flavor to use, or which process to follow. Like the carpenter with one hammer that sees every problem as a nail, organizations mandate a particular flavor of agile to be the only flavor permitted. Agile leaders sometimes think of their personally adopted agile techniques as the only tool. Arguments about what is the right way and what should never be done have escalated to almost religious war status.

Ironically, agile is not helped by the popularity of agile. It is suffering from its own success. As everyone wanted to go agile, more and more books, articles, and blogs were written claiming a new way of doing agile. For the most part, these books focused on the technical side, and anything else was vague and general, kind of a "miracle happens here" kind of approach.

For example, agile books are almost unanimous in their omission of team skills. Agile teams are "cross-functional," which means that everyone on the team does everything: requirements elicitation and analysis, stakeholder management, design, testing, coding, change management, release management, database analysis and design, and on and on. Who can find such a superstar developer, not to mention being able to afford one if found? This is one of the unrealistic ideas that this book tries to remedy, and to explain how it does work.

I hope to debunk the myths, or point to formal studies that have; to make clear what agile is, and what agile is not, what has worked for me and others, and what hasn't.

Various agile and pseudo-agile practices are being used every day, and both the number and diversity of these practices can be confusing. This confusion, and the unusualness of agile practices, is an obstacle to quick adoption by traditional organizations, organizations that have been doing software development their way for perhaps decades.

A Guide for the Perplexed

Before agile, project management used the "the predictive process," characterized by long-term and detailed project plans, detailed requirements specifications, and no development work before all the requirements, analysis, and design documents were completed. The "waterfall process," a subset and ugly cousin of the predictive process, made this process famous. At the time it was documented, waterfall was known as a "suboptimal process," that represented the worst of the predictive process. It is easy to kick a methodology when it is down.

This book attempts to help the new project manager get on board with agile practices quickly, to sort out the hype and dogma of pseudo-agile practices, and give a practical guide to new agile practitioners. It is hard to write a book like this because agile's inherent nature is based on values and principles, and not procedures. The specific agile processes need to be tailored by the team members to individuals and the problem of the project—one style does not fit all.

This book lays out the general guidelines for running an agile project but from the position that the project team may be working in a traditional environment. (By traditional, I mean one that complies with the long-standing predictive process, of which waterfall process is of PM-1.)

Many agile techniques have been proven, but like any tool, the tool depends on the situation. There are simply some projects or situations in which agile does not work well. The greatest threat to successful agile is that management may not buy in on the approach because they are looking at issues other than product development techniques. Very large projects are a challenge to agile because strict agile does not scale well, unless the large project team is broken down into small subteams. Fortunately, small teams are all that is needed for most software projects. The project manager or agile coach can help change the situation and project perspective. At least they can learn the language and show the due diligence needed to convince upper management to allow them to try.

Who Should Read this Book?

This book is intended for project managers, upper business management, technical team members, project management offices, technical team members, those trying to transform their organization from traditional to agile, and the idly curious. It is for those beginning to use agile methods in an organization that may not have tried agile projects before. Of equal importance, it speaks to the comment I frequently hear from business leaders or project managers, "Oh I believe in agile, but in the real world. . ." This tells me that they don't really believe that agile practices are useful in daily practice. They may believe in the theory, but when it comes to working the project, they do something else.

Project Managers

For those who want to run an agile project, especially if they are coming from a traditional environment, I provide a particular approach that I have used with great success. I also show the decision points and perspectives as the agile project moves forward from one step to the next. I wanted to allow new agile project managers to choose between the benefits of various flavors of agile and the benefits of other methods.

If you want to become a project manager (or an agile coach) for agile projects, read the first two sections to understand upper management's perspectives. Try to follow Chapters 4 through 7 closely—a project fails at its beginning, but the failure is not known until the end, usually when it is too late. Skim through the role-specific chapters (Chapters 8 through 11), but study Chapter 12, where it is all brought together from the project manager's point of view. It gives a good ground-level view of the agile project manager's responsibilities.

Upper Management

This book will explain the principles behind agile, and how agile can address the traditional needs behind business decisions. Projects are still selected for the same reasons, but project failure is greatly reduced and product value is greatly increased. See how agile practices play into portfolio management, improving ROI, and increasing spending efficiency. Agile also provides easy-to-use tools for Earned Value Management (EVM) for more predictable project tracking. Although the techniques are different from what might have occurred in the organization before, the fundamental principles of product development that aligns with the business's goals have not changed.

If you are in upper management, particularly a stakeholder in a new project, read Chapters 1 through 3 on portfolio management, business alignment, and capacity planning. (I have been surprised by organizations that did not know how much they were actually spending on their projects, or didn't know how many projects they could complete in a certain period of time. They had no capacity planning to know whether they could take on more projects or not.) Also read Chapters 4 through 7 on project startup. Both upper management and traditional project managers will recognize the similarities in those artifacts for justifying, managing, and tracking a project.

Skimming over Chapters 8 thorough 12 will allow you to better understand what the product team is doing. Attend a few of the team's daily stand-up meetings. Get engaged. It should help smooth the way and keep the project turmoil to a minimum.

Technical Team Members

This book contains templates and sample project artifacts to assist in learning agile techniques and hopefully, to be used as exemplars for the new practitioner's own project. Although this book tries to lead the practitioner down a clear road to success for their initial agile project, it does not delve into technical details of established techniques, unless these may be used in agile project in a new way. It points the way so the professional technical team member can learn more about these techniques elsewhere.

If you are a technical team member who wants to follow agile techniques, skim through Chapters 1 through 7. Read carefully though Chapters 8 (a process overview) and Chapters 9 through 12, and follow the particulars that apply to your profession: BAs, developers, testers, and agile project managers (APMs).

Many agile techniques can be used on traditional products too. Use the templates and case studies to shorten your learning curve. Agile is easier experienced than explained, and can be picked up easily with practice. Agile is a set of values that must be internalized, and that is the harder part.

The Project Management Office (PMO)

The first three chapters focus on portfolio management. It explains, for the agilists' benefit, how projects are selected and approved, and why projects have an inherent "shelf-life" that results in hard deadlines that may seem arbitrary. The PMO needs to understand how and why the agile team members are more involved in project management, business goals, and even vendor selection, than in typical traditional organizations. It explains how a PMO can help agile projects and teams. I attempt to establish a common understanding between the goals of business management and those of the technical team.

All Agile Practitioners

This book gives insights into how to sort out myth from fact. There are agile practices that are good ideas and others that are not. Some agilists distain, and agile books omit, many good project management techniques. There are also some agile practices that are bad ideas, and by that I mean that there is no success data to support that idea.

Agile Transformers

For those trying to change the culture from traditional to agile values, it is hard to instruct a culture on only facts. Any counter-cultural statement will seem unrealistic, and the advocate can easily lose credibility. As the saying goes, "You can't tell a fish it's wet—they don't see the water." A strong series of successful projects speaks the loudest, so tread slowly with a pilot project and scale upward. Be careful of using non-agile practices that call themselves agile; it runs a high risk of ruining agile's reputation as an effective process.

This book does not contain a how-to guide for organizational change, but there are tips and recommendations about what may be done at the project level. The best transformation will start with a pilot project and expand from there, letting success breed success.

The Idly Curious

If you are merely trying to find how agile fits into the industry practices for software development (agile practices are now more pervasive and successful than traditional practices), then reading Chapters 1, 4, and 8 may suffice. Chapter 1 shows how agile fits in with traditional project management theory, Chapter 4 is an overview of how to get projects started in Iteration 0: initial requirements, infrastructure, team forming, and architecture.

There are many good courses on agile project management available, and this book is the basis for two professional certifications (PMI-ACP and ICAgile), as well as a source book for a capstone course taught at the Ohio State University computer science department. Many different techniques can be used, and some are different than are described here. Whatever specific steps you take to augment your career in product development, this book should be a good foundation for moving forward to your better success.

How Is this Book Organized?

This book is broken into three sections of multiple chapters. Each section is placed in the order one would initiate, plan, execute, monitor and control, and close a project—the Project Management Institute's golden braid through project management, but from the agile perspective. Each chapter within a section elaborates an important point of the section's theme.

Part 1 *Getting Started* is about why an organization would want to start an agile project, and how to get a project chartered with a project manager and team. (Chapter 1 describes the evolution of agile: how it fits into the context of project management, its history, and its greater benefits over traditional practices.) It applies to project management and organizations independent of agile techniques. Hopefully, it gives the agilist a perspective on what the executive is thinking, and gives upper management a perspective on what the agilist is trying to accomplish when (and by) not adhering to traditional practices.

Part 2 *Iteration 0: Getting to Ready* discusses the critical project actions before any product can be produced. This initial and essential period of time, before the actual value-delivering iterations of 1 through N, has become known as Iteration 0. Interestingly, the time it takes to complete these project-independent activities is an organizational scaling indicator for the project. If iteration zero takes one week in one organization and one month in another, then that same project will take about four times longer in the second organization. (Chapter 4 gives an overview of activities that are crucial in Iteration 0; initial scoping requirements, team acquisition, infrastructure, and architecture.)

Part 3 *Iterations 1 to N* contains the chapters on the actual day-to-day work within an iteration of project execution. It follows the actual roles of the BA, developer, tester, and APM as their work dovetails, merges, or runs concurrently with each other. Each chapter explains the individual's role in agile change management, the user demo, and the quality aspects for the product, shown in context with each other. Each chapter explains the responsibilities and tasks of the various team members from that role's point of view. (Chapter 8 gives an overview of a particular agile process that can be used as a guide, with focus on the business analyst, developer, tester, and agile project manager.)

Comparing Agile vs. Traditional

Each chapter has an explicit section called PMI Parallels that shows how the agile techniques comply (or contrast) with the traditional principles of project management, although quite diverse from traditional practices. The PMI Parallels section addresses all ten of the Bodies of Knowledge defined in the PMI's certification guide (PMBOK, fifth edition, 2013): Integration, Scope, Time, Cost, Quality, Human Resources, Communications, Risk, Procurement, and Stakeholder Management. These comparisons show that Agile is only one of many methodologies that comprise all product development methodologies. I hope that a traditionalist can find some common ground to begin productive discussions with the agilist.

Side Notes

There are several kinds of side notes used to enhance or clarify points made in the text. Each note is indicated with a suggestive icon, and is boxed for emphasis.

Variants   This book describes a recommended way of implementing a particular principle or point, but it isn't the only way. There are other ways that may work as well. To indicate that the reader may need to decide on a different approach according to her or her needs, a veering road icon is used.

Examples or Implementation Anecdotes   To provide more clarity to some points, or give examples that I have encountered while working projects, I added more material in a side note that uses a hammer-and-wrench icon, which represents the machinery grinding down the work. Some are like mini-case studies, and the lesson learned should be directly applicable to the reader; some are anecdotes, and some are metaphors.

Key points and Recommendations   Important principles or points are emphasized by a key icon to indicate that this is an idea that the reader should remember. Sometimes the key is also used to distinguish a recommendation from a set of options that could be chosen.

Warnings   Occasionally, the text will guide the reader to a particular kind of action, but the novice may produce an error because of an unintended or non-intuitive consequence. The thundercloud icon is intended to dramatically emphasize actions not to be taken, or errors that can likely occur, in the situations described in the surrounding text. I tried to use this icon sparingly, whenever an action taken at face value would seem to be the proper action but would in effect be an error.

Bibliography and References

I believe in these techniques, and have proven them, or even developed them further in my projects. Some of this book contains original ideas and techniques. However, wherever possible I try to reference other research, practices, and literature for the point I made. The bibliography is lengthy, and originally my reviewers thought it too academic and not suitable for the trade press. I muted the style but maintained the references so skeptical readers can investigate further on their own.

PART I

■ ■ ■

Getting Started

CHAPTER 1

■ ■ ■

Evolution of Project Management

People have been running projects for centuries, and those experiences have led to a science of project management. When people began building software, however, applying initial project management theory to software development did not work out as well as expected. Later, manufacturing practices were applied to create software engineering, which worked only slightly better. Recently, project management theory and software engineering practices have made an evolutionary improvement, and agile software development is part of that improvement. The current state of project management is the culmination of centuries of experience and theory. It is especially important for software developers of all kinds and their management to understand that *agile* is not another new fad.

There has been great controversy over the *new agile practices* and traditional practices. Agile practices use a preconfigured subset of traditional practices from the predictive theory called PM-1. Agile practitioners have incorporated "soft-skills" explicitly into software development practices: cultural, psychological, and sociological aspects of people, teams, and their roles in the organization. With these additions, agile has moved into a level of PM theory called PM-2, which describes higher evolved practices. These PM theoretic levels have been around for some time. (There is also a PM-3 for complex and chaotic systems, and a PM-4 for systems automatically optimized by artificial intelligence agents.)

A project's organizational culture and structure, how people work together, and how stakeholders perceive the project and results are equally as important as the technical aspects of software product development. This chapter shows how practices originating in ancient times have grown and evolved into the software practices of today, a decidedly better way of developing software. A clearer understanding of this evolution will allow a more precise understanding of how and why it works better, and allow agile practitioners, *agilists*, to better describe and manage the forces that drive success.

Modern software project management—that is, principles and practices in the last 20 years or so—have made three major advances.

- The anatomy of a successful project is divided into three regions: (1) the technical, where the product is constructed; (2) the organizational project context; and (3) the business framework and structure by which project contexts are defined (institutional). The first two will be discussed in detail; the third is out of scope for this book.

- Both the project and project context for a successful project depends on the social, political, and psychological forces of the team and stakeholders. Although these factors were recognized by successful project managers, they were not explicitly part of traditional project management theory.

- Technical aspects have emerged to increase the probability of successful projects with the advent of agile practices. Agile practices still rely on the traditional principles of project management, but have reconfigured their implementation somewhat. Agile practices also included the social, cultural, and psychological forces into Region 1, which have been shown to be superior, in most cases, to traditional software project management practices.

Project managers who understand the concepts and values behind the practices, and the principles that have worked and have not worked, and why, will be able to adapt the variety of methods to their project, culture, and teams. As with any evolutionary step, new practices have produced confusion. The role of agile project manager and business analyst are two important cases, but an understanding of how those roles are played inside and outside the agile project clarify those issues.

First, let's look at how project management has developed from ancient times to modern times; what has changed, what worked, and what didn't work. As George Santayana said, "Those who cannot remember the past are condemned to repeat it."

Ancient Project Management

We can start with the projects that built the Great Wall of China, the cities of Babylon, or the Great Pyramids of Egypt. Leaders have been producing great works for centuries. Let's look at one example of an ancient work that illustrates both a wrong way and right way of doing it.

King Xerxes of Persia sponsored a three-year project in 483 BC to dig a canal across the isthmus of Mount Athos to better attack the Greeks. The Persian workers dug vertical walls and lifted excavated dirt on tall ladders. The vertical walls collapsed on the workers, killing them and slowing down the project. Xerxes enlisted the Phoenicians to help. The Phoenician workers excavated dirt along ramping walls, carrying the excavated dirt out in baskets. Although they dug 50% more dirt, they finished sooner than the Persian teams (Herodotus 2002, 426).

Figure 1-1 comically illustrates the difference between the Persian and Phoenician approaches. Who would have thought that taking longer to excavate the dirt would result in completing the entire project sooner? The Persians had not accounted for the rework from collapsing walls and dead workers. Successful project practices often are counterintuitive and countercultural.

Figure 1-1. *Persian vs. Phoenician project management (courtesy Dave Campbell)*

The first case of a written project management record comes to use from the Roman era. A Roman project manager by the name of Frontinus, who built Rome's viaducts and irrigation systems, was the first to write down engineering project information in 97 AD: political patronage, stakeholder management, project policies, and technical specifications for the waterways. In Frontinus's case, it was a matter of politically protecting himself, since he had no experience and was assigned to save a failing project. His contribution to project management was that he was the first to record operational procedures to be used after the project completed. Frontinus recognized that operations and development follow different sets of rules (Walker and Dart 2012, 4–16).

Despite building of the ancient great wonders of the world, like the Inca, Mayan, and Egyptian pyramids, or the Great Wall of China, and despite hundreds of lesser works that were built, such as numerous merchant and war ships, city infrastructures, and other large projects, no known project information was recorded until Frontinus decided to compile his project data. Prior to that, project results were the focus, and how those results were obtained was not considered.

Eventually, as commercial projects replaced governmental projects, which proceeded on project goals changed from building public infrastructures for service to that of delivering commercial products with least cost and minimal risk *predictably*. The "how" of achieving that took center stage.

Project data were collected and dispersed to apprentice engineers as a way of delivering the best products in the shortest amount of time. Unfortunately, the data were specific to an industry or a profession, and nothing was joined for a general approach to project development. Many of the practices were based on reputations of experienced engineers and project leaders, with a "measure-twice, cut-once" philosophy. These processes were personality-dependent and industry-specific, and project success was only as good as the PM skills of the lead engineer. Project management was seen as a craft, and not a science.

Although the technology improved to make the technical work easier and more accurate, no significant improvements were made in project management for two thousand years. What changed? First, it became recognized as a science, with practitioner- and academic-based research. Second, software development as an industry was invented. Software development is a unique enterprise with unique challenges. With new levels of PM theory, and the application of agile principles, project management leapt forward to a science of the twenty-first century, and its practices to a level of success never seen before.

Formal Development of Project Management

Faced with ever-larger projects and project budgets, and the risk (and history) of massive failures, the US Department of Defense (DoD) formalized project management in the 1960s as a way to manage risk and keep costs under control. (During the Roman Empire, slave labor and emperor-sponsorship removed the need to monitor cost and risk.) The software development effort was sponsored by the DoD, and monitored and matured by the Software Engineering Institute (SEI) at Carnegie Mellon University.

About that time, the Project Management Institute (PMI) developed a community of practice to offer professional certification, much like lawyers and doctors defer to law and medical boards, although PMI never reached that level of authority.

Project management for years used a *predictive life cycle*, also known as the first evolutionary level of project management understanding, or PM-1.

> *The focus is on the forward planning of specific approaches and action plans (e.g., planning phase, achievement of objectives). The approaches…consider the goal and object-oriented system (product) rather than the project participants (Saynisch 2010, 5–6).*

Formal project management of that time, made famous by the *waterfall model*, or *waterfall method*, used a series of stages in which validation and verification occur before proceeding to the next stage, with feedback to inform changes in a preceding stage. Not all predictive life cycle projects are waterfall-based projects, but the waterfall method became famous, despite its being known as a suboptimal form of the predictive life cycle (Boehm 1981, 36).

Traditional project management is based on a *system view* of inputs, processes, and outputs, with selected monitoring and control procedures. You can see this approach used in PMI's Project Management Body of Knowledge, the standard reference book used to certify professional Project Managers (PMBOK 2013, 54). The system view includes feedback cycles—outputs are added into future inputs as adjustments to the process involved need to be made—which causes the outputs to be *nonlinear*.

Why do we care about nonlinear processes? Although nonlinear process outputs can be calculated, they are not intuitive, and people are not good at predicting nonlinear results. Ironically, the system view behind the "predictive life cycle" has unpredictability built in. To compensate, detailed plans and rigorous specifications with close monitoring are necessary. The controls and documentation are many, and once that structure is in place to drive a project, it is hard to for the PM to go against that inertia to change direction or adapt to unforeseen circumstances. The infrastructure and artifacts needed to control unpredictability and risk works too well, and does not handle well the unpredictability of executing the project.

✖ **Example**   A developer working a traditional project asks a stakeholder for feedback on a requirements feature. The customer requests that a change be made. It is apparently a minor change, so the developer quickly gives an off-the-cuff estimate of one hour to make the change—an impact that can easily be absorbed by the schedule. Unfortunately, the developer did not take into account the time to revise the tests, retest the system around the change, and to rewrite the technical and user documentation. Also, the PM must get the change approved by other stakeholders (which can take days), adjust the project plan, and recalculate the schedule and cost due to extending the time. What the developer thought was a one-hour change in fact turned into a two-day impact, with an increase in cost. The later in the development cycle that a change is made, the more costly the change. The effect is exponential, a characteristic common of nonlinear systems, and one of the main driving forces that produced one of the first agile methods, *Extreme Programming*.

The system view of project management applies to construction and manufacturing processes very well. The assembly line is a good illustration or model of the system view: raw materials are input, the product is consistently built along the assembly line, and the output is sold to the customer. In the early days, this system view was formally applied to software development. Software developers began developing software the same way that manufacturing built products.

While keeping the system view, the theory of project management evolved into a new conceptual model called PM-2. It includes a key principle Saynisch calls "controllable planning":

> *This "controllable planning" functions according to the principle: "Better plan roughly and control quickly (frequently) than plan in detail and control slowly (sparingly). Whoever plans too much detail loses time and chances."...But applications or practical works use integrated, holistic, or systemic processes and mode of actions, not analytical categorizations. Such an integrated higher level of approaches and processes points out a characteristic of "continuum." (13)*

With the development of a spectrum of development life cycles, practitioners could choose between the fully traditional method of the predictive life cycle PM-1 (sometimes called a *software factory*) to a highly reactive, or adaptive, method of PM-2 (originally called a *skunkworks*).

Software Development As a Manufacturing Metaphor

One of the first attempts to develop software project management used an assembly-line process, and applied the project management engineering concepts to software development in the early 1990s with *Concurrent Engineering* (ConcEng 2014; Cline 2000). It may have been the first of the *incremental development* techniques. Instead of developing a detailed plan for the duration of the project, requirements, analysis, design, construction, and testing of one module was done concurrently with the requirements, analysis, design, construction, and testing of a different module. Teams leapfrogged along the project stages instead of building the whole project in sequence. Plans and designs were done in parallel and the overlap resulted in faster release cycles.

Concurrent Engineering became popular in Japan under the manufacturing name of *Kaizen*. Another manufacturing process applied to software borrowed from lean manufacturing, or just-in-time manufacturing, and later, provided a popular task tracking technique for agile projects: the Kanban board.

Incremental development, with its shorter and faster feedback cycles (typically quarterly), evolved to *very short* feedback cycles, often daily feedback to software developers, and biweekly feedback cycles to the customer or business units. Some referred to the process as mini-waterfalls, or incremental-iterative. Shortening the feedback cycles and revising the product much sooner decreased the product's development cost and time to delivery, but to evolve to *agile* required another conceptual jump.

Moving Toward Software Engineering

Traditional project management principles are based on a system view of the product under development, and suggest a dynamic for project execution. Although these principles were applied to develop software projects, they were inadequate. It was time for software development *as a practice* to develop more into a science, called *software engineering*.

Projects up to the end of the twentieth century have rarely completed on time, within budget, or with complete user satisfaction. Software projects have failed to complete successfully 84% of the time. Lalonde, Bourgalt, and Findeli (2010, 21–36) summarize the state of Project management evolution:

> *According to this international report [Standish Group 1995], only 16% of software projects meet set performance standards and deliver outcomes with time and cost objectives. Moreover, 31% of projects are failures: projects are either abandoned or canceled. Furthermore, 53% of projects are carried out but do not meet customer specifications.*

There are several reasons for this project failure rate. One centers on how well the system view, developed initially for construction and manufacturing projects, fits software development practices. Manufacturing processes create hundreds or thousands of identical products, and repeatability is key. Tight requirements specifications are created to define the product. However, software development creates a single product once, and is subject to the whims of change influences as the product is developed. The "predictive" method of product development is not predictive at all, or at least, it is not reliable in its predictions because circumstances and requirements are so fluid in software development, and product repeatability is not relevant.

The second reason that the manufacturing metaphor can fail is that *people* do software development, and people are not workstations on an assembly line. They have good days and bad days, they interact with a dynamic that parts of an assembly line do not have. People, whether stakeholders or the development team, are not necessarily repeatable but can adapt to situations. They can quickly change the way they do business, but formal project management did not recognize this as an influencing factor (or an asset) at the time.

To combat the low for software projects, more formalism was added by the DoD, PMI, and practitioners themselves. There were somewhat successful attempts to have programs written by other programs from design diagrams, things such as *executable UML*. Software practices were moving toward a rigorous science known as *software engineering.* [1]

Software Engineering As an Immature Science

There were great debates about whether software development was an art, a science, or a craft. My university could not decide for years whether teaching computer science belonged in the engineering school or the applied math school, and there were emphatic debates on both sides of the faculty. Software engineering advocates took the science-based approach to formalize the system view of development. If software development was a science, then at best, it was an immature science that could grow; or at worst, it was not applicable enough to software development.

The groundbreaking book, *The Structure of a Scientific Revolutions* (Kuhn 1970) identifies key indicators for whether a science is mature or not. These indicators do not imply that immature sciences are less valuable than mature sciences, but they are more application oriented, which may be inherent in the nature of the science. This should not be surprising since the existence of software development is less than 60 years old.

As applied to software engineering:

- *Software engineering is largely practitioner-based applied research.* Computer scientists in academia provide theory and practices, but the software development community provides the vast majority of progress in the form of new tools, languages, and procedures. Agile did not originate in academia, but from the accumulated efforts of software developers.

- *Software engineering at the project level lacks experimental rigor.* Although there are many agile variations being practiced, few are based on experimental results that indicate a new and improved way of working a project. The best we can hope for is to apply the accumulated experience of veteran developers, experience garnered from years of projects that succeeded or failed. Their conclusions are then based more on anecdotal evidence than experimental rigor. In this regard, agile is moving in the wrong direction: agilistas encourage guess-and-check development. One hears phrases like "discovery through delivery" or "fail fast."

- *Software engineering is technology-driven engineering.* Software projects are driven by technology more than solid theoretical principles, although that may be justified in that the technology is moving faster than the research can keep up. Many products come and go as technologies rise and fall. The businesses are in a clamor over the next marketing opportunity, such as the next mobile app because competition in that space is fierce. For example, the explosive proliferation of mobile phone apps was a result of the technology of the smart phone, and not a theoretical drive to expand communications worldwide, or any other theoretical principle.

---

[1] I include software development in this science of software engineering, but do not count software development as rigorous a practice as software engineering.

- *Software engineering is social-directed progress, like law or medicine.* The problems being solved depend on the pressures of culture and society. Basic sciences, like astronomy, explore the scientific principles of the day, driven by scientific questions derived from prior research. By contrast, software development initiatives arise from social forces. For example, currently, a lot of interest has focused on Internet vulnerabilities that cause commercial and financial loss. I think because of this last factor that software technologists will always be playing catch-up with the malware practitioners that exploit software security vulnerabilities. In general, developers are not looking at the principle of how to solve malware cases, but how they can plug a specific security hole and quickly fix a specific virus.

- *Software engineering is authenticated by certifications and board reviews*, based on experience and courses offered by the standards organizations, instead of academic degrees justified by research contributions to the industry, the basis for PhD programs. PMI and other professional organizations have grown a handful of certifications in the last few years. There are no less than eight certifications from PMI in variants of project management, and at least four certifying organizations for the professional PM from which to choose.

There is a plethora of certifications for law and medicine, but law and medicine degrees require at least eight years of formal university schooling. Software engineering requires at most a four-year degree. Only recently has software engineering certifications become recognized as valuable in the industry, to be preferred by employers who want experience in a particular domain or technology.

- *Software engineering does not apply lessons learned to the next project.* Until recently, project teams did not hold lesson-learned sessions as a matter of practice, or if they did, the lessons learned were not carried over into the next project. Subsequent projects were run as if they were done for the first time. Mistakes were propagated across projects and teams, unless a team member brought a personal goal to the team to change project practices. This is ironic considering the previous point that employers prefer experienced individuals to degrees or certifications, and experience did not capitalize on lessons learned.

All this is to say that software engineering is an immature science, or one that is inherently an applied science. As an immature science, the practitioner must realize that many things advocated in the software world may not be based on scientific data or principle, but on someone selling something. What can we, as software developers and project managers, rely on to guide us toward success? What works and what is hype? We need a workable project management practice for today's needs in the twenty-first century.

Project Management for the Twenty-first Century

Modern project management—that is, practice and theory developed during the last 20 years—has shown itself to vastly increase the chances of a successful software project over traditional projects. First, the organizational context of a project (cultural, political, and stakeholder influences) is recognized to be equally as important as the project team's technical execution (Morris and Giraldi 2011). Second, the addition of sociology, psychology, and team dynamics has provided a deeper understanding and more tools for project success (Saynisch 2010); and third, practices have independently evolved to implement and extend traditional software development.

Morris and Giraldi (2011) explain the two regions of a successful project that must be considered and managed. Region 1 is the technical core, where the project team designs, builds, and releases the software to operations. It is heavily execution-oriented, and agile practices center in that region. We will delve into that in Chapters 8 through 11.

Region 2 is the more strategically oriented region. It is defined by the organizational structure and culture. It captures the front-end project definition stages, where concept and feasibility are considered, business alignment and return on investment (ROI) evaluated, the project is chartered (obtains a sponsor and authorization), and stakeholder management is started.

Unfortunately, agile practices tend to minimize the importance of Region 2 in an attempt to avoid "big upfront design" or "big upfront planning," but Region 2 is as equally important as Region 1. If the project isn't chartered, there will be no project team; and the way that the management culture or stakeholders view the agile team affects the success or failure of the project. Region 2 practices are discussed in Chapters 4 through 7.

Both Regions 1 and Region 2 have existed traditionally, so are called PM-1 project management theory, one that is based on the traditional predictive life cycle (Saynisch 2010). What is new is the evolutionary project management step that has added the "soft sciences" to project management, and is applied across both Regions 1 and 2. Saynish calls this level PM-2 project management theory.

PM-3 covers the institutional context for defining the organization structure, culture, and support for PM-2, and to a lesser extent, PM-1. It defines the external environment of the organization, and is outside the scope of this book.

Figure 1-2 shows both Regions and the layers of PM-1 and PM-2. Region 2 contains the organizational support and processes to initialize a project. A few keys artifacts are listed as examples below Region 2. It has not changed too much from traditional project management, but PM-2 principles can be applied to make it more effective.

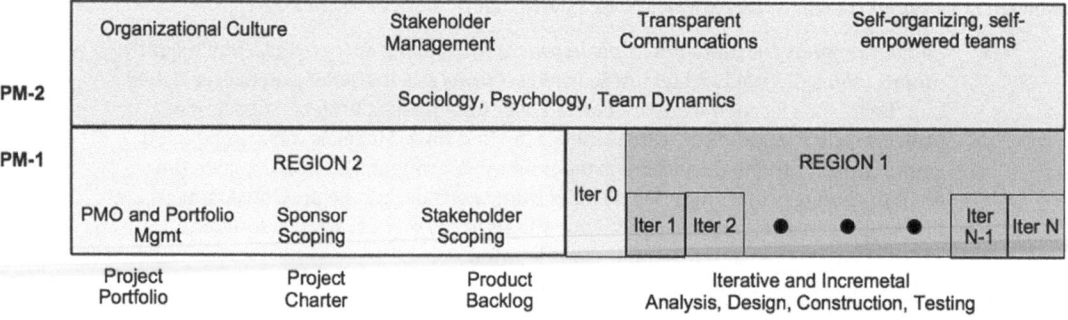

Figure 1-2. *Modern project management structure*

Region 1 is the iterative and incremental processes followed by the technical team of an agile project. Although iterative and incremental product development is not new, agile has adopted it to produce high-quality product to deliver fast business value. Region 1 is segmented into time-boxed iterations, where analysis, design, construction, and testing are performed concurrently. All productive work (delivering business value) is accomplished in Region 1.

PM-2 applies practices from sociology, psychology, anthropology (culture), and team dynamics over both regions. Applying the PM-2 aspects to development teams has resulted in current agile team practices of creating self-organized and self-empowered teams. Also, the breakdown of Region 1 and Region 2, within the "soft sciences" wrapper, helps to clarify how the PM and BA are used in agile projects. These characteristics are discussed in detail in later chapters.

In Figure 1-2, Iteration 0 is special, and distinguished by a color that is neither that of Region 1 nor of Region 2. It is an overlap area that could be argued to belong to either region. Iteration 0 is a time-boxed period of work in which the team builds their infrastructure, defines product architecture, identifies team working practices, and other necessary prep work before productive value is started. Iteration 0 is discussed in detail in Chapters 4 through 7.

With this background in place, we look at how agile got started and how it grew out of the predictive life cycle approach. Agile does not have a prescriptive method; rather, it has several frameworks from which agile values and principles are applied to the team, project, and organization specifically. Although there are many agile approaches, such as Scrum, XP, and Crystal, there are more hybrid methods being used than any others. Practitioners moving to agile must make the adjustment to move from following a procedure, to working from a set of values and applying those values to a real team.

Evolution of Agile Development

In the late 1990s, software project management took a step forward to solve the inadequacies experienced in traditional software development. Extreme programming (XP) was the first of the modern agile practices, developed to solve a particular problem, and that led to an adaptability that evolved software project management to the next level, PM-2.

Extreme Programming: An Early Agile Method

Changes made in the product life cycle are exponentially more expensive than changes made earlier in the cycle. For example, a change that cost $1 at the specification phase may cost $300 or more if that same change were made for the product in operations.

Barry Boehm (1981) showed from multiple studies that the later in the project that the defect is found and repaired, the more it costs, and that cost rises exponentially with the later the defect is repaired in the product development cycle. He showed that there are two cost curves: one for large teams and one for small teams. The larger teams have the greater cost per defect. The cost of change depends on project size: changes to smaller projects have a small cost increase with phase. He also showed that more defects originate if up front requirements and design work is not done before coding.

> ...[I]f we proceed to write code without having performed the earlier requirements and design activities, there will be many more requirements and design errors in the resulting product... [T]hese errors will be much more expensive to correct in later phases, leading to a less successful software project and product (Boehm 1981, 41).

Kent Beck wanted a development method that would solve many symptoms of traditional project development, but most importantly, to flatten the exponentially high cost of defects that appeared late in the project. A lower cost of change was important to allow his method of constant change (refactoring[2] and experimentation) to be successful. As he says in his book on extreme programming (XP):

> What if the cost of change didn't rise over time, but rose much more slowly, eventually reaching an asymptote? ...This is one of the premises of XP. It is the technical premise of XP. If the cost of change rose slowly over time, you would act completely differently from how you do under the assumption that costs rise exponentially. ...The flattened change cost curve makes XP possible, a steep change curve makes XP impossible.

---

[2] *Refactoring* is rewriting code to improve its internal design without changing its external behavior or appearance (Fowler 2000).

Beck partially succeeded with his innovative extreme programming approach. However, XP also uses smaller teams, which means the cost-change curve is less because of that fact alone. XP works on the lighter line, and not the darker line of large project teams, which most organizations used in those days to develop software.

The 2013 Standish CHAOS report agrees that project complexity and size affects project results more than methodology for small project teams (total labor costs of less than $1 million). In fact, traditional and agile projects fared roughly the same when compared after compensating for the fact that traditional projects work mostly on large projects.

> *Size of a project trumps methodology. The agile process benefits from small projects. Overall, small projects have a better success rate than agile projects and waterfall projects when you include other types. In the last 10 years, 45% of agile projects were less than $1 million in labor cost. In contrast, only 14% of waterfall projects were less than $1 million in labor cost. Head to head, small, agile, and waterfall projects have almost the same success and failure rates (Standish 2013, 25).*

XP became highly successful, not because of the reduction in cost of changes, although that was a factor, but because the methodology produced higher quality results. It also provided quicker business value to the customer because of its shorter feedback cycles and higher quality. Developers found working on an XP team less tedious and more fun. The real success with XP came from its absorption of customer-developer relations. Beck had added social and psychological principles to software development, the defining next step in the evolution of software project management.

Progressive Elaboration

On the spectrum between "big upfront work," which agile tries to avoid, and the small repeated iterations of XP, there is a process of discovery to learn more about what is needed to develop the product. All work done within the project level—detailed design, coding, and testing—lie within the project, Region 1 of PM theory. The work done before the product development gets started—project sponsorship, stakeholder management, architecture, and initial requirements—are part of the organizational Region 2. This *progress elaboration* starts when the project is chartered in Region 2 and continues until the project is completed by the development team in Region 1. How much time and effort is spent in either region distinguishes traditional from agile methods.

Figure 1-3 shows the certainty curve for a typical traditional project. Risk decreases as scope is *progressively elaborated*; that is, refined into knowledge that is more detailed. From charter to detailed requirements, the team goes through a controlled discovery process. The uncertainty about the product decreases as the product develops until it reaches the lowest level of knowledge, a level of *unpredictable volatility* that can safely be called "noise." This is the level at which the programmers find themselves each day, coding, testing, debugging, rewriting, and so forth. The noise is a result of *entropy,* the amount of disorganization resulting from constant changes as the developers write, debug, and rewrite code. Production progress is predictable only down to this level of activity, which in agile projects, is within a daily scope. One hundred–percent certainty doesn't occur until the product release, when the work is completed and the project is history.

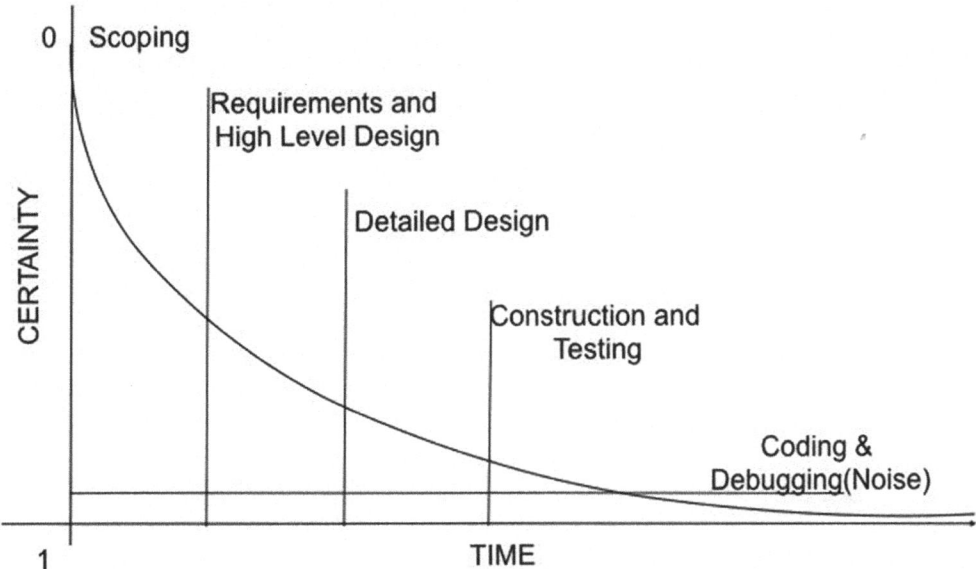

Figure 1-3. *Progressive elaboration for traditional project*

In contrast, a highly iterative approach like XP has repeating, low-risk elaborations, as shown in Figure 1-4. There is still uncertainty but the uncertainty is less to start with although it repeats. Within each iteration, detailed design, coding, and testing are applied to new requirements. The uncertainty starts again in each iteration with new requirements, but is worked to certainty before the end of each iteration (within the noise level).

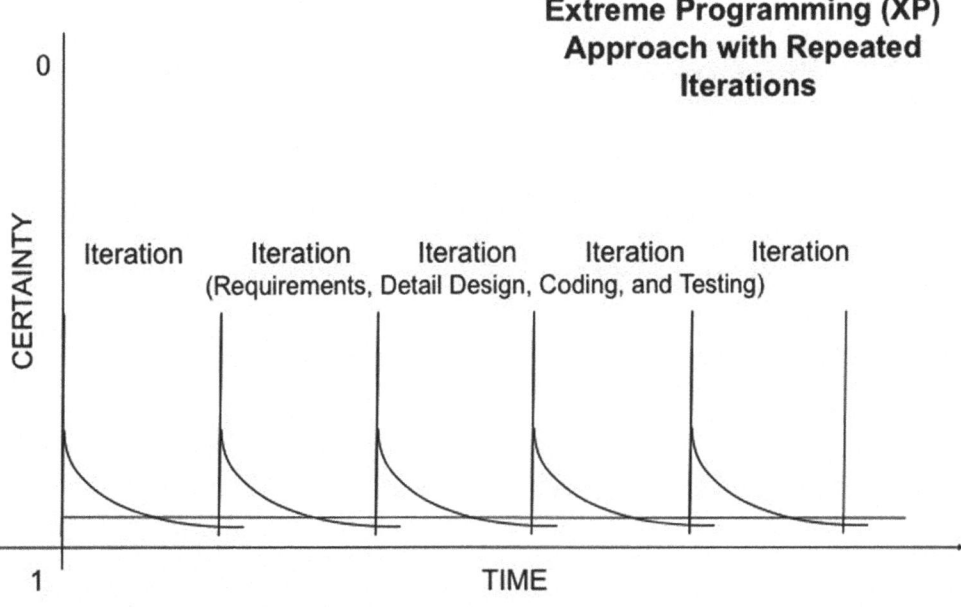

Figure 1-4. *Full iterative agile approach*

There is no upfront work with XP[3]; code starts very quickly after the project is authorized. Most documents that are considered standard for traditional projects (e.g., requirements specs) are not written. Contrast that with the almost 40% up front work done in traditional projects (see Figure 1-5) before code gets started.

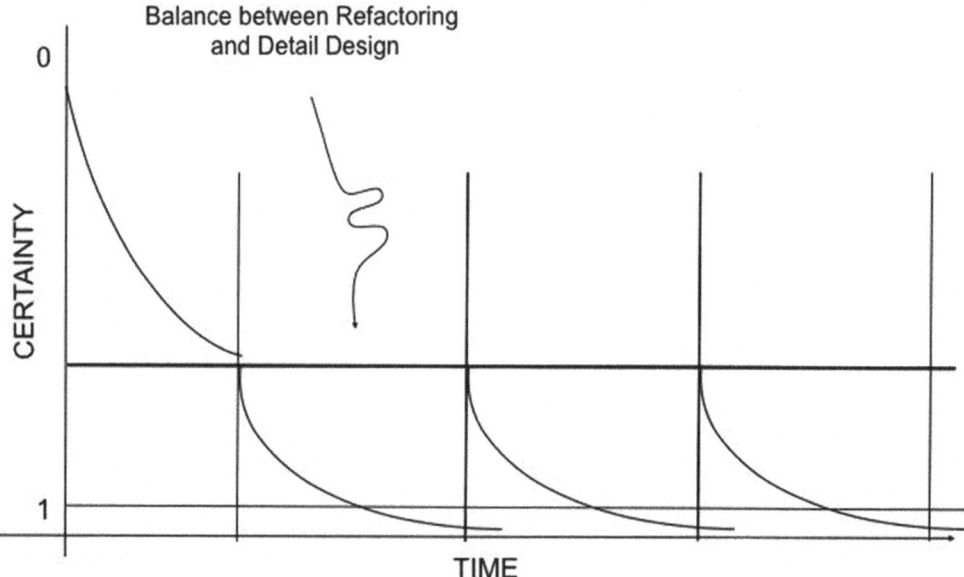

Figure 1-5. *Balanced agile iterations*

Figure 1-5 shows a balance between some upfront work and iteration work. Work above the horizontal line is "upfront work"—discovery work like architecture and design before coding; work below the line is iterative work—coding and testing during the iterations. The horizontal line can be moved downward to represent a full traditional project, or moved upward to represent a fully iterative project, like XP.

Where this line goes—that is, how much upfront work the team should do before moving into iterations—must be tailored to the team, the project, and the organization. At project startup, the technical team has not been selected, so it is left to the project manager to decide how much upfront work is appropriate, taking into account any organizational and cultural constraints.

Effort vs. Planning by Project Method

The project method chosen will affect the amount of time and rework needed. Figure 1-6 shows a qualitative curve of the relationship between the project method used and the effort required, all other things being equal.

---

[3]There is no up-front *product* work, but there is still infrastructure work, team formation, and the other activities on which product development depends.

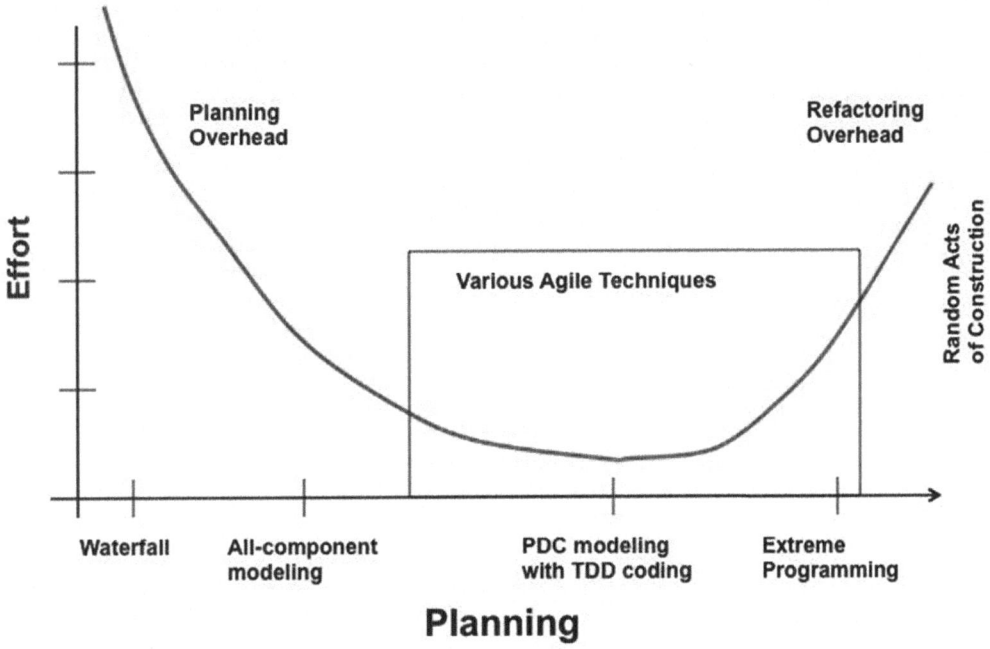

Figure 1-6. *Effort vs. planning by project method*

With the waterfall approach, everything is planned upfront before any design is started. For each change "downstream," the planning must be reworked, followed by a change to the code and tests. By planning ever-smaller pieces of scope, the effort is reduced accordingly.

Planning overhead decreases with increased scope decomposition, and reaches a minimum of effort when the requirements' problem domain component (PDC) validation and the quick feedback cycles of Test-Driven Development (TDD). (These concepts are discussed again in Chapter 9.) The overall project effort increases again for XP because of the constant changes and refactoring required to fix what was missed by not planning. Of course, if no planning is done and bits and pieces of code are stuck together in what I call "random acts of construction," then the effort is even higher from repeated reworking—product development with almost as high an overhead as too much planning.

The optimal level is a combination of two techniques that focus on very small pieces of scope in a coordinated way. First, use the proper architecture to maximize separation of concerns so *refactoring*, a kind of guided rework, has very small units to change (Fowler 2000). Second, use TDD so that developers write unit tests while writing code.

The Agile Manifesto: Values and Principles

Agile methods fell into the higher evolutionary scale of project management when it added sociology, psychology, and team dynamics. Natural selection processes driven by business value, speed to deliver, team collaboration, and the needs of individual team members have honed the various resulting approaches for agile methods. The principles are the same, but *agile projects*—that is, projects using agile methods and teams—exceed the results of traditional software development projects.

At the same time PM evolutionary theory was growing, various agile-style thinkers independently developed the *agile movement*. I call it a movement because it was started by developers for developers to deliver successful software in a countercultural way, thus Beck's label calling it "extreme."

Advocates who pushed agile practices gathered in Sunbird, Utah, in 2001 and signed the *Agile Manifesto*, a statement of the values and principles that underlie agile practices (Manifesto 2001). The Agile Manifesto emphasizes a different set of values than traditionalists (see Figure 1-7). The 17 signatories of the Agile Manifesto are computer scientists, designers, and programmers, with varying degrees of interest in applying sociology and psychology to the developers as people. Most worked in large-scale to small-scale commercial applications, and a few signatories worked in real-time embedded systems. These patriarchs of the agile movement have banded together since in professional organizations to guide and propagate agile in their quest for how to build successful software products best.

Manifesto for Agile Software Development

We are uncovering better ways of developing software by doing it and helping others do it. Through this work we have come to value:

Individuals and interactions over processes and tools

Working software over comprehensive documentation

Customer collaboration over contract negotiation

Responding to change over following a plan

That is, while there is value in the items on the right, we value the items on the left more.

Kent Beck	James Grenning	Robert C. Martin
Mike Beedle	Jim Highsmith	Steve Mellor
Arie van Bennekum	Andrew Hunt	Ken Schwaber
Alistair Cockburn	Ron Jefferies	Jeff Sutherland
Ward Cunningham	Jon Kern	Dave Thomas
Martin Fowler	Brian Marick	

Figure 1-7. Agile Manifesto and signatories

With these four basic values, the Agile Manifesto contains twelve agile principles (Agile Principles 2001).

1. Our highest priority is to satisfy the customer through early and continuous delivery of valuable software.

2. Welcome changing requirements, even late in development. Agile processes harness change for the customer's competitive advantage.

3. Deliver working software frequently, from a couple of weeks to a couple of months, with a preference to the shorter timescale.

4. Business people and developers must work together daily throughout the project.

5. Build projects around motivated individuals. Give them the environment and support they need, and trust them to get the job done.

6. The most efficient and effective method of conveying information to and within a development team is face-to-face conversation.

7. Working software is the primary measure of progress.

8. Agile processes promote sustainable development. The sponsors, developers, and users should be able to maintain a constant pace indefinitely.

9. Continuous attention to technical excellence and good design enhances agility.

10. Simplicity—the art of maximizing the amount of work not done—is essential.

11. The best architectures, requirements, and designs emerge from self-organizing teams.

12. At regular intervals, the team reflects on how to become more effective, then tunes and adjusts its behavior accordingly.

Formally speaking, agile is an implementation of PM-2 using a subset configuration of traditional project management. Saynisch (2010) says about agile development:

> *The agile operating mode is very similar to the previously described "evolutionary acquisition model" of DoD. Ultimately, it is also an application of the cyclic evolution process "variation-selection-keeping." Therefore, the agile project management corresponds to the principles of PM-2, a precise cooperation of World 1 and World 2. But the phenomenon of the evolutionary overlapping of traditional methods…emerges at this point, because the evolutionary elements are realized unconsciously. (Emphasis added)*

Agile project management started as a sometimes covert, developer-driven, grassroots movement; mostly because upper management could not understand the drastic changes project teams wanted to follow agile practices. The first book written on agile methods is called *Extreme Programming Explained* (Beck 2000) because the author knew it was very different from how software was usually developed, and that using it would take strong cultural adjustment.

Management was sometimes justified in banning the practice because it did not consider aspects of product development that management thought essential: alignment with business goals, business risk, total-cost-of ownership for a product, and return on investment. Agile almost completely ignored the influences of Region 2. XP centered itself in the mind of developers. Other later agile methods have gotten around this developer-centered problem, and XP has broadened its scope to improve over its first version.

Since the *Agile Principles* were published in 2001, many other methodologies have surfaced using the same principles and values. PMI certifies agile practitioners (PMI-ACP) on four of them: *Extreme Programming Explained* (Beck 1999); Ken Schwaber and Jeff Sutherland's *Scrum* (Schwaber and Beedle, 2001) (Scrum 2013); *Kanban* (Anderson 2010); and *Lean Software Development* (Shalloway, Beaver, and Trott 2010); along with key principles of other flavors like DSDM, FDD, and Alistair Cockburn's *Crystal Clear* (2004).[4] The big difference between them, since by definition of *agile* they must all follow the agile values and practices, are the various practices that are followed during the up-front work or by the technical team during the iterations of the project.

---

[4]Originally, PMI-ACP prep material included two books: John Goodpasture's (2010) book for study and either Mike Griffiths's (2012) or Andy Crowe's (2012) test prep guide. Recently, PMI provided a list of 11 books to help agile practitioners pass their PMI-ACP test.

Later chapters will pull from these various agile methods, but before we examine the detail, let's examine the differences in the bigger picture: agile vs. traditional practices.

Comparing Agile and Traditional Practices

Traditional and agile approaches differ in their driving values. Traditional project management techniques were based on cost- and risk-control and predictability. Agile is based on more team-oriented and customer-value drivers. These fundamental differences have manifested as a series of practices that are characteristic of agile.

The following sections describe some points of contrast between running a traditional project and running an agile project.

High-Quality Product Development

There are two ways to improve product development. One may improve the quality of the product by improving the *product*, or improving the *process* of building the product. Improving either or both of these areas will improve the product's quality.

As an example, imagine the assembly line in a car-manufacturing factory. One can improve the quality of the car built by using high-quality parts and highly skilled mechanics and assemblers (product components). One may also improve the quality of the car by using clean processes, statistical QC controls, lower tolerance to defects, and so forth. Project management is all about improving the product *and* the process.

By augmenting traditional development practices with improved team communications, sociological and psychological concerns, the project processes have improved. By using automated testing for improved test cases and testing, the project components have improved. New *continuous improvement* tools have also improved product components through better process and standards verification.

Traditional Approach

Traditionally, improving quality meant verifying each and every detailed step of the plan and the work. Before agile became formalized in development and IT shops, long specifications and long lists of tests (even unit tests) were written before construction started. It would take weeks and months to develop the requirements before the product actually began to be built. The traditional approach incorporated poor practices that led to poor project success—practices that agile has solved to produce successful projects.

- *Up-front requirements and design.* The end result of the business planning activity was a *software requirements specification* (SRS) that contained stakeholders, capabilities, and a feature catalog (although it was not called that) for the entire product. Design and coding would not start until the SRS was approved by all management stakeholders. Getting through the SRS process could take months of effort, and no value was delivered to the business in that time.

  From the SRS, the PM would build a hierarchical *work breakdown structure* (WBS) for the whole project, decompose it into middle-sized tasks and small tasks (activities), and then sequence them in the order that they would be worked to make a schedule. All that would occur before construction started.

- *Overly precise and under-accurate specifications.* The specifications were intricate, overly long, and time-consuming. (One company had an acronym for these all-too-common kinds of specs, referring to how they were treated by developers who were to review them: TLDR, meaning "Too Long, Didn't Read"). Tens of thousands of dollars were spent before the programming team had the information they needed to build the product.

- *Cost of change exponentially high.* Too frequently, those specs would change before coding started (wasting the time to build the requirements), or during coding (causing rework through refactoring and changing the code and tests), or worse, after the code and testing was complete, resulting in the exponentially rising change costs shown earlier.

- *Lack of sufficient customer interaction.* After this long requirements and design process was completed, the product would be built without intervening customer feedback. The specs were "tossed over the wall to IT," built by IT without sufficient business context or detail, and then "tossed back over the wall" to the customer. The product was installed by the IT department whether it was what the customer wanted or not. If the product was not want the customer wanted, and the customer had some clout, the product was not installed (or uninstalled) and the work, time, and money were wasted.

- *Technology diversification and redundancy.* Two or more years could go by from initialization to release of a large application. By that time, the business sponsor who wanted the application was long gone, transitioned to another department, had left the company, or more frequently, found a purchased work-around that remained in place. In the worst cases, many business departments, reacting to IT's lack of success and late delivery schedules, would try to develop their own technology workforce within the business units. The economies of scale and integration of technology that justified a separate IT department was lost. The technology was duplicated across business units, and technical resources were redundant. The IT department became in-house "contractors" to fill the gaps of what the business units were building, so the IT department devolved increasingly to order-takers and decreasingly toward having a partnering relationship.

Agile Approach

Today, agile processes improve product quality by improved project factors. The following list describes a quick summary of the approach agile takes to solve the traditional problems mentioned earlier. I will describe how agile approaches these problems by using the best example I've heard. A customer wants a painting, say of the Mona Lisa. First, the artist delivers a rough sketch of a woman. If the customer likes that, the artist fills in a more detailed sketch—facial expressions, angle of the head, background. Then, if the customer likes what he or she sees so far, the artist does a quick color sketch, perhaps in oil. If that is approved, the artist can put the finishing touches on the detailed oil painting. After the customer approves the painting "for release," the painter can then "lock it down" with varnish and a frame.

- *Little upfront requirements and design.* Agile uses a technique called adaptive planning. Only the rough requirements and design are used, then each level is progressive elaborated into more detail as that level of detail is about to be implemented. Each iteration the product's requirements and implementation are reviewed before collecting information that is more detailed from the customer.

- *Historically driven and accurate specifications.* Traditionally, the specs for the *Mona Lisa* example would try to describe every aspect of the painting in detail, with the intent that the customer could pass off the spec to the artist and get the finished product sometime later. Of course, rarely does a spec cover, or a customer think of, every aspect of anything, so there are always changes to the product. In this case, the changes wouldn't occur until the customer views the final painting. By reviewing partial progress periodically, as with agile, written specs are minimized in exchange for an actual (but partial) product.

- *Cost of change low.* During product development, the cost of change is higher the later the change is made. With a partial product reviewed periodically, the cost of change is kept to a minimum because extensive work has not been done between reviews, so there is less to change. The time-boxed iterations also keep risk and risk costs to a controllable minimum.

- *High level of customer interaction.* The periodic reviews require the customer to be closely involved in describing what he or she wants, even if the customer does not know at the beginning of development. As the customer sees the partial product, it allows the customer to change aspects of the product he hadn't thought about before. Some changes will be improvements to the current partial product, so in this way, the product is constantly improving through periodic reviews.

- *Technology support for unification.* The *Mona Lisa* example doesn't apply to this topic, but agile uses a strong projectized approach to product development. Agile teams can sit in business units to be closer to the customer, or they can sit in IT departments; either way, agile teams are kept small so that the benefits of small team dynamics can be leveraged. A series of studies by QSM that showed that large teams (30 people) do not deliver significantly faster than small teams (3 people) (Putnam Jr. 2014; Armel 2012; Putnam 2005). The increased productivity of having more resources is compensated because the larger teams create more rework, and have larger communications problems than smaller teams. Better to have a few small teams and save the expense of a large number of resources. Agile is best when worked in small teams, regardless of what department the resources are from.

You can see that each of these factors is closely related, which is why agile is considered a *holistic* process of product development. Agile requirements are written with use cases, small chunks of scope that define a user-system interaction, or user stories, even smaller chunks of scope. The developer writes each of these mini-scenarios, tests its logic with unit tests, has another person test it more comprehensively with integration and GUI tests, and then reviews it with the customer in a user demo. This process may occur several times within an iteration. Often, in that cycle of review, the customer comes up with a change to what they thought they wanted, and the build will be revised quickly, where it is least expensive.

This holistic approach works very well to deliver a high quality product. The cost of change is small for small projects because the scope of work is small. Traditionally, projects have failed to complete successfully 84% of the time (Lalonde, Bourgalt, Findeli 2010, 21–36), but with agile approaches, not only do projects complete almost all the time, but 80% of the products are without defect (Lalonde et al. 2010). Their paper says that the sociological aspects of project management has improved project success.

Comparing Agile vs. Traditional Results

There are compelling reasons to use agile on software projects. According to most studies (perhaps all studies), most traditional software projects are late, over-budget, or are cancelled; and if they do finish, they are rife with defects that must be repaired (Standish 2013). Agile projects almost always complete on budget and on time, and most have zero defects when released (Standish 2013; Forrester 2013). The industry is moving quickly toward agile project methods, and their popularity is skyrocketing.

Rico, Sayani, and Sone (2009) reported the researched benefits of agile methodologies over traditional Project management evolution:

> *[The studies] cited an average of 29% improvement in cost, 71% improvement in schedule, and 122% improvement in productivity performance. Quality improvement averaged 75% and customer satisfaction improvement averaged 70%. Over 29 of these studies had the data necessary to estimate the average return on investment of 2633%.*

Agile Transformation Inc. (2012), a training and consulting company, quoted Gartner in their training course on the rise of agile methods in the future. Gartner predicts that in the next couple of years "agile development" methods will be utilized in 80% of all software development projects.

PM Network magazine (Gale 2011), published by conservative PMI, reports the results of the latest report from The Standish Group, famous for its IT report card on projects since 1994. Over the last several years, they have published dismal reports of IT project results. Their last few reports, conducted for 10,000 projects around the world, showed that only 37% of projects succeeded; that is, came in on time and budget (32% in 2008 and 28% in 2004).

However, "the 2011 results represent the highest success rate in the history of [those reports]" (Gale, 10–11). The drastic uptick in project success was attributed partly to economic market recovery, and partly to the new way that organizations are approaching project management. They are installing Project Management Offices (PMOs) to integrate fast-reacting, adaptive project management into their organizations, and targeting projects in a way that fit agile practices best. The latest Standish Group report (Standish 2013) shows how, for small projects, success has risen over the last ten years. Many of these top success factors are agile practices.

- Executive management support and user involvement speak directly to the business/technical team relationship from frequent to continual feedback from the stakeholders. This is a Region 2 focus.

- Skilled resources are more often used on agile teams. Team members work together, sometimes at the same workstation, and general competency levels rise in agile teams. This is a Region 1 focus.

- Optimization refers to portfolio optimization for project selection, which is not necessarily an agile practice. This is a Region 2 focus.

- Project management expertise. Agile methods have a lot of PM practices (and quality techniques) built in, including using an agile coach to facilitate the development process. This inherency, and simpler monitoring and reporting artifacts, and smaller iteration-level scope, make it easier for PMs to be successful. This is both a Region 1 and a Region 2 focus.

Agile projects are now included in the Software Engineering Institute's (SEI) Capability Maturity Model (CMMi), one of the most conservative software development standards organizations (SEI 2008). Furthermore, the SEI recognizes the PMI-ACP as a professional milestone and incorporates it into their CMMi assessments. Organizations have become CMMi Level 2 and 3 using agile techniques.

PMI Parallels

The Project Management Institute (PMI) has introduced in its latest edition of the PMBOK (Project Management Body of Knowledge) a new knowledge area for Stakeholder Management. It recognizes the newer project management techniques of "Iterative and Incremental Life Cycles" and agile "Adaptive Life Cycles" (PMBOK 2013, 45–46). It also offers a new professional certification for agile PMs to distinguish those who have demonstrated experience and proficiency at agile project management—the Agile Certified Practitioner (PMI-ACP), which requires 1500 hours of agile experience, and detailed knowledge of multiple agile methods.

The SEI and the International Institute for Business Analysts (IIBA) also recognize the PMI-ACP and recommends those practices.

Conclusion

Agile development is an evolutionary approach that arose independently, but consistent with, the directed progress of a theoretical framework for project management. Agile demonstrates much better results than what came before because the sociological aspects and human dynamics have been factored into a dynamic, high-feedback set of values.

Applying the values forced evolutionary practices. For example, stakeholder management forced project leaders to consider the cultural, psychological, and sociological principles behind a project's success. The self-empowered and self-organized team forced project leaders to consider the team dynamics behind a project's success.

Agile practitioners have been vested by the software practices standards groups—the PMO of the United States—and accepted by software practitioners. Scrum, XP, and its hybrids are currently the most used software development techniques throughout the world.

The twenty-first century is a different place to do business than that of the mid-twentieth century. Today's businesses are driven by faster global communications, faster business delivery, the Internet, mobile devices, better business-to-technical partnering, and the value of individuals. Products that are released annually lose to products that are released and updated weekly. Software project management has evolved from the foundations of ancient product development to emerge into a success not seen before in software development.

In 480 BC, King Xerxes and his advisor General Artabanus had a parting of the ways, differing on many points of view. General Artabanus is quoted as saying,

> ...the best man, in my belief, is he who lays his plans warily, with an eye for every disaster which might occur, and then, when the time comes, act boldly.

To which King Xerxes replied,

> Certainty, surety, is beyond human grasp. But however that may be, the usual thing is that profit comes to those who are willing to act, not to the overcautious and hesitant.

What do you think about planning? When is planning too much? As a project manager, software developer, stakeholder, or someone else who is involved in developing products cost-effectively, your personal opinion on this issue will affect the project development methods you prefer to use in your day-to-day business.

I would like to close this chapter with a quote from the brilliant astronomer Sir Arthur Eddington, as cited by James Newman (1956). What he says about science in his day aptly fits the current evolution of software development as a science today:

Science [software development] has its showrooms and its workshops. The public [developers] to-day, I think rightly, is not content to wander round the showrooms where the tested products are exhibited; the demand is to see what is going on in the workshops. You are welcome to enter; but do not judge what you see by the standard of the showroom.

We have been going around a workshop in the basement of the building of science. The light is dim, and we stumble sometimes. About us is confusion and mess, which there has not been time to sweep away. The workers and their machines are enveloped in murkiness. But I think that something is being shaped here—perhaps something rather big. I do not quite know what it will be when it is completed and polished for the showroom. But we can look at the present designs and the novel tools that are used in its manufacture; we can contemplate too the little successes which make us hopeful."

CHAPTER 2

■ ■ ■

The Birth of a Project: Portfolio Management

Business executives and developers look at projects differently. This chapter focuses on what the business executives need to authorize a project, and how to separate one project from another in terms of selecting the "best" project for the organization at the time. It explains what information is needed to get a project started, and how its scope is refined to prepare it for the development team. The project manager and business analyst must understand both the business management and development team perspectives to maintain the goals of both groups.

Selecting a project is part of Region 2 of the project management domain—the organizational and project context, as described in the first chapter. The product development itself is part of Region 1, the technical region. Project team members often focus so much on the project that they often miss the bigger picture that defines the context around the project. Region 2 is as equally important to success as Region 1.

Before a project manager takes responsibility for a project, someone must select which project needs to be done. The project is selected from a list of proposed or existing work called the *portfolio*, as determined by the organization's upper management. The people who manage proposals and select the project are called the *portfolio team*, typically comprised of upper management, including the CIO for software development. Selecting whether a project will use traditional or agile methods does not apply at this time. All projects start in the same way.

For a proposal to become "a project," it must be culled from the various other endeavors management has in mind. The project starts with a project proposal and goes through these various stages:

1. Submit a project proposal.

2. Align the proposal with existing business goals.

3. Find a sponsor.

4. Build a business case.

5. Prioritize the project portfolio.

6. Authorize the project with a project charter.

7. Review the portfolio periodically.

Each of these activities is described in detail in the following sections. Without these steps, one would not have a project, agile or otherwise.

Submit a Project Proposal

Anyone can submit an idea for a project, but more is needed than an idea. What is expected to be done for the project? What will the product look like when it is ready to be used? These questions must be answered before a sponsor puts any money, time, or effort into the project, or authorizes that to happen (even a compliance project must have a sponsor).

A successful proposal, one that will entice a sponsor to back it and fund it, must align with the business goals of the organization. All proposals and current in-progress projects are contained in the project portfolio, and managed by a team whose job it is to select "good" proposals that benefit the organization. A good project proposal is one that meets the business goals for the organization and is feasible. The more that the person who submits the proposal knows about the business goals of upper management, the less work must be done to get it approved, and the more likely management will approve it.

Before discussing how a proposal can align with the business goals, we must talk about what typical business goals are, and how they are expressed in the project portfolio.

Align the Proposal with Existing Business Goals

All projects currently being executed or considered by the organization are captured in the project (or program) portfolio. The word *portfolio* comes from the financial industry, where portfolios are collections of investment types to manage risk. Portfolio diversity prevents an investor from putting "all his eggs in one basket" and losing everything in case that basket breaks.

Project portfolios diversify project types and goals for the same reason. The project portfolio is a mixture of projects that achieve strategic (long-term) objectives, tactical (short-term) objectives, operational objectives (infrastructure support, sometimes called "keeping the headlights on"), and compliance (externally or internally "must do") objectives. The mixture of project types chosen reflects the project culture of the organization as aggressive or conservative, risk-adverse or risk-tolerant, and so forth.

Business Alignment

The portfolio team's first priority in approving a project is to ensure that it aligns with the business's goals and objectives defined by upper management. The executives define business strategies to ensure that the organization moves in a sustainable direction within their market segment. Companies that build products that are inconsistent with their marketing segment are soon out of business (unless the company is trying to move to a new market segment). Additionally, portfolio managers want to maximize gain. The project mix affects the value of the portfolio; therefore, the portfolio manager must evaluate different "mixes" to determine the highest value of a portfolio.

The portfolio of approved projects is organized to bring the best use of resources (personnel, funds, materials) to the organization's benefit. Companies make products that satisfy a certain market segment to build profit; even a nonprofit company's existence depends on attaining positive revenue to sustain itself.

Risk

Risk is the second priority for selecting a project. Qualitatively, at the portfolio level, negative risk can be seen as the probability of a project hurting the organization, or of taking the organization in a different direction than defined by its business strategies. Positive risks (*opportunities*) are identified and responses developed as part of project selection too. Quantitatively, risk is measured as the probability of the risk occurring times the impact if the risk event does occur. Risk has many aspects, but business risk and technical risk/complexity are two of most relevant aspects that affect how projects are selected.

Formal project management was invented as a way to manage the risk of building products. Every project has known and unknown risks, and at first few of those risks are known. Although risks are sought and discovered by the project manager (PM) as the project progresses, some project risk must be known enough for the portfolio team to make a selection decision. Some organizations are more tolerant of risk than others are. The nature and contingency of those risks, and how they are handled, is specific to the organization, the portfolio team, and the project team.

The portfolio team must justify why they are committing organizational resources to the selected project. The PMI dictum favors high-value, high-risk projects first, because if something goes wrong, the project team will have more time to correct the problem. High-value low risk projects are selected next, followed by low-value low-risk projects; low-value high-risk projects should be discarded.

After project risks are identified at the high level, the project constraints (scope, cost, time, and quality) can be adjusted to *avoid* some of the risk, *mitigate* (prevent) it, *transfer* it (such as with insurance or certain kinds of vendor contracts), or develop a *contingency* plan ("Plan B") for a particular risk event. Contingency plans also have budgets and schedules, so have similarities to subprojects. If the risk is improbable enough, or has low enough impact, the risk can be acknowledged and *accepted* (the organization will live with whatever happens).

Return on Investment (ROI)

If the project is strategically aligned, and deemed to be worth the risk, then the questions become, "How much investment in time, cost, and resources will it take to get the results desired?" and "How much will it increase or retain revenue?" The product is profitable whenever its revenue has exceeded its investment (funding) and the net revenue is higher than the maintenance or operational costs. These questions are answered quantitatively by the project's expected *return on investment* (ROI).[1]

A desired project should not be done if the company will have a negative ROI, which means it will lose money. Compliance projects and operational improvement projects are exceptions to this rule; they are accounted as the cost of doing business. Of course, contingency plans and mitigation costs from project risk must also be factored in, because they indicate the probability of a cost increase.

If the project is short, say, less than nine months in duration, then typically the ROI may be based on a *payback period* technique. Payback answers the question, "How soon will the product's revenue equal the amount of investment made?" The payback period is the project's fiscal breakeven point as measured by time.

If the project is long, then the time-value of money should be taken into account: a dollar today is not worth a dollar two years from now. For large investments, Net Present Value (NPV) is often used. If money is borrowed for the project, then the interest cost of the loan is accounted to the project cost. NPV is measured in terms of percent increase, or projected dollars.

Any revenue achieved before the investment is completely paid back can be counted into the revenue for the project as part of the ROI. Consequently, project funding is delayed as long as possible, dispersing the funds over time and balancing costs against partial-product revenue. Typical financial practices will fund a project in increments to maintain this balance between gain and loss, a practice consistent with agile's practice of delivering incremental business value as soon as possible.

Projects are funded based on how long it will take for the revenue to exceed the cost, and the longer the project takes, the most costly they become. This means that after a certain point, the project will lose money for the organization, and should be terminated. In other words, projects have a *shelf life*: there is a time when a project begins costing more than the benefits its product or service produces.

Instead of pushing a project to completion "just to get it done," or allowing it to move forward out of ignorance, the "stale" project (one that has exceeded its shelf life) should be cancelled so the organization doesn't continue throwing good money after bad. The PM needs to be aware that at some point, the project will have outlived its worth, and if it isn't completed by that time, it should be terminated.)

---

[1]ROI is meant here in the general sense: a payback of the investment made, and is not to be confused with the very specific calculation called ROI.

Unfortunately, the development teams sometimes do not recognize or understand these real boundaries because they are focused on the development aspects of the project. They are focused on the Region 1 work, and often ignore the Region 2 causes of failure. They too often see cost and schedule limits as arbitrary management restrictions with little meaning to their "real work." It is the PM's job to protect against the inherent project deadline, the fiscal point of no return.

Example Acme is building a $100,000 agile project slated for completion in ten months. However, at the end of the first three months, Acme sells the basic product and achieves $30,000 in new revenue, which offsets part of the $100,000 project cost. Each month the project team releases a newer, improved version of the product and gains another $10,000 in revenue. After four months, depending on operating costs, the product has paid for itself (up to its planned value) and is entirely self-sustaining financially; so $60,000 could be given back to the sponsor. Any new releases of the product will be pure gain. In contrast, traditional projects would not start gaining revenue until the product was released ten months after starting, and the entire $100,000 would be needed. The initial investment would not be paid back until ten months after product release.

Agile software development-project costs are lower than traditional projects, for several reasons (Rico, Sayani, and Sone 2009).

- Agile projects deliver business value sooner, so revenue begins sooner. Payback period is shorter and ROI is greater.
- Small agile teams have a lower cost of development, both for the team itself because it is small (there are no 75-person agile teams) and the software tools involved. Many software tools are low cost or free through open source. Agile teams usually do not need large, complex, and expensive tools.
- Agile projects have a higher quality, both during development and after release. Therefore, maintenance is much lower due to decreased defects, so the effort and money spent on the project is less. The product's ROI is increased and total cost of ownership (TCO) is reduced.

The agile PM must make the new economics of software products reflect these results to the boardroom and portfolio. There are plenty of statistics that show significantly improved risk management, ROI, cost, delivery speed, and quality. Rico, Sayani, and Sone's book discusses the financial benefits of many of the aspects of agile projects. (See also the references in Chapter 1.)

Product Life Span

One of the gaps in perspective between the agile team and upper management is that the agile team focuses on the *development of the project* and not the entire *life of the product.* However, the lion's share of cost and time goes into the product once it is in operation. Development is typically only 20% of the time and cost of the product, with maintenance accounting for 80% of the product's life span, and 60% of the cost (Boehm 1981).

The three phases of a product's life span, starting at release, are informally called *sunrise, zenith*, and *sunset*. (The military calls the product life span "lust to dust," in that the product goes from a much-desired idea to one that is retired.)

- *Sunrise phase:* Figure 2-1 shows the empirical relationship between development effort and maintenance effort once the product is in operations; that is, in the production environment. The product development time is shown by the hump of effort at the beginning of the product life span. The product moves to operations and enters its early maintenance stage.[2] The sunrise period is often called the "warranty period," the amount of time after the product is released that some part of the development team is retained to repair newly found defects. Typical warranty periods are 30, 60, or 90 days. If no defects are discovered in a time equal to the development time, the product is called a zero-defect product.[3]

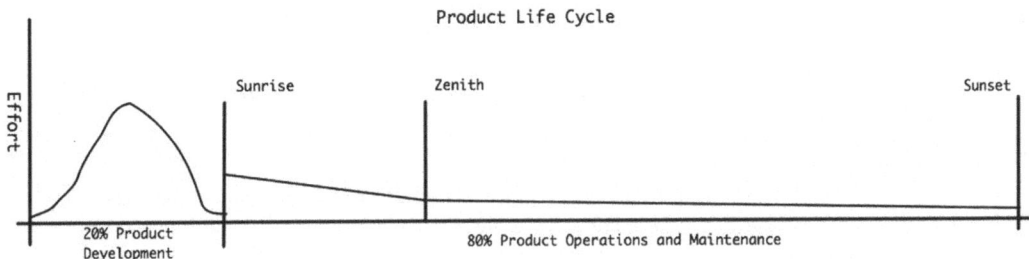

Figure 2-1. *Product life span*

- *Zenith phase:* During the Sunrise period, some defects may be found, but as they are repaired, the effort on the product decreases until it is stable and the product is in use full-force, its zenith period.

- *Sunset phase*: After a long time (sometimes ten years or longer), the product is phased out, and reaches its sunset period. It is eventually replaced with something else and retired completely.

The full product life span must be known to calculate the total cost of building and operating the product. When the product will be retired or phased out is usually not known, and thus frequently ignored. A rough estimate of how long the product will survive, plus the time and cost estimates for development, is usually sufficient to select a project at the portfolio level.

Total Cost of Ownership (TCO)

The portfolio team must be concerned not only with project cost, but also with the total cost of the entire *product life span*. Their first priority is not *how* a team gets the product built, but *when it starts delivering value to the customer,* and how much it costs to keep it running: cost of materials, tools, and resources to

---

[2]The sunrise period shown in Figure 2-1 is equal to the product development time, a common metric for determining zero-defect products.
[3]By statistical standards, there is no such thing as a zero-defect product because the product must be monitored for an infinite amount of time before such a claim can be made. The newer definition was announced at an OOPSLA conference in 1996.

build the product, cost of product release, cost of training, and cost of maintenance and support.[4] All this is the total cost of ownership (TCO) for the product. TCO must be less than the product's revenue and benefits, and the longer the product is in development, the higher the TCO. This is another factor inherent in the project's shelf life.

For traditional projects, the ROI for the project doesn't occur until the product is well into the zenith stage or later. For agile projects, ROI can occur after as little as 30 days. Project managers must keep the total cost of the product in mind, which is usually not the first thought of the technical team. You can be sure the sponsor, and most of the stakeholders, keep the TCO in mind if they are contributing to the project funding.

The product does not start producing revenue until it is in operations, whether that is through a single traditional release, or through multiple agile releases. The longer development takes, the more investment and time needed to get the investment back. Spending too much money up front in the development phase could mean that the return on investment may take longer than the product will ever be able to recover.

There is a breakeven point at which time the product begins to lose money for the organization, by decreased revenue or accumulating operational and maintenance costs. When that happens, the product should be retired (unless it is a compliance project or explicitly selected as a special investment, such as moving the company into a new market.)

Find a Sponsor

The sponsor fills a critical role: funding, guidance, and project championship. The sponsor pays for the project (by definition), and subsequently will define its initial scope and milestones (roadmap). Because project success depends on political influence most of the time, the sponsor must also resolve conflicting influences from the stakeholders, and escalated project problems from the technical team. In many cases, the sponsor submits the project proposal and drives the project. In that case, the sponsor is filling the Scrum role of Product Owner (there is no specific role called "Sponsor" on a Scrum team).

It is important that the management team and its infrastructure *show support* to allow the assets of the organization to be used to develop the project. Those assets include budgeted funding, revenue, staff resources, physical assets like computers and office space, and eventually sales and marketing if necessary. The stakeholders will expect the project to have a sponsor, or they will not see the project as truly viable. It is not uncommon to see projects fail as stakeholders avoid project team meetings—they don't want to waste time on what they consider a failed effort.

The portfolio team usually wants answers to such questions as: Why should our organization approve this as a project? What happens if we don't? Will this project accomplish something that is aligned with our company's mission, vision, and goals? How much time and money will it take to accomplish? If the sponsor does not provide these answers, the portfolio team may ask for a little investigative work before the project—its *due diligence*, that partly justifies doing the project; a *feasibility study* is performed to get that information. Sometimes a sponsor won't step forward until these data are known.

Build a Business Case

The sponsor or portfolio team decides if the proposal warrants the time and effort of a *business case*, sometimes called a *financial feasibility study*, to collect the data the portfolio team needs to decide if the project should proceed. The business case is not a technical study to determine design options, but to support the decision to add the project to the organization's list of projects to do, and at what priority. Sometimes a business case is included in the project proposal as a way of shortening the decision process.

---

[4]TCO can be affected due to insufficient documentation and support materials resulting in future maintainers having to spend extra time "learning" the code and other factors of maintaining existing software. This will usually result in a higher TOC.

The project proposal provides the structure and framework from which the feasibility team can collect the initial financial data. They can add the business case data to the proposal. After authorization, this same document is the basis for the project charter. Since the portfolio team meets periodically (it is rarely a day-to-day decision event), a proposal with a business case will move faster through the decision process than the three-step process of proposal, feasibility, and authorization. I recommend always submitting a fully prepared proposal if the sponsor is available and willing to commit to the project at the time the proposal is written.

The project's business case can be handled in one of several ways.

- Some organizations will assign someone to build the business case, and write off the expense as the cost of doing business.

- An upper manager may claim tentative or conditional sponsorship and allot a small part of his or her budget to do the study, or charge the study to operating costs.

- Often, the business case is built by the person delegated who is later assigned as the PM for the project. (The PM and other roles of the project have not yet been selected, nor have they been *authorized* to be selected.)

- If a standing technical team exists, then the business case is better prepared by both the business and technical team members.

The data to answer these questions can usually be collected within three to ten days, depending on the complexity and size of the project.

Prioritize the Project Portfolio

How should a portfolio be prioritized? What is most important to a company when each customer department has different needs and their own priorities? There are many ways the team may characterize and sort portfolio projects: strategic, tactical, compliance, risk, business complexity, technical complexity, value delivered, urgency, enterprise impact, cost, resources, duration, dependencies, and many more. This section will discuss project types and multiple criteria for getting the best benefits for the resources and time committed.

Project Types

The portfolio team evaluates each project proposal to select the best combination of project types (strategic, tactical, operational, compliance) to fit or align with upper management directives. These project types are described briefly next.

- *Strategic*: The project is typically long-term to meet a long-term objective. Strategic projects often have higher levels of risk than the others do. Building a new product for public release for next year is an example of a strategic project.

- *Tactical*: The project is typically short-term to meet a short-term objective, but bigger than what might pass as a task. Installing an enterprise-level help desk turnkey application would be an example of a tactical project.

- *Operational*: Operational projects[5] are projects that support the enterprise as a whole, whereas a project usually enhances or enlarges the business processes of targeted business units. Installing a new set of computer databases for all departments is an example of an operational project.

---

[5]An "operational" project can get confused with operational tasks. A project is a "temporary endeavor that is undertaken to create a unique product, service or result" (PMBOK 2013), and is very different from operational tasks, which are recurring and provide continual support for the organization. Operations and projects follow different sets of rules.

- *Compliance.* The project must be done to comply with an external regulatory body, internal organization standards, or a law. There is often no business value or gain from completing a compliance project but the organizational *must* do it. Removing all personal data from the medical history database to comply with HIPPA[6] laws and regulations is an example of a compliance project.

Of course, as organizations change, their directives and goals change, and the portfolio of approved projects will change. Organizational-direction changes contribute to imposed deadlines for a project. Organizational change is one of the reasons that the portfolio must be reviewed periodically to ensure that existing projects are still beneficial to the organization.

A good mix of project types optimizes the portfolio to minimize risk and maximize benefits. The portfolio should be sorted first by project type—strategic, tactical, operational, or compliance projects—then within each type, prioritized by multiple criteria that represent the organizations business profile: prioritized as to which projects are the most important ones to do first so the company can get the most value fastest (an agile principle). Portfolio diversification allows the company to achieve long- and short-term goals while still maintaining operational activities—"keeping the headlights on."

Many PMOs (and portfolio teams) cannot tell how many projects their organization has the capacity to execute, thinking they don't have enough resources. Actually, they have not organized the portfolio properly, and if they did, they would find more resources available. Improper portfolio organization is the second largest waste of a PMO. (Trying to multitask teams across multiple projects at the same time is the first largest waste. We will deal with this counterintuitive principle in later chapters.)

✖ Metaphor   Prioritization examples commonly use a metaphor of placing large rocks, middle-size rocks, and pebbles into a jar to maximize how many can be put in: the portfolio should contain a few strategic projects (big rocks), a majority of tactical projects (small rocks), and as many operational projects (pebbles) as necessary. Compliance projects must be added when they are demanded, and of course, adding them will affect the number of projects of the other kinds the organization can accomplish with their finite resources— the jar has a fixed size called *organizational capacity.* Sometimes compliance projects must preempt existing projects in the portfolio.

The rocks-in-a-jar metaphor can be extended to include "sand," which is the work that provides no business value. Some activities that have no business value are required for support, such as important meetings, prioritizing the portfolio, and acquiring project teams. Other activities are not required but are done anyway, such as unnecessary meetings and unnecessary documentation. One of agile's principles is to ruthlessly pare aware unnecessary activities. The "sand" metaphor emphasizes the idea that "motion," as agile calls it, is not always progress. The more sand in the jar, the fewer rocks of business value can fit. Significantly, when rocks rub together, they produce sand, and so trying to do too many projects at the same time creates the sand that prevents more business value from being obtained, sometimes excluding the rocks (business value) that created the sand.

---

[6]The Health Insurance Portability and Accountability Act of 1996 (HIPAA) protects the privacy of individually identifiable health information. See http://www.hhs.gov/ocr/privacy.

Project Selection Criteria

For the portfolio team to approve, deny, or defer a project proposal, the proposal needs enough data to determine business alignment, the stakeholders who are involved, ROI, TCO, general risk factors, rough-order-of-magnitude (ROM) estimates for cost and duration, and other information collected to justify the project.

Selecting the right mix of projects for the organization is important. Forrester Research (Symons et al. 2008) recommends that projects should be selected from multiple criteria for each project type. The criteria depend on what is important to the portfolio team and the organization, within each type, such as alignment with the business strategies, risk to the organization and the candidate project, return on investment, and total cost of ownership of the product. Each organization will have its own selection criteria, but this chapter discusses a few of the most important ones common to all portfolios.

Within each project type (strategy, tactical, operational, or compliance), each criterion (business alignment, project risk, ROI, or TCO) provides one value by which the portfolio team may objectively compare and select the best project for the organization. For example, each criterion can be given a value from 1 (least valuable) to 10 (most valuable) and the sum of all criteria characterizes a project. The projects can then be sorted to determine which ones have the largest value.

The completed project proposal should provide sufficient information about the project to support a go/no-go decision to move forward. To decide whether it is a viable project, some of these questions would be good to ask when evaluating each within the organizational and portfolio context.

- *Does the product align with business strategy?* The sponsor (or portfolio team) has probably already decided if the product or service, the result of executing the project, aligns with current business strategy. The business case will verify that earlier decision. If the project does not align closely enough with business strategy, it is not a candidate (compliance and operational projects excluded).

- *Does the project have acceptable risk and cost?* The feasibility study has identified risks and costs at a high level. The budget needed is then determined by these factors along with the risk response. If either the investment cost or TCO is too high, or the ROI too long, the project is no longer a candidate. If the cost is acceptable, but the funding is not available now, then the project can be deferred until the next portfolio review. It is increasingly common, and almost always for agile projects, to fund the project in small increments during the project's life span, and augment it by any revenue attained by partial releases.

- *Where should the project fit into the portfolio?* The portfolio is sorted by the value of its multivalued criteria. However, dependencies can change the portfolio order. Typical dependencies may include the following: one project must be completed before another; an essential system or resource is not available until after a certain date; funding is not yet available; or the culture is not mature enough to develop or accept such a product. Of course, prioritization works the other way: certain projects are urgent, and must be moved to the top of the list. This is common for projects that must comply with legal mandates, standards policies, or political decisions.

- *Are the resources available?* If the project is viable, are there enough people to work on the project now? Each project proposal in the portfolio may list a first guess of the project team members, how many people of what skill set (role) need to be involved. If they are added to the new project being proposed, how much will the other proposed projects be delayed? This is especially important for NPV ROI's where the time value of money is involved.[7]

---

[7] An important Agile rule says to never use the same *core* team member for multiple concurrent projects (multitasking), but some people are not needed full-time, such as database analysts, tech writers, or representatives from the help desk or operations team.

The portfolio team queues the projects from the highest priority to the lowest (exactly the way an agile project handles its feature backlog). The projects are assigned (or continued) as warranted by the capacity of the organization.

🔑 Recommendation　An important and valuable way to prioritize the projects within a portfolio includes looking at the project mix and determining how the mix affects value. The proper prioritization can increase portfolio ROI by doing projects in an order that reduces times to realize the portfolio's ROI (or other benefits).

If a common sizing metric is used, then it can be used as a way of estimating how fast new projects can be started. However, unlike agile projects that typically use story points and team velocity to predict progress achieved, story points are relative to the team, and cannot be used for cross-project comparisons. A better way of scheduling projects starts by comparing the milestone schedule and completion dates of currently executing projects with the proposed project.

Ironically, portfolio teams usually run through some multivalued selection exercise, but then pick the projects in the order they want to do them anyway. Strong political factors play into the project selection process. However it is defined, the final prioritization may come down to a subjective evaluation at some level of granularity. Depending on the political, emotional, and cultural environment, subjective evaluation usually does not provide a best solution to the project mix. Various techniques have been developed around this problem. One of them is the Delphi technique (Wood and Silver 1995), a group nominal multi-vote technique that is used for emotionally laden decisions, or decisions made in highly political environments. A description and tutorial for using the Delphi technique is included in the *Additional Tools* section.

A good strategy to use: fill the portfolio list with slightly more projects than the organization has capacity to do, whether limited by people, money, or something else. Give up on the really low-priority projects—by the time that those projects are ready to go, business and circumstances may have changed, and newer proposals will preempt the low-value potential projects. It is important that the organization knows how many projects they can support in a given time period, usually one fiscal year, so they can optimize their resources and finances.

⚡ Warning　Novices to portfolio management think that by making a list of many projects, they will do them all eventually in the order listed. That is the intent. However, during the time that top-priority projects are being completed, new projects arise and are added to the portfolio list. Most new projects are added at a higher priority than the existing low-priority projects; partly because they are rationally justified by circumstances and partly because they are evident in the minds of management and seem more important to them at the time. The lower priority projects will never get done because they are constantly being preempted. Assume that only the top 70% of this "project buffer" will ever get selected for completion—a maxim from the agile method DSDM (Cohn 2006).

Authorize the Project with a Charter

The project *charter* is a key document for a project, and many projects have failed without one. It is the next step after a proposal has been approved, which usually is tentative depending on more detail from the sponsor.

The charter does not have to be big—one or two pages is sufficient. The charter will contain the sponsor's vision, mission, and roadmap for the project. The roadmap can be monitored to act as high-level success criteria for project progress. The project will also need an estimate of ROI to justify the funding from upper management.

The Project Vision and Mission

The project *vision* is the sponsor's dream. It is <u>why</u> the sponsor is providing funding, support, and how he or she expects the project result to fit into and contribute to the organization in the future. The *mission statement* is the practical implementation of the project. It is the tactical description of *how* the project will accomplish its business goals.

If the sponsor is going to add money, and ensure that the project will be completed in time to see a positive return on investment, he or she will estimate how long the project will take. Toward that end, he or she will define interim waypoints of completion at a high level, a series of *objectives* for the project. An objective is a *key event or deliverable* that contributes to the progress of the project goal consistent with the objective. Common agile objectives include the feature backlog (a list of features from the stakeholders), working code for a key feature, a demo of the partially delivered product, and a key stakeholder approval meeting.

Milestones and the Roadmap

Some objectives will have dates (either rough estimates or mandates) associated with them at this point. Consider a *milestone* as an objective with an associated completion date (and sometimes a start date.)

Milestones should follow the SMART guidelines; that is, each milestone should be

- *Specific* – target a specific area for improvement.

- *Measurable* – quantify or at least suggest an indicator of progress.

- *Assignable* – specify who will do it.

- *Realistic* – state what results can realistically be achieved, given available resources.

- *Time-related* – specify when (a date) the result(s) can be achieved.

It is this last characteristic—the completion date—that distinguishes a milestone from an objective.

The project roadmap is the sequenced collection of milestones to accomplish the sponsor's mission. Each milestone has a clear success criteria, a "definition of done." The project roadmap is not a project plan in the traditional sense; it is merely the list of dates that the sponsor *expects* the project to accomplish before it is completed.

The Project Charter

The *project charter*, usually one or two pages long, contains the initial definition of the project and product scope, as defined by the sponsor.

- *Vision statement*: The reason that the sponsor drives or supports the project.

- *Mission statement*: How the mission will be achieved (strategy or tactical statement).

- *Roadmap*: Chain of interim waypoints (milestones) of partial project success.

- *List of key stakeholders*: People who play a key role in the project, and can help determine the success or failure of the project.

- *Business case*: Optional financial feasibility study to justify the project.

- *Budgeting model*: How often funding will be allocated, especially if it is different from what's normal for the organization.

These five (or six) elements are all that are needed for the project to move forward to the next level of detail. They are enough to assign a project manager, and often enough to convince the organization to back the project. Traditional charters will contain much more information about the project up front but agile projects will use this "barely sufficient" charter, allowing it to grow as new information is discovered during the project.

The project charter serves the portfolio team, project manager, program manager, and others in many ways. The following list describes some the many uses for this key document.

- *Portfolio team:* The project charter structure, being of standard format, provides a common point of comparison between other projects so they can make easier and quicker to compare projects "apples-to-apples." The portfolio team can evaluate and prioritize the portfolio easier and more quickly.

- *Upper management and sponsors:* If enough information is collected to complete the project charter, upper management may be less averse to sponsoring the project.

- *Project manager:* The project charter is sufficient after the project is approved. The key constraints of scope, cost, and schedule are listed, and if desired, financial reporting and progress updates can be added to the charter. Later, quantitative goals from the stakeholders are provided, which help the PM manage expectations and keep the project goals in sight. The charter defines the scope at the highest level, but allows the PM to get a jump-start on the project right out of the portfolio gate.

- *Stakeholders:* The project charter can serve as a working document after project approval for status reporting, periodic updates as milestones are achieved, risk management, financial reporting, and general info. The charter is a logical place (but not required) for the PM to update project status so the business stakeholders can use the on-going proposal like a status report if they want more detail than a simple red/yellow/green dashboard report. For agile projects, the charter would document the business metrics while periodic user demonstrations would communicate the product progress with burn-up (or burn-down) charts.

- *Program managers and the PMO:* Whether PMO means *project management office* or *program management office* in your organization, the standard format of the charter provides a point of commonality for program managers to compare various projects within their program,[8] and find dependences between the program's projects.

This version of the project charter is not final; as project knowledge changes, the project progress should be periodically reviewed to see if it should continue, or be cancelled. Unfortunately, once a project is underway, few stakeholders review the project status to make that determination.

It usually falls to the PM to monitor and recommend that a project be cancelled if necessary. Unfortunately again, the PM is invested in the project, and usually tries to save it even against overwhelming odds ("heroic efforts").

A portfolio team drastically increases the likelihood that "good money isn't wasted on bad projects." Some PMs will fight to save a sinking project, and sometimes will succeed; but a better PM knows when the project will sink, and will evacuate the stakeholders from the wreck in time. Fortunately, most agile projects finish successfully on all counts: schedule, budget, scope, and customer satisfaction.

---

[8]The PMBOK (2013) defines a *program* is "a collection of related projects, subprograms, or program activities managed in a coordinated way to obtain benefits not available from managing them individually" (553); and a *portfolio* as "project, programs, subportfolios, and operations managed as a group to achieve strategic objectives." (551).

An example of a project charter for an ATM project, with field descriptions and notes as illustrative examples that the reader may use to adapt to his or her own organization and needs can be found as Source Code under www.apress.com. Reading through this material provides detailed information on the chartering process.

☞ Recommendation   If I am assigned as the project's PM, and the project charter does not exist, or is incomplete, I find it invaluable to have this two-page document. It is my first step in gathering all the data needed to proceed. Usually it takes not much more than a conversation with the sponsor. Usually, the roadmap will not have dates, and those can be worked out later when all the stakeholders are known, and the product scope is better known.

Review the Portfolio Periodically

Managers are aware that long-range estimates (say, longer than one year) are not reliable, so increasingly, portfolio teams review the portfolio for changing priorities, and the progress of in-flight projects and their ROIs, typically each quarter. The frequency of portfolio review usually coincides with the funding allocations, which can be allocated a fiscal quarter at a time. This approach allows the organization to make quicker adjustments to their funding spending, business strategies, and minimize the risk of bad estimates. The review may also be driven by how often upper management wants status. Annual reviews of project status are not likely to be frequent enough.

If the project charter is the standard way organizations start and identify projects within the portfolio, then the charter is updated each time before the portfolio is reviewed. Budgets, status, milestones, financials, and other information of each project can be updated in the project charter, and is usually rolled up into an executive level red/yellow/green dashboard report that communicates the status visually at a glance.

According to The Standish Group (Gale 2011), 21% to 42% of started projects should be stopped before completion because they failed or did not deliver as expected. The portfolio review allows the portfolio team to evaluate these projects and stop them before they consume unrecoverable assets. It helps the team to "stop throwing good money after bad." In this case, the PM joke applies: "What's worse than beating a dead horse?" Answer: "Betting on it." Throwing more time and money onto a project that should be killed is like betting on a dead horse.

Differences with Agile

For some reason, projects using agile methods have gained a reputation that some have mistakenly interpreted as not using schedules, using guess-and-check development methods, and ad hoc feature definition. From management's point of view, this approach is undesirable because it fails to answer the questions needed by the portfolio team, sponsor, or the project manager.

For these kinds of agile projects, there are no measurables (metrics) by which the portfolio team can choose a project, and they are not likely to select a project that is a shot in the dark. If the technical team moves the project forward regardless, without management approval or knowledge— so-called *stealth projects*—managers can get annoyed. It also puts the stealth project at risk when management assigns a (different) approved project to the stealth project team, who then must drop the stealth project and work on the approved one—a huge waste of time and effort.

Fortunately, those metric-less characteristics are not part of the agile approach. Agile projects do have schedules and costs, some upfront scope, and deal with risk—albeit these elements are first estimated at the broadest levels. The major difference between agile projects and traditional projects at the portfolio level depends on how the following questions are answered.

- *How much detailed product information is predefined before work begins?* Traditional projects try to define all detail before any coding gets started; agile projects collect only enough information to move forward.

- *How much formality (documentation, standards, and ceremony) is required as part of the project deliverables?* Agile projects minimize the amount of documentation needed.

- *How short are the feedback cycles between the development team and the customers or stakeholders before the product is revised?* Agile teams try to work with customers and stakeholders daily, and recommend including a customer representative on the development team. Feedback cycles are frequent and intrinsic to agile practices.

- *How often are product releases?* More frequent releases increases feedback to increase product quality, decrease the overhead of producing a release, and support earlier revenue returned to offset project cost.

PMI Parallels

The project charter, as described earlier, complies with what the PMI calls a project charter, although traditional projects have required much more predictive documentation and more guarantees before proceeding. For agile projects, the charter is sufficient for the portfolio team and PM as described.

The PMI focuses on ten "bodies of knowledge" (or BOKs): *Integration, Scope, Time, Cost, Quality, Human Resources, Communications, Risk, Procurement,* and *Stakeholder Management.*[9] As many aspects or BOKs as desired can be identified in the project proposal or charter, although some are inherently defined later, like the people assigned to the team (Human Resources). In Region 2, the PM and BA play roles similar to those in traditional projects; the big differences between agile and traditional projects show up just before the repeating iterations start in Region 1.

After the portfolio team authorizes the project and the PM with the charter, the PM of a traditional project begins to build the various management plans, which are often voluminous. Agile projects rely on the principle of "barely sufficient documentation," and these subordinate plans are not built. They are either not needed the data is not well enough known until project execution gets under way, or because the policies are built-in to the agile practices, a kind of preconfiguration of project management approaches.

Agile development uses a predefined subset of project management in general, and consequently, many management plans are unnecessary because they are defined by the agile process itself. The agile PM will not write those plans, except for the project schedule and milestones, which are, or should soon be, in the charter. (Later, the sponsor, PM, and technical team will build other documents, most notably the *release plan*—a schedule of iterations.) What may be called a "management plan" for agile projects is the one- to two-page charter.

---

[9]The ten BOKs can be easily remembered by the mnemonic "**I** Saw **T**wo **C**rows **Q**uietly **H**aving **C**offee and **R**eading **P**oetry **S**lowly," referring to Integration, Scope, Time, Cost, Quality, Human Resource, Communications, Risk, Procurement, and Stakeholder Management, respectively. Special thanks to Richard Vail of Vail Training Associates.

Conclusion

Regardless of how the project will be executed, agile projects and traditional projects both originate from a portfolio of possibilities and ideas. At the portfolio level, the portfolio team must evaluate the project proposals *to maximize the value delivered to the customer* while balancing these considerations:

- Best aligned to the business strategies

- Minimize risk, both during the project and after the product is released

- Maximize the project's return-on-investment (ROI)

- Minimize the product's total cost of ownership

This chapter discussed how the portfolio team selects a project for execution, using the project proposal as the key artifact. We looked at the different perspectives between *agilists* (those who practice agile techniques well) and upper management. In the past, these perspectives have produced a conflicting relationship.

The project proposal gives management enough information for each of them to get project momentum started and a leg-up on getting the product out the door. The project charter is the melding document for a great partnership between the technical team and the business team going forward.

Most agile books focus on the technical aspects of the project itself: Region 1 of the technical domain; but equally important is the organizational context and culture that supports the project, Region 2. Fortunately, both groups want the same thing: the quickest business value to the customer with a minimum of ceremony and cost. Agile teams interpret this as getting a product to the customer as quickly as possible with short feedback cycles and controlled rework (refactoring). Management interprets the goal as obtaining high ROI with low maintenance costs for a product that benefits the organization.

At this point in the project process, a kernel of a product idea has been defined, a sponsor to fund and support it has stepped forward, and a project manager can be assigned to continue to drive the project, refining detail and estimates as needed. For Region 2, there is little difference between traditional projects and agile projects, except the expectations of the respective members of those schools of thought.

In summary, Table 2-1 shows the key artifacts of this step in the process, and who probably takes ownership of that task. This table identifies the general deliverables for progressing a project from proposal to initial execution, and could be used as a general charter structure.

Table 2-1. *Initial Objectives When Starting a Project*

Objective	Owner
Submit a project proposal	Anyone
Align the proposal with business goals	Proposer or Sponsor
Find a sponsor	Executive management or proposer
Build a business case	Sponsor or delegate
Prioritize the project within the portfolio	Portfolio team
Build project charter	Sponsor

In the next chapter, we talk about how the project manager travels through Region 2 to the boundaries of Region 1 and what must be accomplished along the way.

Additional Tools

Prioritization Process Using the Delphi Technique

Background and Motivation

The Delphi technique[10] was developed by the RAND Corporation in the late 1960s as a forecasting methodology. Later, the US government enhanced it as a group decision-making tool with the results of Project HINDSIGHT, which established a factual basis for the workability of Delphi. That project produced a tool in which a group of experts could come to some consensus when the decisive factors were subjective, and not knowledge-based.

Delphi is particularly appropriate when decision-making is required in a political or emotional environment, or when the decisions affect strong factions with opposing preferences. The tool works formally or informally, in large or small contexts, and reaps the benefits of group decision-making while insulating the process from the limitations of group decision-making; for example, over-dominant group members, political lobbying, or "bandwagonism."

Delphi has worked well when prioritizing national funding for projects among different states with conflicting goals, or if the scale of the decision-making problem is very large:

> *The size of the budget for ASSIST, and the large number of proposals submitted, generated a complex decision problem. For example, the number of possible ways of funding is far more than could be considered individually. In view of this, and the need to identify secondary criteria and allow them to influence the funding decision, decision makers at [National Cancer Institute] decided that a formal modeling approach should be used. [Hall92]*

Taiwan used the method to prioritize their entire Information Technology industry, and they conclude:

> *Finally, these decisions reflect the experts' world views, life experiences, cognitive feelings and perceptions. Thus, these results are based on the participants' subjective assessments, which may also be influenced by data. Decision-making in itself is subjective. However, the use of experts in a systematic manner will yield a satisfactory solution to sociotechnical problems. [Madu91]*

Delphi has the added advantage that it works as an informal, subjective model when the decisions are based on opinion, and can be directly converted to a formal model, when the data is more knowledge-based.

Delphi Prioritization Procedure

The remainder of this document describes the general procedure for defining key criteria and prioritizing items that use those criteria (for example, project funding). It is a variation on the classic Delphi technique adapted from the National Cancer Institute to fit the particular problems of corporate project prioritization.

---

[10]Adapted from a white paper first published at www.carolla.com by Carolla Development, Inc. (Cline 2000)

The prioritization process enumerated next allows the stakeholders and subject matter experts to produce a list of project rankings, or several lists, from which the decision-makers in upper management may apply other criteria to make a decision. The process can be completed in a few short meetings by a panel of experts, by the corporate associates at large in a series of questionnaires, or by a hybrid of the two. The following description is vague when company policy or facilitator discretion may be used to invoke a variation.

1. *Pick a facilitation leader.* Select a person that can facilitate, is an expert in research data collection, and is not a stakeholder. An outsider is often the common choice.

2. *Select a panel of experts.* The panelists should have an intimate knowledge of the projects, or be familiar with experiential criteria that would allow them to prioritize the projects effectively. In this case, the department managers or project leaders (even though stakeholders) are appropriate.

3. *Identify a "straw man" criteria list from the panel.* In a brainstorming session, build a list of criteria that all think appropriate to the projects at hand. Input from non-panelists is welcome. At this point, there are no "correct" criteria. However, business alignment, risk, ROI, technical merit, and cost are the usual criteria; secondary criteria may be project-specific.

4. *The panel ranks the criteria.* For each criterion, the panel ranks it as 1 (very important), 2 (somewhat important), or 3 (not important). Each panelist ranks the list individually—and anonymously if the environment is charged politically or emotionally.

5. *Calculate the mean and deviation.* For each item in the list, find the mean value and remove all items with a mean greater than or equal to 2.0. Place the criteria in rank order and show the (anonymous) results to the panel. Discuss reasons and assumptions for items with high standard deviations, which indicate high levels of disagreement. The panel may insert removed items back into the list after discussion.

6. *Re-rank the criteria.* Repeat the ranking process among the panelists until the results stabilize. The ranking results do not have to have complete agreement, but a consensus such that the all can live with the outcome. Two passes are often enough, but four are frequently performed for maximum benefit. In one variation, general input is allowed after the second ranking in hopes that more information from outsiders will introduce new ideas or new criteria, or improve the list.

7. *Identify project constraints and preferences.* Projects as a whole are often constrained by total corporate budget, or mandatory requirements like regulatory impositions. These "hard constraints" are used to set boundaries on the project ranking. More flexible, "soft constraints" are introduced as preferences. Typically, hard constraints apply to all projects; preferences usually apply to only some projects. Each panelist is given a supply of preference points, about 70% of the total number of projects. (For example, give each panelist 21 preference points if 30 projects have been defined.)

8. *Rank projects by constraint and preference.* Each panelist ranks the projects first by the hard constraints. Which project is most important to that panelist? Some projects may be ignored. For example, if the total corporate budget is 100 million, the panelist allocates each project a budget, up to the maximum requested for that particular project, and such that the total of all budgets does not exceed the $100 million. Some projects may not be allocated any funding. Next, each panelist spreads his or her preference points among the project list as desired. Some projects may get ten points, others may get none, but the total may not exceed the predefined maximum (21 in the preceding example).

9. *Analyze the results and feedback to panel.* Find the median ranking for each project and distribute the projects into quartiles of 25th, 50th, and 75th percentiles (50th percentile being the median). Produce a table of ranked projects, with preference points, and show to the panel. Projects between the 25th and 75th quartile may be considered to have consensus (depending on the degree of agreement desired); projects in the outer-quartiles should be discussed. Once the reason for the large difference in ranking is announced, repeat the ranking process.

10. *Re-rank the projects until it stabilizes.* After discussing why some people (minority opinion) ranked their projects as they did, repeat the rankings. Eventually the results will stabilize after now more than four passes: projects will come to a consensus. Not everyone may be persuaded to rank the same way, but discussion is unnecessary when the opinions stay fixed. Present the ranking table to the decision makers, with the various preferences as options, for their final decision.

Alternate Method for Secondary Passes

After the first pass using the preceding procedures to obtain a ranking, second and subsequent passes can be use multipoint vote to set a clear prioritization. Instead of asking the panelist to assign values 1, 2, or 3, ask them to assign points to each item, up to a maximum of N points, where N is 70% of the total number of items in the list. (For example, if there are 50 items in the list, then every panelist assigns no more than 35 points to all items.) This approach forces some item to have zero points, and allows the panelist to reflect higher priority items with more points.

The resulting ranking of mean and standard deviation is more granular, and allows better discussion and stability of the prioritized list. High standard deviations still need to be discussed for hidden assumptions.

CHAPTER 3

■ ■ ■

Project Startup

Overview

In the previous chapter, we saw how and why the portfolio team selected the project. It ended with a project manager being assigned to move the project forward, guided by the project charter. Before the actual product construction gets underway, some preparatory work is necessary, which is critical to cultivating the fertile ground for both the business and technical team and sowing a good working partnership between them.

In more general terms, this chapter will describe the objectives in Region 2 (organizational preparation) with the sociological and psychological aspects that differentiate PM-2 from PM-1. It also addresses the differences between traditional and agile upfront work and roles before the actual construction work starts.

Preparatory work (non-developmental work) is divided into two parts: project startup and Iteration 0. Project startup work includes activities that are done with the initial business team for initial scoping. Iteration 0 is the pre-development work that both the business team and technical teams must do before the actual product construction iterations start. Whether activities should happen before or within Iteration 0 is not clean; the tasks can be moved as needed. Generally, the acquisition of the technical team and the technical team meeting initiates Iteration 0. This chapter covers project startup; Iteration 0 activities are discussed in Chapters 4 through 7.

During the project manager's discovery trek through Region 2, he or she must pass certain milestones (objectives or artifacts[1]) to maintain project momentum. Each step informs later steps in the project. The artifacts comply with the agile axiom *barely sufficient documentation*; each one is one to two pages in length.

Each objective and artifact is achieved through a group facilitation with the PM, business analyst (BA), stakeholders, and team members, as appropriate.

1. Hold a *business kickoff meeting* to identify all stakeholders, schedule future meetings, and set stakeholder expectations. Assign business abstracts (initial project expectations) to stakeholders to collect before the next meeting

2. Develop the *project abstract*, a high-level view of what is, and what is not, in the project scope, all stakeholders' objectives, and relevant business workflows. Approve it (get a consensus) at the next business team meeting.

3. Develop a *communication plan*, a simple action plan of how certain stakeholders will be engaged, and how they will receive or provide information of certain kinds. This is a key artifact (a one-page table) for managing stakeholder expectations.

---

[1]Here *artifact* is used as a key document that informs later parts of the project, or members of the project. *Interim* or *working documents* are also created, used somewhat like a scratchpad, and discarded, so are not considered artifacts.

4. Build the *feature catalog*, a list all the features of the product, prioritized by business value and estimated for size; also called the *product backlog*.

5. Build a preliminary *release plan* with the business and sponsor, defining iteration lengths with high-level scope content, and applying release milestones to the calendar.

A common point of confusion is where the PM and BA fit into agile projects. The PM and BA play the traditional role in Region 2 (project selection and pre-development work), and they play a different role in Region 1 (technical development during project execution). Although the roles in Region 2 are more traditional, the relationship between the PM and stakeholders are improved if agile values are added into Region 2 activities. The PM and BA facilitate with the stakeholders to get a group understanding of the requirements, and the result is always a work in progress that is refined and improved later. The more the stakeholders understand about agile principles, and are willing to use them, the better the relationship and product.

The Project Manager

Before continuing, I need to define better what I mean by a project manager. Some organizations do not authorize a person to manage all aspects of a project. Some aspects of the project are kept from their control. Often, this kind of "project manager" is delegated to keeping track of project activities, reporting status, and other administrative tasks. They have no control (and sometimes, no input) over resources, budget, or key decisions. This person is more correctly referred to as a *project coordinator*, or *project administrator*, and is not a fully functioning project manager. All further discussion in this book will refer to a fully functioning project manager, and not a project administrator or coordinator. The points in this book are still applicable to them, but at a much narrower scope.

Once the selected project manager is handed the charter, he or she is now authorized to begin the project. His or her responsibilities in Region 2 include:

- Define and gather the stakeholders and customer SMEs to form the business team. (The charter only contained some of the stakeholders; the PM must discover any others that are missing from the charter.)

- Identify with the business team their objectives and expectations, and reconcile them with the sponsor's vision, mission and success criteria.

- Identify how best to engage and communicate information of interest to each stakeholder involved in the project; that is, create a one-page communication plan.

- Proceed from the charter to gather the high-level scope with the BA to build the preliminary release plan.

The duties of the PM will change significantly when Iteration 0 starts; the PM becomes the APM.

The Product Owner

Agile Variants The Scrum agile method defines a role called *product owner* (PO), a single person, usually the sponsor, who represents all requirements and needs of all stakeholders. All requirements are the responsibility of the PO, and all stakeholders must go through the PO to get their desired features into the product. The PO and all project team members work together to perform all actions—requirements, analysis, design, coding, testing, and change management.

Other agile methods, such as XP, do not have a single person control all the requirements, but allow the technical team to discuss requirements directly with each of the stakeholders who wish to present their feature. The entire team will talk with each stakeholder and work out exactly what needs to be implemented. Refinements and changes will occur at the code level as the customers think of new features or change their minds.

If the product is small, and the sponsor wants to get directly involved, these variants can work well. However, there are several practical problems with this approach being applied in Region 2.

- The technical team is not available at this point in the project. It is the PM's job to define and form the team for the project.[2] Most agile books do not address this issue, but assume the technical team already exists and focuses on Region 1 aspects of product development.

- The sponsor is rarely available for the amount of time recommended by agile books to work with the team. Many agile books expect daily engagement, which is ideal but rarely occurs. The sponsor usually has many projects and executive responsibilities to perform, so the sponsor will delegate a PO for large or complex projects. It works equally well to have multiple customer SMEs talk with the BA, and by spreading the work, does not take as much time from any single business individual (except the BA).

- The requirements discovery process takes much-needed time, and developers are usually on the critical path designing, coding, and unit testing. They have no time for non-development tasks. If these tasks can be given to someone else to validate and cull down to their essence, then the developers can spend their time to produce better code sooner.

- Once the PO is assigned, can he or she really speak for all the stakeholders and customers at the proper experience level needed? Many customers think not, and prefer to speak for themselves, and represent their own needs. Reconciling business requirements among multiple stakeholders is not a skill that the PO usually has, nor do developers, testers, and other non-BAs. Agile books that address the PO's responsibility (or the customer-developer requirements sessions) in Region 2 are rare or nonexistent.

---

[2]Agile organizations prefer that an agile team is always in place for forthcoming projects, and work is brought to the team instead of, as is often the case, forming teams around new projects then disbanding them after the project. This book is about PMs trying agile techniques in organizations that have not yet completely embraced all agile practices, so I assume, as a worst case, that new teams are formed for each project.

If an organization resists supporting the sponsor as PO and to work directly with the project team, most agile books advise to "educate the management." Because of the demonstrated benefits of agile development, many managers will cautiously comply with this request. However, managers are also familiar with the downside of "the tail wagging the dog," that is, the detail trying to define the whole. Managers generally do not want to defer to technical people on matters of business and strategy, and resist doing so; the higher the manager, the greater the resistance. I think that perspective caused much of the early tension between management and agile project teams in the early days.

From this point forward, I will assume the BA is the stakeholder liaison for requirements purposes, and the PM (and later, the APM) is the liaison for stakeholder expectations and project facilitation and reporting.

The Business Analyst

During Region 2 activities, before the actual product construction starts and the product fundamentals are identified, deeper aspects of requirements discovery are needed, such as defining core features, examining business flows, and defining business rules. For example, automating a large complex payroll system is quite different from setting up a web site to track sales. Although agile books discuss defining large-grain scope features (*epics* and *themes*) during Region 2, they primarily focus on Region 1 requirements, which are stripped to single-statement "headlines" (user stories) of how a user interacts with the system.

At this point in the project, a professional business analyst (BA) should be involved. The BA needs to elicit requirements and validate them; that is, ensure that the requirements at this level of (high) granularity are complete, logically consistent, have no missing data or control flows, and are defined for all user types. More detail is given on the techniques of *business flow analysis* in Chapter 7.

The BA's responsibilities in Region 2 include the following:

- Analyze the business workflows with the business team to define the features (and themes, epics, and use cases) within the scope of the project. It is up to the BA to ensure that the right product is being built, and up to the technical team that the product is built right.

- Elicit, discover, and refine the high-level requirements scope of the project: collecting their expectations (business abstract), merging individual expectations into an agreed set of project objectives (project abstract), building a catalog of features with the business SMEs, and helping them prioritize the feature catalog by business value into a product backlog.

- Maintain and encourage partnering relationships with the customers and stakeholders.

Warning Some agilists may argue that detailed valid requirements are not needed at this point because requirements cannot be known completely and changes can be made whenever it occurs to someone to change them. Yes, requirements always change and *detailed requirements are not needed at this time*.

Agile projects are fairly stable in the face of frequent changes, but performing unnecessary changes because the requirements were not done *sufficiently* before implementation is what another agile method, *lean*, calls "waste," and is the requirements' equivalent of *technical debt*, a violation of an agile rule. Both result in repeated and time-consuming changes to the code and tests that could have been avoided.

The requirements discovery process takes much-needed time, and developers are almost always on the critical path designing, coding, and unit testing. They have no time for non-development tasks. If these tasks can be given to someone else to validate and cull down to their essence, then the developers can spend their time to produce better code faster.

Manage Stakeholder Expectations

The stakeholders' *perceived satisfaction* of the project's results defines the success and failure of the project. The PM should keep in mind the maxim: *Success is political, not technical.* A perfectly built doghouse is a waste of time and money if the dog won't sleep in it. Ensuring that the stakeholders will "sleep in their house" is foremost the responsibility of the PM, and to a lesser extent, the BA and technical team.

During the stakeholder kickoff meeting is also the time to identify and get consensus on the value the stakeholders expect the project to return. Of course, different stakeholders have different expectations, and the PM must reconcile these differences into a single list of objectives for the project. The context diagram (discussed later in the chapter) is essential for this task.

The end users are often overlooked as key stakeholders who contribute to the ultimate success of the project. They should be counted as stakeholders, and customer representatives should be invited to the business kickoff meeting and the user demos as much as practical. If the end users are public customers, then focus groups or equivalent techniques are used to collect their input.

The following are the recommended ways to set the stakeholders' expectations at this point:

- *Hold a business kickoff meeting.* Collect individual expectations from each of the stakeholders to discern what they expect from the project. Ensure that the sponsor is involved to make it more "official." Get a consensus on grounds rules so that the business team and technical team know how to work with each other; such as, the agile approach, the change management approach, what they should expect for reporting, contributing to regular requirements meeting and periodic user demos.

- *Clarify stakeholder relationships.* Analyze the stakeholder's level of influence to define who wants what from the project (engagement grid), and how they are informed of project information (communication plan).

Warning   The project manager is held accountable for the success of the project, and the project's success depends on the stakeholders' expectations being met. For a project with a single product owner, that removes the onus of success from the PM and puts it on the shoulders of the PO. If they are not skilled at this delicate task, stakeholder expectations may be disappointed. Even if the project technically fails (or have unnecessary problems), the PM will still take the blame for it. I always prefer to be responsible for my own success, which is why I don't want "not-me" to manage stakeholder expectations.

Anecdote   On one large project, the client manager agreed to discuss project status with the sponsor at least monthly. He worked in a way similarly to that described by the single PO. However, he did not meet with the sponsor as agreed. After several months, I bumped into the sponsor in the hallway, and he asked why I was still there—he thought the project had finished weeks ago—although, unknown to him, it was proceeding on schedule. When he found out the actual situation, he was reluctant to continue his funding because he had already decided to use the "leftover money" from my project for a different project. He terminated the project so he could use that "leftover money." I resolved for all future projects that I would maintain a touch base meeting with the sponsor at least monthly for all future projects.

Hold a Business Team Kickoff Meeting

The business kickoff meeting is the first meeting in a series of business meetings for the project's duration. Projects where the stakeholders hand off the requirements and then disappear for months or years are doomed from that day forward.

The purpose of the business team meeting is to gather the business partners of the team, officially begin the project, collect expectations, and set up a working agreement ("the ground rules") between the business team and the technical team. This working agreement is sometimes called "the ground rules." They outline how the business team will develop the product, but there is plenty of room for adjustment, especially in a full partnership relationship. It is not the business unit's job to tell the technical team how to do its job, and it is not the technical team's job to tell the business unit how to do its job.

There is a discovery part and a logistics part of every kickoff meeting. A template for the business team's kickoff meeting is given in the "Additional Tools" section, and a description of the meeting objectives follow.

- *Official launch.* The sponsor explains his or her mission and objectives for the project, which should be on the agenda. By spending five or ten minutes at the beginning of the meeting to introduce his or her expectations, and to introduce the PM for the team, many issues that might later arise are defused. The sponsor's presence gives official authority to the project and the PM as she or her explains his or her mission and objectives. Although the sponsor's contribution may be only five minutes long, it is one of the most important aspects of the kickoff meeting.

- *Identify all stakeholders.* The project charter rarely identifies all the stakeholders, nor does the associated business kickoff meeting. People who represent key organizations, such as the helpdesk, operations, or other shared resource organizations, are usually missing. Also frequently omitted are those who represent the external systems that will impact, or be impacted by, the new project. Frequently, the currently identified stakeholders will know of others who should be stakeholders, and when, and not all stakeholders need to be engaged with the same frequency. Example: The helpdesk can get involved a few weeks before launch, unless they get involved in product testing, which is earlier and better; in contrast, customer SME's should be involved frequently, whenever their features of concern are discussed.

- *Business roles and responsibilities.* All high-level roles and responsibilities of each member are identified, with details of how each member will contribute. The business roles are typical and the same as for traditional projects. They are listed here for completeness and to clarify what is meant about a particular role. Of course, a role may be filled by multiple people, or one person may fill more than one role.

    - *Sponsor:* Champions the project to higher management and peers, defines the vision and mission statement, and provides funding.

    - *Key stakeholder.* Manages the product development on the business side to protect their business units' interests and ensures that the project delivers the expected value. Key stakeholders are usually delegated by the sponsor or they are primary customers in the business unit.

    - *Business subject-matter expert (SME).* A specialist for a particular topic or business workflow. SMEs enter and leave the project as they are needed, and are engaged during requirements elicitation and user interface design.

    - *User acceptance tester (UAT):* A member of a business unit who will exercise the requirement feature when the build is released to them; provides feedback on the user demo each iteration.

- *Agile project manager (APM)*: Many small agile projects do not have a PM, so the work is delegated during the iterations to an iteration coach. When a PM is involved, usually that person is involved in the business aspects for the project, working in Region 2 to coordinate with upper management, and liaise with the iteration coach. It is common for the PM and iteration coach to be the same person, but the skills sets are different enough that sometimes that person is referred to as an APM. The PM is not considered a technical person. For agile projects, the same person can work as PM outside the team, and as an APM inside the team.

- *Business analyst*: The BA is introduced in this meeting, and is used to collect stakeholder business abstracts, the starting point for requirements elicitation and expectations. BA responsibilities were discussed earlier.

The roles for the technical team are described in Chapter 4.

- *Stakeholder engagement.* What is the level of engagement for each member of the business team? Daily meetings? Weekly meetings? Monthly meetings? The project will move at the rate of these meetings. Describe how escalation issues will be handled. The PM needs to know what kind of data goes to whom, and how, and through what channel; such as e-mail, meeting minutes, or a shared documentation database—the docBase. This information is written in a communication plan, and a one-page table is all that is needed.

- *Project approach.* Why do the stakeholders care about the project approach? It affects the business team: feature catalog as product backlog, frequent requirements meetings, product demos after each iteration, status reports, change requests, task tracking, communication, and so forth. They may want to modify it somewhat, through other constraints on their time or because of their own preferences. The PM reconciles and adopts suggestions. It is part of the tailoring needed to best fit the approach to the business side of the project team.

- *Meeting Minutes.* The meeting minutes are the PM's most powerful political tool. Key meetings will have agendas, minutes, and action items, are distributed to each member. It is especially important that each attendee's manager be informed, so should always be on the cc list (see the "Meetings, Agendas, and Minutes" section.)

- *Business abstracts.* The business abstract is a statement by the stakeholder about what they expect the product to do for them. It is necessary to help define the project scope, and their expectations of the result. Make it part of the meeting's action items, with a deadline. The project abstract, which is the conflation of all stakeholders, objectives and expectations, will be the focus of the next meeting. See the upcoming sections for more on business abstracts and project abstracts.

- *Shared documentation repository.* All documentation will be placed in a shared documentation repository (the docBase) for review and archive. Tell the group where the shared documentation repository will be located. It is usually in a document management system, a version control system, or a dedicated web server.

- *Subsequent meetings.* Schedule regular requirements meetings, user demos, and project reviews with appropriate delegates and assigned SMEs. It is easier to schedule it now and skip it later if necessary, then fight the calendar each time a meeting is needed.

Usually one or two hours is sufficient duration for a business meeting, and no meeting should be longer than two hours without a break (Friedman and Weinberg 1990, 434).

Clarify Stakeholder Relationships

The sponsor's mission statement defines the project and product scope's *outer bound* because all product features must fall within the mission statement. The stakeholders' expectations for the product must be verified against the sponsor's mission statement and their own requirements. If the stakeholders are expecting something inconsistent with the mission statement, those expectations need to be clarified immediately. A conversation with the sponsor will usually resolve the disconnect quickly, or change the mission statement, or determine that the person is actually not a stakeholder for the project.

It is best if the technical team has a *full business partnership* with the business units. The PM, technical team, and stakeholders are the embodiment of that relationship. Some organizations have an order-taker relationship—the business units dictate what the team will develop, and in the worst case, micromanage how and when they will develop it.[3] The converse relationship—that the project team will develop a product with little or no feedback, and deliver it to the business units who must then live with the result—is no better. That relationship is an example of the "throw it over the wall to IT" syndrome where the stakeholders wait in silence for delivery. These relationships don't yield a satisfied customer or a superior product. Consequently, these poor relationships add to the formal risk of the project, to be noted so by the PM. If the culture expects that is how projects are managed, then that is another stakeholder expectation that must be changed and managed for the agile project to move forward successfully.

If a partnering relationship doesn't exist between the business units and the IT department, then beginning a history of projects that are delivered with full satisfaction will build a good relationship, one that will be built on credibility, trust, and respect. *Full project success* means *delivering the product with all requirements met, on time, within budget, with zero defects, predictably.*

To maintain a good relationship with the stakeholders, the PM should be "transparent," which means that the PM should

- Never undersell or oversell the product (report status accurately, for good or for bad)

- Always be honest with what the product will and will not do in a timely manner

- Provide clear reasons, either shared or developed with, the stakeholders, as to why decisions were made

- Adopt a "no surprises" policy to the stakeholders and the project team

Most of the time, the PM facilitates group sessions so that all attending stakeholders come to their own conclusions. Transparency is a good policy in personal and business relations. Misleading the stakeholders never ends well.

⛧ **Key Point**   Many people have a misconception about the role of project manager. Some people think PMs "control" the project, and have the right to deny scope, cost, or schedule changes. The PM is a facilitator, and the stakeholders often outrank the PM. If the PM takes a hard stand against the wrong kind of stakeholder, the stakeholder can roll right over the PM and flatten their career. The PM should provide project data to offer consequences of stakeholders' decisions and propose solutions, but they are never a "project controller."

Define Roles and Responsibilities

Stakeholders evaluate a project's success from their own point of view. A stakeholder should at least feel comfortable with the project, and at best, feel that they are making an important contribution to it. If a stakeholder gets confused as to how they should be involved, or do not get what they are expecting, they will evaluate their satisfaction low, and rate the project as poorly run. Lack of good definitions for roles and responsibilities is a key cause of project failure, even with cross-functional agile teams where the roles are not strongly distinguished from each other.

Regardless of which agile methodology is used, actual skills must be used to produce the product, and some people are better at certain tasks than others. Each team member has a contribution to make, and the role that each fills is fairly standard throughout the industry. Traditionally, the team member's name, role, and responsibilities were collected in a Responsibility Assignment Matrix (RAM) so that it is clear to all who does what. It is equally important to define what the person should not do, to prevent confusing the team or redirecting project momentum. For Region 1 agile projects, these roles are relaxed in certain ways.

Table 3-1 shows a partial RAM for an agile project before the iterations start (Region 2). Keep in mind that these roles are to identify skill sets, and are not strict roles for particular people on the team. Developers and testers may also be involved, but usually they are part of the Region 1 project team, and not involved in the pre-work of the project. See Chapter 4 for technical team roles.

Table 3-1. *Sample Responsibility Assignment Matrix (RAM) for Region 2*

Objective / Role	Sponsor	Stakeholder	Project Manager	Business Analyst
Project Charter	A	C	O	R
Business Abstracts		C	A	O
Project Abstract	A	R	O	C
Communication Plan	R	C	O	
Feature Catalog	A	C	R	O

C = contributor; O = owner; R = reviewer; A = approver

Table 3-1 is a CORA[4] chart, because each role **c**ontributes, **o**wns, **r**eviews, or **a**pproves the artifact. In agile projects, the interaction with the team is informal. In fact, the CORA chart does not need to be explicitly written down for agile team members.

Stakeholder Analysis and Engagement Grid

The PM must identify the stakeholders who need to be involved or engaged, and determine how the stakeholders should be engaged and how they will work with the technical team to maximize good working partnership. The engagement grid is an interim document that captures sponsor and PM insights on how the stakeholders should work together on the project. The engagement grid is a working tool, and with the RAM, leads naturally to the communication plan.

Some stakeholders are not as engaged as they should be, and others are engaged more than they should. There are usually political factors involved in working properly with the stakeholders and managing their expectations. Stakeholders can be classified into categories:

- *Critical*: Clearly, they can make or break the project, such as the sponsor. They should take a *leading* role, like project champion.

- *Essential*: They are influential with the project, or perhaps other critical or essential stakeholders, such as key business SMEs or customers, or friends of the sponsor. If their expectations are disappointed, they also can sound the death knell for the project. The PM needs to nudge them into a *supportive* position.

---

[3]There is an even worse relationship: when the business units duplicate the information technology (IT) services and resources within their own units so that they bypass IT. The business units hire their own software staff to act as "personal programmers" on the whim of the upper management. This kind of fragmentation and vote-of-no-confidence for IT leads to a breakdown in the economies of scale that justifies a centralized IT relationship in the first place.
[4]The RAM is a general term, more commonly known as a RACI chart, for Responsible, Accountable, Contributing, and Informed. I think that the alternative CORA is more self-evident as to who does what in a role.

- *Nonessential*: They may be curious about the product or project, or need to know about it later, after development, such as the helpdesk. The helpdesk often is unaware of a product until it is in production and the helpdesk personnel are forced to field questions about it. They would fill a *neutral* role. If the PM can get them to help with acceptance testing, then they would move to a supportive role, perhaps even essential.

- *Resistant*: These stakeholders resist the product or project for various reasons. Perhaps the project took money away from the stakeholder's project that they were attempting, or the stakeholder is against the entire agile approach. These resisters can hurt a project, especially if new techniques or approaches are being tried. The PM should try to move all resisters into at least a neutral position. Be especially aware of the grapevine. Resistant stakeholders have no official stand (otherwise they would be doing something official), and may use the grapevine to spread false and damaging rumors The grapevine is a dangerous place, fertile with ways to make projects fail. Because of the political nature of project success, sometimes it is not about the truth of the project, but about its image (or the PM's image).

- *Unaware*: All stakeholders start unaware, except the sponsor. The PM must move the stakeholders from ignorance to the appropriate category of neutral, supportive, or leading.

Figure 3-1 shows a sample engagement grid, visually represented as a set of sliders. Each slider shows a stakeholder's current engagement (blue circle), and the engagement desired (X crosshatch) to match their categorization. The arrow shows the direction the PM needs to move the stakeholder's engagement by what kind of information should be given to that person, how frequently, and by what method.

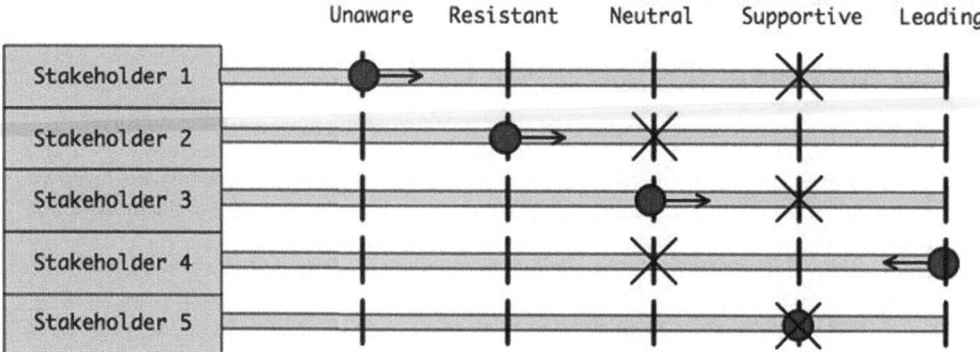

Figure 3-1. Sample stakeholder engagement grid

There are strong political factors at work oftentimes. Sometimes a little "ninja management" must be exercised behind the scenes (unofficial channels) to work with the stakeholders to move them in the right direction. Often stakeholders will get more involved if they are contributing in some way, so asking them to review or attend user demos or project reviews can change their position.

In the sample grid in Figure 3-1, stakeholder 1 is unaware of the project, and the PM needs to move that person into a supportive role. Stakeholder 4 is too engaged, and taking on leading tasks which they should not be doing (perhaps a "busybody"); the PM needs to move that person back to a neutral or supporting role. Stakeholder 5 is currently where he or she needs to be, so the PM has no action to take.

Build a Communication Plan

The communication plan identifies *what* type of information is sent to *whom* by *when* and *how*. The PM can use it to assist changing the engagement level of stakeholders by the amount and frequency of the communications they receive.[5] The plan needs only to be a single page or less.

It is critical that the sponsor monitors the progress of the project, and the stakeholders are engaged at the proper level. They have many activities going on around them, and it is easy to forget about a project. A project that is out of sight is out of mind, and soon out of budget. It is easy to lose stakeholder support in the flurry of other activities and projects that have their close attention, either because the projects are more urgent (not necessarily more important), or have their attention at the moment. It is necessary that the PM maintains and transfers an excitement about the project to the stakeholder so they continue to want to be part of a successful outcome. The PM should be one of the best cheerleaders for the project and the product champion. If the PM is cynical or pessimistic about the project, she is poisoning her own well; especially if the sponsor is optimistic, which is likely since the sponsor is funding his or her vision.

Table 3-2 shows a sample communication plan. Note that information intended for customers, stakeholders, and senior management are sent by e-mail, but will be stored on a central server in a shared codebase so it is accessible whenever they want to retrieve it. Some information is generated in a meeting, and may or may not need documents to go with it. The team's working documentation (technical documents, code, and tests) are stored in a central server enabled with version control.

Table 3-2. *Sample Communication Plan*

WHAT?	PROVIDER	TO WHOM?	WHEN?	HOW?
Project Charter	Sponsor	Senior Mgmt, Technical Team	As revised; reviewed each 1-3 iterations	e-mail; project review mtg
Release Plan	APM, technical team	Senior Mgmt, Technical Team	As revised; reviewed each iteration by team	business team mtg minutes; e-mail
Business team working agreement	Sponsor, stakeholders, APM, BA	Senior Mgmt	Before Iteration 0 and weekly meetings	Business team kickoff mtg minutes; e-mail
Product Backlog	Customer SME's and BA	Senior Mgmt, Technical Team	As revised; reviewed each iteration	Requirements Meeting; e-mail
Technical team working agreement	APM, technical team	Technical Team	Iteration 0	Technical team kickoff meeting; e-mail
Iteration Backlog	BA, Technical Team	Technical Team	Each Iteration	Team taskboard

(continued)

---

[5]If the project uses the SCRUM agile variation of a single product owner, the PM does not need to write a communication plan because it falls to the PO to manage the stakeholders' expectations.

Table 3-2. (*continued*)

WHAT?	PROVIDER	TO WHOM?	WHEN?	HOW?
Daily team synchronization	Technical Team	Technical Team	Daily	Daily Standup meeting
Project and iteration status (burnup chart, iteration status, QA Report); demo of working software	APM, Technical Team	Project Community	Each Iteration	Iteration Review and Demo
Team process changes	Technical Team	Technical Team	Each 1 – 3 iterations	Team Retrospective meeting

The portion at the top of Table 3-2 refers to Region 2 artifacts, and bottom part of the table refers to Region 1 artifacts. The BA is considered part of the technical team in the table.

Define Stakeholders' Scope

The sponsor's mission statement defines the ultimate scope of the project and product. All features expected by the stakeholders must be a subset of that mission statement. Anything identified by the stakeholders that do not agree with the mission statement is by definition out of scope. It is important to find what the stakeholders expect the product to do; if they have any expectations outside the project scope, get those expectations resolved immediately.

At the business team kickoff meeting, the PM requests they write their expectations (business abstracts) which are then conflated into a single series of responsibilities and objectives (project abstract), high-level workflows (context diagram), and then update the project charter accordingly, with the sponsor's approval.

Business Abstracts

The PM (or BA) asks each stakeholder to write a quick one or two paragraph description of what problem the product will solve when it is delivered and in use. They are asked to answer the following questions:

- "What is the business problem you are trying to solve?"

- How will this new product (system) contribute to its solution?"

- How do you expect to interact with the system?

It should not be more than one page long. The one-page limit is arbitrary so that they don't go into too much detail, and end up designing the system, which they are wont to do. It is also premature to collect a long list of features at this point. I ask that it be sent by e-mail to the BA for discussion at the next business meeting.

The business abstracts are an interim artifact used to build the project abstract for approval. It is a high-level "definition of Done," a result of progressive elaboration from the mission statement and sponsor's objectives to a more detailed project scope, and is critical to help the PM manage stakeholders' expectations.

Here are two examples of business abstracts.

BUSINESS ABSTRACT (BANK MANAGER)

We need to perform the business duties of the teller as closely as possible to how we do it now, but with an automated facility. We want the ATM to perform these functions:

- *Deposits:* We expect the customer to be able to deposit money, whether that be checks, money orders, or cash; and give receipts for the amount deposited.

- *Withdrawals:* We expect the customer to be able to withdraw cash. The machine should be able to have enough money to support a day's activities, about $5000. Our staff of managers and tellers does not have a withdrawal limit, but some limit should be defined for security purposes for the ATM. A reasonable limit should be put on the customer, and our ATM's should talk to each other quickly enough to keep a customer from making multiple withdrawals from different ATM locations to exceed the limit.

- *Transfers:* A customer should be able to move unlimited amounts (up to their balance) between their own accounts after their authorization has been established for the accounts.

- *Balance Inquiry:* A customer should be able to obtain their account balances without having to execute a transaction.

- *Security:* We need to check the security of the customer account so that only authorized account members have access to their account—not only should bank members have access, but also bank members should not have access to each other's accounts. The machine should verify the proper ATM card as well as the proper account and account balance. It should not allow more money to be removed from the account than $100 above the balance. We do not want the account number to be entered at the ATM, but use a decoding device, such as an ATM card with PIN number. Physical security is not important to this discussion—an outside vendor is taking care of it.

- *Control ATM accessible accounts:* We should be able to control which customer accounts can be accessed via the ATM. Normally, account accessibility would be set to whatever the customer requests. We should also be able to disallow certain transactions against accessible accounts (e.g. disallow withdrawals against savings).

- *Transaction logging:* At the end of the day, the ATM needs to report the total number of transactions by type, dollar amount, and accounts accessed (with totals). The ATM should reconcile the total dollar amounts of deposits and withdrawals with the cash dispensed and remaining in the cash box within the machine.

BUSINESS ABSTRACT (CUSTOMER)

We need to have the ATM machines fulfill the same functions as regular tellers. In addition, the ATMs should allow us greater access to our accounts and account-related information. We should be able to:

- *Make Deposits:* We should be able to make deposits to both checking and savings accounts. We should be able to deposit any items a regular teller would take (cash, checks, …).

- *Make Withdrawals:* We should be able to make withdrawals to any of our accounts that allow direct withdrawals. This would be mainly checking and savings but should include established lines-of-credit and withdrawals against checking overdraft protection.

- *Transfer Money:* We should be able to transfer money from any account that allows withdrawals to any account that allows deposits.

- *Obtain Account Balances:* We should be able to obtain balances on any account including loans and credit cards.

- *Pay bills:* We should be able to make loan and mortgage payments, pay or transfer money toward credit card balances, and make utility company payments.

- *Get cash advances:* We should be able to obtain cash against our available credit card limits.

- *Time availability:* The ATM network should be available 24 hours a day, 7 days a week. An individual machine could be out of service but if it is just out cash then it should say so up front (rather than waiting for you to put in all your information) and should also give addresses for nearby machines.

- *Physical availability:* Machines should be placed in well lighted, high traffic, public areas. Some of the machines should be accessible without leaving your car, those that are not should provide some protection from the elements.

The Project Abstract

When all the business abstracts are collected, the PM and BA reconcile each of them into a single project abstract. Within the collection, there will be some objectives that are repeated, some that are unique, and a few will be out-of-scope; sometimes, there will be objectives that are hard to determine if they are in scope or not.

The PM reconciles them into a single summary of objectives, listed in frequency (priority) order. The objectives that are in scope can be listed by the number of times they are mentioned in the business abstracts, with the assumption that the more people who mention it, the higher priority it is for the project. Usually the same objective in multiple business abstracts must be merged for wording.

If a stakeholder lists a particular objective (or responsibility) in a business abstract, then it must be mentioned somewhere in the project abstract, *especially* if it is out-of-scope. To drop an expected objective from the project abstract without mention is a sure way to break that stakeholder's expectations, and potentially dissatisfy that stakeholder. If the stakeholder insists that the objective be in the project, the stakeholder always has recourse to the sponsor to include it. It is one of the duties of the sponsor to handle stakeholder objections; the PM is only a facilitator.

At the next business meeting, the agenda will cover whatever action items are listed from the previous meeting, and the project abstract (containing a preliminary context diagram). The meeting's objective is to get a consensus on all the responsibilities and objectives listed in the project abstract, and resolve any that are out of scope.

A sample project abstract, a reconciliation of the ATM business abstracts, is shown inin Table 3-3.

Table 3-3. *ATM Project Abstract*

Automated Teller Machine Sample Project Application	Carolla Development, Inc. January, 2016
Project Mission	Increase customer access, bank profit, and security by implementing an automated teller (ATM) network that customers will accept as a suitable alternative to regular tellers for their demand deposit transactions.
	System Responsibilities
Objective 1	*Customer Transactions:* Enable processing of simple (deposit, withdrawal, transfer, balance) transactions against demand deposit (checking, savings) accounts. Each transaction must be individually verified against transaction limits and account accessibility. Account balances must be updated at transaction commit.
Objective 2	*Security:* Provide robust transaction security and customer authentication. Customer need only be authenticated at beginning of ATM session. Cashier needs to be authenticated for administrative transactions.
Objective 3	*Administration:* Cashier has special transactions to (1) load money and initiate ATM software, (2) collect reconcilement report, and (3) to shut down ATM system software.
Objective 4	*Performance:* Provide for nominal transaction volume to be 30% higher than current volume, and peak volume to be 100% higher. Network should be available 22 hours per day, 7 days a week. Hold cost per transaction, at nominal transaction volume, at least 20% below that of regular teller transactions.
Objective 5	*Logging:* Provide transaction logging which is consistent with current transaction reporting.
Not Included:	Loan, mortgage, utility bill payments, credit card transactions (not demand deposits). Customer control of permissible transactions (account either available or not). Complex security issues.

Workflow Context Diagram

The context diagram shows the highest-level workflow of the project. All use cases are derived from the workflows shown. The list of objectives in the project abstract is often enough to start writing a context diagram before the next meeting. If that is available, it can be refined for consensus. The context diagram can be discussed to ensure that the BA understands the proper workflows and data at the highest level. At the end of the meeting, most stakeholders will understand what every other stakeholder is expecting from the project, and how their needs fit into the project context.

The context diagram (or a table that contains the equivalent information) that shows the business workflows represented by each user type. The context diagram is a crucial document. It defines the actors, data, and work flows for which the project is responsible. Unlike most data flow diagrams that show product, the circle of the context diagram shows the boundaries for the responsibilities of the project. Anything that is within the responsibility of the project is *inside* the circle, and anything for which the project is not responsible, is *outside* the circle.

An *actor* is a user or an external system that interacts with the new product when it is in operation. Actors may be external systems, real people, or *personas*—that is, idealized users. The business team stakeholders may interact with the project team when it is executing, but may never actually transact with the new system; their staff will use it. In that case, although they are stakeholders, they would not necessarily show up on the context diagram as actors.

The context diagram shows the workflow between the new product and the actors. These workflows are defined at a high level, and show the direction and kinds of data (or control) that the new product provides to, or receives from, particular actors. It does not show a sequence of interactions or conditional interactions. Later, the workflow can be broken down into sub-flows (use cases) during requirements elicitation.

For example, if a database is under control of the project, then it does not show up (it is eclipsed by, or "inside," the circle). If the database is under control of a database staff member outside the project, then it shows up as an actor outside the circle. The PM (ad BA) must involve all the people that represent the demands and interactions of all the actors.

Figure 3-2 shows an example, the ATM project context diagram. It has three actors.

- The customer, who performs transactions to deposit checks or money orders, and receives cash and account balance information. The customer must be authorized to perform these transactions.

- The ATM admin, who loads the cashbox and deposit envelop bin, and starts up the ATM machine each day, and at the end of the day, shuts down the ATM machines to retrieve the deposited funds, and balances the reconcilement report.

- The Bank Data System is a non-person external system that interacts with the ATM machine. The ATM machine connects periodically to the central banking system so that it can retrieve new and updated customer accounts. It also cross-checks the daily session log against the Admin's reconcilement report.

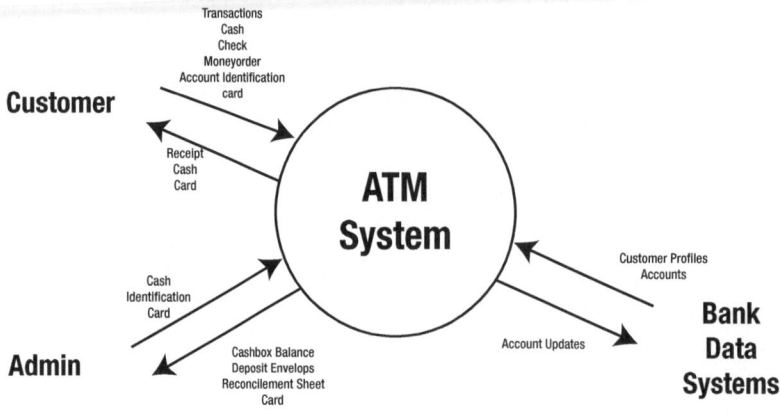

ATM System Context Diagram

Figure 3-2. *ATM context diagram*

The context diagram for most projects takes about 20 minutes to draw. The same data can be shown with a table, but the visual image is more engaging, as shown in Figure 3-2.

Meetings, Agendas, and Minutes

It is important to make a few comments here about meetings. "Meetings" have a reputation as a waste of time, in which no decision gets made that couldn't have been made better or faster without the meeting. This bad press may be warranted in many organizations, but there are good reasons to have particular meetings, and a few important reasons to have them. These are the real questions: When should you have a meeting? What should be captured during a meeting?

- *Memory is unreliable.* The agile community prefers to have "conversations" with business team members instead of meetings, but what happens after the meeting or conversation? Many decisions were made, and usually not everyone was present. However, verbal decisions but often quickly forgotten—memory is too fragile. Meeting minutes are important to remind people of joint decisions, and sometimes a gentle reminder is needed to refresh the working agreements, or change management policies, or other project policies the teams are following, and to communicate to those who were not part of the meeting.

- Minutes are not written to hold someone's feet to the fire about earlier decisions. If the person wants to change something, they should be able to do so with the consensus of the other people involved. Agreements even in writing are not written in stone.

- *Communication among the team.* If decisions are made, but not everyone on the business team was present, it may or may not be important to the absentees (whether they were invited or not). However, the more decisions made without the entire team means that communication is out of sync, and different stakeholders will have different expectations about what will happen as the project moves forward. Product backlog priorities are especially sensitive in this regard. Lack of consistent communication will disappoint some stakeholders' expectations, and is not good for the health of the project.

- *Meetings, and the lack of them, have a political aspect.* If a decision is reached without a particular person present, that person may think that the development team is making decisions without their input; or worse, conspiring with other business people to work around those who did not attend. This practice, real or perceived, will sow distrust and lack of respect among the project team members, which will erode the business relationship. It could force the technical team back to an order-taker relationship, which will severely hamper the agile approach.

- *Minutes are your most important political tool.* When you distribute meeting minutes, send them to all invitees—those who attended and those who did not. Also send them to anyone else that should see them; that is, those on the cc list. Then, equally important, send them to all the managers of the invitees.

- First, copies to the attendees give them a record of what was agreed, and includes the action plan (who will do what by when).

- Second, non-attendees will be informed of what decisional (strategic of tactical) progress the project team is making.

- Thirdly, send the minutes to managers of invitees to inform them of what progress their reportees are making on a particular assignment. Be leery of stakeholders who do not want their actions to be reported to their manager. It may indicate that the person may be trying to avoid accountability. Are they fully committed to the project? It may also indicate that they may be trying to provide plausible deniability for his or her manager. Is the manager fully committed and working transparently? In either case, the sponsor should be made aware of these political issues. (It is an organizational issue as to why a manager does not want to know what his or her reportee is doing.) See the "Wake-up Call" anecdote in the upcoming sidebar.

The agile approach requires few meetings and even fewer meeting minutes. However, there are a few times that meeting and minutes are necessary. Most business meetings should have minutes because they involve stakeholders' expectations and involved certain political aspects for the projects. Here are the key meetings I would recommend to distribute meeting minutes.

- *Business team kickoff meeting and subsequent meetings*[6]: These meetings identify the project members and determine how they will work with each other. They set up the working agreements and "ground rules" by which the business and technical team will engage, how their business partnership relationship will work. The business team kickoff meeting minutes confirm that all the stakeholders have approved the scope of the project.

- *User demo*: This is the most obvious meeting in which minutes need to be distributed. It contains the agreement of changes and defects for the product, and action items for what was agreed next. The team is put in a hard place if the some stakeholders think that something should (or should not) have been done, and then it wasn't. Stakeholders' expectations are not met, and that could be fatal to the project.

- *Team retrospective*: Every two or three iterations, the technical team gets together to review their working agreement: what is going right, what needs to be changed, and things they want to try. For example, the team may modify how they tailored their agile method (e.g., moving from a physical taskboard to an online Kanban board); or add or remove a particular step they were doing (e.g., add a "late jar" to remind people to attend the daily meeting on time).

- *Project retrospective*: These meetings are held less frequently than team retrospectives, but they involve the stakeholders to reviews the project process. They may discuss how to see status reports differently, or decide on different release schedules. These meetings are as important and the user demo meetings because they deal with the expectations of management and stakeholders.

---

[6]The technical team kickoff meeting is done as part of Iteration 0, but all comments apply to that meeting too.

⚒ Wake-Up Call Anecdote   During one project I was mentoring, the customer SME (say, Mike) promised to deliver a set of requirements to the team the following meeting. His task was part of the action plan recorded in each set of minutes. At the next meeting, Mike didn't deliver anything. OK, things happen. During the next two weeks, Mike continued to promise the requirements but failed to deliver anything. The PM finally announced that the project was on hold because the team could not move forward without requirements. Mike ran off to tell his manager the bad news. Let's call her Julie, a key customer stakeholder.

Within minutes, Julie angrily strode into the office of the PM's manager, the department's director (Andy). The PM and I could see those two, and hear Julie, through the glass walls. She was shouting about how Andy always gave her projects short shrift and looked for any excuse to delay or kill them.

Andy listened calmly, and then retrieved a set of papers from a basket on his desk. He had highlighted all the relevant parts of the project meeting minutes in the time it took before Julie arrived. He showed her the bright yellow highlighting. As he told me afterward, he said, "Look Julie, Mike has not delivered his requirements to the team, even though he has promised them for the last three weeks. It clearly shows his commitment in these minutes. Notice also that your name is on these minutes. *You knew* he wasn't delivering, and you let him get away with it. Also notice, that your boss's name is on these minutes, so *he knows that you were letting him get away with it.* The question now is—What are you going to do about it?"

Julie went from a feet apart, hand-on-hips stance to hands at her side, head bowed, in about 15 seconds. She left Andy's office, grabbed Mike by the metaphorical ear, and dragged him into a conference room. By the end of the day, the technical team had all the promised requirements and the project moved forward, without losing even one day. Julie and Mike only needed a wake-up call about how the teams work together, a reminder about the agreement they made a month or two earlier.

The unfortunate side of this story is that on every project I have worked, someone on the technical team or business team needed at least one wake-up call incident like this one.

Recommendations for Writing Minutes Easily

Another reason that minutes are disliked is because of the format and hoopla that corporations use to write minutes. Unless you are in an organization, like the military, government agencies, or regulated industries where intensive record-keeping is required, minutes do not have to be onerous.

Minutes can be done quickly and succinctly. The consensus of each objective can be collected easily during the meeting, so writing minutes is almost automatic. Here are some tips for easily writing meeting minutes and the key elements.

- *List of objectives:* There is no need for a separate agenda and minutes. Make a list of objectives that can be augmented during the meeting with each objective's resolution. No one really cares who said what when, and no one needs to follow Robert's antiquated Rules of Order. They only want to see what was decided about a particular item. The minutes can be mere augmented agendas that are completed in the meeting, and then cleaned up a little and sent.

- *Action plan and open issues*: During the meeting, tasks will arise that someone must perform. Make a table at the bottom that shows what must be done, who will do it (owner), and when it will be completed. Do not leave out any of these elements. A task with no owner (or something generic like "team") will not get done because all others will assume someone is doing it.

- *Issues that can be investigated, escalated, or deferred in the action plan table or a separate table*: Both the action plan and issues list is the core of your agenda for subsequent meetings, to be reviewed at the beginning of each meeting. Tip: Phrase the issue in the form of a specific question that can be answered to resolve the issue. If the "issue" cannot be phrased as a question, then it is likely *not an issue*, and could merely a task that needs to be done.

- *Purpose and invitees*: Make the purpose (what everyone should achieve when they leave the meeting) as clear as the place, time, and duration of the meeting. I put a check box beside each invitee on the agenda. The agenda is displayed with a projector, and as people arrive, I check off the box next to the attendee. I also have a cc list on the agenda so that others can see who will get the minutes (and who showed up and who didn't).

- *Recording the agenda item resolutions*: During the meeting, I type directly into the agenda items the resolution that was made in the meeting. Since the items are displayed, all in the meeting can see what was written, and can change it if it is incorrect.

- *Post-meeting cleanup*: After the meeting, clean-up any errant statements, grammar, and so forth, and send them to all the invitees, and members of the cc list. Minutes need not take more than 10 minutes after the meeting to distribute.

☞ **Meeting Recommendation**   Start on time and end on time, even if not every item was completed. Carry over any undiscussed items to the next meeting. If the meeting ends sooner than scheduled, all the better. The business team will realize that meetings you run are prompt, concise and to the point, that each meeting will achieve its purpose and then end. No meetings should be held merely because it was scheduled, and do not fill up the time with unproductive discussion. As facilitator, keep the meeting focused and the attendees on topic. Future meetings will go more smoothly as the group begins to work in this mode.

Update the Project Charter

The PM updates the project charter with the data from the project abstract. The PM adds new stakeholders, objectives, and the context diagram. The out-of-scope features or objectives from individual stakeholders can be added to the charter to ensure that they don't silently come back into scope as expectations. The charter can be approved at the same meeting in which the project abstract is approved.

The stakeholders and their objectives are more of interest now to the sponsor than the details are later. Updating the project charter is one way to keep the project community in touch.

After the stakeholders have progressively refined the project scope, several things can be added or updated in the charter.

- A modified mission statement (perhaps a stakeholder won his case with the sponsor to modify the project scope).

- The refined roadmap; that is, an expanded or revised set of objectives with dates (milestones) from the business team meeting.

- The context diagram, which usually is not part of the initial charter. It is extremely helpful if the project is part of a program.

- A modified set of stakeholders for the project, which usually grows in this first pass.

It is important for the charter to stay up-to-date for the portfolio team and any program manager over the project to have a consistent way of comparing projects equally: "apples to apples." Saying "This is an agile project, and the rules don't apply" will not work. These kinds of statements have thwarted agile projects on traditional organizations to the point that some management will not permit agile projects. As developers know, *separation of concerns* is an important principle in software development and applies here as well. The portfolio team does not really care how the project is done—that is the team's job—but agile projects can report progress and status the same as any other project at this high level.

Define the Features Catalog (Product Backlog)

The feature[7] catalog is a list of all the identified large-grain scope items within the project. In agile terms, the feature catalog is called the *product backlog* and is used to drive the more detailed iteration scope later. A sample feature catalog is shown in Figure 3-3.

- Authenticate customer and authorize access to accounts
- Deposit funds to checking or savings account
- Withdraw funds from checking or savings account
- Transfer funds between accounts
- Inquire about (get) the balance of an account
- Reconcile transaction done on the ATM
- Load cash into ATM cashbox

Figure 3-3. *ATM sample feature catalog*

The stakeholders, or more likely, their delegates, will further define the product features. These features will be elicited as high-level requirements by the BA. As features are identified, they are categorized as in-scope or out-of-scope, depending if they align with the sponsor's mission statement. It is usually easier to determine if features are in scope by comparing them with the lower-level stakeholder expectations in the Project Abstract, which has already been confirmed to be within the project scope.

---

[7]A feature is a rather amorphously defined aspect of the product that contains value to the customer. It is similar to the checklist of items advertised on the back of many product packages.

Prioritize the Feature Catalog

Using the agile principle of delivering to the business the greatest value first, the stakeholders need to prioritize the feature catalog for business value, risk, and dependencies. Prioritizing the features is accomplished similarly to the way the projects were prioritized in the portfolio: select a multiple set of business criteria so that all stakeholders agree that the list is in business-value-first order (see Chapter 2).

A prioritized list tells the project team what features to implement first. Secondly, riskier features are pushed to the top of the list over less risky features (given equal value). Risky features are implemented first so that if something goes wrong, there is more time to correct it and get the project back on track.

There is little detail about the features at this point, so the typical Delphi technique may be overkill or not worth the effort. Two other methods may be more useful here: MoSCoW (2014) and Kano (2014).

- *MoSCoW*: Organizes the features by four categories: *Must have* (must be included for project success); *Should have* (critical to have but may be worked around in a worse case); *Could have* (desired but of lower priority); and *Won't have* (explicitly excluded or deferred feature that will not be in the current project scope).

- *Kano Model*: The Kano model, developed by Dr. Noriaki Kano (Kano, Nobuhiku, Fumio, and Shinichi 1984) uses five categories with a slightly different slant:)

  - *Threshold:* Must haves; a failed product if any of these kinds of features are missing.

  - *Satisfiers:* Core features, satisfaction if present, and the more, the better.

  - *Delighters:* Attractive; satisfaction if present, but does not cause dissatisfaction if omitted. These features are like the "sizzle on the steak": not critical, but customers love to have it, they think it's "cool."

  - *Indifferent:* Does not matter if the feature is present or not.

  - *Dissatisfiers:* Reverse quality; dissatisfaction if too much of that quality is present; satisfaction if none or little is present.

Prioritizing on business value is fairly straightforward, and either Delphi or a multipoint prioritization scheme can be easily used, even across e-mail, which is more convenient than yet another meeting. Of course, each stakeholder will have a different prioritization value for these, and it is up to the BA to get a final reconcilement, and assure that each stakeholder can live with the final prioritized feature catalog.

If there are many stakeholders, Delphi technique works fairly well across e-mail for this. Do not use an *average* value between stakeholders because usually that means the priority is not what either of the stakeholders want, but something in-between. There must be agreement on the product backlog among the stakeholders.

One of the common problems with getting priorities from stakeholders is that they want to give everything a priority of 1. To overcome this, use a priority card system, which is adapted from the estimating techniques used during the iterations; it works extremely well.

When using the *priority card technique*, give the group of stakeholders a set of 3×5 cards on which each card contains a single feature and a summary description. Have stakeholders *as a group* place the cards in a stack, highest value at the top. *A stack of cards cannot have physically more than one card at top*; it cannot have multiple number-one priorities, or multiple values for any priority. Record the position for each card to indicate the priority of each feature in the product backlog.

Estimate Relative Feature Sizes

The relative feature size indicates how long it will take to collect detailed requirements and implement (that is, design, code, and test) each feature. However, detailed requirements have not yet been collected, no design is done, and the skill level (that is, speed of development) of the resources working on that feature, are all unknown. (The technical team is not yet in place.) Therefore, this estimate, although better than the ROM[8] estimate that was used to charter the project, is insufficient to deliver the product predictably. The estimate will improve as requirements and implementation proceed during the iteration in which the feature is built. Traditional project management would spend the time to calculate these durations, but agile practitioners think that the resulting estimate is too rough (unpredictable) to be worth the time. The time would be better spent on progressively elaborating during the iterations.

There is a good solution to this problem. First, do not try to estimate *time to complete*. Time depends on many factors: resources assigned, skill set and knowledge of the resource, interruptions, time allocated to the task, and other factors that cannot even be guessed at now. The approach is to estimate the *relative size* (scope) of each feature. Those relative values are easier to handle later when predictability is an issue.

For example, it is easier to know that a large dog eats more than a small dog, and a medium-size dog eats some amount in-between. Given the relative ratios of large, medium, and small dogs in a kennel, the kennel owner can accurately estimate how much dog food to buy for all the dogs.

Similarly, the features in the catalog can be scoped for later allocation to the time-boxed iterations. Several agile scoping metrics can be used for this task.

Scoping Metrics

Traditionally, scope is measured in person-hours or person-weeks. Agilistas have introduced a different metric that does not include time: *Story points, T-shirt sizes, ideal-hours,* or *ideal-days,*[9] and time-based metrics are avoided. All the scope metrics are defined in arbitrary units relative to each other: one piece of work is smaller or larger than another by a little or a lot. Scope sizing is like trying to determine if a dog is large or small, which depends on what "small" and "large" mean. However, I can say that a Great Dane is larger than a collie, which is larger than a Chihuahua. The top three most popular scope metrics are described next.

- *Story points*: If I say that a Great Dane is an 8, and a Chihuahua is a 1, then I can rank all the other dogs accordingly. Due to a psychological fact that people estimate more poorly the larger the entity being scoped, story points are assigned to elements of the Fibonacci series: 1, 2, 3, 5, 8, 13, and 21 (and larger); the values of, say 4 or 16, are never used. The ever-increasing gap in the numbers reflects the lack of accuracy in the estimate due to its size; a value of 8 or 10 is the same within the accuracy of the estimate. The story points of a feature or use case or other scope amount is done in that way. Story points are typical for agile projects, but team members new to this kind of scope sizing have trouble thinking in these terms.

- *T-shirt sizes*: Instead of a Fibonacci scale from 1 to N, as with story points, T-shirt sizes refer to only four sizes: small, medium, large, and extra-large. Only four sizes are used (although the team can choose others) because at the feature level (before requirements are collected sufficiently), there is not enough information to estimate a feature more closely. The metric tries to avoid being "overly-precise and under-accurate."

---

[8]Rough-order-of-magnitude estimate

[9]"Ideal days" and "ideal hours" are actually a metric of scope, but because it includes the word "day" or "hours," it often causes confusion. How to handle this issue is explained later.

- *Ideal days (or ideal hours)*: Another popular metric is ideal days (or ideal hours), or the amount of time a "typical" person would take to complete the task if they were not interrupted, had to attend meetings, and were as fresh during the task as when they started. Although "time" is in the name, this metric is one of scope, and not of duration. Team members often can relate to this metric easier than story points, and feel that it is more accurate than T-shirt sizes. This metric is often using in training or for new teams until they get more comfortable using story points.

✖ **Metaphor**   I walk into a store to purchase a thermometer to measure the temperature in my house. I find an inexpensive red alcohol thermometer, and it indicates the store temperature as 75 degrees, plus or minus 5 degrees, because the calibration markings are relatively far apart from each other. I also see a more expensive digital thermometer that indicates the store temperature as 69.3719 degrees. Which is the better thermometer? *It depends on the store temperature!* If the temperature in the store is actually 77 degrees, then the alcohol thermometer is better for why I need it. The extra precision is farther from the truth than the less precise alcohol thermometer. Do not confuse precision with accuracy, which is often done when building scope documents like product backlogs or project plans.

For the team to come to a consensus on the scope of a use case or user story, they must have the same idea as to (1) what metric to use, and (2) what that metric means. Let's assume the team decides to use story points. I can use the dog-sizing technique shown earlier, where I give a range of dog sizes, and all other dogs fall within that range. That is the technique called *triangulation.*

Let's say that an "average" user story takes one day to complete, and let's assign that story five story points. Now all user stories can use the calibration point of 5 with which to compare other user stories, in a range of 1 to 13. This is a technique sometimes called *affinity estimating.* Either triangulation or affinity estimating is fine, but it is essential for the team to have a common understanding of the scoping metric it uses.

Estimate the Top Part of the Features Catalog

The BA and stakeholders break down the top-most features into smaller levels of scope and estimate only those features that are likely to be completed in the first few iterations. They estimate the scope in detail corresponding to when it will be implemented: the sooner a piece of scope will be implemented, the more detail is unwrapped; the later pieces of scope are estimated at a larger granular level. This technique is called *adaptive planning*, and is used throughout agile for all estimation activities. Features are broken into themes (use cases) or epics. Decomposing scope to the most detailed level, user stories, should wait until the iteration in which they are implemented, and the technical team is involved.

Once the feature catalog, or at least the top part of it, is prioritized and size-estimated, the sponsor and project manager can apply it to a calendar in the preliminary release plan.

Develop a Preliminary Release Plan

The *release plan* is a simple calendar schedule showing when each fixed-length iteration starts and ends. At a minimum, the release plan will have an *Iteration 0* (start-up), a number of productive iterations (delivering business value), and a *release iteration* at the end of the project. There may be other release iterations within the release plan for multiple releases, and there may be *hardening iterations*. Each iteration is labeled with the high -level scope (a feature or two) to be accomplished in that iteration.

The preliminary release plan is mostly a guess, but release plans must be reviewed periodically anyway as requirements are added, removed, or reprioritized. The preliminary release plan is completed before the iterations start and revised by the technical team when they come on board in Iteration 0. This double pass technique (1) communicates the scope and objectives to the team, and (2) allows the team to improve the release plan.

Iteration 0

The first iteration of the project, one in which the technical team is acquired, development and test environments are set up, tools put in place, architecture defined, and the first pass of the requirements completed. This first iteration is called *Iteration 0,*[10] and no real productive value will be delivered at the end of it. *This iteration cannot be skipped.* The project will literally not be able to proceed without its infrastructure and support in place.

■ **Warning**   *Do not skip Iteration 0, or try to blend it with Iteration 1.* I was involved in two projects at different times that tried to do Iteration 0 and Iteration 1 concurrently—develop the tools as you need them—that's the agile way, right? Wrong. The productivity expected to be delivered in Iteration 1 wasn't completed until Iteration 3—at least four weeks wasted. Tasks and user stories were constantly being deferred or blocked, waiting for infrastructure dependencies. There were more cracks for the tasks to fall through than the highways after a San Francisco earthquake! The philosophy of trying to do both iterations at once reminded me of the Dilbert comment from the pointy-haired manager: "We don't have the requirements yet, but start coding anyway so it looks like we are doing something."

The release plan (sometimes called *iteration schedule*), at this point, is a list of say, two-week calendar intervals that are labeled Iteration 0 to Iteration N. Each iteration is time-boxed so regardless of the scope being implemented in those iterations, each iteration has a fixed start and end date. As the features from the features catalog (product backlog), are known, each iteration can take the name of the primary objective of the features going into the respective iteration.

There should be two other kinds of iterations in the release plan within the normal product-producing ones: one or more *hardening iterations*, and one *release iteration*.

Hardening Iteration

A *hardening iteration* may be scheduled into the release plan every three or more iterations; like team velocity, the number of hardening iterations needed depends on the product and the team. During this time, all technical debt is repaid: refactoring that should have been done, gaps in requirements filled in, necessary documents completed, and any other work that resets the project to full production quality. A hardening iteration also allows the schedule to reset somewhat, providing a little margin on a schedule that is not based on history yet. A hardening iteration can be shorter than a normal iteration; usually it is one-week long.

---

[10]Scrum calls their first iteration Sprint 1 instead of Iteration 0. The process and goals are the same, but the terminology is different.

Theoretically, a hardening iteration should never be needed because refactoring is done continually within an iteration, and technical debt never goes past the end of the iteration. (Of course, theoretically, there will never be any bugs in the code and testing will not be needed either.) I have never seen, or even heard of, a project that didn't need a hardening iteration, even if it is treated as a normal iteration. At any rate, it is a common enough event that that kind of iteration has its own name.

Release Iteration

The last iteration that releases the final version of the product and closes the project is a *release iteration*. There may be multiple release iterations, just as there are multiple user-demo iterations, but the last iteration closes down the project by definition.

The release iteration is performed just before the product goes to operations. It contains activities that span individual iterations. It is the time that any last minute defects are repaired, documentation that is needed external to the project is written or collected (such as operations manuals, user manuals, or technical support docs), final project-level status reports and overall test results are compiled, and other general cleanup activities. It may also have load testing, performance evaluations, and other system-wide activities. This iteration can be shorter than a normal iteration.

⚷ Recommendation   After the stakeholders have identified and prioritized all the features in the product backlog. A prioritized backlog will have a combination of small, medium, large, and extra-large features in it, and over the length of the project, will average out to roughly the same number of story points per iteration. Try to avoid ideal-hours as much as possible because it is often confused with *time* of completing a feature instead of its *scope*.

Example: A product backlog contains 400 story points, comprised of features, use cases, or epics of different sizes. Assume the technical team will have a velocity of say, 20 story points per iterations, so the project will need 400/20 = 20 iterations. Distribute approximately 20 story points of scope into each iteration. Add an Iteration 0, a few one-week hardening iterations (say every five iterations), and a final Release iteration, to complete the project duration. Add start and end dates for each iteration, and you have the initial release plan. Review the release plan after each iteration to ensure that it is still on schedule. As team velocity becomes better known, the release plan will change to reflect the team's historical rate of progress. After the first five iterations, the velocity is averaged to forecast the project's end date. It should be very accurate and reliable, but review it each iteration anyway to ensure that it is staying on track. Any changes should be brought to the sponsor and stakeholders at the next iteration review.

How Long Is an Iteration?

There is an optimal iteration length in which the least amount of effort is spent to get the most value. The length of the iteration depends on the agile method chosen (such as Scrum or XP), the size of the project, upper-management considerations, team dynamics, and the quality approach. For example, iteration length is affected by how often unknown scope is in an iteration, or how often the stakeholders want to see results. However, the iteration should not be less than one week or more than four weeks (Leffingwell 2007).

Different agile methods, with different overhead ratios, have different time box recommendations. The most popular iteration is two weeks in length, which makes sense since agile methods are applied best to small projects. Having the same amount of work each iteration fixed to the calendar also makes it easier to pre-schedule regular events, like user demos.

Leffingwell gives a list of reasons for recommending the two-week iteration. By having periodic feedback sessions, showcased by the iteration's user demo, the team gets feedback so that they can revise the product. If the feedback comes too late, then they must rework that part of the product, which wastes time. If the iterations recur too soon, time is wasted doing a lot of setup and teardown work. There is a balance between the productive value of building the product uninterrupted with quick feedback, and the overhead of starting and closing an iteration.

The iteration length also depends on the size of the project. For most projects, a two-week iteration allows enough time to develop and test a "chunk" of business value in the form of product code. For large projects, or those involving high levels of research, three- or four-week iterations work well. Iterations longer than four weeks produce unnecessary rework because the feedback cycles are not short enough; and the agile acid test (working software within 30 days) is not met.

Iterations less than one week are not recommended. They are overwhelmed by iteration overhead: regression testing, collecting requirements, coding and unit testing, reporting activities, and acceptance testing the user story. The team cannot get up to their peak speed. It is like trying to race a car through a neighborhood with a stop sign at every block.

Variant As an alternative, you can use the Kanban method: no iterations. User stories are done a few at a time as the team member(s) currently working the story passes it through requirements, analysis, design, coding, and testing, like a product on an assembly line. One of my open-source project teams consists of volunteer members who are committed to working on the project only 2 to 4 hours per week, and they only meet once a week. We found the Kanban method to work better for our team than the other agile methods.

However, Kanban can be time-boxed for convenience for reporting and user demos. The team velocity needs to be measured over time, and user demos are better pre-scheduled. There is a satisfying closure when an "iteration" plans what is being put in the build that will be demoed in two weeks.

PMI Parallels

At project startup, how do agile development and traditional practices compare to the PMI's Body of Knowledge (BOK)? The following are the knowledge areas from the PMI, which differ from agile practices.

Scope: The PMI would say that project startup, as described in this chapter, is in the stages of scope definition, although only the high-level scope is defined and the lower level scope is deferred until later. There is no hierarchical work breakdown structure, but the feature catalog (product backlog) provides a breakdown of the work by scope and business priority. As with the WBS, time-based tasks are used to define sequence and schedule, which is done by agile projects during the iterations.

Time: The project schedule works almost as a template into which scope is inserted, instead of a list of WBS tasks allocated across the calendar. The schedule is addressed only as a high-level view of iterations, without detailed work assigned into them. The iteration schedule is bracketing by an Iteration 0 for setup, and an Iteration N for project release and closedown.

Quality: There are no quality standards defined yet; the technical team will develop them during the technical meetings later.

Human Resources: Resources are only treated in the abstract, as a set of roles and responsibilities, instead of people's names. The RAM discussed is exactly the same as that of the PMBOK, and forms the basis of the communication plan. The role and authority of a PM at this point (Region 2) is dependent on the organizational structure, such as functional, matrix, or projectized, as that defined in the PMBOK.

Communications: The communication plan is a one-sheet table of who gets what information, when, and how.

Risk: No differences here: risks are identified and collected as found, and the risk responses that go with them. The project charter may identify a few risks, and it continues to grow as the project progresses.

Stakeholder Management: Stakeholder management is the same as the PMBOK, even down to plans on how to maintain the engagement.

Integration: The integration of the various aspects of the projects are addressed by the business and technical sequences of how this all comes together in the various meetings and artifacts described earlier.

Conclusion

The agile project characteristics are just beginning to show themselves, as scope and schedules are not defined to the full-detail of the project. As shown in the history of agile vs. traditional progressive elaboration, the agile project undergoes *some upfront* work before moving into the iterations in which real productive business value is built and delivered.

The project stakeholders are brought on-board, and the project team is oriented on the agile approach. The critical business abstracts and project abstracts allow the scope to be decomposed in alignment with the sponsor's mission statement and all the stakeholders' expectations.

At the end of this stage, the PM should have key deliverables: a project abstract, a prioritized and size-estimated product backlog (features catalog), an iteration-based release plan (project schedule), and a written agreement of the business team's working agreement ("the engagement ground rules") from the business kickoff meeting, the RAM (CORA matrix), and a communication plan.

Everything is ready now to move forward into Iteration 0 to set up the technical team kickoff meeting, the architecture, infrastructure, and initial requirements to prepare for delivering business value to the customers.

Additional Tools

Table 3-4. Business Team's Kickoff Meeting Template

Meeting Information

Meeting Name	Kickoff		**Coordinator**	
Date				
Location				
Time				
Purpose				
Expected Outcomes	[results and decisions to be made]			
Invitees	[Name], facilitator [Name], scribe [Names...]			
CC				
#	**Topic**		**Time**	**Presenter**
1	Introduction by executive sponsor or project sponsor		0000 – 0000	
2	Determine stakeholders			
3	Review project proposal			
4	Set project meeting schedule			
5	Set ground rules			
6	Determine deliverables			
7	Assign date of completion for business abstracts			

PART II

■ ■ ■

Iteration 0

CHAPTER 4

■ ■ ■

Preparing the Project

Some Upfront Work Is Necessary

In the early days of agile, agilists wanted to avoid all upfront work before the iterations of requirements, coding, and testing started: no architecture, no initial requirements, not even getting their development environment set up. (The emergent design fans still use this approach.) I think this is an overreaction to the waterfall method. The pendulum of popular development style swung from too-much-upfront work to no-upfront work. Fortunately, that pendulum is swinging back to some upfront work that some agilists call upfront learning. [1]

Early agilists' argued that developing detailed anything (plans, design, requirements, or tests) on an unknown product is a waste of time. That is partially true. However, the problem with no upfront work is two-fold. First, development iterations depend on certain things being in place before work actually starts so that the iterations can run smoothly, like the team and development environment being in place. Secondly, much of the rework that resulted from no-upfront-anything was excessive, and not a refinement of original knowledge. Product changes are more time- and effort-intensive at the code and test level than they are the paper (planning) level. Agile uses a principle of *refinement,* not wholesale replacement.

Many agile approaches are distinguished by how much upfront work they recommend. Some things, like architectures, are very difficult and time intensive, to change. The team must walk a balance between what is too much, and what is too little, upfront work. This preparatory work is called "getting to ready" and is packaged into a pre-productive iteration called *Iteration 0.*

The sections that contain what I consider the activities that must be accomplished to reach that balance, a bare minimum to minimize the rework of product refinement later, namely, setting up the infrastructure, designing an overall architecture, collecting initial requirements, and setting up the team's working agreement in a technical team kickoff meeting. Agilists may complain that this is too much Region 2 work, too much like waterfall, but it is not. These tasks are merely preparing the project and the team into being productive fastest.

What Is Iteration 0?

Agile projects run as a series of time-boxed iterations[2] (usually two to four weeks) in which the project team develops the detailed requirements, writes the code, tests small units of work, and ends with a user demo and progress report to upper management. The project flexes on the scope delivered, as defined in the feature catalog, constrained by time and cost. Not all projects will flex scope, but will flex cost or time. The overview I give here will flex scope because it is the most common approach to agile. Agile projects will

---

[1] Alistair Cockburn, one of the agilist patriarchs, announces this idea at a recent NFJS conference in Columbus, OH. Meyer (2014) and Guiteri (2011) have also published on the topic.

[2] Lean and Kanban are two of the popular agile approaches that do not require iterations, but work is often packaged into iterations for reporting purposes, and for periodic and frequent user demos.

deliver business value for each of the 1 to N iterations. Before Iteration 1 starts, some preparation work must be done, and that work is done in what is called *Iteration 0*.[3] Iteration 0 is so-named because it is the period of time in which prep work is done before any productive value can be delivered, before the productive iterations of 1 through N. Iteration 0 starts after the project is selected. For purposes of this discussion, the following things should assume to be completed by this time in the project.

- All the steps in the previous chapters are completed: the project is chartered; the PM and BA are assigned; stakeholders are identified and their kickoff meeting completed; and the feature catalog (product backlog) has been prioritized by business value, risk, and dependencies.

- At least one business unit SME is allocated to provide requirements during the requirements sessions. These sessions will start in iteration 0 and continue throughout the project.

- At least one developer and one tester are assigned as part of the technical team.

- The project is committed by management, stakeholders, and technical team to follow agile principles, and Iteration 0 in particular.

This chapter discuss the technical team kickoff meeting and agile tailoring, and introduces the architecture, infrastructure, and initial requirements activities discussed in later chapters. The product architecture must be defined to set a framework on which to base the product (see Chapter 5); the infrastructure must be put into place so the technical team has something with which to work (see Chapter 6); and initial detailed requirements need to be started so that the technical team has something on which to work during the first iteration (see Chapter 7).

Count from Zero

The technical team revises the preliminary Release Plan. Using the detail revealed during the progressive elaboration of Iteration 0, they refine the project's schedule and cost from the rough Release Plan done previously.

The next estimate with the level of accuracy for schedule completion, scope, and costs is based on the actual performance of the team. It will be much more accurate and precise. The team's history will continue to be applied and compared against the latest estimate and can change if the team's rate of progress changes. These historically based estimates (actuals) will have a margin of error that merges toward less than 10% of the final result as work results are applied. Agile projects usually finish on the day predicted, and within the budget.

■ **Warning**   The tasks of Iteration 0 simply cannot be skipped, and skipping it should not be attempted. It is not possible to skip the hardware and software setup of Iteration 0, but it is possible to do it under some other name or iteration and falsely think that time has been saved. Some teams try to prepare for the work at the same time as they do the work of Iteration 1. This is a common "time-saving tactic" that does not work. Projects that have tried to develop code, collect requirements, and build the infrastructure (development and testing environment) concurrently have slowed as a result of their support procedures, tools, and architectures being in flux or late. Often, the developers have nothing to do because the requirements aren't ready, or their development machines and tools are not yet available. Development cannot actually start until Iteration 0 is complete. It is like trying to drive your car without first getting into it.

---

[3]Scrum has no iteration 0, but does the same work in what it calls Sprint 1.

The good news is that Iteration 0 may take less than two weeks, but depending on culture, it might take longer. The time needed to complete Iteration 0 provides a scaling factor that can be applied to the other iterations. The duration of Iteration 0 is mostly independent of the product, but depends on culture and organizational factors that apply throughout all the iteration activities. The detail of this is outside the scope of this book.

Acquiring the Technical Team

Ideally, the technical team already exists and project work is directed to the team. However, most traditional organizations have resource managers who assign people to the team, and the PM must negotiate to get the best people and their time. Unfortunately, the resource managers usually assign people with the mistaken idea of multi-tasking: more will get done if the workers are spread across multiple projects. Agile teams are dedicated and the core team members must be assigned full-time to the project.

Once a new team is in place, then the team members develop a working agreement among themselves, with coaching from the APM, in the technical team kickoff meeting. They follow up with choosing how to apply agile to their team, project, and organization in a agile tailoring session. For new agile teams, the APM plays a key role.

Avoid the Myth of Multitasking

The term *multitasking* has provided a cultural paradigm of mental efficiency that is incorrect and ill serving. It is essential that core team members be dedicated to the project and not be allocated to multiple projects at the same time. Multitasking not only reduces team productivity and quality, but also deteriorates team communication and increases the individual's ability to be distracted more easily. All these factors work against what is necessary for *empowered team*, an important agile principle.

Resource managers who believe the myth of multitasking mistakenly think that developers who swap between different projects are covering more ground, are more productive. The opposite is true. Projects get done sooner if the team is dedicated, and resources are *not swapped* between projects. These kinds of resource managers often complain about not having enough resources, when actually they have created the very bottleneck they were trying to avoid. A comprehensive report from Realization Corp (2013) contains case studies, raw data, and proposed solutions to this problem at the organization level.

> *Job seekers around the world still tout their ability to multitask as a desirable skill, and in many organizations, multitasking is worn as a badge of honor; however, research consistently shows that people who attempt to multitask suffer a wide array of negative effects, from wasting 40 percent of their productive time switching tasks to experiencing a heightened susceptibility to distraction. (Realization Corp. 2013).*

People cannot multitask well. What is commonly called multitasking is actually context-switching, time sharing, partial consciousness, and other variations. *Multitasking* is a term borrowed from the computer industry referring to how a computer processes multiple threads of computation simultaneously. People do not think the same way that computers do. People-based multitasking is slower than doing two tasks in sequence, and reduces the quality of each task by as much as 50% (Craig-Hart 2014). For example, look at the increase in the number of car accidents as people try to drive and phone-text at the same time, an effect recognized by lawmakers, resulting in prohibitions against texting and driving in many states.

The closest people get to multitasking is *context switching*: quickly (and sometimes subconsciously) stopping one task to start another, and then stopping that task to return to the original task. Rinse, wash, repeat. Switching from one task to do another takes shutdown and startup time each time the person switches. It is faster to do two tasks in sequence than to try to do two at once; the greater the shutdown and startup times, the greater the difference between sequencing the tasks and trying to multitask (Foroughi, Werner, Nelson, and Boehm-Davis 2014).

Depending on the amount of time to shift from project (or task) to another, and then back again, the time to complete two projects concurrently can be 40% longer than working the two projects (or tasks) sequentially (Bregman 2010). Multitasking produces other negative effects to schedule and quality, such as 50% longer to accomplish a task, and 50% more errors (Foroughi et al. 2014; Rosen 2008, 105–110). These data partly explain why agile projects, centered on single project teams, are more effective than traditional projects that have team members distributed across multiple projects and organizational units.

Another term we can borrow from the computer industry is *thrashing*, which is when the time needed to shut down a current task and start up a second task (or restart the first task again) takes longer than the time allotted for the work to be done on the task. In that case, no work is done; the computer spends its entire time thrashing. This can happen to people too.

Multitasking also applies to interruptions, which forces a kind of multitasking. Interrupting a person in *deep-think* mode, someone who is intensely focused on a task, can also cause a sudden drop in productivity: a five-minute interruption can cause a loss of an hour of productive time (Venezia 2014). The Software Engineering Institute reported that a person takes about 20 minutes to recover from a deep-think interruption. If a person is interrupted on the average of three times an hour, then that person will get nothing done. Programming and testing is a deep-think activity, which is why it is part of the APM's job to shield the developers and testers from interruptions, and it is part of the team member's responsibility to redirect those interrupters to the APM.

As an implication of multitasking at the task level, the same is true at the project level as at the organizational level (Realization 2013). It is essential that team members be dedicated to the project and not be allocated to multiple projects at the same time. However, there are always downtimes, so having a low-priority alternative task is not a bad idea, and will not delay the project. Sometimes, urgencies arise that cannot be avoided, so the team will need to accept the preempted time spent. Sometimes, urgencies arise that cannot be avoided, so the team will need to accept the preempted time spent.

There is an upside to multitasking, which is enabled by the agile team room and osmotic communications. There are always downtimes, so having a low-priority alternative task does not affect the project. Multitasking allows necessary backburner projects in the downtimes of first priority projects, and the people on those projects can relax their previously held intense focus (Silverman 2010). It is a matter of the right tool for the right job.

Hold a Technical Team Kickoff Meeting

The technical team has a different set of ground rules than the business team does. The technical team kickoff meeting is held after the business team kickoff meeting because the business direction must be set first, the needed technical skill sets identified, and some features and requirements need to be ready for the technical team when they start. Once the context is in place for the technical team, their kickoff meeting defines the iterational *working team agreement*.

The following are some recommended goals for the technical team kickoff meeting.[4]

- *Technical launch.* The PM leads off with what is known about the project so far: the latest version of the charter, the objectives from the project abstract and feature catalog, and facilitates a consensus for defining grounds rules for the team. The ground rules contain the assumption that the team will follow some form of agile, and that a separate meeting will be held to define the details. As with the business team kickoff meeting, it is a good idea to have the sponsor share his or her vision of the product. The business-technical working relationship also benefits if the chief customer or stakeholder is introduced, and that person shares their goals for the product.

---

[4]I assume that the PM working in Region 2 works as the APM in the iterative Region 1 but this is not necessarily so. The APM should work on one project, but a Region 2 PM may work with many projects at a time, and sometimes called a program manager.

- *Describe the project approach.* Familiarize the technical team briefly with how an agile project affects them if they are new to it: iterative, incremental, daily builds, repeated scope estimation, daily meetings, thin-thread development, concurrent development and testing, frequent requirements meetings, product demos each iteration, burn-up charts, change requests, task tracking, communication, and so forth.

- *Roles and responsibilities.* Agile team roles are fairly predefined, although agile technical team members wear many hats. These roles are not as cleanly delineated for agile teams as they are for traditional teams because an agile team works together on all aspects of the work to be accomplished within an iteration. Each team member contributes something to the team, and has a specific role, and perhaps a secondary role. There are no functional silos on an agile team as on traditional teams. The typical roles and responsibilities that follow are actually skillsets that one or more team members may have.

  - *Agile project manager (or iteration coach):* Organizes and mentors team members on agile process development and changes, and iteration and project progress reporting. For agile projects, sometimes this role is called the agile coach, especially if the PM is filling this role when working inside the agile team.[5]

  - *Business analyst:* Within an iteration, the BA elicits detailed requirements and user interface artifacts (e.g., screen mockups) with the business SMEs. Once a use case[6] requirement or a set of user stories are completed at this level, they are refined with the developers and testers.

  - *Developer:* Designs the software, writes the code for the user story, and writes unit tests. The developer is responsible for removing all defects and ensures that all code integrates seamlessly with existing code from other team members.

  - *Tester:* Writes the test cases for the requirement while the developer writes the code, and tests the requirement when the developer is finished. The tester also organizes test cases, defect reports, and final QA aspects of the build before the user demo. Defects to the developers are reported as soon as possible, typically within a day of the code being submitted to the code base.

- *Identify other technical team members.* For large projects, others may work part-time on the team. A *technical writer* is sometimes needed on large projects or when documents are required by those outside the team, (e.g., operations and user manuals, special management reports or documents, or white papers that spin off from the project). A *user interface design expert* helps ensure that the user interface design is conducive to a clean and friendly user experience. A *database analyst* may help organize the data, especially if the database is being shared with multiple applications. A *network specialist* may be needed for web applications and architectural integration. These other technical team members may not be needed every day, but as often as practical to complete the necessary work.

- As with the business team, members of the technical team may be aware of others who should be involved on the project. The APM should investigate to see if they actually should and can be on the team. There may be extra funding or resource allocations to consider. If more resources can be secured, add them to the RAM.

---

[5]For convenience, I will refer to a PM when talking about Region 2 activities, and APM when talking about Region 1 activities, where *APM* and *agile coach* are synonymous.

[6]A *use case* is comprised of a set of interactive paths, each one being a *user story*. It provides context for a set of related user stories, and is similar to an agile *theme*.

- *Technical team member engagement.* How much time will each member be able to commit to the project? Stakeholders and customer SMEs need to be available full-time. Weekly meetings with stakeholders can work, but those who provide detailed requirements need to be available almost daily. Many organizations do not have such an arrangement, especially in matrix organizations.

- Ideally, the technical team is in place always, instead of acquiring them for each project. The overhead of team forming, storming, and adjourning is removed (and most of the overhead of Iteration 0), and high-performance teams develop products like an assembly line: projects requirements in and products out. See the "Avoid the Myth of Multitasking" section.

- *Shared infrastructure.* Similar to the shared docBase the stakeholders can access to see project documents, the technical team will also need to select a shared infrastructure for coding, automated testing, code versioning, tracking, technical specs, and whatever else they think they can use. Almost all infrastructure software is available through open source at no cost, and commercial tools recommended by the organization may already be in use. If not, their cost will need to be approved and added to the project budget. Details about what might be in the infrastructure are described in Chapters 4 and 6.

- *Daily meetings and two-week iterations.* The technical team meets each day for 15 minutes to discuss the tasks each has *completed*. Each day, each member describes (1) what they completed yesterday, (2) what they will complete today, and (3) any impediments (blockers) that they have encountered that needs more time, a response from someone else, or escalation. Daily meetings and two-week iterations are the standard for agile projects for good reasons, but they can be modified in the iteration tailoring session.

- *Schedule an iteration tailoring session.* What agile approach will the team follow? Kanban, Scrum, XP, something else? The approach will be specific to the organization, culture, project, and the team. Schedule a follow-up meeting to allow the team to tailor the iteration approach (see the next section).

Tailor an Agile Iteration Approach

In many organizations, management polices prohibit the PM from choosing whether to use agile or not. The PM is required to follow the organization's policies, using traditional methods or agile methods, regardless of what approach fits the project best. The one-size-fits-all approach contrasts strongly with the agile approach of customizing an approach that works best for the organization, project, and team.

By default, agile is the preferred approach because of its benefits, quality, speed, and success rate of agile projects, but early approaches should adapt the approach to their organizational culture and project team for a best fit. More experienced agile teams can adopt more intense forms of agile.

According to Jeff Sutherland, the acid test for an agile team is *Deliver working software within 30 days*. If this cannot be done, the project is not agile (Schwaber and Sutherland 2012), regardless of the various agile ceremonies that the team might have used.

The key factors to keep in mind when customizing a team for the agile project's success are (a) developing very small chunks of product with very short feedback cycles with the customers; and (b) delivering the highest value first as the product is released into use, and thus begin to accumulate its value to the organization.

The project moves forward best when all the technical team members can use what they know, learn what they need to know, and work together as a tight-knit performing team. The APM should facilitate a meeting in which the team leverages the standard agile principles (Manifesto 2001) to define an agile approach specific to the particular project and team. The APM frequently recommends one to start.

If the team seems to get bogged down in committing to an approach, remind them that the proposed agile approach can be revised as questions arise. Some of the technical team may have preferences on how they do their work, and these should be acknowledged and respected. Be sure to mention that at the end of the first iteration, and periodically afterward (at least each third iteration), there will be a *retrospective* to collect lessons learned and make changes to the approach. If changes are large enough to ripple out to the business stakeholders, they must agree also.

The team's biggest decision to make when tailoring is which flavor of agile the team prefers to use, such as Scrum, Kanban, XP, Crystal, or some other. The choice will affect the balance between effort and planning, quality, and amount of rework the team is willing to experience. Figure 1-7 showed the relationship between effort and planning by agile techniques. In addition to this, the team needs to decide the durations of their iterations, something between two and four weeks.

Details on the various options are discussed in the following sections, but the end result of the tailoring session is a rough procedure, with full consensus of the technical team, for the aspects of each iteration:

- How features are moved from the product backlog to the iteration backlog.

- How requirements are elicited and refined.

- How concurrent development and testing occurs.

- How much will be contained in the product demo (at full production quality) each iteration.

- How will iteration planning be performed? Poker planning, brainstorming, scoping metrics?

- What task tracking devices will be used? Kanban boards, sticky notes on a wall, Excel spreadsheets?

- What tool to use for progress tracking? Burn-up charts, burn-down charts?

- Do they want to use test-driven development (TDD)? Behavior-driven development (BDD)? Something else? With what are they already familiar?

- What tools will they use—for version control, continuous improvement, development IDEs, change requests, automated testing, and so forth.

- How will coding and testing work together in the various shared codebases and builds?

- How will the different environments of development, testing, staging, and production interplay with each other? Is support from outside the team needed?

- What standards come into play, both external and internal to the team?

- How will compliance (to team standards, regulations, or external policies) be measured, and with what tools? What non-compliances will stop a build from going into the codebase?

The technical team member who comes in late to the project is at a disadvantage, because he or she will be expected to follow the current team practices. Those practices may be new or painful, but fortunately, the iteration approach can be (and should be) reviewed and modified every few iterations to improve the process, and adjusted to fit team dynamics.

Quality Approach: Risk vs. Rigor

The business and technical team should resolve, with guidance from the APM, how much "quality" they want to instill in the product. Before first saying, "As much as possible," consider that the higher the quality, the more effort that goes into the validation and verification (V&V) of the product, and more overhead means more time and effort needed. There is a balance between how much quality can be built in, and how much it is needed. Software quality for an astronaut's life support system is justified at a higher level than a mobile phone video game.

Conversely, developers will want to write code immediately, and anything that prevents that is met with resistance. Writing code directly from user stories is often the developers' choice, but other team members, or even the sponsor, may want a more rigorous approach. If someone else applies the rigor, such as the BA doing requirements modeling, then it more acceptable to the developers. The APM should also remind the team that they will get a chance to revise their decision after a few iterations when a team retrospective is held. A try-and-see approach is usually more acceptable to the team.

Figure 4-1 shows a qualitative diagram of how the respective development approaches map to effort. As the granularity of the scope increases (from features to use cases to user stories), the risk drops because more is known about that unit of scope. In moving from features to user stories only, the curve mirrors the progressive elaboration curve. If test-driven development (TDD) is used, the unit tests are written as the code is written; this low-level validation removes additional risk.

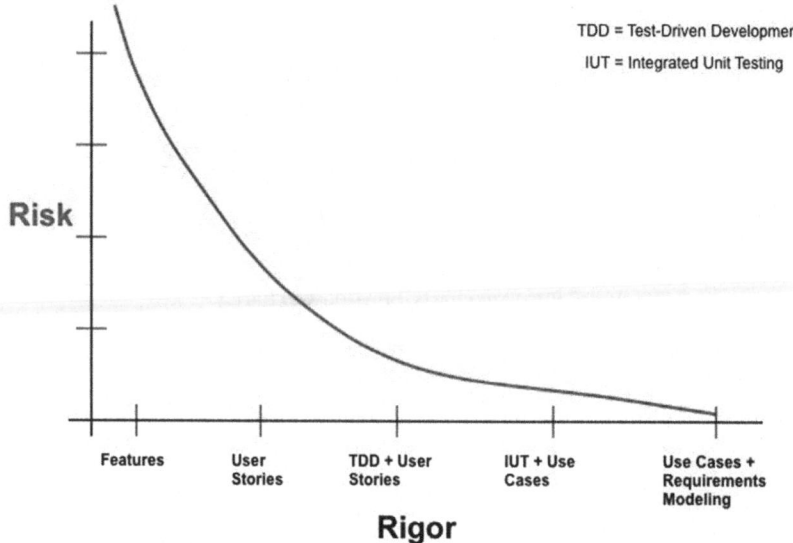

TDD = Test-Driven Development

IUT = Integrated Unit Testing

Risk

Features | User Stories | TDD + User Stories | IUT + Use Cases | Use Cases + Requirements Modeling

Rigor

Figure 4-1. Risk vs. Rigor by project method

User stories alone can be fragmented, but a use case gives each user story a context, and contains more detail. Use cases in conjunction with integrated unit testing (TDD plus automated integration testing at the use case level) allows more validation and lowers even more the risk of a defect. Finally, if the team goes to the trouble of rigorously validating the use case with requirements modeling,[7] then almost all defects can be removed from the requirements and the risk is close to nil. Since requirements defects account for over half

---

[7]Requirements modeling refers to building an object model of the problem domain, and validating it with a XUML sequence diagram to guarantee that no logical, control, or data errors exist; most ambiguities are removed too. This activity takes a few hours per use case, but does not impact the developer because the BA performs this exercise. The requirements model also helps the testers write test cases faster because they can leverage the model for testing. See Chapter 9.

the product defects (Alberts 1976), performing requirements modeling at the use case level removes over half of the product defects before the coding even starts. This of course takes longer, but the risk of a defect-ridden product is lowered. Although the business may find defects in the user demo, it is quicker to prevent the defects than remove them after an iteration or more has elapsed.

Integrated unit testing (IUT) refers to integration testing at the use case level. Uses cases define a logically related set of user stories, and provide the context. Testing done at the user-story level increases the quality even more. IUT is similar to acceptance test cases. Despite the thin-thread approach of agile, testing at the use case level (integration testing) is important. Like the wit said, "Although an airplane has over a million parts, none of them can fly." It is important that all pieces of the product work together properly.

The business team may (but often not) define some level of quality they want for the product. It is up to the technical team to choose how they will achieve that quality; that is, how and what sort of validation and verification they will do. The team chooses what level of rigor they want for the project, and much depends on what they are comfortable with. Many developers prefer user stories to use cases, or business analysts may not have the time for requirements modeling; many things factor into the choice. Choosing the development approach is like anything else: the quality you get depends on the time and effort spent getting that quality.

Architecture

Software architecture is a description of a software system at a high-enough level of abstraction that the system can be viewed as a whole, and supports the structure and functionality of the product at multiple levels. It does not address the implementation details, although it is commonly defined in term of components, relationships, and connections.

Unlike traditional architectural definition activities, where all components and structure are laid out ahead of time, agile defines as little as possible in advance, delaying all decisions as late as possible until they are actually needed. The idiom YAGNI ("You aren't going to need it.") has become a commonplace for agile projects. After a certain point, system architecture is also progressively elaborated as changes in design warrant them.

However, *some* architecture must be defined, or at least implied. There is a big difference between doing web applications, desktop stand-alone applications, mobile phone apps, service-oriented architectures (SOA), and so forth. *Some* upfront planning is needed to get started. The question for the technical team is how much planning is done beforehand, and how much is deferred until coding starts? If too much planning is done too early, the work may be wasted because of later changes. If not enough planning is done beforehand, then work is wasted because of frequent rework during the iterations. With architectural concerns, the amount of rework is frequently the most difficult, and can be massive. This is an area that planning should not be skipped, but optimized. As one programmer quipped, "Weeks of work can replace hours of planning."

The architectural concepts described in this book apply to all applications and systems. They originate from Kruchten's 4+1 Views (logical, development, process, physical, and thin-thread requirements to merge them together) (Kruchten 1995) and an updated version of Coad's Four-Component Model called MVP (Model-View-Presenter) (Coad and Yourdon 1991); all applications need a strong separation of concern for logical robustness and maintainability.

According to the MVP architecture, the application is divided into components for the problem domain, user interface, data management, eternal system interfaces, and a user interface validation component into which automated test tools can be inserted. Protocols are defined to allow clean communications between components. Except for the problem domain module, an implementation of one component can be swapped quickly and seamlessly with a different implementation of that component.

For more information, techniques, and recommendations, see Chapter 5, which discusses this topic in much more detail.

Development Infrastructure

Setting up the infrastructure with which to build the product is not as progressively elaborated as many of the other activities. Certain tools—hardware, software applications, templates, techniques—are needed before the team can start.

Full product support (development, testing, and product management) can be accomplished without a tool budget by using *open-source tools*. Programmers will need a computer to write code, and automated unit testing tools like JUnit. Testers will need ways to run the product to test the GUI code, and need tools for automated testing, and defect tracking as generic as spreadsheets or specific to the task (such as Bugzilla for defect tracking). Later, continuous improvement tools can be added.

Many tools should be added sooner than later or else the benefits will be less. It is hard to export results from an interim tool (or no tool) back into a new tool. The chapter of development infrastructure gives a list of the tools with respect to the role and environment in which they would be used: developers, testers, business analyst, agile project manager and those that the entire team share.

For more information, techniques, and recommendations, see Chapter 6, which discusses this topic in much more detail.

Functional Requirements

Requirements are collected, refined, and analyzed throughout the project, starting before Iteration 0 in Region 2. Each workflow of the project context diagram is comprised of use cases, which is comprised of user stories. Features are not as mappable to use cases, as are workflows, but often features are all that the stakeholders provided. Each feature is progressively elaborated into its constituent use cases within a workflow. Changes are identified, tracked, and prioritized for stakeholders' approval. The following list summarizes the sequence of activities along the "requirements track," and explored in more detail in Chapter 7.

- *Features to use cases.* Using the product backlog[8] and associated workflow, convert the associated workflows into use cases (transactions) and collect into a *use case catalog* until needed by the iterations. The use case catalog is only a collection of the name and goal of each use case, where each name is a simple phrase summary, or "headline," of the use case. Each use case name in the use case catalog is also ordered by priority, risk, and dependency, which reflects the priority order in the product backlog. There is no need to have a separate document called use case catalog; the use case summaries can be placed at the top of the product backlog as more refined product backlog items.

- *Use cases to user stories and test cases.* During each iteration, select the use cases to implement, and disaggregate them into their constituent user stories. The number of user stories that can be implemented in an iteration will depend on the team's average velocity from previous iterations. Non-functional requirements, such as screen mockups or system quality attributes, are discovered at this time also. Only a few use cases need to be defined in Iteration 0, enough for the development team to start work. During iteration 0, the focus is defining the initial requirements—building the use case catalog from the feature catalog.

---

[8]I will refer to the feature catalog *after* is it prioritized as the product backlog.

- *Use case validation.* Rigorously validating the use cases is not used on many agile projects, but under certain conditions, the project team (technical and business members) may choose to have the business analyst validate the use cases. The project team may choose to validate use cases if

  - the product is complex or large

  - the quality requirements are high

  - the time to validate the use cases more than compensates for the time that rework will consume

  - the business units insist that they have the highest quality they can get within the schedule limits

  - the technical team prefer that they have zero-defect requirements to minimize their refactoring efforts

- *Requirements Traceability Matrix (RTM).* The RTM ensures that all the scope is accounted for and tested. Add to the RTM each feature or workflow, its corresponding use cases, and the use cases' corresponding test cases. This mapping enables change management and defect localization. The RTM is updated continually throughout the iterations. (I add use cases to the RTM and not user stories because user stories are too fine-grained for the RTM, which is a summary-level artifact.)

- *Change management.* As testing reveals defects in code, requirements, documentation, or even defects in the test cases, the defects are collected and repaired. A few team members meet to decide if those defects imply repairs or requirements changes; all changes are analyzed to determine the impact on development. The stakeholders involved must decide the priority based on accepted change impacts so that changes can be scheduled into the product. Change management and its governance are discussed in Chapter 7 and Chapter 12.For more information, techniques, and recommendations, see Chapter 7, which discusses this topic in much more detail.

Project Support Tools

Tools in the sense used here means software aides, application project artifacts (e.g., the RTM), and techniques (e.g., use case validation). The tools for the roles of business analyst (BA), developer, tester, and PM are listed in Chapters 9, 10, 11, and 12, respectively. The following tools are used by the entire team.

- The *Requirements Traceability Matrix* is done well using a spreadsheet, such as OpenOffice Calc. The BA adds features, the stakeholder who requested the feature, use case summaries, and references to supporting user experience (UX) artifacts; the tester adds the date the use case passed its tests; and the APM uses the data for stakeholder reporting.

- *Change management*: Not all changes can happen immediately, or even in the current iteration. Changes can occur that must be scheduled into future development. The team sorts out the proposed changes for impact analysis and scheduling during the iteration, but the APM must reflect new scope in the various progress reports (such as, burn-down charts) and project schedules. A spreadsheet works fine for this activity also.

- *Task tracking*: Agile is known for its 3×5 card or sticky-note approach to track tasks. I prefer, and all of my project teams have preferred, an online Kanban board, a special version of task board. Each user story (or task or use case) to which the team commits is put in the iteration backlog column as a card, and as it is worked, the card moves from requirements to development to testing to completion. The card moves along an "assembly line" of work zones on the board for construction and testing, a visually easy way to see what work is in progress, and leads directly to progress status reporting. The online boards have the advantage over the physical-card-on-the-wall system in that it is accessible by anyone with a browser in any location; great for virtual teams too. A popular, open source online Kanban board is available at www.trello.com.

- *Progress reporting*. A spreadsheet that can draw line charts from data is all that is needed. The progress reporting uses iteration-duration and project-level burn-up charts (or burn-down charts), updated daily. A burn-up chart shows the planned work vs. the actual work accumulated. Fixed term projects can also show the contracted amount of work on the chart to predict if scope creep is likely.

For more information, techniques, and recommendations, see Chapter 12, which discusses this topic in much more detail.

Reestimating the Project

Near the end of Iteration 0, several artifacts are completed.

- Many of the highest-priority features in the product backlog have been converted to use cases

- New tools that might affect the project cost, and lack of tools that may affect development speed, have been identified.

- Progressive elaboration has revealed enough detail that the project team can make a more refined project schedule and budget for the given (expected) scope.

The technical team revises the preliminary Release Plan that contains for each iteration its start and end dates, scope size, and primary topic to be completed with that iteration. They walk through at least the top 50% of the product backlog and estimate the relative scope (read: story points) of each item in the product backlog that can be completed within which iteration. Often, the content within an iteration will change as scope is moved about within each iteration's time-box; sometimes the number of iterations will change.

The Iron Triangle

Traditionally, a project's core controllable factors are scope, cost, and time, and their ever-changing relationships. These *triple constraints* depend on each other such that the third constraint results from setting the other two. These constraints are not arbitrary factors, but derive from the physics of the project itself. If two of the constraints are fixed, say scope and cost, then the project will take as long (time) as scope and cost will carry it, regardless of any managerial dictates. Because these three constraints are hard constraints, the keys for project management, they are often referred to as the *iron triangle*. If anyone changes, the other two must change to compensate.

Quality, among other things, is a consequence of how well the triple constraints fit together. If, say, the time is insufficient (that is, the project is rushed) to complete the scope for the given cost, then the product quality will suffer. How often has your project been rushed through testing because of a mandatory deadline? How often has your management tried to cut corners on cost, which resulted in a lower-quality product?

Figure 4-2 shows, a little whimsically, an iron triangle, and gives an example of increased scope, causing the time and cost to be insufficient, such that quality "leaks out at the bottom and sides."

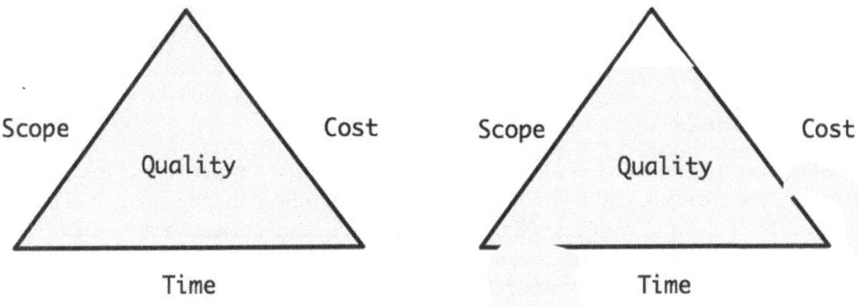

Figure 4-2. *Balanced and unbalanced iron triangle*

There are empirical relationships and complicated derived equations to show these relationships (Putnam and Myers 1992, 26–41) but the PM in the field does not sit down and calculate these involved equations. The PM needs a more practical approach.

Most agile projects are given a fixed cost and schedule, but a flexible scope requirement. Less common is fixing the scope and flexing the cost or project duration. Although iterations are, by definition, time-boxed, and characteristic of all agile projects, not every iteration must be the same length. Some iterations can be larger—but not more than four weeks; and some can be smaller—but not less than one week.

Some agile methods, such as Kanban and XP, allow iterations to have differing lengths at different times as necessary. When iterations are not the same duration, the APM must do a little extra work to recalibrate the team productivity into team velocity per day or week, but it still works well.

Agilists prefer not to use the iron triangle because it refers back to traditional predictive life cycle practices. They have replaced scope-cost-time of the traditional iron triangle with the agile triangle, whose corners represent value (extrinsic quality), intrinsic quality (technical excellence), and Agile constraints (scope, cost, time). Highsmith (2009) points out that if the key driving factors have changed, then the project needs to change the way it is executing and measuring progress. Since the triple constraint is included in the agile triangle, those factors must still be considered. (Perhaps the agile triangle should be called the agile pentagon.)

Impossible Projects

Some constraints make compliance impossible regardless of how much the other constraints are flexed. For example, there is no amount of budget or resources that can build the space shuttle's software systems in 48 hours. No project can be built with a zero-dollar budget[9] or without resources.

For less extreme cases, if management has set time, cost, and schedule, with no flexing of any of these three parameters permitted, the project could be impossible to complete. The project manager's first job is to determine if that is the case. During the execution of the project, there will necessarily be some flexing and counterflexing of scope, cost, or time. It may be that the project is entirely feasible within the given parameters, but it is better to know earlier than later if you are dealing with a doomed project, and inform the sponsor of that as soon as possible.

---

[9]As an exception, I recall one case of a networked application, built with open source tools by university students without a hard deadline, and the only cost was that of the CD on which to back it up.

With a cooperative sponsor, something may be adjusted to give the project a better chance of success. If the sponsor insists, against the PM and team's recommendation, then the team must go forward anyway, but the PM has done his or her job and made the situation known. It is a management and stakeholder issue; the stakeholders don't want the project to fail either, so they may be able to exert some diplomatic pressure on the sponsor.

Fixed-Term Agile Projects

Increasingly more projects are written under a fixed term contract, meaning that one or two of the constraints of scope, cost, or time are fixed. This takes most of the project risk from management, and puts it all on the vendor doing the project. Some agilistas will not take on a fixed-term project because they think fixing any of the constants, particularly scope, is contrary to the agile paradigm. It is equally hard to determine the exact end date of a project (or final cost or scope) for agile or for traditional projects.

The entire product backlog must be sized for fixed-term projects but that is already a Scrum technique. Using history to forecast project results is pervasive to any agile flavor (except Kanban where the product backlog size is not needed). Scrum asks the team to estimate all items in the project backlog to identify the project scope, and apply team velocity after a few iterations to forecast project schedule. Fixed-term agile projects are not as hard as previously thought.

Fixed-term projects have been around as long as project development. Whether agile or traditional, in-house or vendor-provided, the PM must investigate whether the triple constraint makes the project impossible or not. If it is, then adjustments must be made, or it would be foolish to take on a project knowing it will fail.[10]

Agile is based on the idea that a product being developed is not well enough known during Region 2 that doing upfront requirements, analysis, and design are not worth the time and effort. This concept begs the question: how to determine realistic scope, cost, and time estimates before there is enough data to know those values? Estimating project metrics before sufficient detail is discovered leaves only analogous or parameterized estimating. How long did it take a team do produce a similar project? How long did it take to produce similar components (user interface screens, database modules, etc.) in an historically similar project?

Function points, a classic way of estimating, uses this parametric approach to count these kinds of components. However, during contract negotiations, that amount of detail is not available, or the contract must be delayed until the vendor makes a good guess at how the scope decomposes into those components.

Forecasting from Team Productivity

The best solution is a blend of some advance estimating, some upfront work, and some adjustment afterward, based on what is discovered as the project proceeds. Measuring team productivity allows the rate of building the product to extrapolate a finish date as scope completed per unit time.

Team productivity is typically measured as story points per iteration for this very purpose. This metric is called *team velocity*, and is averaged over a rolling five-iteration window. Team velocity is used to predict how much work the team can get done in a single iteration, the team's *capacity* for that iteration. It is also used in the long term in making the end schedule predictable and precise.

Agile projects progressively elaborate until they have at least a three-iteration window to calculate the team velocity.[11] At that point, the APM can go back through the product backlog to calculate how many iterations are needed to complete the entire catalog, and revise the release plan. That approach yields an

---

[10]I have seen some cases where the PM took on an impossible project knowing that he could make changes later in the project. This approach depends on the flexibility of the management, and creates less of a career impact for the PM than saying "No" at the beginning of the project.

[11]Typical team velocity might be 14.3 story points per iteration. The decimal figure comes from the *rolling window averaging* of accomplished scope over five iterations.

accurate date (within a small margin) of completion for the entire project. This approach works great for large projects, and analogous estimating works great for smaller projects, so either way, estimating a fixed-term agile project is doable.

It seems that doing three iterations before knowing the end of the project is waiting too late. Actually, the project cost and duration are estimated in Region 2 for funding, and the team velocity is used to *refine the estimate*. Adjustments can be made after a couple months, as would happen on any project, but agile revisions are more accurate because they are based on historical actuals history, and occur sooner than if a traditional project was adjusted when a potential failure came into sight.

PMI Parallels

The material in this chapter is compared against the traditional approach using the PMI's 10 knowledge areas.

Scope: The PMI recommends PMs build a hierarchical work breakdown structure (WBS) instead of a feature catalog. With agile, the features are decomposed into use cases instead of work packages. The purpose is the same: to breakdown the scope into more detail to estimate time and cost better. The agile approach uses *adaptive planning:* the more imminent the product backlog item, the more detailed in which it is estimated; items to be implemented later are given a larger granularity. For example, a prioritized product backlog will have user stories and use cases at the top; use cases, epics, or themes in the middle; and features and themes near the bottom. Periodically, the product backlog items are *pruned;* that is, the team reviews the product backlog's larger items that come to the top, and disaggregates them into smaller units of scope before they are moved into the iteration backlog.

Time: There are no time changes between traditional and agile except to define a series of iterations that comprise the project schedule. At best, the use cases that can be built during each iteration is applied into the iteration in feature priority order and recorded in the Release Plan.

Quality: There are no quality standards defined yet, except for those the technical team will develop during the technical meetings. The default quality goal for successful agile projects is to let no defects "escape" into production, on-time delivery to stakeholders, repeated on-time releases, and all within budget.

Human Resources: All roles and technical members should have been defined and on-boarded by the end of Iteration 0, preferably those with agile experience for the agile project. However, technical prowess is preferred over agile experience when acquiring team members. Most of the agile methodologies do not have roles defined as distinctly as they are for traditional projects, probably as a reaction to avoid the siloes that cause inefficiencies as information is handed off from one role to another. Agile projects have team members who work together on many tasks regardless of skill sets, but people tend to gravitate to the skills they do best.

Variant   The agile Scrum methodology has only the roles of "product owner," "Scrum master," and "Scrum team." The product owner serves as sponsor and requirements authority; the scrum master serves as the agile coach or agile project manager (APM); the duties of the scrum team are not defined further, although the team members as a whole are responsible for requirements, analysis, design, coding, testing, and documentation.

eXtreme Programming (XP) has the same lack of role definition within the technical team. XP defines only "the customer" and "developer," with extended roles of "tracker" and "agile coach." The "developer" of an XP team is regarded as anyone on the development team: analyst, designer, tester, programmer, or anyone else.

Communications*:* Although daily meetings between BA and customer SME are preferred, agile allows weekly meetings between them, as with traditional projects. Agile teams also have *information radiators* (big visible charts of self-evident progress) and daily stand-up meetings. Stakeholder meetings for progress and demonstrating a working product occurs after each iteration. Typical weekly status meetings are not needed.

Procurement: Fixed-term *agile* projects are relatively new, and agile vendors are reluctant to agree to that kind of contract, although these kinds of projects are becoming more common as vendors adjust agile practices to accommodate them.

Stakeholder Management: Iteration 0 uses the stakeholder meetings to elicit requirements and elaborate the feature catalog. At this point in the project, stakeholder engagement is more intense and frequent than for traditional projects.

Integration: The integration of the various aspects of the projects are addressed by the business and technical sequences of how this all comes together in the various meetings and artifacts. The following chapters on architecture, infrastructure, and initial requirements contain more detail on these topics.

Conclusion

Iteration 0 is a required step to prepare the project. This chapter explains the work that needed to be done before the actual product iterations started: acquiring the technical team; tailoring the agile approach to best fit the team, project, and organization; defining the product software architecture; setting up the infrastructure environment and tools, and refining the initial requirements in "getting to ready."

The technical team ideally is a team already in place, and projects are passed to the agile team like car parts into a car assembly line. Guidelines were given for facilitating the technical team kickoff meeting and facilitating the agile tailoring session, with a special note about defining quality levels and practices to achieve them.

For architecture, the Model-View-Presenter (MVP) approach was recommended as a standard application architecture because of its separation of concerns, robustness, ease of maintenance, and implementing automated testing.

For infrastructure, the definitions and interactions of the various environments (development, testing, staging, and production) were shown, and how the team worked with them.

For initial requirements, the requirements refinement from feature catalog to product backlog, and then refinement of those features into use cases and user stories was introduced, showing the progressive refinement in scope and priority, were introduced.

More information is in Chapters 5, 6, and 7.

CHAPTER 5

■ ■ ■

Architecture: Product Foundation

Introduction

So far, both the business teams and technical teams have been formed. Before any productive work gets done in the actual iterations from 1 to N, the teams can start thinking about the architectural principles underlying their product. This effort may not involve any coding, but includes the highest level of design.

This chapter addresses a general architectural strategy with a view to the fastest construction and minimal maintenance, and allowing architectural changes with a minimum of effort, cost, and design impact. Specifically, this chapter describes the following:

- What software architecture is, and is not. The software architecture is the driving overall design for the system, and all other architectural sections (such as the data architecture and the technical architecture) are subordinate to this architecture.

- A user-scenario-driven approach to a four-view perspective consisting of a logical view, a process view, a development view, and a physical view.

- The data architecture of the system, which references the Object Model and outlines how the persistent data corresponding to the object model will be managed globally; and where appropriate, specifically within the subsystems.

Agile assumes a user-scenario (thin-thread) driven development. The 4+1 Component Model is based on the key principle of *separation of concerns,* a best practice that applies to all projects. Data management will be discussed only as it is differentiated between relational data base tools and object-oriented data base tools. Object-oriented architectural models, languages (e.g., Java), and databases (e.g., db4o); or procedural languages and databases (e.g., RDMS and SQL) is independent of the development approach used.

This chapter also tries to show that *some* up-front work is needed. Changing architecture is time-intensive and difficult. Later sections contrast architectural work performed in planning and development against code-first, architect-later approaches such as the *emergent design.*

What Is Software Architecture?

There are many good definitions for (and arguments over) software architecture. For clarity, the one used in this book is one I've found operationally useful from Bredemeyer (1999).

Definition

Software architecture is the high-level structure of a software system that has the following properties:

- It is a high-enough level of abstraction that the system can be viewed as a whole.

- The structure must support the functionality required of the system, thus requiring that the dynamic behavior of the system be taken into account.

- The structure, or architecture, must (1) conform to the system qualities (nonfunctional requirements), which include performance, security, reliability, extensibility, flexibility, and the like; and (2) accommodate future functionality at a reasonable cost of change. These requirements may conflict, and trade-offs among alternatives are an essential part of designing an architecture.

- At the architectural level, all implementation details are hidden.

- The architecture is commonly defined in terms of components and connections.

Software architecture is *not* low-level design; that is, component internals, algorithms, or implementation. It is not a description of hardware or the physical system, although both hardware and the physical system are informed and framed by the software architecture. It is not the data model, which must comply with the policies of the software architecture. This chapter includes many of these non-software architectural concerns, but note that they are subordinate to the driving software architectural principles.

Architecture is an upfront-framework that will be built up to become the product. Architecture, especially enterprise architecture, has its own set of requirements, system qualities (sometimes called the "-bilities"— as in reliability, available, scalability), and most of the nonfunctional requirements (NFRs). Without knowledge of the NFRs, the product is being built in a context-free environment—a picture without a canvas. Unfortunately, the product must be placed into operations in the enterprise's context-constrained production environment. Without some upfront architecture, a lot of unnecessary refactoring will follow. Architectural requirements and NFRs are an overarching concern that often gets missed with agile methods.

Defining the architecture is required for both traditional and agile projects. Most agile projects focus on the low-level granularity of user stories and the refactoring needed to change the implementation until it matches. The difference is how much is defined before implementation it is started.

Balance

Architecture, because of its all-encompassing scope on which the project is based, is difficult and time-intensive to change. At one extreme, a project can do a huge amount of up-front work before *any* development gets started; at the other extreme, user stories (lowest level granularity) are implemented and a huge amount of work is spent rewriting or refactoring afterward. When user stories are implemented without a cohesive set of architectural principles, then any user story can be implemented without regard for context. I call this approach "random acts of construction" (as shown by Figure 3-7 of Chapter 3), and it has a very high rework cost. It is not much better than guess-and-check construction. It violates the woodworkers' principle of "measure-twice, cut-once." Instead it is a "measure-none, cut-many times" approach until one exhausts the deadline and resources, then cries, "We're doing Agile! We don't use schedules."

Building a product without *some* up-front architecture is like building a house without regard to the location and size of its foundation, or where the walls and electrical and plumbing systems should be located. This could result in rebuilding the house, not refactoring it. Refactoring has a price, and some things are not as easily refactored as others are. A product that is built using a guess-and-check approach will require huge amounts of rework, perhaps even more than the traditional project with much effort done in advance: both can neutralize the benefits of agile practices. The large-level granularity of databases, network connections, and large components are equally important, and time-consuming to refactor.

Of course, I am not saying that guess-and-check construction is a common way of building software. I mention it here as an extreme example of what not to do. The reader will have to find their own balance between full up-front architecture and design and none at all.

Refactoring vs. Rewriting

Refactoring refers to changing the internal structure of the code without changing its behavior or appearance, and helps clean the code in progress. Refactoring applies typically to small granular items such as code API, methods, and classes. . Refactoring is considered good practice to keep the code clean, efficient, and easy to maintain. The overhead is worth the resulting robustness of the code.

Rewriting refers to changing the structure and the behavior of the code, and applies typically to larger granularity, sometimes even the architecture. Both refactoring and rewriting are forms of rework but rewriting is pure redo, and should be minimized as much as possible. Refactoring is addressed in detail in Chapter 10.

Application Architectural Views

Phillip Kruchten's 4+1 Views (Kruchten 1995), consists of four views, integrated around the user requirements of the system, as illustrated in Figure 5-1. It is a standard model, taught in some universities.

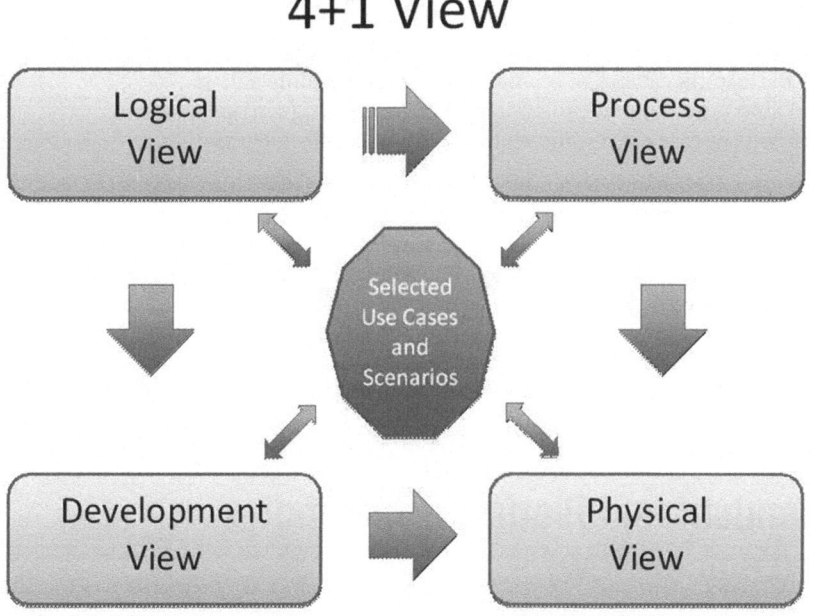

Figure 5-1. *A high-level view of a software application and its subsystems (adapted from Kruchten 1995)*

- *Logical view*: Describes the components in the system (or subsystem), their contracts/interfaces, and their relationships and interactions with each other. For example, the recommended Model-View-Presenter (MVP) model will lay the foundation for the system, how it separates concerns, the internal component interfaces, and their relationships.

- *Process view*: Describes the details of the dynamics of the system such as the concurrency and synchronization aspects, where appropriate. These are usually represented in Business Process Model Notation (BPMN) or swim-lane diagrams. This view is often included in requirements and workflow analysis documents. They are discussed further in the chapter on requirements.

- *Physical view*: Describes the mapping(s) of the software onto the hardware or technology components; a variation on Coad's Four-Component Model (Coad and Yourdon 1991) is a general strategy for structuring all applications.

- *Development view*: Describes the static organization of the software in the development environment. The view is directed toward the developers of the system and it is not included here, but it is defined in detail during each of the project iterations. Development views are sometimes shown as UML class diagrams and originate as part of requirements validation, and are used for producing high-quality products.

- *Requirements view (the +1 view)*: The requirements view (shown as features, use cases, and scenarios) serve as the fifth view (or the +1 view) that anchors all the others. The stakeholders' original list of desired and needed features and capabilities are collected in the features catalog, or product backlog. Each feature and its supporting workflows (shown in the project abstract's context diagram) are analyzed to define the current use case catalog and requirements traceability matrix.

To get the requirements view, each feature is iteratively broken down into scenarios—a short descriptive summary statement that executes the product to deliver that feature. These scenarios, or *use cases*, are captured at the top of the product backlog (which contains highest degree of scope granularity), or in a separate *use case catalog*. The use cases are expanded and detailed into user stories during each project iteration. Each feature and corresponding use case is recorded in the requirements traceability matrix (RTM), and later mapped to test cases, defects, and test results. The RTM is a key artifact for change management and impact analysis, and knowing when all the requirements have been fulfilled; that is, in knowing when "done is done. See Chapter 9 for more about elicitation and validation for use cases and other requirements.

Platform-Independent and Platform-Specific Design Models (Logical View)

The high-level process view of business workflows is decomposed into usage scenarios, which become the +1 requirements view. Detailed use cases or user stories (paths through use cases), which are annotated with nonfunctional requirements, form the basis on which to build platform-independent models (PIMs), and later, platform-specific design models (PSMs). These scenarios, or use cases, are captured within a use case catalog and are detailed during each project iteration.

Platform-Independent Model (PIM)

During each project iteration's *analysis* activity, the four views are integrated, made more detailed, and embodied as Platform-Independent Models (PIM). Optionally, but increasingly less common these days, the PIM is represented by UML class diagrams and sequence diagrams that map the logical and process views to the development view for validation.

The object model is the main core of the PIM. The object model at the analysis level for an application describes the problem domain. Object decomposition is different from functional decomposition, but these two views are critical for checking the consistency of the data, control flow, and behavior of the objects. Each class of the model is defined by scope-of-control decomposition. The major classes are defined through an inheritance map of Components and their derived classes, and another diagram shows the relationships between the classes. The object model may also include UML sequence diagrams that are detailed during each iteration.

Platform-Specific Model (PSM)

During each project iteration's *design* activity, the analysis diagrams of the problem domain are expanded into design models using implementation class diagrams, use cases at the technology level (design cases), and sequence diagrams to map the development view to the physical view. The result is a set of platform-specific models (PSM) with enough detail to include in an implementation.

During later design stages, the classes of the PIM's object model are extended at a more detailed implementation level for components other than the problem domain, and comprise the main parts of the PSM.

Agile Practices

Increasingly, the work that goes into the PIM and PSM is neglected, or intentionally dropped, in exchange for rework or refactoring. The higher the level of change, the more rework is needed. A small design change might be refactored in a day or less, but an architectural change can take weeks. It is the agile team's decision as to how much plan-ahead they want. The penalty is the rework needed to remove the entropy that results from constant change. As a bare minimum, the development team should adhere to the 4+1 Component Model (sometimes call Model-View-Presenter, or MVP) to minimize architectural changes, and support automated testing. The details on how MVP contributes significantly to automated testing are described later in this chapter.

A note about customer involvement. Most of the time, the customer is intimately involved with the functional requirements, user interface design, and perhaps the high-level design. In general, they do not care, nor need to know about the architectural choices of the technical team. However, by all means, if they do care, it certainly does not hurt to their allow input and discuss the architectural choices with them. The customer is key to defining the requirements that pull all the other four views together.

Architectural Layers (Physical View)

When most people think of an *application*, they think of one monolithic program that must be loaded into the system and configured for that platform. Today we have the technology to think of an application as a collection of modules that can be deployed at any time, depending on the module wanted and ready to be deployed. The standard OSGi architectural framework has demonstrated this principle remarkably well.[1]

---

[1]OSGi is taking center stage in the development community. It is built into some development tools like Eclipse. Originally, developed by the Open System Group for Internet deployment, the tool itself is referred to as OSGi, without any claim that the term is an acronym.

Knoernschild (2012), an experienced architect, illustrates an important set of logical units and relationships at the physical (implementation level) that characterize an application. He defines a hierarchy of layers, each representing various levels of (1) separation of concerns, (2) interoperability and process relationships, (3) testing, and (4) release cycles and deployability. Together they optimize reusability, maintainability, and defect control.

At the lowest level are the *classes* that constitute the units of integrated state and behavior (function). Classes are the atoms of object-oriented systems. The classes are organized into logically related groups that work together, known in Java as a *package*. Each package comprises the software architectural components discussed in the section on the 4+1 Component Model. Just as classes can be run independently, as when unit tested, packages can also be designed to run with minimal or no coupling.

Groups of packages that work together to implement a high-level feature are placed in modules called *bundles* by OSGi, an interface standard from the technology consortium Open System Gateway Initiative.[2] It is through bundles that applications can be deployed for the most flexibility because bundles can be deployed and run independently of each other when designed properly. This deployable modularity allows users to add, remove, and share models within the various libraries without affecting other areas and users. The OSGi framework is key to this aspect of behavior because features can be added, updated, or revised "on the fly" by installing and uninstalling bundles while the application is still running; sometimes called a "hot fix." Merging Kruchten's 4+1 Views with Knoernschild's modular anatomy yields a table that organizes architecture into subordinate topics.

The four Kruchten views (logical, process, development, and physical) are organized into three layers of decreasing granularity (class, package, and modules). Table 5-1 not only describes the architectural organization and artifacts of the product, but also illustrates, from top to bottom and from right to left, the progressive elaboration of design.

Table 5-1. *Architectural Layers at Three Levels of Modularity*

	Class	Package	Module
Logical	Unified Object Model	Coad's 4-component model	Application subsystems
Process	Use cases per iteration	Use case catalog	Business process workflows
Development	Core classes	Design scenarios	Subsystem integration
Physical	Use case designs per iteration	Hardware technologies	Integrated product technologies

Agile takes a scenario-driven approach to developing the architecture, which is also consistent with best practices in project management. This approach employs progressive elaboration, iterative development, and test-driven design.

The following list summarizes the sequence of team tasks in the "architectural thread." It is explored in more detail in later chapters.

- *Map use cases to logical or subsystem components:* The use cases are "threads" through the subsystem components likes pearls on a necklace. Each object is a pearl, and the use case executes through each one on its thread. Starting from the prioritized use case (or feature) catalog, decide which parts of the use case thread is handled in which subsystem or component: user or system interface, problem domain, or data management.

---

[2]"The OSGi Alliance is a worldwide consortium of technology innovators that advances a proven and mature process to create open specifications that enable the modular assembly of software built with Java technology. Modularity reduces software complexity; OSGi is the best model to modularize Java." See `http://www.osgi.org/About/HomePage`.

- *"Script" the scenarios* against the architecture in order to identify new major abstractions (classes, mechanisms, processes, subsystems). This helps merge individual threads into common components that support those threads. These scripts are written as detailed use cases. Detailed use cases start in Iteration 1 and continue throughout the project.

- *Revise and repeat:* Throughout the following iterations, add any newly discovered architectural elements to the architecture. Periodically review the architecture for improvements, simplifications, and reuse. Feedback from design and implementation steps will usually result in changes to the architecture. For both these reasons, the architecture document should not be thought of as "cast in stone," but rather as a living artifact that evolves with the development cycle.

Software Architecture (Development View)

Following Coad's Four-Component Model (Coad 1991), shown in Figure 5-2, each subsystem is comprised of four major components: Problem Domain Component, Data Management Component, Systems Interface Component, and Human Interface Component. Later, with the advent of the Model-View-Presenter model, another specialized component was added for automated testing—the CIV. Each component results from a scope-of-control decomposition of the system that separates that component's respective concerns. The four components communicate through well-defined protocols to ensure ease of maintenance and fast changeability.[3]

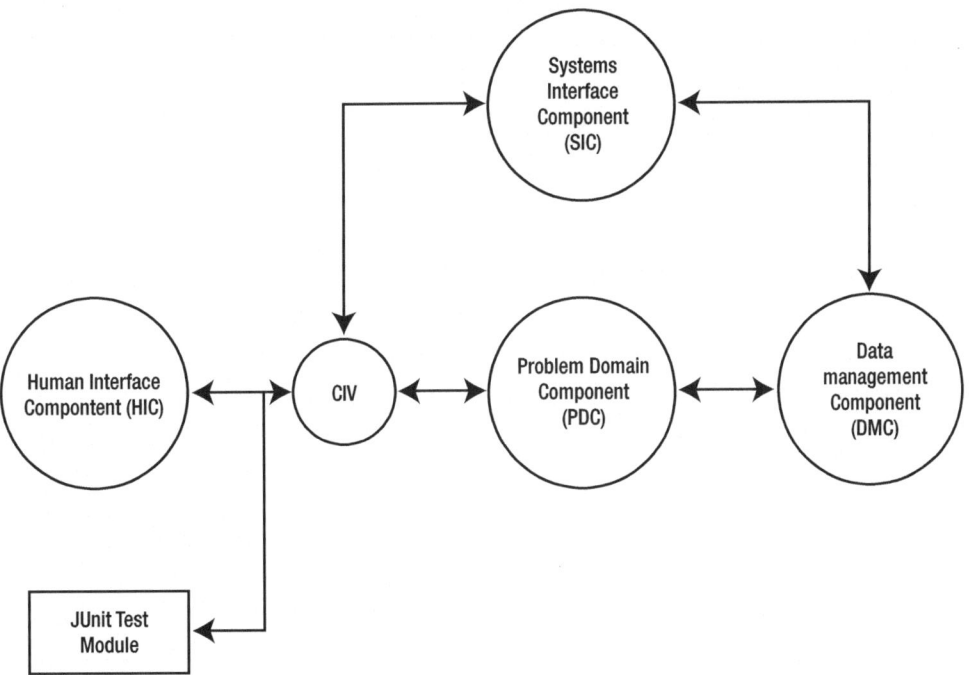

Figure 5-2. *The Model-View-Presenter Architecture*

---

[3]Coad and Yourdon's 4+1 Component Model should not be confused with Kruchten's 4+1 Architectural Views, an unfortunate naming coincidence.

Problem Domain Component (PDC)

The PDC manages and contains all business logic and objects that are independent of any concerns outside the system. All data is used internally in its theoretically optimal format. The PDC works at the informational and logical level of data. The PDC verifies that the business rules are not violated, and assumes that proper syntax and semantic data is being sent to it. The other components (see descriptions next) must ensure that the PDC does not receive corrupted data.

Data Management Component (DMC)

The DMC manages the persistence data and mechanisms for storage, such as file systems, database management systems, XML parsers/writers, permanent media, and the like. The DMC works at the semantic level of data and communicates with the PDC. Although both the PDC and the DMC work at the semantic level, the PDC is concerned with business logic, and the DMC is concerned with data management and storage. The DMC is not permitted to communicate with the HIC (and vice versa) without going through the problem domain (PDC), which would result in a two-tiered model that are higher maintenance and less robust (Gallaugher and Ramanathan 1996).

✖ **Implementation**   There is an irony here between theory and practice. I give two examples. Relational Databases are theoretically one of the slower database management systems, and yet, despite the optimal alignment between today's object-oriented systems and object-oriented databases, relational databases are still the most popularly used. I suspect that their ubiquity rests on the fact that programmers)are most familiar with that technology, and many support tools are available.

Second example: The two-tiered architecture was shunned in preference to the three- or N-tiered architectures in the late 1980s, but with the plethora of web applications and mobile phone applications being built, many web-based applications are again based on the two-tiered architecture. Multiple supporting technologies must be used to support them (e.g., HTML, CSS, XML) and consolidation technologies sprung up to make them easier to handle, such as AJAX. Today we see the more powerful programming languages, such as Java and C++, giving way to easier-to-modify scripting languages, such as JavaScript. Perhaps the ease of change and low level of technical expertise needed has contributed to the fallback to 1980s technology. The massive development of mobile applications is another example of social forces driving software engineering practices, as discussed in Chapter 1.

✖ **Implementation**   The architectural pluggability of the DMC was key to one of my projects. My team replaced a relational database with an object-oriented database in the main corporate accounting application. We replaced one database with another, and changed some interface coding. There was no coupling between the database and non-DMC concerns that did not go through the data interface in the DMC. The entire system swap, including testing, took only three weeks!

Systems Interface Component (SIC)

The SIC manages any communication to external applications or systems outside the application, which includes handling local and remote networks, connection pools, XML protocols, and talking to other applications. The SIC can talk to all other components at the semantic and informational level except the HIC. All output data to the HIC is reformatted in the CIV.

Human Interface Component (HIC)

The HIC manages all input and outputs that originate from or pass to a user, such as screen views, printed reports, and device control. In a Graphical User Interface (GUI) application, the HIC uses only visualizations and string formats, and is responsible to interact with the user with the desired technology and (mostly) the PDC. The HIC works at the syntax level of data; that is, it ensures that the user input data is correct and consistent. The HIC is not permitted to communicate with the DMC (and vice versa) without going through the problem domain, which would create the less preferred two-tiered model again. The HIC can only talk to the CIV in order to assure the separation of concerns and a more pluggable component. Some of the HIC restrictions enforce the three-tiered domain model, and some enable easier automated testing by using the CIV.

The reader should note that the HIC contains objects that support the GUI, interface design, and its behavior and is not the user experience (UX) itself. The user experience is a psychological interaction between the user and the GUI to allow for a satisfying (or dissatisfying) experience while using the product. Sometimes the interface screen designs are called *UX artifacts* because they are the visible part of the UX.

Component Interface Validator (CIV)

The CIV (pronounced "sieve") is a special component that validates and formats data between the HIC and the PDC. All GUIs input data through strings that are syntactically validated at the HIC and semantically validated by the CIV. The CIV also reformats the input data to the application's internal format (and vice versa for outputs to the GUI). Ideally, there is one CIV object for each GUI widget. CIV objects in most cases do not need to talk to each other, but can if necessary.

Because GUI objects are difficult to test, the HIC contains as little functional logic as possible, relegating the GUI code of the HIC to pure aesthetic display; the logic is contained in the CIV. This approach allows the testing engine to "plug into" the CIV, and ensure that as much semantic and informational logic as possible can be tested automatically. The GUI code (about 15% to 20% of the total in my projects) can be verified easily through periodic manual inspection. This approach complies with a "pluggable" philosophy that allows front-end interfaces to be more easily replaced as technologies or demands change.

Architecture Recommendations

To balance the application architectural effort with the minimalist and thin-thread approach of agile, three recommendations are made here.

- Use the MVP model as an abstraction from which to define the design and concrete implementation for the product.

- At Iteration 0, define the lowest common denominator framework, a thin-thread from input to output. Establish the "Hello World" analogue of all connectivity needed for the simplest thing first. This is often the uninteresting use cases of initialization and termination.

☞ **Recommendation** I like Diego Fontdevila and Martin Salias' recommendation in the March issue of *The Architecture Journal*: "[I]nstead of spending a lot of time designing and implementing the different moving parts around layers and tiers, crosscutting concerns, and so on, we build the minimal amount of code that is needed to connect all of the pieces and start building the actual functionality on top—providing an early end-to-end experience of the results. Indeed, the focus is more on the API level of the infrastructure, and not the actual implementation, which is usually mocked up for the first few iterations." (Fontdevila and Salias 2010).

- Maintain an architect (or someone with equivalent skills) on the team—at least an on-call or a visiting architect that comes every two or three iterations. As mid- and low-level designs emerge, the architectural requirements, enterprise environment, design context, and NFRs will change. The architect needs to work with the team to accommodate those changes. Architects become stakeholders, bridging the gap between business cases and technological solutions in the large, at the enterprise level (Bedell 2014a).

☞ **Recommendation** Maja Tibbling, principle architect of Con-Way, Inc. recommends: "…use an Iteration 0 to address any major new or changed architectural requirements. During that iteration, technical spikes that may require more time are identified and accommodated for in the iteration planning," she said. "A technical spike may include the introduction of a new technology, data migration, etc." (quoted by Bedell).

The application architecture is clear, but where Agile and enterprise architecture fit together is still being worked out—the application architecture must integrate with the enterprise architecture, the application's context architecture, cleanly.

> *We have not found anyone who has disagreed with the need to have this up-front leading vision of where the projects and architecture are going and what is intended," Albert said. "The trick is how to do that so it's not over engineered, but just enough so that Agile teams can keep moving at their rapid pace." (Bedell 2014b).*

As an alternative to up-front architectural design, a new movement has appeared on the scene: emergent design. This point-of-view advocates *no upfront design*, but writes the code and let the design evolve around it; the architecture and design will form. If you write the code, the architecture will come.

I am not a proponent of emergent design, but for the sake of fairness and completeness, the next section describes emergent design, as contributed by a software engineering practitioner and advocate of emergent design. Tim is a software/hardware engineer at a communications-product defense contractor, which is the last place I would expect to see Emergent Design practiced.

Emergent Design: An Architectural Alternative

Special Contribution by Timothy Armstrong

Emergent Design recently gained popularity as part of the eXtreme Programming (XP) movement pioneered by Kent Beck, which eventually has been adopted by the agile community. Emergent design can be understood best by looking at what it is not. It is not "Big Upfront Design." We all sit down, before any code has been written, and decide the best way to develop each part and parcel of a software solution. Now, if this is a team of experienced developers working in a familiar domain, there is a chance that the group can come up with a pretty good approximation of what the end product should look like.

Proponents of design would say that a small or simple project could be developed using "emergent design," but for any serious undertaking, we need to get the design right before we build it. If the plan isn't laid out at the beginning, then a series of haphazard fixes to address mistakes and problems will result in a mess of spaghetti code grown in the garden of "code and fix." Planned design emerged as an alternative to the "code and fix" style of early software development. As opposed to the "code and fix" problem that occurs if a team or individual abandons the premise of design, planned design offers a path (that looks nice on PowerPoint slides) toward the finished product. The path may not ultimately be the correct one, but it is a path nonetheless.

Of course, no designer can fully appreciate all the complexities in the body of code that will develop over the course of a project. As Moltke the Elder once said, "No plan of operations extends with certainty beyond the first encounter with the enemy's main strength." Which Mike Tyson summarized as, "Everybody has a plan until they get punched in the face." It is inevitable that at some point in a project's life, there will come some unexpected change or problem that must be dealt with. However, the further into a project a team gets, the more complicated and expensive it is to make a large-scale change. How can we balance these opposite forces? This is where emergent design comes into the picture.

When do you know the most about how the software should work? A reasonable answer, if not the best, is "once you are done writing it." After a team of developers has hashed out all the issues in a project, they can look back and see all the poor choices that hampered their progress. It stands to reason then, that by delaying implementation decisions until later in a project, that a software developer will have a better understanding of the best solution, and so will be prone to make better decisions. This is one of the principles behind Emergent Design. By postponing major decisions until later in a project, it is more likely that the decisions will be correct, and it is less likely that the decisions will need to be undone later.

Emergent Design does not say that a developer can simply decide that he is "not going to do design anymore" because he doesn't want to. For Emergent Design to be truly successful, the software must be flexible enough to be altered significantly late in the development phase. Conventional wisdom holds that the later in a project's development a change is made, the more expensive - time and cost - that change is. This is the same reason that planned design can run into issues when unanticipated difficulties arise. So, how is it possible to practice evolutionary design then?

So, now we will consider the reasons that cost of changing software is high. If a major change is made to software, this requires extensive regression testing, and that is a major expense. Using automated testing brings down the cost of these tests exponentially. By using test-driven development (TDD), there is an existing body of tests wrapping the software and ensuring the classes and methods still work as intended. Automated testing, at both the unit and integration testing levels, reduces the cost of large-scale testing.

Another way that late changes can have a high cost is by introducing additional bugs with the changes. While TDD gives us confidence that our code is still in the same state that it was prior to the change, there is the possibility of concurrency issues or some other failure that is not easily caught by tests. In this case, the continuous integration can keep the software ready to deploy, or in our case to re-deploy, at any given moment. In continuous integration, developers are regularly merging code into the main branch, running tests, and building the project. This can lower the cost of introduced bugs by allowing the developer to move a fix into test or production very quickly.

Third, changes to software can become unwieldy late in a project because the code base tends to rot a bit as it grows. The original solid design has been compromised to deal with unplanned changes, or new requirements, or unanticipated complexity. Methods have innumerable branches, classes grow to hundreds of lines, and some of the developers and their knowledge have left the team. In this case, a developer may not have the confidence or ability to make a change to the codebase without creating more issues. The agile answer to gnarly code is refactoring.

Refactoring is considered so important to agile developers that it is one of the phases of test-driven development. Following the patterns laid out by Martin Fowler's key work, *Refactoring: Improving the Design of Existing Code* (1999a), the behavior of code is not changed, but the other attributes like readability, maintainability, and simplicity can be improved. In this way, the cost of changes also decreases drastically. When methods are short, descriptive, wrapped in tests, and self-documenting, changes can be made without fear of unearthing some ancient evil.

When all these practices, test-driven development, continuous integration, and refactoring are combined, the end result is a code base that can be modified with low cost at any point in the development cycle (Fowler 1999b). In the end, emergent design is not the enemy of planned design. Every software developer writes code first in her head and then on a screen, and in this sense, every bit of a software project is planned before it is written. Emergent design is an attempt to address the known shortcomings of planned design. Lowering the cost of making changes late in the development cycle allows a software artisan to make choices about a particular problem, when he knows the most about it.

PMI Parallels

This chapter focused on technical aspects of software architecture, and the different perspectives that one can take, reconciling them together through the product requirements to come to a consistent and tight framework on which to build the product. The PMI does not address software architecture, so there is nothing that deviates from the PMBOK.

The big exception to the principles behind the PMBOK is contained in the concept of Emergent Design, which advocates no up-front architecture or design, but uses an evolutionary approach to both. This is strictly different from the PMBOK, which teaches building a full-blown work breakdown structure (WBS) before starting construction (Of course, agile does not recommend using a WBS either.) Emergent design is being attempted in agile circles, but is too new for any studies to measure it benefits or effectiveness.

Conclusion

Software architecture was defined with Kruchten's 4+1 Views model, showing how user scenarios tie together the logical, process, physical, and development architectural views. The MVP software architecture model was described, emphasizing separation of concerns and how that contributes to easier construction change and maintenance. With the ideas of PIM and PSM, we see that it is important to define a platform-independent architecture to make changes easier, and not "build to the metal." Final implementation makes it more platform-specific for efficiency. Agile techniques enable bring quick and easy changes at the implementation level.

The end result of an agile project is a code base that is "able to be modified with low cost at any point in the development cycle," as Tim Armstrong writes. There is some question about *how* agile projects are able to save money over traditional projects. As Boehm showed, the cost-change curve is flatter for small teams than for larger teams, and traditional projects typically use larger teams. Fowler added that the cost-change curve is flatter for agile projects than non-agile projects. Agilistas argue that the flattening is because of the practices or TDD, CI, and refactoring combined, enabled by architectures and designs that allow fast changes. Why agile projects have a flatter cost-change curve is still controversial, and perhaps not important from a practical sense.

A recommended architectural design strategy was given, which is a good place to start, even if it gets revised during the iterations. Emergent Design is more extreme; it skips up-front architecture design before coding. I think the best approach is in agreement with Martin Fowler, and that is to plan more on the things that are hard to change, but allow evolutional change as needed. In summary, I close with Martin Fowler's (2000a) words:

> *So my advice is to begin by assessing what the likely architecture is. If you see a large amount of data with multiple users, go ahead and use a database from day 1. If you see complex business logic, put in a domain model. However in deference to the gods of YAGNI, [4] when in doubt err on the side of simplicity. Also be ready to simplify your architecture as soon as you see that part of the architecture isn't adding anything (2000a).*

---

[4]"You aren't going to need it." An agile maxim to maximize simplicity.

CHAPTER 6

■ ■ ■

Infrastructure: Supporting the Project

Overview

The product is built by a team of differently skilled people, each using their own specific set of tools and procedures, and working in different system environments to accomplish their tasks. They also require a set of tools and procedures used by the team as a whole. The project infrastructure must include environments (hardware plus software tools) for analysis, construction,[1] testing, managing, and sharing information. The staging and production environments must also be considered before the product goes into operation. Frequently, an additional environment must be set up for training the users, the helpdesk, and others.

During Iteration 0, the project's infrastructure is put in place; that is, the combination of all the different tools, systems, and facilities needed to begin the actual delivery of business value. The infrastructure supports the technical team both as skilled professionals and as people. The developers will need hardware and software for programming and unit testing, and will need build and configuration tools. The testers will need an isolated system for integration, system, and GUI testing; tools to track defects, and preferably, a separate place to stage a final build before it is released. Analysts will need spreadsheets and document tools for requirements. The agile project manager (APM) will need task tracking and reporting tools. The training environment is an exception in that it is not set up during Iteration 0, but before the product goes into production.

The team as a whole will need shared tools, such as code and document repositories. Agile teams characteristically use a special team room called an "agile room" or "war room" to work together. Agile rooms facilitate more frequent communication than team members who work in the typical isolated cubicle. Agile rooms also support pair programming techniques, another characteristic of agile development. Each is described in detail later in this chapter.

Although the product is built by a team as a whole, the environments can be described by focusing on key skill sets: requirements, construction, testing, staging, production, and project-integration environments. These environments are described next, partly to describe the kinds of tools needed for the development iterations, and partly to clarify in further discussion what is meant by these various environments.

---

[1] I use the word construction to distinguish it from the more general word development. "Construction" refers to the practice of writing code, unit testing, and integrating the code into the shared codebase. "Development" is the more general term to refer to building the product as a whole: requirements, construction, testing, and so forth. The technical team, working during iterations, is called the development team, and the programmers who perform the design and construction are called developers.

Infrastructure Environments

The product-in-flight, the *build*, goes through different stages of development during each iteration. The product grows as use case is added to use case. The build is developed like a ball of string, one functional thread added to another. Each iteration the build moves along from development environment to test environment to staging environment; periodically or eventually, the build moves into the production environment. The purpose of Iteration 0 is to build those environments to support those flows. Since requirements, construction, and testing are executed concurrently, then these environments usually must be in place for the iterations to start. Staging and integration environments may come later if necessary.

Figure 6-1 shows an abstract view of the environments and how the build moves from requirements to release. Each element is keyed to the following numbers. Although the environments are separate in the figure, usually the hardware and software environments are mostly the same for the team, but are shown here for descriptive purposes, and reflect the team interactions.

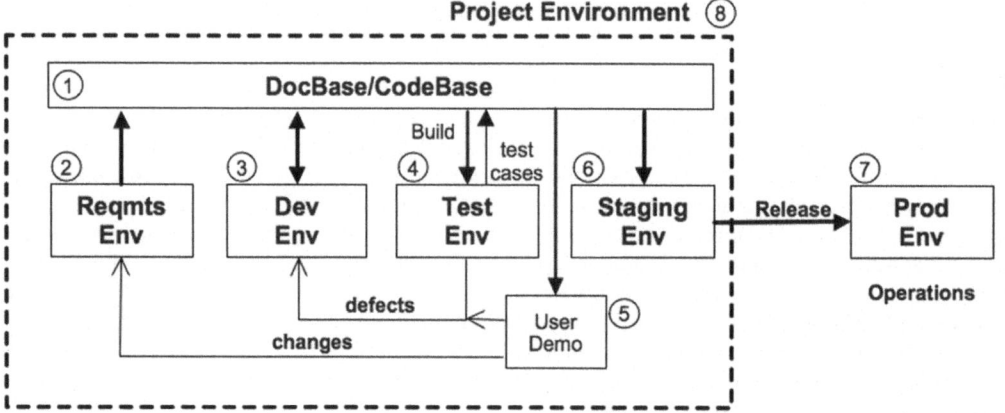

Figure 6-1. *Overview of project environments*

- *docBase/codebase:* The docBase is the shared repository for all documents pertaining to the project: requirements, code, unit tests, and related project artifacts. The codebase is the shared repository for all the code, tests, and builds. Both the docBase and the codebase are part of the same version control system shared by the team to ensure that all team members have the same (latest version) artifact or build. Stakeholders may also access certain portions of the docBase, usually project progress reports, current requirements, or special meeting minutes.

1. *Requirements environment:* Contains the standard tools and hardware for building the requirements artifacts, such as the iteration backlog, user interface designs, and requirements traceability matrix. These, and other collective memories of the group of what the product should look like and how it should behave, are stored in the docBase.

2. *Development environment:* Contains the specialized development hardware and software tools for constructing and unit testing the build. Each developer contributes his or her part to the build, and downloads other developers' contributions to the build, at least daily.

3. *Test environment*: Contains the production-similar hardware and software for testing the build. Note that the build is extracted from the codebase, and only test cases are uploaded. Any defects found while testing the build are sent back to the developers for repair.

4. *User demo:* At the end of each iteration, the team holds a user demo to allow the stakeholders to review the part of the product completed in the current iteration. The stakeholders will usually find changes to the requirements, which are returned to the business analysts to update the requirements. Sometimes the user demo will reveal defects, which are returned to the developers for repair.

- *Staging environment:* If the user demo is approved, then the approved build is set aside as ready for release. This is called the staging environment, although it may be nothing more than a specially marked branch of the version control system. Sometimes special kinds of testing are performed on the staged build: configuration testing, multiplatform testing, and performance evaluations. In that case, there may be a separate staging environment. The *training environment* can be part of this staging, but is should be separate, with its own user IDs, licenses, and training data.

- *Production environment*: As the team upgrades the product each iteration, the staged build becomes a compilation of all the builds that went before. Eventually, the business units decide to release the build as the first (or next) version of the product. The build is moved to production environment into operations.

- *Project environment*:. The integration of all the other environments except the production environment. The team controls the project environment until the build is released into operations, which controls the production environment. The APM makes most use of the project environment in that he or she builds the project-level performance reports that originate between other team members, such as, team velocity, project progress, and defect repair rates.

Each of these environments is described in more detail in the following sections.

The Requirements Environment

The requirements environment supports the business analyst specifically, and the team as a whole. It usually contains word processors for writing use cases and stakeholder meeting minutes; spreadsheets for the features catalog, use case catalog, and the RTM; and graphic tools to build wireframes or screen design prototypes. If use cases will be validated, then diagramming tools for UML diagrams are needed. The analyst needs a place to store shared documents (the docBase), particularly requirements artifacts, with the business and technical teams.

As the analyst takes each use case designated for the iteration and elaborates it into a detailed use case, and works with the team to produce user interface artifacts, he or she makes them available to all in the shared repository. There is no need to wait until all the use cases are completed before making them available—the sooner the developers receive each use case or user story, the sooner each can be implemented, integrated, and tested. Recall that a single use case may contain many user stories; two or three use cases may keep the team busy for the entire iteration.

The Development Environment

The development environment supports the developers, and contains the hardware and software tools to implement the next version of the product—the *development build*, as defined by the scope of the iteration. The development environment contains the machines and tools that support coding, unit testing, version control, configuration management, and various compliance checkers. The developers need a place to store the current codebase with unit tests. They need build tools, like the open source products Maven or Ant, which package the build and run automated unit tests and compliance checkers, like CheckStyle. Many of these support tools are integrated with language compilers, unit testers, metric calculation applications, and compliance checkers into a single integrated developer environment (IDE) such as Eclipse.

The development environment should be set up to provide the fastest and best services to the developers, which is why new product releases often run on the latest, and most powerful, technological machines. Once the product is built on these powerful machines, it is hard to scale them back to "standard" machines that most users have—one of the factors why customers must upgrade to new hardware when new software becomes available.

The developers need access to the requirements environment to pull down all requirements artifacts (use cases and user interface artifacts) from the docBase. When the developers have completed all coding, unit tests, regression tests, and possibly compliance checking, for each use case, then that part of the development build is copied to the test environment and becomes the *test build*. There is no need to wait until all use cases are completed before sending it to testing—the sooner the testers receive and test it, the sooner defects can be repaired. There are usually as many development builds and test builds as there are use cases.

The Test Environment

The test environment supports the testers, and contains the hardware and software tools to verify the test build, which is a copy of the latest development build. The test environment contains the machines and tools that support all *automated* testing: regression testing, integration testing, user acceptance testing (UAT), system capacity and stress testing, and performance evaluation. (The test build inherently supports unit testing too, but that is a role of the developers.) The test environment has defect tracking and reporting tools.

Agile developers require automated testing, with the arguable exception of GUI testing. If automated GUI testing is not going to be used, the test environment must support *manual* GUI testing.

After the testers verify that the test build meets requirements (with all defects repaired), then the test build is passed to the staging environment. The build is now marked "Ready for release."

The Test Environment Is Not the Development Environment

Too many companies think they can get away with having the testers run their tests on the development environment. The development environment and test environment need to be separated for several important reasons.

Although developers and testers start with the same version of the build when it is copied from the development environment to the test environment, the development build soon changes as developers add, remove, delete, or refactor the code. It also is unstable as code changes and high-impact defects crash the system under construction. The development environment is commonly *unintentionally unstable*.

The testers must test a stable version of the build in a stable environment, one that can be ready to go to the users, and it must be immune to the many changes that occur in the development build. Ironically, the test environment supports system crashes (or may cause them) as part of various kinds of testing, so the build is *intentionally unstable* on occasion.

The test environment must be more similar to the production environment that it is to the development environment. The testing environment should be as much of a clone of the production environment as possible. For some performance tests, common operational applications in the production environment are run in the testing environment to simulate the load of the production environment during normal operations. The testing will be less effective and waste more time if the production environment is too different from the testing environment. There is little point in testing a build differently than how it will be used.

Developers should not have access to the test machine, or no more than read-only access. The testers can move the development build into the test environment when they are ready to test. It is too easy for developers to make a "trivial" change to the database or code directly without the required discipline (regression testing at least) that assures the test build is still defect-free.

✗ Anecdote   A payroll project was using copies of production database tables in the test environment, but simulated data in the development environment. A developer changed some database tables in the test machine without proper regression tests (or authorization), just before the test build was to be released to operations, pending a final user demo. The system crashed during the user demo. Staging and the subsequent release was delayed one week while everything got sorted out, and the data tables were returned to their previous state. Fortunately, the testing environment was using read-only copies of the real data but that one-week delay, and changes to the production data, could have affected the paychecks of thousands of employees.

Why did that developer make a change to the testing data? He didn't want the defects he found in the development environment to be seen by the testers or at the user demo. By changing the data, the development defects would not occur (he thought). Unfortunately, the test data and development data were now not the same, and caused the subsequent crash.

The Staging Environment

The staging environment supports the testers, and contains the hardware and software tools to execute the user demo. The staging environment serves two purposes.

First, it serves as a holding area for the fully tested build from the iteration, and is now called the *staged build*. The staged build waits until the business units decide the product, or partial product, should be released to operations in the production environment. Each test build that comes from the testing environment is an updated version of a previous build, so the test build replaces and augments the older staged build as the new releasable product.

Secondly, as mentioned earlier, the development machines are usually close to the state-of-the-art technologies, and the production machines are not. (In fact, they are usually old machines that are updated as late as possible and sometimes have outdated versions of commercial software or hardware.) The staging environment allows the configuration and scaling problems to be worked out before the build moves into operations. These tests can be done on the testing environment, but if the staging environment is more similar to the production environment than the testing environment, then the staging environment is a better place to test configurations and scaling.

With the advent of configuration and version control tools, and the complex branching abilities of shared codebase tools like Git or Subversion, a separate staging environment is not strictly needed. The staged version of the build is usually a different configuration of the test environment, but can be the same machine. (It can simply be a separate branch in the version control system.) After final testing and debugging, the test build can be redefined as the staged build version, and can reside on the test machine. This version is augmented as more test builds are approved and added to the staging.

🌲 Variant   Some organizations use an external QA team to verify the build after it is approved by the testers and stakeholders in the user demo. Agile practices do not need a post-iteration QA team because after the iteration, the build is already production quality. An external QA team is an organizational safety to confirm the build when it is outside the jurisdiction of the team that developed it. An external QA team is redundant, and often wasteful, especially when the QA groups typically use the tests created by the test team. A user-written set of tests would be more useful, and agile has a counterpart with its practice of automated acceptance testing.

On the plus side, an external QA team will move the staged build to their own environment, which may have better tools, and more skilled and knowledgeable testers. The agile team usually tests the build for functional, and perhaps configuration, considerations, but the QA may test the build for other things. The QA team may give the staged build a more through testing at a level not available to the agile team, such as for load or stress testing, performance evaluations, and compliance checks.

The *training environment* may be part of the staging environment, and just before product release is a good time to set it up. The training environment should be a separate environment, isolated from the development and test environments, with its own user IDs, licenses, and training data. Although the staged build is stable and clear of *known* defects, the user in training can sometimes crash the system, either from undiscovered defects, configuration problems between environments, or strange actions by new users.

There is no inherent reason that the training environment be part of the staging environment, except that it is needed at this time, before a stable release goes into production, and the staging environment is not otherwise active. The training environment is a good last minute effort in finding unexpected defects.

The Production Environment

The production environment[2] supports the applications running for the organization, usually for the entire company; for online applications, the user base could be global. The production environment does not contain any tools that affect the project development, but it often contains procedures by which new products can be added into the production environment. The production environment is where the new product lives until it is retired. When a product is released, it "goes live"; or for online applications, it is "thrown into the wild" where it is expected to survive on its own for at least until the next release.

Release procedures are strict QA gates to ensure that this new application does not jeopardize the existing applications, and perhaps damage the user base and reputation for the company. There are also strict maintenance guidelines about how long the product will be closely monitored (often called *the warranty period*) before defects found are repaired by the project team, instead of repaired by the maintenance staff as change requests.

The business units decide when to release the staged version, based on how much functionality (business value) is in the product before it is released. A staged build is not released each iteration for several reasons. First, the first several iteration builds do not have sufficient value to move into operations.

---

[2]When a product moves into the production environment, it is often called *in operations*, and I use it interchangeably here. The operations domain works under a different set of principles than product management for development (usually ITIL principles) and is outside the scope of this book, except for the transition of products from development to operations.

Secondly, there is overhead to a release, and tasks that need to be done before release: train the Helpdesk, train the new users for internal projects or prepare marketing programs for external users, write release notes to inform user of changes in their day-to-day work and the new product. Perhaps field settings or machines need to be reconfigured. Often pilot programs are set up to *field test* the new product before propagating to the entire field what might be a problematic product (technical term: *lemon)*. Pilot projects are a common risk-management mitigation technique.

Subsequent releases to the initial release also need to factor in support calls, revisions to help documentation or mechanisms, and other change requests. Change requests that originate from the field (production environment) often comprise high-priority changes to releases in progress, and may change the development direction.

The Project Environment

The project environment supports the agile project manager specifically, and the project team in general. The APM needs reporting tools and task tracking tools, which are shared with the whole team. The project environment includes at least the following.

- *Task tracking*: The team selects items from the iteration backlog to complete by the end of the iteration. One of the most famous of the agile techniques to track progress is the *agile wall*—3×5 cards or "sticky notes" are placed on a wall to designate the user story or support tasks of the iteration. Each card contains a user story or a support task, and the person currently doing the work. The cards show who is doing what and when. The visual status of the iteration is apparent at a glance by anyone, very useful for the stakeholders. See more on the iteration process in Chapter 8.

  An alternative and popular task-tracking tool is the online *Kanban board*, which simulates the agile wall. The online aspect of the board means it is not restricted by physical location, but can be seen during any meeting anywhere with online access. My team members often keep the online task board on one workstation screen while they work on their virtual "card" on a different screen.

- *Reporting*: The Kanban board (or agile wall) provides tangible and definite status. Each task on a card is either complete or not. When the card is compete, a spreadsheet can automatically convert the card data into a burn-down (or if preferred, a burn-up) chart for visual iteration progress, and to calculate team velocity. Some online task boards can do this automatically. See more on reporting in Chapters 8 and 12.

- *Agile room and facilities*: An agile team works differently than a traditional team. Instead of each member working alone in cubicles and getting together occasionally to check status or information, agile teams work in a large open room most of the time, and retire to private meeting spaces occasionally.

  Most organizations have rules about "moving the furniture," or defining the agile room: it is not permitted. Kent Beck (1999, 80) comments on putting the product ahead of facility constraints, which also emphasizes the value of putting the software (business value) first:

All this screwing around with the furniture can get you in trouble... I say, "Too bad." I have software to write, and if getting rid of a partition helps me write that software better, I'm going to do it... Taking control of the physical environment sends a powerful message to the team... After all, the organization spent a gazillion dollars for all that flexible office furniture. All that money would be wasted if you didn't flex the furniture a little... Whatever works, stays. Whatever doesn't is sacrificed to the experiment.

An agile also room needs plenty of wall space for *big visible charts* (BVCs), also called information radiators, especially if online task boards are not being used. Regardless, burn-up charts and other progress devices populate the wall space of an agile room. See more about agile-specific practices in Chapter 10.

- *Osmotic communication*: The agile room allows conversations to be overheard, and that accidental communication is significant: people find out things they didn't expect to find out, contribute information that was overheard and needed, all to the benefit of the team and product. Alistair Cockburn (2004) calls this process *osmotic communication.* Kent Beck says in his XP book (79):

The team member needs to be able to see each other, to hear shouted one-off questions, to "accidentally" hear conversations which they have vital contributions.

- *Pair programming[3]*: A full open room also engenders the second most known characteristic of agile projects: pair programming. Two people work at the same machine at the same time, changing off partners as they need. This is common for mentor and mentee relationships, but agile makes it a standard practice. One may argue that during routine pair programming, for a particular technical point, one person in the pair knows more than the other person, and so the mentor-mentee relationship is temporary and an ad hoc affect. More on this technique is discussed in Chapter 10.

- The agile room should also contain as many whiteboards as possible, and power outlets for the various computers and work screens. Mobile phones with cameras have replaced the printing whiteboard. If the team is a virtual team, then videoconferencing tools, such as TeamViewer or GoToMeeting or many others work well. There is no need for expensive videoconferencing equipment that was commonplace years ago. Conference calling on a phone does not work nearly as well as communication among a collocated team, but is adequate as a last resort.

- *Other practices*: Agile has many, many practices that are different from traditional development, some from that are inherent from the principles, and some purely from the organizational culture. The reader may find it useful to refer to Scott Ambler's agile model at www.agilemodel.com. Scott is an influential and proactive agilist and trainer; sometimes these people are called *agilvangilists*.)

---

[3]Pair programming started for programmers, but the practice has moved to any two people working together simultaneously at the workstation—testers, BA and stakeholder, programmer and tester, and so forth. *Pairing* is the more proper term now.

Tools

The topic of tools is broken out into its own section to keep the mainstream flow of the various environments cleaner; each environment's tools are discussed separately, instead of in line with the environment descriptions. Specific tools used on my projects are listed for the various associated environments.

Full product support (development, testing, and product management) can be accomplished without a tool budget by using *open source tools*. Products like OpenOffice[4] Writer, Draw, and Calc serve well for word processing, diagramming, and spreadsheets, respectively, and they integrate seamlessly. (There are, of course, the commercial equivalents.) There are plenty of shared document repositories available, like Google Docs for stakeholders and nontechnical documents.

Regardless of the tools used, make sure that all the formats are compatible and standard. Building a diagram with a proprietary format that cannot be read by other members of the team is not productive, and tends to make that person perceived as a poor team player. Even if the formats are compatible, the artifact must be editable by all those who need to edit it.

Requirements Environment Tools

Business analysts work fine with the standard office tools such as OpenOffice. If they are validating requirements, simple open source UML editors are available, such as Violet and Green, but Draw is also sufficient for this. I particularly like CS Odessa's ConceptDraw Pro for diagramming. It is not an open source product, but it is reasonably priced. Business analysts may also need Business Process Modeling Notation (BPMN) tools to analyze business workflows and derive use cases. Whatever the tools used, they must be compatible with the other team members for shared communications, and possible shared editing.

Development Environment Tools

The developers will need workstation software for design, programming, and unit testing. They will also have tools to support those activities, such as IDEs (integrated design environments). Most of my teams in the last decade have written code simultaneously for both the Apple Mac OS and Microsoft Windows machines, with only a few platform-specific differences.

- *Programming*: One of the most popular IDEs for Java applications is the open source Eclipse product.[5] It comes with intelligent syntax editors, a boatload of options and shortcuts, and full developer team support: version control, Ant and Maven (an object-oriented evolvement of the standard Ant) scripting tools, OSGi architecture bundling, deployment tools for web applications, plug-ins, and desktop applications. It is a product that *feels* like it was written by developers for developers, and has a myriad of those small nice-to-have features that eventually the developer cannot do without.

- *Documentation*: (1) For developer documentation to describe the Java code API (packages, classes, methods, and fields), Javadoc is the standard tool. It reads specially formatted comments in the code and builds the API documentation automatically. Other languages have similar autodoc tools. (2) For general documents, such as user manuals, charts, and graphs, the standard team tools suffice. (3) Our team puts technical documents inside our codebase repository in a technical document folder.

---

[4]www.openoffice.org

[5]At the time of this writing, Eclipse Mars *(August 2015)* was the latest production version. It can be found at www.eclipse.org.

- *Documentation standards:* Whatever the documentations, documentation standards are needed to define what *should be* and *should not be* in the document. Sometimes, documenters elaborate too much. Not only is it confusing, but violates the agile principle of barely sufficient documentation."

- *Unit testing*: JUnit is the standard for unit testing Java applications. For other languages, there are corresponding developer test tools referred to generically as xUnit. (For example, CppUnit is used for C++ applications.) Maven automatically will run all JUnit unit tests each time it invokes the build process, thereby providing automated regression unit testing. Both Maven and JUnit come with the Eclipse IDE.

- *Design*: Most designs for an agile team are informal. Designs can be drawn on a whiteboard and a picture taken with a nearby camera phone. More formal design diagrams can be built with Green or Violet, an intuitive UML design-diagramming tool. There are many general diagramming tools, like OpenOffice's Draw tool; all are open source tools. The most important aspect is to have a single tool for a consistent format, so that only one tool and format is needed by the team to edit diagrams.

- *UX artifacts*: Although the business analyst defines the requirements, the developers are often asked to build screen mockups. Open source tools like Windows Builder are simple enough that the BA can use it to draw their own screen mockups, and yet powerful enough that developers can define a screen layout using expert knowledge of the technical programmatic underpinnings of the user interface. Windows Builder has the additional benefit of generating code from the design.

- *Version control*: All developers work on a single codebase; the code is communal. The code is shared and stored in a version control system, such as Subversion (SVN) or Git. The developers update the build with new code daily, and eventually, when the build is ready for testing, the build is extracted (versioned) for testing, and the developers continue with coding, unit testing, and updating the development build.

- *Continuous improvement (CI)*: Some open source tools automate script building and standards compliance. They can run automated regression testing, or warn of errors moving into the shared codebase. Not all agile projects use CI tools, but when they are used, the developers and PM have found them to be indispensable. Open source CI tools Jenkins, Gherkin (focuses on behavior-driven design), and Maven (a build scripting tool that is easily extended for CI purposes).

- *Programming coding standards*: A good consistent coding style (syntax, grammar, structure, and commenting) and high readability reduces defects, and their subsequent rework and cost of repair. Coding standards define how to write these kinds of styles. In a shared coding environment, multiple developers write (and overwrite) to the same codebase, and the testers, documenters, and others who may not be well versed in the language but need to read that code. Coding standards of some form are needed. Checkstyle[6] is one of the tools that automatically checks for compliance during the build process.

    - *Programming* styles are emotional and personal, and "religious" wars have started over minor things like on which line a brace must reside, or how many spaces to indent subordinate lines of code, or how long a line of code should be before it wraps. There are more than a few perspectives on coding standards.

---

[6]See http://checkstyle.sourceforge.net.

- *Enforce consistency*: The code is shared, so developers should create the most consistently readable code by using the same language style. That style is agreed upon by the team and tried for a few iterations, revising as needed. With this approach, most of the developers will have to adopt a new style, which is personally uncomfortable, and usually outside the developer's coding habits. Initially, the disciplined developer has to undo his or her coding frequently at first. Some developers merely ignore the standard, intending to go back and revise it later, which rarely happens. Therefore, this approach is initially error-prone and can lead to inconsistencies. To enable following an objective standard easier and Java code less prone to error, Google has a freely available set of Java standards and an application to go with it for just this purpose (Google 2014).

- *Allowing diversity with formatters:* Many IDEs come with formatters so that the developer can write in whatever style they want, invoke the built-in formatter, and it will reformat the code to whatever style is desired. (Traditionally, these were called "pretty printers.") Everyone can write and read the code in their most comfortable style. However, each time the code is reformatted, all changed files will be rewritten, causing them to be uploaded to the version control system and then downloaded by each developer trying to synchronize their code (at least daily). At first, if many files are changed frequently, upload/download time can be significant. It may discourage developers from making frequent updates to the codebase, which is more important. Eventually, the developer will not take the time to reformat the code, and gradually get accustomed to reading an unfamiliar style, which will become familiar. The result is a built-in evolution to a de facto code standard.

Testing Environment Tools

The testers will need the standard team tools for writing their test cases, executing the test build, writing defect reports, and updating the RTM. They will also need tools to support their activities, such as defect trackers. The test machine should be isolated from the development environment so that it is not easy for the developers to change the test build. Keep in mind that these are tools, and not specific practices. See the relevant chapters for the practices of developers, testers, analysts, the APM, and others.

- *Integration testing*: Testers who write integration tests will need a programming IDE to write the integration tests, and run both the integration and regression tests. The integration tests are written in JUnit for Java applications (or xUnit for other languages). They also need to access the version control system to retrieve the latest development build. The Eclipse IDE has a built-in SVN and Git client, automatic JUnit regression testing (with Maven), and Javadoc.

- *GUI testing*: I have not found any suitable open source tools for automated GUI testing, despite periodic searching. GUI testing is often performed manually, and so will GUI regression testing, which is laborious. There are many GUI test tools from the commercial sector, but even those leave much to be desired. The effort of running manual GUI tests is one of the prime reasons that the MVP architecture should be used, which minimizes the amount of code that must be manually retested.

- *Defect tracking*: Defects are defined and added to a tracking system, such as the open source product Bugzilla. The tracking system should have good reporting capabilities because all defects are listed, sorted, and selected in various ways for review each week. Defect tracking reports of various search and sort criteria (number of defects, number of open defects, mean time to repair, etc.) are important for the APM reports.

- *Test reporting:* Most of the artifacts the testers produce are test cases; OpenOffice works for that. The testing results can be stored and updated in any spreadsheet, such as OpenOffice's Calc.

- *QA testing standards*: These standards aren't as controversial as developer standards. They describe how to write complete and useful test cases. The one standard that I strongly push is the NEBS method. There is no software needed for this; NEBS is a *technique*, not a program, used to convert use cases to test cases (see Chapter 11 for details).

PMI Parallels

The PMI does not involve itself in particular tools or vendors, and therefore does not address infrastructure configurations or tools. They do recommend standards and documentation practices, but not as prolifically as discussed here. Documents in agile teams are written for communication purposes, and are not the same as big upfront detailed specifications found in the traditional approach.

Traditional change management and configuration control are addressed in a broad manner in the PMBOK, and is consistent with agile practices. The RTM, critical to change management and scope tracking, is a staple artifact of both the PMI and the Software Engineering Institute (SEI), which now recognizes agile projects as complying with the SEI Capability Maturity Models.

Conclusion

Setting up the infrastructure to support a project team is not an easy task. Most organizations have cultural norms or rules on how teams must work with management and stakeholders. Fortunately, the APM is the lynch pin between the team, stakeholders, and upper management to make this work.

Most organizations have predefined infrastructure that they expect the project team to use for development. The IT department, for example, must support the production environment and allow the new product to be maintained as easily as possible when in the production environment. A Linux production environment would take a lot of work to absorb a large MS Windows application, and vice versa. A Java-heavy production shop may find it hard to absorb a new COBOL application.

Moving a project's product from its development software and hardware to the diverse software and hardware of the production environment is an aspect of infrastructure that is often the least flexible. The team must adapt where it can. There are always design, risk and budget trade-offs, some better and worse than others.

Probably the most important aspect of the infrastructure (a stick-your-sword-in-the-sand position) that I see violated in most organizations I work with is: do not allow the development machine to be the test machine. You need two different environments, as explained earlier. If there is only one step that you can do, ensure that the development environment is separated from the testing environment. It is as easy as keeping a separate branch in the version control repository. This is true of traditional or agile infrastructures.

Iteration 0 contains a lot of nonproductive but valuable work: facilitating the business team and technical team kickoff meetings; defining the base product architecture; tailoring an agile method to the team, project, and organization; and decomposing initial large-grain requirements. None of these will be of use unless the infrastructure for building the product is not available.

Chapter 7 talks about eliciting[7] the initial requirements so that the development team is ready to implement and deliver the first pass of the product at the end of Iteration 1.

---

[7]Later, the requirements chapter makes a strong distinction between the passive phrase "collecting requirements" and the more accurate and active phrase "eliciting requirements."

■ ■ ■

Initial Requirements: Defining the Product

Overview

The previous chapters explained how the project manager collected initial project information: project charter, mission statement, stakeholder expectations, project abstract, and feature catalog. In this next step of progressive elaboration, the business analyst will drill down another level and collect the initial requirements.

This chapter describes general principles of requirements elicitation, a few do's and don'ts, and gives a recommended practice for the business analyst (BA) to drill down to detailed requirements that the developers and testers can use during the development iterations. Examples from the ATM project are shown throughout. Differences in traditional and agile requirements practices are discussed.

Now that the business objectives are agreed by the stakeholders and business workflows identified, the BA can begin to derive the high-level requirements from those workflows and stakeholders. In the two-weeks (Iteration 0) that the developers and testers are putting their parts of the infrastructure in place, there is time for the business analyst and stakeholders to decompose the business workflows from the project abstract context diagram, and to refine the features from the feature catalog, into detailed use cases. It is the detailed use cases from which the development team derives *user stories*— the implementable-sized parts of requirements—during the construction iterations.

The Requirements Traceability Matrix (RTM), a mapping of each feature to its supporting use case is started as use cases are defined. Later, test cases, associated defects and test results are used to update the RTM. The RTM is critical for change management, and defect control and tracking.

The business analyst may also want to formally validate the detailed use cases for high-quality products. Formal validation ensures that the requirements, which contributes to over half of all defects in the product, are clean before design and coding start. When Iteration 1 starts, the developers should have the use case catalog, at least one detailed use case (possibly validated), and the proposed user experience mock-ups needed for the detailed use case design.

High-Quality Product Development

Some applications require high quality, such as applications in the field of medicine, aerospace, security, communications, and finance, or any complex application. Rigorous proofing and validation techniques may be needed and can be applied to the use cases (Cline 1999). The quality overhead of this level of verification and validation is not always justified, but the effort will guarantee *zero-defect requirements*. A rigorous technique to validate detailed use cases is explained in Chapter 9.

Every couple of years a new piece of data is published showing that the greatest source of defects originate from the requirements and functional design step of product development, not from coding. The programmers are not the problem. The oldest study I have seen, and one of the most cited, is from Alberts (1976, 230–238). Although it was done in 1976, it was still typical of projects until about 2010. Not much has changed in requirements results in the last 30 years!

What happened to change that? Agile and its depth-first way of collecting requirements arrived. The agile way of collecting requirements using progressive elaboration, thin-thread development, continual stakeholder involvement, automated testing, refactoring, and use case validation, changed requirements results. Agile techniques have made it possible to double the quality of the product by removing the requirements defects, if not by validation, then by repeated conversations with the stakeholders and customer SMEs to refine what they wanted until they got it.

Functional Requirements

Requirements can be placed into two major categories: functional requirements and non-functional requirements. Sometimes requirements get confused with design. All three groups can be separated by keeping this quick guide in mind.

- *Functional requirements* define WHAT the business unit wants: the appearance and behavior of the product.

- *Design requirements* define HOW the product meets those requirements. There are an infinite number of designs for a single set of requirements. Requirements reflect a higher level of abstraction than design. The UX artifact is a design requirement, and bridges the gap between abstract functional requirements and design.

- *Non-functional requirements* (NFR) include quality or system attributes (the so-called "-bilities") that constrain the design.

Eliciting requirements and converting them into a working product is difficult and error prone. Requirements are captured at the beginning of product development, but few defects are caught then (Alberts 1976). The longer a defect propagates through the project, the more that must be undone to repair it or collateral work. Most requirements defects are not detected until the end of the project, which is why requirements defects result in the greatest project cost and maintenance costs. Recall Figure 1-3 from Chapter 1.

Requirements Hierarchy

The requirements, like the product itself, have a hierarchy that is revealed as it is progressively refined or elaborated. Initially, the product is decomposed into workflows from the context diagram of the project abstract, which in turn are decomposed into use cases, and eventually into their constituent user stories. (Both detailed use cases and user stories may have UX artifacts associated with them.)

The BA uses progressive elaboration to discover and distill down from larger scope to smaller scope. Unlike traditional requirements elicitation that collects all requirements in one document before construction (*breadth-first*), the agile BA works *depth-first* to refine detailed use cases one at a time so that construction can begin before the entire product scope is defined.

Figure 7-1 shows the cone of scope relating project and requirements artifacts with team members as they are produced through the requirements hierarchy. The requirements artifacts are shown on the right side of the cone, and the people providing those artifacts are shown on the left side. It illustrates the widening requirements scope hierarchy before and during iterations.

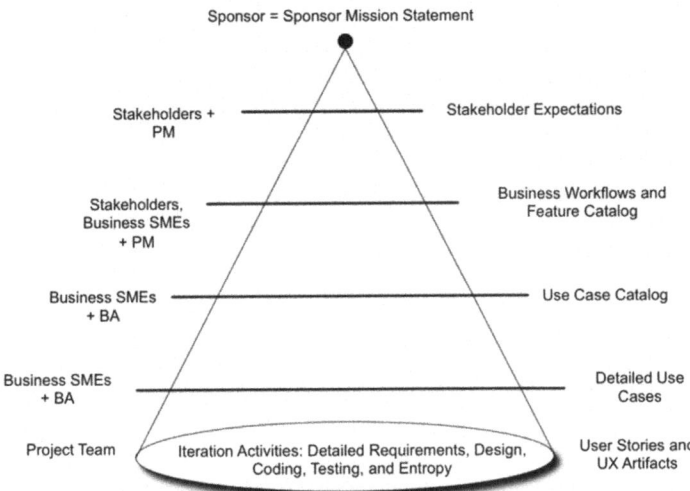

Figure 7-1. *Requirements cone of scope*

- *Mission statement*: The ultimate goal of the product is to meet the expectations and needs of the sponsor, who is paying for the project. Anything outside his mission statement is out of scope. The PM should have collected this in the project charter previously.

- *Stakeholder expectations*: Each stakeholder has expectations and needs that to justify their involvement with the project. Each stakeholder captured those expectations and needs in their business abstracts, which the PM should have reconciled previously to build the project abstract.

- *Business workflows and feature catalog*: Each stakeholder has an idea of what features are needed for the product, and sometimes enlist the aid of business SMEs to help. At first, these are "desirements": features that are like market points on the back of a product box when it is sold. They become requirements after they are vetted against the mission statement and practical considerations. They are prioritized by business value, risk, and other factors (see Chapter 3) and listed as the feature catalog. Unlike an approved, and voluminous, software specification document, the feature catalog is only a prioritized list that can be revised as needed before construction starts with little or no project impact.

- *Use case catalog*: Each workflow is comprised of multiple transactional threads or use cases, and each use case is known (at this time) only by its single-statement goal. Each use case summary is a name and short description of the usage transaction. The list of use case summaries are collected in priority order, correlated to feature priorities, into the use case catalog.

- *Detailed use cases*: Each use case is expanded into a detailed use case, which contains the conditions in which the use case applies, detailed actor-system dialog, and all data required into and from the system. The data is defined for default values, min and max field lengths, optional data elements, and other attributes. The detailed use case is a rigorously written one-to-two page document that drives design, programming, and testing. Detailed use cases are collected both before, and during, the iteration in which they are implemented.[1] If the use case follows the simple IEEE 830 standard-compliant use case template, they may be validated for zero defects, and have an associated validating object model.

- *User stories*: During the iterations, further detail can be defined for each use case. Each use case contains a series of normal and error paths; each path through the use case is a user story, or a particular scenario. User stories are easier than a use case to implement and test. Many agile teams work directly with user stories and skip the use case stage. Chapter 9 discusses the pros and cons of use cases vs. user stories, and how they relate.

- *User experience (UX) artifacts*: During the iterations, the detailed use case or user story will be associated with a user screen mockup, picture, navigational map, or some other similar document that describes the user's interactivity and one aspect of the product's appearance. Both use case and UX artifact are part of the functional requirements, although the UX artifact is actually a bridge between design and requirements. Some use cases have multiple screen mockups, and each is referenced in the detailed use case. Both user stories and UX artifacts are described in more detail in Part 3: Iterations 1 to N, Chapters 8 through 12.

Figure 7-1 reflects agile's adaptive planning technique, as applied to requirements and stakeholders. As the requirements are progressively elaborated from charter to implementation, the artifacts go through the stages shown.

Other Useful Terms

There are two other concepts under the requirements hierarchy, although they are arbitrary distinctions for convenience. They both are useful when rearranging features or use cases in the product backlog. The terms stem from XP and are helpful for talking about groups of user stories or use cases. It helps to use these words when discussing how to sort through the product backlog to extract groups of use cases.

- *Epic*: A large use case or very large user story. It may be that the use case is not broken down enough, or there is lots of work in that one use case. An epic usually cannot be implemented within one iteration, or is the only piece of scope that can be implemented. An epic must be decomposed into more detail before it is truly testable and buildable.

- *Theme*: A collection of logically related use cases or user stories. Unlike an epic that is not decomposed into enough detail yet, a theme is a collection of multiple pieces of smaller scope. As an example, the ATM Projects has a theme of user demand transactions: deposit funds, withdraw cash, and transfer funds. The use case inquiry for balance may or may not be included in this theme.

---

[1]If the detailed use case reflects design choices, they are called *design cases*.

Requirements Elicitation

Professional business analysts refer to the process of obtaining functional requirements from the users as requirements *elicitation*, instead of requirements *collection*. Requirements collection gives the impression that requirements are already defined and can be easily picked up from where they are sitting, like pebbles on a beach.

That is far from the truth. Stakeholders have a concept in their head, but usually not specifically enough to express, and definitely not enough to specify a product. The business analyst helps the stakeholder mold that concept into a buildable, testable, and usable set of requirements for the developers and testers. The business analyst must ferret out the information that is omitted, verify it, and then put it into a detailed use case, which works as a specification.

Merging Different Perspectives

The BA must be able to look at the various perspectives of the product. Everyone on the team will have a different perspective, and different people see product attributes or features as more important than others. One business SME may emphasize or see something different from another; a tester is looking at the requirements very differently than the developer. It is similar to the old Indian folk story about three blind men examining an elephant, shown in Figure 7-2.

Figure 7-2. *Elephant and Three Blind Men*

As the story goes, each blind man feels the elephant to try to get an idea of what an elephant is. One touches the trunk, and thinks of a snake. Another touches the tail and thinks of a rope. The third touches the side and thinks an elephant is a big leathery wall. When they get together, they might become the various facets that make up an elephant. (In the worst case, they may think the elephant is a shape-shifter.) It is the BA's job to ensure that he or she gets a real picture of an elephant after talking with the various "blind men" (and women) on the business team.

Quenty Twestions: Interviewing Is Not a First-Approach Technique

Most people trying to collect requirements will schedule a meeting for the business SME or user to ask what they want the product to do. They often come armed with a list of typical questions, sometimes overly technical. This is a bad technique for at least three reasons. First, the users or SMEs do not know specifically what they want, which is partly why business abstracts were collected earlier. Second, close-ended questions will bias the results, and give flawed requirements. Third, it sets up the business SME to change his or her mind more often because their first answer was not well thought through.

As an exercise in my training classes to demonstrate the point, I ask the participants if they know the parlor game Twenty Questions: a small group of people ask questions to a "target person," who answers only Yes or No. The object of the game is to come up with what the target person is thinking in 20 questions or less. It requires skill on the part of the questioners to efficiently pare down the answers into what the target person it thinking.

Then I introduce the class to a new version of the game called "Quenty Twestions," because it is Twenty Questions with a twist. I break the class into groups of four or five. They select one person as a "target person" who will answer the questions, one to track the questions, and the others will ask the questions. I meet privately with the target people of the various teams and tell them to answer completely randomly. I ask them to write down random Ys and Ns on a piece of paper before the questioning and answer accordingly, but without contradicting themselves, or divulging the secret.

After 10 to 15 minutes of this game, (almost always) all groups will have a very definite object that they think the target person had in mind: a black beetle in the Peruvian rainforest, a new computer system currently being installed in the IT department, a young unicorn with silver hair and blue eyes. Where do these objects originate since *no information* was transferred by the person answering the questions? The objects came from the questions! As a business analyst, do not ask questions for initial requirements. Use your questions for clarifying or probing into missing data or operations later.

The users or business SME's often aren't sure how they will work with the new system. They expect the development team to tell them. Sometimes the users or SMEs are not really stakeholders but were delegated to the task and may not be sure of their role—someone else thought they would be a good source of information. To avoid the "Quenty Twestions" syndrome, ask the users or business SME, as a first step, to write the business abstract page, discussed in Chapter 3.

Twenty Questions was inspired by John Wheeler, a theoretical physicist and cosmologist from Princeton University, in discussing our "Observer Universe." He says that the questions we ask determine the answers we receive. Add Heisenberg's principle: "When we look at something, we change it." Both of these are principles of hard physics, but are easily manifested in psychological settings like requirements elicitations sessions, as the game demonstrates.

Prefer Use Cases to Features

A *feature* is a topical perspective of the product scope, instead of a functional perspective like a use case. Features encourage component-based development; use cases encourage agile thin-thread development, which is the agile approach. Unlike features, use cases can be mapped from workflow to objects[2] to code to test cases, and the RTM shows the mapping. Also, unlike features, use cases can be put into a canonical form as a specification, and validated using rigorous proof techniques.

---

[2]The word *objects* are used here in the object-oriented sense of analysis, design, and programming.

Produce Detailed Requirements

The business analyst starts with the feature catalog and the project abstract, which contains the context diagram (see Chapter 3), as his or her key artifacts. He or she uses both to convert, in conjunction with the business SMEs, to produce a list of prioritized use cases in the *use case catalog*. It is important to note that the BA is not expected to convert the entire feature catalog during Iteration 0.

Lessons learned sessions from multiple projects and companies recommend that the business analyst prepare the detailed use cases before the iteration in which the developers implement them. The BA needs to develop just enough use cases for the developers to get started in Iteration 1. The BA returns to finish the feature catalog and grow the use case catalog, always staying ahead of the development team. Ideally, he or she works one or two iterations ahead eliciting requirements.

The following is a summary of the typical sequence of steps followed by the business analyst.

1. Associate features to business workflow.

2. Decompose each workflow to use cases into the use case catalog.

3. Write the detailed use case for approval.

4. Develop the UX artifact.

5. Start the Requirements Traceability Matrix (RTM).

6. Repeat through the features catalog.

Each step is discussed in more detail in the sections that follow. Note that the validation step for a detailed use case is not listed. Although that should be done for some projects as part of validating the detailed use case, those more technical details are described in Chapter 9.

Associate Features to Business Workflow

Ideally, the BA is available before the business kick-off meeting, and can help build the business workflows before or during the first business team meeting that builds the project abstract. The project abstract contains a context diagram that illustrates the high-level workflows of the new product and how certain actors (stakeholders, users, and external systems) are involved with each workflow. The BA starts with the project abstract, which contains the context diagram and project objectives, and develops the feature catalog. The feature catalog is merely a value-prioritized list of features from the stakeholder of what they want the product to do.

The BA meets with the business SMEs and focuses on the first priority feature, and they identify the workflow associated with that feature. (Be aware that some features are related to non-functional requirements and have no workflow.) The SME describes the various interactions the actors have with the workflow that expresses the feature.

A note about features. Features are rather large granule requirements, scoped randomly as stakeholders think about what they want. Features are not cleanly mappable to use cases and serve only as an anchor point for the stakeholders to "know" what is in the product. Features-driven development is reminiscent of traditional bottom-up or top-down development, instead of thin-thread development, which agile uses exclusively. Ideally, the BA should steer the stakeholders (and customer SMEs) into thinking of user interactions instead of features, and deriving use cases directly from the business workflows.

Decompose Each Workflow to Use Cases into the Use Case Catalog

The workflow is a functional description (inputs, process, and outputs) of behavior at a high level, just as the use case is a functional description at a lower level. A single workflow will contain one or more use cases. A *use case* in software engineering is an interactive scenario between the actor and the system,[3] explaining *what* must happen, without explaining *how* it should happen internally; the "how" is the domain of design. In some cases, the agile team may choose to write user stories with the stakeholder, and develop no use cases or requirements specification.

The BA breaks down the workflows of the one-page context diagram into more detail. The more detail one extracts from the workflow, the easier the constituent use cases are to see. Workflows below the level of the context diagram can be annotated with *Business Processing Modeling Notation (BPMN) diagrams, state transition diagrams,* or *state charts,* which were invented to model and document the behavior of systems (Satzinger, Jackson, and Burd 2004). Both are primary tools of the BA. The one that the BA uses is often a personal preference. Workflows shown as state charts are sometimes better received by the technical developers, because use cases can also be represented with state charts. That means that a single notation can be used for both workflow decomposition and use cases. Either way, the BA should pick the tool that fits his or her preference and communicates best to the team.

For example, the user's workflow may be to log on, withdraw money, and get their account balance. These three use cases make up a single workflow session at the ATM machine.

The Unified Modeling Language (UML was developed to model object-oriented systems, which was the paradigm of choice before agile. It is still valuable. UML includes state transition diagrams and a notation specific to UML called a sequence diagram, which has largely replaced state charts. Sequence diagrams are not particularly useful at the higher BPMN level, but UML Activity diagrams work sufficiently well for that. Check out Booch (1994) for a full description of UML and its many uses. Although developed over ten years ago, it is still a modeling standard of the Object Management Group (OMG) and the International Organization for Standardization (ISO), and organization to which the PMI belongs (http://en.wikipedia.org/wiki/Unified_Modeling_Language; June 24, 2014).

The decomposed workflows will show the data flow transitioning from inside to outside the system, and vice versa. A use case is generally limited to a single actor providing input data, and perhaps the same or different actor receiving output data. This heuristic helps to delineate one use case from another.

Figure 7-3 shows a mid-level workflow (within the context diagram) of the ATM system, using a UML Activity diagram. It represents a mid-level flow and use cases can be read directly from the diagram—the easiest way to identify use case summaries. The state transitions are labeled in bold as use case summaries.

---

[3]"In systems engineering, use cases are used at a higher level than within software engineering, often representing missions or stakeholder goals. The detailed requirements may then be captured in Systems Modeling Language (SysML) or as contractual statements." See http://en.wikipedia.org/wiki/Use_case, June 24, 2014.

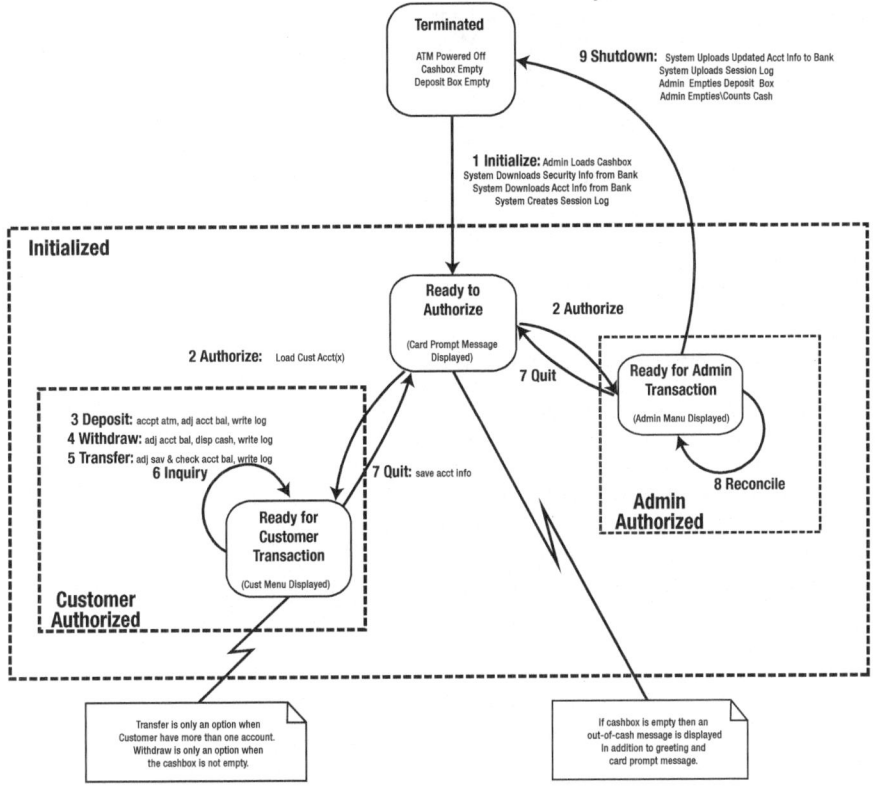

Figure 7-3. *Sample mid-level workflow (UML activity diagram)*

All use case summaries are collected in a list—the *use case catalog*, prioritized roughly the same as the feature priorities. (The use-case catalog priorities may change later, when the team helps identify technical and implementation dependencies during the working iteration.) The use case catalog contains only the summary goal statement of the use case, and is associated with at least one of the features in the feature catalog. An inconsistency between the workflow, features, and use cases is the first indication that a feature may be out of scope, or a workflow is incomplete.

In Figure 7-3, one of the Admin workflows is the sequence of use cases 1 (Initialize), 2 (Authorize), and 9 (Shutdown). Use case 8 (Reconcile) is optional because the system state can change with or without that use case. One of the customer workflows is use case 2 (Authorize), one or more of use cases 3, 4, 5, or 6, and then use case 7 (Quit).

It is critical for an agile team that some of the use cases get detailed before Iteration 1. The BA works to identify the use case summaries (scope breadth) only as far as necessary to detail the first few use cases (scope depth). Once the developers and testers move forward with building and testing detailed use cases, the BA can return to the workflows and features catalog to widen the scope with more use cases.

It is important to understand that the use case catalog is *derived by* decomposing workflows; it was not *collected* as a set of arbitrary features during requirements elicitation.

Use cases that define initialization and termination (*initialization* and *shutdown ATM* in the example) are more design-centric than the others, but are always use cases, and are dependencies. These two use cases are always included in Iteration 1, and often augmented in subsequent iterations (see Figure 7-4).

Customer		Administrator	
		1	Initialize ATM
2	Authorize	2	Authorize
3	Deposit Money into Account		
4	Withdraw Cash from Account		
5	Transfer Money between Accounts		
6	Check Balance of an Account		
7	Quit	7	Quit
		8	Reconcile
		9	Shutdown ATM

Figure 7-4. *Sample use case summaries for ATM project*

Write the Detailed Use Case for Approval

Starting with the highest priority use-case summary in the use case catalog, the BA progressively elaborates that summary into a detailed use case. The use case is a scenario that describes how the user's business value is achieved with a dialog between the user and the system. The use case can be captured in many forms, but I prefer the IBM format: The business goal of the use case is stated, the desired actor-system dialog defined, Input and Output sections give a concise summary of what input data is required or optional, and what output data will always, or sometimes, be produced. See Figure 7-5 for an example detailed use case Withdraw from Savings/Checking Account from the ATM project.

UC4	Withdraw from Savings/Checking Account	
Actor	Customer	
Objective	Give cash to customer from their account, deducting that amount. Provide a receipt of the transaction.	
UX	UX01. Transaction Receipt	
Pre-conditions	Cashbox is not empty.	
Post-Conditions	o Account balance decreased, AND o Session log is updated and saved, AND o Cash has been dispensed	
Invariants	Customer is authorized for the transaction.	
Detailed Description		
Step	Actor	System Response
1	(a) Selects Withdraw from the Customer transaction options (b) Selects checking or savings account, if more than one account exists (c) Enters withdraw amount	(a) Verifies the withdraw amount is • A multiple of $20, greater than $0 and less than maximum 24 hour transaction limit of $200 • Less than or equal to cash amount in cashbox • Less than or equal to savings account balance for savings withdraw • Less than checking account balance - $100 for checking withdraw If verification fails, or an invalid withdraw amount is entered, restart use case with an error message.

Figure 7-5. *Sample use case: Withdraw Money (ATM project)*

	If the requested amount exceeds the capacity of a non-empty cashbox, then an info message is displayed indicating the amount remaining (so the actor can readjust their requested amount). (b) Updates destination account with the withdraw amount (c) Posts transaction to log (d) Prints receipt (UX01). (e) Displays Customer transaction options (resets for next use case)
Input Data	Savings or Checking account, Withdraw Amount
Output Data	o Printed receipt: Bank ID, ATM Stations Number, Transaction Type, Date/Time stamp, Customer ID, Account number, Transaction amount o Log data: Transaction type, Time stamp, Amount, Account number o Cash
Notes	1. If the cashbox s empty, then an out-of-cash message is displayed (in large, highly visible text in lieu of the withdrawal menu option) as well as the greeting and ATM bank card prompt message. This implementation allows customers to perform deposits, transfers, and inquiries without the frustration of authorizing only to discover the machine is out of cash and cannot perform cash withdraw. 2. Invalid amounts include those that exceed the current capacity of the cashbox, e.g., a $200 request when the cashbox only contains $60. In that case, an appropriate error message must be displayed, and the transaction asks again. 3. In this use case, the actor could enter all the data at one time without needing to wait for a system response. If the actor had to wait for a system response, then the input before would be step 1, and the input after the response would be step 2, and so on.

Figure 7-5. (*continued*)

There will be many questions for the business SME as the detailed use case is filled out. I have found it most helpful in my roles as BA to ask the SME to fill out the template with me, but I type the text in, controlling the phrasing, which is critically important in a requirements spec. If the SME is not part of writing the use case, they must review and approve it. The SME must have delegation authority to finalize a requirement, or much time will be wasted as the SME repeatedly "goes back and talks to her manager."

No technical details are given in the detailed use case because it is a *functional requirement*: it defines *what* must be done, and not *how*, which is the focus of design. If important design details or non-functional requirements arise during discussion, they are kept in the Notes section so that ideas are not lost while the use case is being defined. The UX artifact, a design requirement, is referenced (linked) in the use case. See the UX field in Figure 7-5.

There is one exception to including technical design details. I have found it useful to the team and the user if the UX is more than referenced in the use case. It is helpful if the use case says something like, *Actor selects the book by clicking on the drop-down selection list*, instead of merely *Actor selects the book*. The detailed use case text may need to be revised after the UX artifact is defined (designed).

The *use case template* in the "Additional Tools" section (see Figure 7-7) contains the use case goal, actor, reference to the associated UX artifact, pre- and post-conditions, detailed interactive transaction steps, and a summary of the inputs and outputs. These last two sections define the default data values, and some syntax requirements, such as field length.

Warning   Some agile teams skip writing use cases and go directly to user stories. Use cases contain a set of related user stories, and provide context for those stories. A series of user stories without their enclosing use case will allow the product scope to get fragmented, and risk conflicts within the requirements, code, and tests. Even if the agile team agrees not to rigorously validate the use cases, the BA should always write use cases for anything but the simplest application.

Bertrand Meyer (2014) criticizes user-story-only requirements with an example of trying to write a square root function by giving only examples of square roots. If an example root is missed, the square root function may not work properly. Not all possible examples can be given, so the square root rule, or equation, must be given. He also argues that the code will be fragmented and prone to more rework. There is a strong difference between data points on a line, and the line itself.

Make the Detailed Use Case a Functional Specification

The use case will be used by the stakeholders to confirm the product will do what they want, by the tester to write test cases, and by the developer to implement code. The use cases are also used by the operations people and maintenance programmers. It must be modifiable because requirements change. It is also important if the use cases are going to be rigorously validated. In short, use cases should meet the IEEE 830 standard to be a *requirements specification* and consequently avoid a critical deficiency.

There is no industry standard form or template by which a functional requirement should be written, but the Institute of Electrical and Electronics Engineers (IEEE) has defined a *specification* in which functional requirements are defined. The detailed use case, written in the template shown in "Additional Tools" section complies with the *830-1998 IEEE Recommended Practice for Software Requirements Specification* (IEEE 1998),[4] characteristics of a requirements specification: correct, unambiguous, complete, consistent, ranked for importance and/or stability, verifiable, modifiable, usable for implementation, testing, and operations, and traceable.

According to the IEEE, if a requirements document does not meet these criteria, it is not strictly a *specification*, but only a requirements *document*, not much more than ideas scratched on a lunch napkin. For agile projects, specifications are informal, and the detailed use case suffices. Many agile projects employ only user stories, which is not a requirement but merely a scenario. The team using this approach exchanges requirements elicitation and analysis time for refactoring and stakeholder feedback to amplify the story at the time of construction. The more complex the use case, the more the team should lean to the former.

To comply with the IEEE criteria, the analyst must verify the use case in several ways. Fortunately, the use case template builds in most of these so the effort is little more than writing the use case.

---

[4]Although the standard was defined in 1998, it was reviewed and reaffirmed in 2009.

- *Product completeness:* The use case is a subset of one of the workflows shown in the project abstract's context diagram. Each use case must be matched to one of those workflows, or it is out of scope. The RTM can confirm that the workflows and use cases correlate.

- *Data completeness*: The workflow shows the data input, output, source, and sink (who or what receives the data), and the use case must indicate those data flows as well.

- *Logical completeness and correctness:* The BA must ensure that there are no logic holes in the usability with the system, and that all the ramifications of the stated requirements are considered. The BA must ensure that no error condition is omitted, or a particular condition is overlooked. Many times the user asks for something without realizing what ramifications may result, what it means to their business procedures, or that it might be subtly contradictory or inconsistent. The analyst must "do what the user meant, and not what the user said." This kind of *requirements defect* is particularly common when user stories are written without the context of the use case, and the developer focuses too closely on the story during implementation.

- *Requirements completeness and consistency:* This refers to the mechanics of writing the spec. Use consistent formatting, unit dimensions (e.g., feet or meters), and structure for clarity. This is a technical writing issue that becomes simple when a use case is written to the use case template.

- *Ranked for importance and/or stability:* The use cases are derived from the workflow and features, which are prioritized by importance (business value), risk, and other factors in the product backlog. Therefore, when the use cases are developed, the BA already knows the priority of the use case.

- *Verifiable*: A detailed use case can be verified in many different ways. Use cases (and the UX artifacts) can be verified with the stakeholders after they are written, through team review before they are implemented, with the testers that the implementation matches the requirements, and by the user demo that the requirements and code are what the stakeholders wanted. If *validation* is assumed to be part of verification, the use cases can be rigorously verified and validated using the UML techniques mentioned elsewhere.

- *Semantically correct, unambiguous, and complete*: Writing specifications, even the detailed use case, in a natural language such as English, is difficult because natural languages are loaded with cultural and semantic connotations. Phrasing and terminology is key—inconsistent terminology between team members can lead the project astray for a long time. Inconsistent terminology is the worst kind of miscommunication because it causes misdirection, which may later cause team friction and conflict, resulting in a lack of productivity or rework. Friedman (1990) has a checklist of words and phrases, with numerous examples, of how specifications can cause more confusion than clarity. The BA should be aware of these terms when writing the detailed use case.

- *Modifiable:* Detailed use cases are short and arbitrarily numbered, and as independent of other use cases as practical. These small units, or their references to other artifacts, can be easily changed without affecting the bulk of other requirements. I like to write use cases using the ACID principle (atomic, consistent, isolated, and durable) that applies to any transaction. See more about this idea next.

- *Usable for implementation, testing, and operations*: After a detailed use case is written and approved by the stakeholders, the BA must verify that the testers and developers must be able to use it. The requirements will drive coding, test cases, and later during operations, maintenance programmers and production support people will need to know how to revise or repair the product. The requirements are initially a living document used to communicate to the project team, but are later used for knowledge transfer after the product is released.

  For agile projects, the testers and developers must understand the use case enough to be able to estimate how long it will take them to test and code that requirement. If they can't, it usually means the BA must go back and get more info, or rewrite it so that it can be coded and tested.[5] Worse yet, the developers or testers may make assumptions about what the unclear requirement means, and code the wrong implementation or test case.

- *Traceable:* The RTM is the control and tracking collection point in which the use case is traced back to the feature and enclosing workflow. Later, the RTM shows what test cases are associated with a particular use case, and when the use case is completed. Some teams find it valuable to also put the object model classes into the RTM. The RTM is key to localizing defects and change management, all enabled by use case traceability.

These specification factors looks like a long and tedious list to keep track of when writing a simple use case, but they are all contained in the use case template. One merely needs to follow the structure of that one page form and usually the use case meets all needs. Remember that after the use case template is filled out and approved, it is still a focal point for team and customer discussion and revision; but having the initial use case first will avoid much rework at the coding and testing level.

Develop the UX Artifact

A user experience (UX) artifact is a piece of design, the behavior or appearance evident from the user interface (UI) of the product. This contributes to the user's experience, which is a psychology reaction to how the user interacts with the product. The artifact is what the user sees; the user experience is how the user "feels." Sometimes a computer-knowledgeable cognitive psychologist or professional user experience designer assists with the design to ensure a positive user experience, but a good BA will have enough UX development experience to build good UX artifacts. I will use the term *UX artifact* to mean the actual piece of UI design, such as screen or report layout, but realize that the artifact is not the experience itself.

The SME and BA have the option of drafting a proposed UX artifact during Iteration 0, or later when the use case will be implemented, depending on how proactive the SME is. Only a proposed UX artifact can be built because building a UX artifact is a design step. It describes how something appears, or how a layout is defined. The designer (or team) must be involved during the implementation iteration to introduce what technology can bring to the final UX artifact solution. The final artifact must be approved by at least the SME before construction, but it will be approved by all the stakeholders in its implemented form at the user demo.

Figure 7-6 shows a sample UX artifact: the layout and labeled data elements of the transaction receipt. In this case, it is the "Deposit to Primary Checking" transaction, but it can contain whatever transaction applies.

---

[5]Bad estimates may also mean that the team doesn't have enough experience, or enough experience in that domain yet. Breaking the use case down into user stories also helps to estimate because the scope is smaller. See Chapter 9 for more on estimating an iteration's scope.

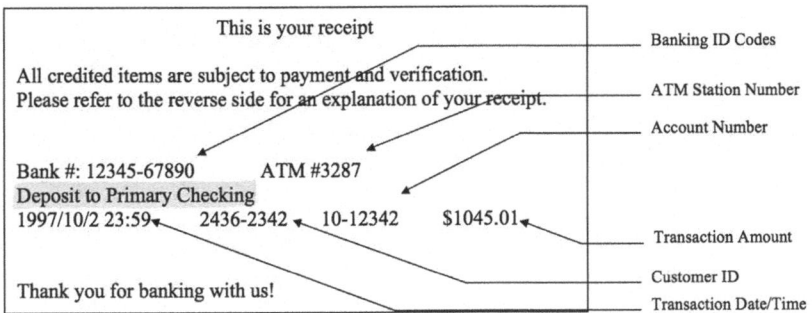

Figure 7-6. Sample UX artifact–UX01. Transaction receipt.

> ■ **Note**   The transaction name is replaced in the highlighted area. For a withdraw, the text should say "Withdraw from Savings Account," or "Withdraw from Checking Account".

Start the Requirements Traceability Matrix (RTM)

The RTM is critical to many aspects of a successful project. As the BA completes a use case, she records each feature, workflow, associated use cases and UX artifacts in the RTM. The RTM is a combined feature catalog, use case catalog, and UX map that also works as a control document for change management, confirming completeness, and defect detection. It will be expanded as the iterations proceed. The RTM is stored in the shared documentation repository for all project team members to review and use.

Table 7-1 illustrates a sample of a partial RTM. The features shown are in priority order, and are mapped to use cases, which are mapped to associated UX artifacts. Except for UC 1, Initialize ATM, each use case has a UX artifact, from which the user triggers the transaction (use case). Compare with the use cases numbered in Figure 7-4.

Table 7-1. Partial RTM for ATM Project

Priority	Feature	UC #	User	Use Cases	UX
1	Authenticate customer and authorize access to account	3	Admin	Login	UX00. Welcome screen
2	Reconcile transactions)	8	Admin	Get Reconcilement report	UX01. Recon report format and sample
		2	Admin	Terminate ATM	UX00. Welcome screen
3	Deposit funds to checking or savings account	4	Customer	Deposit Funds	UX02. Transaction menu
4	Withdraw money from checking or savings account	6	Customer	Withdraw Money	UX02. Transaction menu
5	Transfer funds between account	7	Customer	Transfer Funds	UX02. Transaction menu
6	Inquire Balance of accounts	5	Customer	Get Balance Inquiry	UX02. Transaction menu
7	Load cash into ATM	1	Admin	Initialize ATM	None

Notes: Difference in priority between features and UC# are due to dependencies

By using a spreadsheet,[6] the use cases can easily be sorted in use case priority, designated by the UC number. Use case 1 represents business priority 7 (the stakeholders don't care about the startup of the machine) but the machine must be running before anything else can be working (dependency), so the team decided that UC 1 and UC 2 would be implemented first.

UC 1 allows the Admin to load cash into the cashbox, start up the machine physically, download new and updated user accounts, and initialize the log. UC 2 must upload the transactions log and shut down properly. This symmetry provides the minimal level of functionality, similar to the popular Hello World programs that establish that all support and linkages are in place.

Feature 2 "Reconcile transactions" is broken into two use cases: UC 8 "Get Reconcilement Report," which matches the funds in the deposits box with those reported by the machine; and UC 2 "Terminate ATM," which shuts down the machine and updates the external banking system. The report will be fully functional after all transactions are working; alternatively, the reconcilement report could have been augmented from the log file after each transaction was implemented.

The UC 3 "Login" use case)is listed before the customer transactions UC 4 to UC 7. UC 4 "Deposit" is paired with UC 5 "Get Balance Inquiry" because now the customer will have a balance to check. UC 6 "Withdraw Money" and UC 7 "Transfer Funds" (between two accounts) are done in order of complexity. UC 3 "Login" does not provide business value, but it is a dependency before the demand transactions are permitted. Alternatively, the team could have added login afterward, but since authorization is the number-one priority, the team can show the login functionality at the user demo.

Repeat Through the Features Catalog

After all the use cases for the first workflow/feature have been defined, detailed, and recorded, they can be put aside for the developers when Iteration 1 starts. The BA and business SME now move onto the next feature and workflow. Many features will overlap workflows, so the same workflow may be revisited over time as the prioritized features dictate. It is not important if some of the detailed use cases are left undefined, and not important if not all the use cases summaries are detailed when Iteration 1 starts; but it is important that the developers and testers have at least a few use cases to work in Iteration 1.

PMI Parallels

Only a few PMI knowledge areas have relevant key differences for initial requirements elicitation: scope, schedule (time), and stakeholder management.

Scope: Requirements and scoping is one area that agile diverges in practice from traditional methods, but not in principle. The principle is use progressive elaboration to decompose scope; the practice is *when* that is done. Agile scope is broken down into a prioritized list (non-hierarchical) scope, then further decomposed into middle-sized tasks (thin-thread use cases), and then later, just before implementation, decomposed further into small activities (user stories or detailed use cases). In traditional projects, this work is done in detail before design and coding start; for agile projects, a handful of use cases are defined and implemented while further scope decomposition is done iteratively.

---

[6]There are tools that easily convert spreadsheet lists like the RTM into online electronic "3×5 cards" that allow the team to work in whatever format they prefer.

Schedule: The schedule is pre-defined as time-boxed iterations, but the actual scope is deferred until the team is ready to construct and test it. However, Agile adds the team·velocity concept as a way of predicting when both the iteration scope and product scope will be completed. The Agile final schedule, built incrementally, is based on history, and is therefore more accurate.

Stakeholder management: The PMI has recognized the sociological aspects of project management, and now includes Human Resources (team dynamics), Communications, and Stakeholder Management BOKs as part of its PMP and PMI-ACP training. Agile takes into account team dynamics and sociology much more than traditional project management did, and it is making much of the difference.

Conclusion

This chapter described how the business analyst elicits high-level (initial) requirements from the business SMEs, decomposing the most valuable from the prioritized product backlog into a series of related use cases. After a few use cases are defined and recorded in the use case catalog, the BA elaborates each use case into a detailed use case, which complies with the IEEE criteria for a requirements specification.

If a high-quality product is important, an extra effort to reduce requirements defects to practically zero, the BA can rigorously validate the use cases with an object model and sequence diagrams. Since requirements defects are the greatest cause of product defects, it seems that this rigorous quality approach is always justified, but some agile teams prefer to code and rework after they know more about the product, even though that approach takes longer.

The APM collects features from the stakeholders and helps them prioritize those features for business-value, risk, dependencies, and other factors. The feature catalog is developed for the product as known to date. As soon as the feature catalog is prioritized, the BA decomposes each feature, in priority order, into one or more use case summaries in the use case catalog. (Some agile BA's would convert to user stories, instead). The BA should start the initial requirements elicitation and decomposition process in Iteration 0 so that some detailed use cases are ready for the development team at the beginning of Iteration 1.

Additional Tools

The form below is the use case template I prefer. Its fields are explained below the form. An example of how to use the form was given in Figure 7-5 above.

UC# Use Case Name		
Actor		
Objective		
Pre-conditions		
Post-Conditions		
Invariants		
Detailed Description		
Step	Actor	System Response
1		
2		
3		
4		
5		
Input Data		
Output Data		
Notes		

Figure 7-7. *Use case template*

Descriptions

Each use case requirement conforms to all the characteristics in 4.3 of IEEE Standard 830-1993. Specific requirements are to be cross-referenced to earlier documents that relate. All requirements must be uniquely identifiable. Usually, a use case should not take more than three pages.

- *UC# (use case number)*: Enter the number, used for reference purposes, of the Use Case from the use case catalog, which reflects the stakeholder priority of the use case.

- *Use case name*: The name of the use case, as an imperative (e.g., Add Permit to Reference File, or Withdraw Cash from Account)

- *Objective*: A brief description what the actor will accomplish in executing the use case. Use non-technical language.

- *Actor*: The actor of the system that plays a specific role and drives the use case. Actors may also be external systems. There is rarely more than one actor per use case.

- *Pre-conditions*: The starting conditions that must hold true for the Use Case to be applicable, and made false at the completion of the use case. If multiple pre-conditions are included, the author must specify if all pre-conditions are true (logical AND), or any one or more of the pre-conditions are true (logical OR). Subcases may pre-condition the use case that they are in.

- *Post-conditions*: The final state guaranteed to hold true after completion of the use case that was false before the use case started. If multiple post-conditions are included, the author must specify if all post-conditions are true (logical AND), or any one or more of the post-conditions are true (logical OR). Subcases may post-condition the use case that they are in.

- *Invariant*: The state that is maintained throughout the use case. It is true before the use case starts, and still true after the use case finishes. Only the relevant informative invariants are listed (there are an infinite number of invariants, but not all are relevant.)

- *Detailed description*: The sequence of steps explaining how the use case is performed. The use case steps are written as unambiguous imperative statements to describe the interaction between the actor and the system, without explaining the design of the system. Refer to the [Friedman] for a list of unambiguous words. All conditional (IF-THEN-ELSE) situations should be explained except for error conditions that require minor or obvious handling. Large amounts of detail may be included in the "Additional Tools" section and referenced here. The first step describes what the actor does to trigger the use case.

- *Input data*: A summary list of all external data needed for the use case to be performed. All data elements listed here must be directly or implicitly identified in the detail description. All data elements must be defined as either required or optional. Optional data is placed within parenthesis; default values are placed within square brackets.

- *Output data*: Enter a list of all data produced by the use case execution. All data elements listed here must be directly produced and documented in the detail description. All data elements must be defined as either required or optional. Optional data is placed within parenthesis; default values are placed within square brackets.

- *Notes*: Any other relevant information not included in the preceding sections. Workflow issues and design issues that the author does not want to forget may be recorded here for later use. Open issues may be put here pending their inclusion into the issues log.

■ ■ ■

PART III

Iteration 1 to N

CHAPTER 8

■ ■ ■

Overview of an Agile Iteration

At this point in the product development life, the project has been selected, a sponsor is funding the project, and the business stakeholders have identified their expectations. Within our limited knowledge at this point, the project constraints (scope, schedule, cost, quality, and others) and the product's feature catalog are defined as best as can be.

Iteration 0 was completed last chapter. The developers have their computers for coding and testing. A shared repository, tools, and other infrastructure elements are in place. The business analyst has a prioritized use case catalog and RTM. A release plan of fixed iteration time boxes was developed and a user demo is scheduled in two weeks. The project team is ready to start the first productive iteration. This chapter describes what happens during that iteration, and during the ones that follow.

The approach described in this chapter is a high-level overview of work done within each iteration. It is the core work of an agile team, and explains the threads of activity for requirements, development, testing, and project management. Each subsequent chapter will follow each thread in more detail, and explain the role-specific techniques from that perspective.

The Agile Approach

There is no definitive prescribed "standard agile process," and to attempt that would go against the philosophy of agile. There are many processes—Scrum, XP, Crystal, DSDM, and others—tailored patterns based on agile's tools and values by which a team can build a product. Agile methods are highly tailored for the team, the product, and the culture.

The agile iteration approach described shortly is one of many, and is more conservative than used in many agile projects, but is a good first pass at using agile methods in a traditional environment. It employs a balance between rigor, speed, and short-cycle feedback consistent with the current agile culture, allows a clean mapping between traditional methods at the release level, and agile tracking and tasking at the iteration level.

It is not the only agile process that can be used, but it is a combination of the principles behind any teamwork following agile principles. The process described exemplifies the core process of all the successful agile projects I have run in the last 15 years as an agile project manager. However, in all cases it has resulted in zero-defect products released periodically, within budget, and on time. It should make a good first pass from which your team can apply, modify, and complete a successful project.

Agile Team Roles

Agile teamwork is a melee of requirements, analysis, design, coding, and testing tasks happening almost at the same time. This chapter contains an overview of the roles of *agile project manager* (APM), *business analyst* (BA), *developer*, *tester*, and *business SME* working within the agile process. Each agile role is a high-level exemplar to describe a collection of skill sets and responsibilities.

Details on each role are described in its own role-specific chapter later: business analyst for requirements (see Chapter 9); developers for design, coding, and unit testing (see Chapter 10); testers for integration, GUI, regression testing, and QA (see Chapter 11); and the PM for team integration, monitoring, and reporting (see Chapter 12).

There are specific skill sets that should be employed that are typically associated with roles. In the overview that follows, the tasks are organized around roles but keep in mind that *anyone on the team may fill one or more of the roles*. Also, not everyone is as experienced in one set of skills as another. In describing the duties of every role, this book will enable individual team members to better perform their own role by making them better aware of the tasks involved. During the agile practice of pairing, team members improve their skills too.

Before we proceed, I need to make a few comments about the general role descriptions.

Some agile teams do not consider project managers as members of the agile team. Some agile teams have a team member called an *agile coach*, who has similar skills within the team as a traditional project manager has outside the team. Both the traditional project manager and the agile coach role are considered here as part of the *agile project manager* role.

The developer role includes several technical specializations. An agile developer may be a programmer, a designer, a database analyst, a web page designer, a network engineer, and so forth. When a task is described as, "Developer designs the UI interface," the word "developer" may refer to a user interface expert, a psychologist, a web designer, or a programmer. All will be referred to as an agile developer.

Similarly, the tester role includes GUI tester, integration tester, test code writer, QA manager, and other distinctions below the level of discussion for this chapter.

Traditionally, people with different skills sets are brought together from different functional departments into a single projectized team. For example, instead of a business analyst being a dedicated member of the team, the BA works on multiple projects concurrently, and can only spend, say, one half day twice a week with the agile team. Role-in-transition resources like this cause process bottlenecks when that person is not available; they also cause functional silos because they are disconnected from the team ("give me the input, and I'll get back to you next week"). It degrades the personal ownership and focus of a dedicated resource to the product because that resource is moving between several projects at once. Multitasking problems also arise, which are discussed in Chapter 10.

⚡ Warning Agile thinking wants to avoid the silos and bottlenecks of role delineation, so some agile practices teach that there are no specific roles reserved for PM, BA, testing, or developing: everyone on the team can do everything.

This is an overreaction, and is not practical. It is extremely unlikely that that one person has the skills to do every single job required on the team, and even more unlikely that you will have a team of these super-people. Imagine a group of people who cannot write code or tests getting together and saying, "There are no roles. Let's all pitch in and build this product." The logical extension of this pseudo-agile thinking would disband the professions of business analysis, project management, and testing—eliminating those programs from university curricula—and let everyone be trained as an agile developer. Moreover, programmer training would not be needed if no special skills were needed, and everyone could build software. I don't think the agilistas would agree with this scenario. (If agile developer training included the skills of BA, PM, tester, and developer, then perhaps it would make some sense for agile projects of the future, but currently, that kind of omni-training doesn't exist.)

I have seen teams with developers trying to collect requirements or perform formal testing, and they do it poorly. Not every individual on the team has all the needed skillsets, or the inclination, to do every task needed to build a product. An agile team is an empowered team of *multidisciplined* people who have multiple perspectives. If everyone on the team is a developer, and thinks like a developer, then one perspective is involved; arguably that is not an agile team. This is especially true if the team is *forced* into a single-role configuration because of a particular dogma.

Agile teams evolve naturally to a higher skill set for all. Agile teams may start off avoiding specific roles—all members work on the product tasks as they can. Eventually, the team realizes that one team member does one task better than another, and likes that task better than other tasks, and two members work together on the same task. Eventually, the team has naturally selected itself into the best configuration of roles for that team. This effect is a key agile practice, and is called a *self-organizing* team. As the team evolves through the stages of forming, storming, norming, and performing, their skill set improves to an average accumulated minimum but focused on individually-preferred roles.

Now that we have described how the agile team roles are defined, we can move on to what they need to do during an iteration. The next step is to move some of the prioritize features defined in Iteration 0 to what will be done during the iteration.

Product Backlog to Iteration Backlog

The *product backlog* contains the prioritized features and use cases that are to be implemented. Even if not everything is known, scope can be added, revised, or removed. The *iteration backlog* contains the scenarios (typically use cases or user stories) that will be implemented during the current iteration. The iteration backlog contains the more detailed and higher priority items from the top of the product backlog, and reflects the timing of implementation.

The first batch of use cases were identified before Iteration 1 started. The BA converted features into use cases, placing them into the use case catalog, during Iteration 0. During Iteration 1 to N, the BA refines use cases into detailed use cases with UX artifacts. The team breaks the use case into comprising user stories (*disassociation*) and estimates how many use cases (or stories) they can do within the current iteration. The BA tracks the use cases per feature in the Requirements Traceability Matrix (RTM).

✖ **Metaphor**   Refining features into detailed use cases or user stories is like making batches of cookies. The stakeholders fill a huge cask with cookie batter (*product backlog*), and the BA extracts some of it into a smaller bowl (*use case catalog*), adding walnuts, raisins, chocolate chips, or other variations (*detailed use case*). During the baking process (*iteration*), the team scoops out final dough onto a cookie sheet a few at a time (*iteration backlog*) to make eatable-sized cookies (*user story*). The size of the cookie sheet (team's capacity or *team velocity*) determines how many cookies can be baked at a time. The BA must keep enough cookie sheet dough available while refining the dough from cask to bowl.

Iteration Process Overview

This section describes the work of the team within the iteration process flow. The iteration starts with the initial iteration meeting: iteration planning. The "Box Numbers" in each heading refers to the boxes in Figures 8-1 and 8-2. The following subsections correspond to the boxes shown in Figures 8-1 and 8-2. Each box is described for a general understanding of the flow through an iteration. Beneath each Box description is a table that shows who facilitates the task, what the task is, what is needed (inputs), and what the task accomplished (outputs). Chapters 9 through 12 give a more detailed perspective of the flow for the BA, Developer, Tester, and APM, respectively.

Each iteration within the agile approach contains detailed requirements, analysis, design, coding, and testing tasks. After the team has completed all user stories, the current portion of the product, or the *build*, is delivered to the user for acceptance. Each completed build should be production-ready for the accumulated scope of the current iteration.

Agile teams focus on one or two use cases at a time, but various aspects of a use case aren't completed at the same time. When the BA finishes one use case, he or she returns to the iteration backlog to work the next use case. When the developer finishes coding one use case, he or she returns to the next approved detailed use case. When the tester finishes writing test scripts, he or she may return to the next approved detailed use case while waiting for a new build to test. These parallel efforts result in two or more use cases being worked concurrently as the people are ready to take on more work. Sometimes one person with the requisite skill set will jump roles and help another team member if they are behind.

To keep the overview simple, terms like story points and two-week iterations are assumed; other metrics could be used, such as ideal hours instead of story points, or three-week iterations instead of two. Do not focus too heavily on the specific terms; they are flexible.

Caveat   The roles shown in the swimlane diagrams in Figures 8-1 and 8-2 are matched with the traditional Responsibility Assignment Matrix (RAM), shown as in Table 8-1. The CORA matrix attempts to explain the workings of an agile team within the traditional context with which PMs may be familiar. The team workings are much more dynamic and interactive, but I can only explain the processes sequentially. *Please consider this overview as a teaching aid, and not a prescriptive agile process.*

Roles are loose in agile, so CORA should be read loosely. The **owner** role means that that person should initiate the meeting, but only as facilitator at most—there is no command-and-control leadership. **contributors** help build the artifacts, and **reviewers** look over the artifact for correctness and understanding; they probably have to use the artifacts for development to proceed. **Approvers** can reject an artifact and are responsible for the correctness of the artifact. Business SMEs are usually approvers.

Table 8-1. *CORA Matrix for Iteration Flow Tasks*

Box Nbr	Activity	APM	Business SME	Business Analyst	Developer	Integration Tester	GUI Tester
1	Iteration Planning meeting	O, A	R	C	C	C	C
2	Develop detailed use cases	R	A	O	R	R	R
3	Validate use case with object model			O, A	R	R	R
4	Develop design cases w/UX artifacts	R	A	C	O	R	R
5	Develop GUI test scripts			R	R	C	O, A
6	Develop integration test scripts			R	R	O, A	C
7	Implement use cases and unit test				O, A		
8	Run regression tests				O, A	C	
9	Transfer build	R			C	O, A	
10	Run GUI tests		R	R		C	O, A
11	Code and run integration tests					O, A	C
12	Run QA and regression tests	R				O, A	C
13	Defect/change meeting	C	R	C	C	O	C
14	Approve build	O		A	A	A	A
15	Build iteration and QA reports	O	R		C	C	C
16	User demo	O	A	C	C	C	C
17	Stage or Release build	A	R	C	O	C	C

C=Contributes, O=Owner, R=Reviews, A=Approves

Iteration Planning (Box 1)

At the beginning of the iteration, the team holds an *iteration planning* session. The meeting allows the team to estimate the size of each use case relative to each other, and to determine how many use cases can be completed by the end of the iteration. Box 1 of Figure 8-1 is in the Technical Team swim lane because the entire team is involved in the planning.

Each role has something to contribute to the estimation—analysis, design, coding, and testing all factor into estimating the relative size of the iteration's scope. The BA may need to revise the detailed use case for clarity, or propose a user experience (UX) artifact for it. Testers need to extract the user stories from each use case to identify the test data needed and build test cases. Developers need to design the UX artifacts, write the code and unit tests, and implement the use case. The team must come to a consensus on the relative size of each use case or constituent user story.

After each use case is sized, and placed one at a time into the iteration backlog, the team decides *how many* use cases from the use case catalog can be implemented by the end of the iteration. The stakeholders' priorities determine *which* use cases are selected for a particular iteration, adjusted for dependencies (which can be added) and risk. Each set of use cases in the iteration backlog focuses on what the next user demo will display.

Once a handful of use cases (or stories) are sized, the team must determine how many they will commit to completing by the end of the iteration. The APM provides the team velocity so that the team knows how much scope they have completed during previous iterations. The team must not commitment to more than their average velocity from previous iterations. (The team can always add more stories later if they finish their commitment, but they should not promise more than they have done in the past.)

When the estimating is completed, each person self-assigns at least one card to themselves. Each user story in the iteration backlog is written on a "card" on the iteration task board, with the story's size, the name of the person who volunteered to work the first task for it.

Iteration planning sessions in later iterations will also include new items that were added to the product backlog during the course of this iteration, approved change requests that have been worked into the use case catalog, and any defects that were deferred out of the iteration in which they were found.

The team leaves with a list of all the use cases to which they committed to show in the user demo. Iteration planning meetings take about two hours.

BOX #	OWNER	INPUT	PROCESS	OUTPUT
1	APM	Selected prioritized detailed use cases (user stories if available)	Iteration Planning (scope estimation)	Committed and prioritized list of use cases to complete

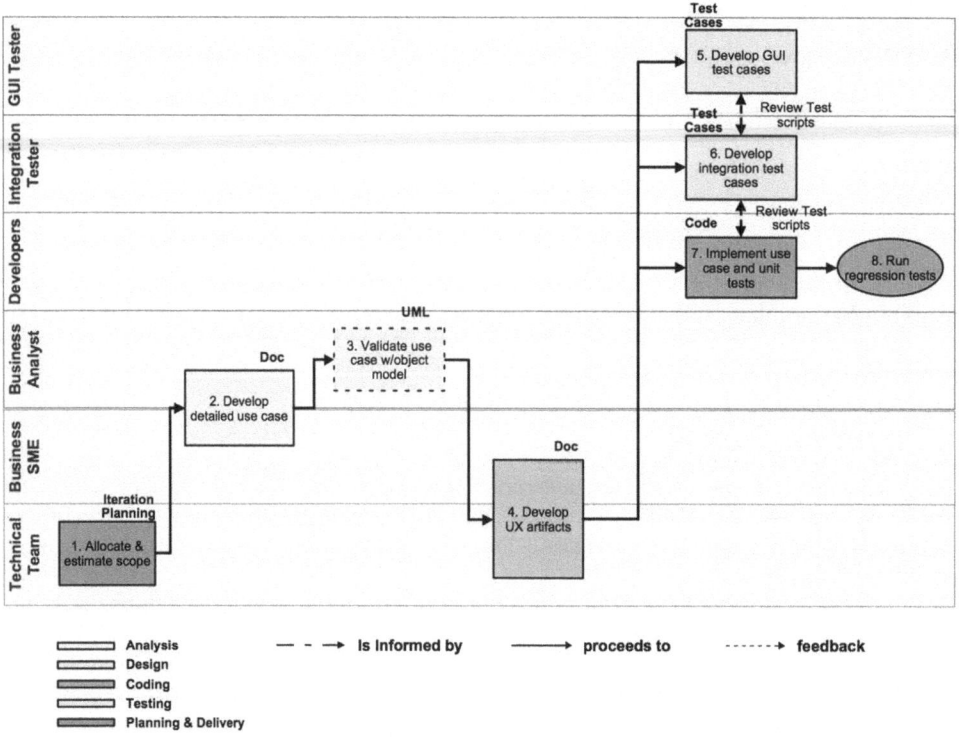

Figure 8-1. *Agile iteration flow (first half); develop detailed use case (Box 2)*

Each use case in the use case catalog needs to be expanded into a detailed use case. Hopefully, this was finished before the iteration started, but sometimes not. (User stories are extracted from the detailed use cases by a process Mike Cohn likes to call *disaggregation,* typically done by the developers).

The business analyst (BA) meets with the business SME and progressively elaborates the highest priority use case in the iteration backlog. Working together, they expand the use case summary into a *detailed use case.* Box 2 in Figure 8-1 overlaps the BA and business SME swim lanes because both are actively involved in this step.

BOX #	OWNER	INPUT	PROCESS	OUTPUT
2	BA	Highest priority use case from iteration backlog	Expand use case into detailed use case (scope refinement)	Un-validated detailed use case

Validate Use Case with an Object Model (Box 3)

The next step is optional, as indicated by the dotted line around Box 3 in Figure 8-1. Use case validation of this kind should be used on complex applications, and are probably not necessary for a simpler product, like displaying a straightforward series of web pages.

Use cases are requirements decomposed using functional (procedural) logic. Object models are decomposed using scope-of-control logic. These decomposition techniques are independent but consistent with each other. A use case validation consists of three artifacts: the use case (procedural), the UML class diagram of the problem domain (scope-of-control), and the XUML[1] sequence diagram that ties them together. When all three artifacts are consistent, then the result is a *validated object model,* and the use case is proven *correct* (see more information in Chapter 9).

XUML validation is an elicitation feedback mechanism. The validation exercise often triggers more questions to the business SME to resolve the inconsistencies and omissions. It is quicker and less expensive to catch the requirements defects here than during coding and testing.

BOX #	OWNER	INPUT	PROCESS	OUTPUT
3	BA	Detailed use case	Validate use case at analysis level with UML (scope validation)	Valid (revised) use case and object model: UML class diagram and XUML sequence diagram

Develop UX Artifacts (Box 4)

User experience (UX) artifacts are mock-ups to show behavior, appearance, information requirements, and navigational flows. They contain and define the widgets[2] needed to allow the user to control the product. UX artifacts may also refer to mock report layouts.

The business analyst presents user experience (UX) artifacts; for example, screenshots and report layouts, and their associated detailed use case for review. The testers and developers review the requirements to ensure that they are testable: all data included, all behavior defined, default and field lengths defined, and other implementation details defined. The BA must revise any of the requirements that are insufficient for the testers to use to test the use case, or insufficient for the developers to build the use case.

---

[1]XUML refers to extended UML notation. It augments standard UML sequence diagrams with data flows, and uses a slightly more concise notation to put more on the page.

[2]"Widget" is a general term for any of the GUI mechanisms to control the user interface: buttons, drop-down boxes, menu configuration, check boxes, dialog boxes, and so forth.

Box 4 overlaps the team and business SME's swim lanes to show that the technical team and the Business SME are involved. The developers need enough information to build the code and unit test it, and they have the knowledge to know how the UX artifact may best be implemented. The testers need enough information of a different kind to write the GUI and integration test cases. The BA or APM must discuss any changes with the SME that may affect the (other) stakeholders' expectations. The business SME is committing to his or her business needs being understood.

The developer (user interface designer) refines the detailed use case with design ideas, how it will work within the system, and how the interface will look and feel. The user experience (UX) artifacts and design features are stand-alone documents, but are referenced by the use case. These two tasks—elaborating the use case with design and defining the UX—need to be done almost concurrently.

The analysis and design review of the use case and associated UX artifact(s) is a form of Quality Gate. The team decides whether the use case should move forward to construction, or be revised.

BOX #	OWNER	INPUT	PROCESS	OUTPUT
4	Developer	Detailed use case	Design user interface, screen shots, and augment use case with implementation ideas. (initial design)	Design case, with UX artifacts

⚷ Key Point: Concurrency   After the design case is approved, the flow splits into two parallel paths: one for testers and the other for developers. The testers build test scripts from the design case, and the developers write code and unit tests for the design case. Concurrency ensures that the tests are written and tested independently, and are based on the requirements and not the code. One Forrester researcher called it *parallelism*, an important improvement to agile practices (Gualtieri 2011).

Develop GUI Test Cases (Box 5)

GUI testing ensures that the user experience is as the business requested or better, and focuses on the appearance and behavior of the user interface. A *test script* describes a particular test: pre-conditions for the test, predefined input data, expected behavior, verification procedures, post-conditions, and expected output data values. A *GUI test script* focuses on the user experience testing. A *test case*, or simply a *test*, is an abstraction of the test script, test execution, and target being tested.

The GUI testers write GUI test scripts from the approved design case. The GUI tester identifies all paths of the use case (user stories), and writes tests scripts for the user interface defined in the UX artifact. All GUI test cases are recorded in the RTM when they are written, and associated with the use case being tested. All GUI test cases become part of standard regression testing.

Some agile testers do not write automated scripts for GUI tests, and perhaps it is not necessary except for complicated and large systems. However, it is essential that the test cases are identified, so that none are inadvertently omitted. The RTM helps the tester ensure that all tests are identified and tracked.

GUI tests are informed by integration tests and the code, so the GUI tester reviews the test scripts with the integration tester and developer as part of developing GUI test cases.

BOX #	OWNER	INPUT	PROCESS	OUTPUT
5	GUI Tester	design case (UX artifacts and detailed use case)	Identify all test cases and expected results for GUI testing (test identification)	GUI test scripts, updated RTM

Develop Integration Test Cases (Box 6)

For agile, an *integration test* is an automated *thin-thread test*.[3] It exercises all the objects and methods along a single path of a use case, and verifies the flow's expected responses. The integration test assumes that all the units (objects) are working correctly, and runs them in sequence: the connections (API) between object methods are being tested to ensure that they pass and receive data between them correctly.

An integration test *script* is a text version to define the integration test, and focuses on a use case or *user story*, which is a single unconditional path through a use case.[4] Each integration test starts from "behind" the user interface (closer to the system than the user), executes through the system along the user story path, and ends at the use story's output point "behind" the user interface. Chapter 5 shows how integration tests "plug-in" to the CIV component, simulate the GUI data, and compare responses that return from the CIV plug-in point. The system thinks that all the test data is coming from, or going to, the GUI.

Integration tests are informed by GUI tests and the code, so the integration tester reviews the test scripts with the GUI tester and developer as part of developing integration test cases.

If the validating XUML sequence diagrams are available, the integration tests are much easier to write. The scripts are written together in preparation for when the build is available for testing (Box 9).

BOX #	OWNER	INPUT	PROCESS	OUTPUT
6	Integration Tester	Design use case, optional sequence diagrams	Identify all test cases for integration testing (test identification)	Integration test scripts, updated RTM

Implement Use Case and Unit Tests (Box 7)

At the same time that the testers are writing the test scripts, the developer will *implement* that use case; that is, write the code and unit test for it. Code is written one user story at a time because a use case is usually too large to code directly. A user story is short and has a single clear objective.

Code and unit tests are informed by the GUI and integration tests. The developer reviews the code and unit tests with the testers before writing the code.

Assumedly, the developer is using test-driven development (TDD), which means he or she writes a very small test, and then writes the code to get that test to pass. The whole process takes a couple of minutes. Next, the developer augments the unit test and code to make *that* test pass. After a series of such test-code-test cycles, the user story is complete. The developer submits the code and associated tests to the *shared code base*, the team-shared repository for all code, tests, and technical documents. The developer repeats the same cycle for other user stories in the use case until the entire use case is complete. It is easy to submit *something* to the shared code base daily.

All unit tests are added to the automated regression test suite.

---

[3]For more detail of thin-thread testing, and a contrast with alternative traditional methods, see Chapter 11.
[4]For more information and a comparison between use cases and user stories, see Chapter 10.

BOX #	OWNER	INPUT	PROCESS	OUTPUT
7	Developer	Approved use case w/UX artifacts	Write code and unit tests for all user stories in use case. (Construction)	Code and unit tests per use case; updated regression suite; updated RTM

Run Regression Tests (Box 8)

Automated regression tests consist of all integration and unit tests built and that passed earlier for the build. After each user story is completed, the developer runs the automated regression tests to ensure that old code was not "broken" by the new code; that is, did not cause new defects. If something was broken, the developer repairs that code, old or new. The regression test will also cover all the other developers' code and unit tests that are downloaded each day.

After the automated regression tests pass for every user story in the use case, the developer updates the use case as "code complete" in the RTM, and the date it was completed. (A use case is not considered "complete" until all tests for it have passed.) The developer uploads any revised code and associated unit test cases to the shared codebase.

Today's continuous improvement tools automate the build process with full regression testing, compliance checking, and configuring, as part of the code submission process. The iteration flow is continued in Figure 8-2.

BOX #	OWNER	INPUT	PROCESS	OUTPUT
8	Developer	Use case code and regression test suite	Run automated regression tests until they pass. (Construction validation)	Regression test results; updated RTM; latest build

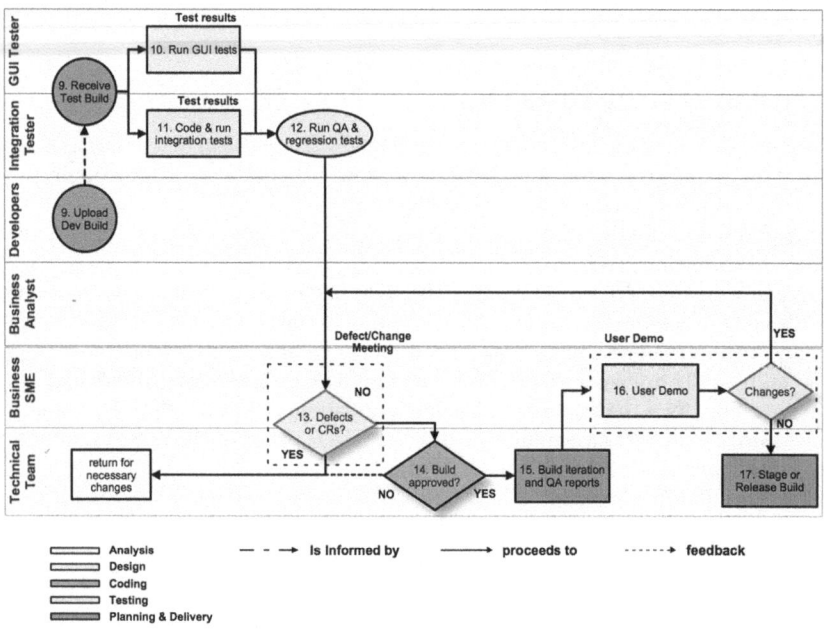

Figure 8-2. *Agile iteration flow (second half)*

Transfer the Build (Box 9)

After the developers think the build is as good as they can get it for the latest use case, with all unit and regression tests passed and compliant in any other standards, they submit (*upload*) the development build to the shared code base and mark it as QA ready. The testers download the build to run their tests against it after all integration tests are written and the RTM is updated.

Most likely, the integration test cases have already been written and added to the RTM because it takes less time to define the test cases than for the developers to code the use case. The team's daily meeting informs everyone which use cases are available for testing, which ones are waiting on coding, and which are not.

One of the testers downloads the build (called the *development build* because it is from the development environment) onto the test environment. The development build is called the *test build* once it moves to the test environment. It is isolated from the developers. The developers can continue to upgrade the development build with new use cases, but it doesn't affect the test build in the parallel environment.

When is the development build ready to become the test build?

- When the developers have (1) written all the code for the use case; (2) written all the unit tests for the use case code; (3) the development build passed all the regression tests 100%; and (4) the "code complete" date is recorded in the RTM for the use case.

- When the testers have (1) written the GUI test scripts; (2) written the integration test scripts; and (3) both sets of test cases are recorded in the RTM for the use case.

- When the test machine is ready for testing.

BOX #	OWNER	INPUT	PROCESS	OUTPUT
9	Tester	Development build	Download last build for testing purposes.	Test build

Run GUI Tests (Box 10)

The GUI tester runs the GUI tests against the test build. GUI testing is fairly quick to do. Failed tests are recorded in the defect log, and passed tests are recorded in the RTM with the date the tests passed. All GUI tests are added to the GUI regression test suite, which for manual testing is often merely a document binder.

BOX #	OWNER	INPUT	PROCESS	OUTPUT
10	GUI Tester	Test build, GUI test scripts	Run GUI test scripts (UX validation)	Defect log; updated RTM; update GUI regression test suite

Code and Run Integration Tests (Box 11)

After the integration test scripts are written, the integration tester writes the *integration test code* for the latest use case. The code is written from the integration test scripts, and run against the test build. Testers should not test against the development build, which is more volatile and can interfere with the expected test results.

Writing the integration test code takes longer than running GUI tests, so the GUI testers and integration testers generally do not have a conflict trying to test at the same time.

Running the automated integration test is much faster than running GUI tests—usually only a couple of minutes. The test build can be tested much faster than the developers can write new production code, so the testers are usually waiting for the next build for repairs or new functionality.

Failed tests are recorded in the defect log, and passed tests are recorded in the RTM with the date the tests passed. All integration tests are added to the regression test suite.

BOX #	OWNER	INPUT	PROCESS	OUTPUT
11	Integration tester	Test build, Integration test scripts	Write integration code and run integration test scripts (functional validation)	Defect log; updated RTM; automated build tests

Variant The testers may not have the ability or skills to write test code. For example, writing automated test code in JUnit is similar to writing product code in Java, and testers are typically not developers. A developer may write the integration tests in JUnit instead as long as it is not the same developer who wrote the product code under test. Under the agile paradigm, the integration tester should learn to write in JUnit, or whatever test language is appropriate.

Run QA and Regression Tests (Box 12)

After all defects for the test build have been repaired (or deferred), the build is ready for user demo and possible release. The tester runs the regression test suite one last time, and the QA compliance tests, before giving it the seal of approval. Any defects at this point are likely compliance issues, and those usually can be repaired quickly.

The tester should run each of the following kinds of tests.

- *Automated regression tests* (unit tests and integration tests) are run to ensure that nothing has changed since the last time the build was tested. Any "breakage" (new defects of old existing code) is recorded in the defect log as a regression defect, and the original pass date is removed (or annotated). Automated regression testing should take only a few minutes.

- *GUI testing* must be regression tested, but GUI tests are tedious and sometime laborious to run if they are not automated. Consequently, GUI regression testing is performed periodically, usually every third iteration. At the very least, the product must be GUI regression tested before release, and given a quick sanity check before the next user demo.

- *RTM update verification:* A tester or the APM checks through the RTM to see if all committed use cases have been implemented and tested, with pass dates. A use case is not complete until all its tests pass. Of course, this assumes that all the tests have been written.

- *QA compliance testing:* QA compliance testing includes other kinds of verifications: style-checkers (ensuring code complies with team standards), automatic documenters (such as ensuring appropriate Javadoc comments were included), all defect log entries are closed as expected, and other tools are run (e.g., performance or profiler tools) to ensure that all standards have been followed. Some QA tests are automated, and others use manual checklists. If a compliance test fails, the tester writes an action item to bring the build back into compliance, and mentions it as a "blocker" at the next daily meeting.

BOX #	OWNER	INPUT	PROCESS	OUTPUT
12	Integration Tester	Test build, QA checklists, regression test suite	Run regression tests and QA tools for compliance verification. (Quality Assurance)	Checklist action items, defect log; updated RTM for passed tests

Defects and the Change Meeting (Box 13)

The defects and change meeting is part of agile's low-ceremony change control process. After the testers run their battery of tests against a use case of the current build, the passed tests are recorded in the RTM, but the failed tests are recorded in the defect log and need to be discussed. Not every failed test is the result of a code defect. Other failed tests are the result of requirements defects, tests defects, or requirements interpretation. Sometimes the SME attends if a change request is needed or for an interpretation to be resolved.

Box 13 shows a decision symbol representing a decision that occurs from a team meeting. For traditional projects, this meeting would be called a *change management meeting*. For agile projects, the meeting is not as formal. It is a defect discussion to decide what kinds of defects are represented by the failed tests. There are several options to resolve.

- The failed test is recognized by the developers immediately as a coding defect, and can be scheduled immediately for repair. A few repairs may not be able to be repaired in the current iteration, so must be scheduled into a future iteration. The APM must be included in that discussion if rescheduling.

- The failed test indicates a difference in interpretation between the developer and tester and perhaps, the analyst. There are several cases: (a) Sometimes a requirement is incomplete or ambiguous, and the requirement must be revised for clarity; (b) Sometimes the test is incorrect, must be revised, and tried again; (c) Sometimes the failed test, after discussion, does represent a code defect, and then must be repaired.

- The failed test may indicate a *small change*; perhaps someone on the team suggests an improvement. If the analyst thinks that the change would be acceptable to the business, then a change request (CR) can be written on a card, with its impact, knowing it is unlikely that the business will not agree with the analyst. The CR impact may be small enough to allow it to be implemented in the current iteration without affecting the schedule; otherwise, it must be scheduled into a later iteration. In any case, the stakeholder must approve the CR and impact before it is implemented.[5]

- The failed test may result in a *large change*; such as the business requests a requirements change because the failed test surfaced some information the business had not considered. A CR must be written and its impact estimated. The change must be estimated and added to the CR. The CR must be approved by the business. Often, these large CRs cause such a significant change in scope, cost, and schedule that the APM must discuss the CR with the stakeholders. Large changes from this D&C meeting are handled the same as an external CR initiated by a stakeholder and going through the APM.

---

[5]The change *can be implemented*, in a literal sense before approval, and the team may take the risk that the change must be undone later if the business does not approve it. The bigger the change, the bigger the risk of rework; and whether the team decides to accept that risk and rework, that depends on the team's aversion or acceptance of the risk.

The team decides if a particular repair can happen in the current iteration, or must be deferred to a later iteration; but deferrals should be the exception and not the rule. Deferrals tend to accumulate over time and repair work tends to escalate exponentially, so the build becomes increasingly difficult to repair because of the *snowplow effect*. For details and serious side effects of the snowplow effect (see Chapter 10).

After the meeting, the team adds any tasks that need to be done as a result to the iteration backlog. The RTM is updated now if it was not updated earlier. See the upcoming "Implicit Change Management Flow Within an Iteration" section.

BOX #	OWNER	INPUT	PROCESS	OUTPUT
13	Integration tester and optional SME	Test results, defects list, QA checklists, change requests, RTM	Decide which failed tests should be repaired immediately, deferred, or have a change request. (Change Management)	(a) Return the build to developers or approve the build; (b) Revise test cases, requirements, and/or code; (c) proposed changes with impact.

Build Approved? (Box 14)

The team decides if the test build is ready for the User Demo. All team members take accountability for the build being ready. If there is more work to do on it, the build goes back to the team, and the cycle repeats from there.

If each member of the team agrees, the test build is production-ready—all of the integration, regression, and QA tests pass 100% and all defects scheduled for repair are repaired—then the team moves the test build into the *staging area*. The build is held in the staging area under version control until it is ready for user demo or release, or both. (A user demo always precedes a release). The build represents the validated partial product to be demonstrated to the user and possibly released into production afterward.

BOX #	OWNER	INPUT	PROCESS	OUTPUT
14	APM	Iteration backlog, regression test results, defect log, QA checklists, RTM	Decide if build is completed at proper quality or more work is needed. (Quality Gate)	Decision: amount of work needed yet on the build, or ready for demo.

Build Iteration and QA Reports (Box 15)

The iteration reports are built from the cards the developers and other team members completed throughout the iteration. There is no special work the team needs to do. See Chapter 12 for more on the iteration reports.

Box 15 may be performed before or after the user demo, depending if there is another opportunity to present the project status to the stakeholders. The Iteration and QA reports are part of the regular periodic information to upper management, and usually part of the release package. The APM writes up the iteration and quality reports, but the team provides almost all the data, which is why Box 15 is in the Team role swim lane. Read more about these tasks in Chapter 12.

The reports produced depend much on what upper management wants, and on what the APM uses to monitor the project. I provide the following iteration reports as part of my iteration closing.

- *Iteration burn-up chart*: Shows the work done during the iteration and whether the team successfully made its iteration commitment.

- *Project burn-up chart (or burn-down)*: Shows the work done for the project so far. It is a merging of the iteration burn-up charts for the duration of the project. It also shows the average team velocity and by extrapolation, a forecast of the team's progress and its completion point.

- *Defect trend chart*: Shows the discovery rate of defects, number of outstanding defects, and their rate of repair, for the iteration (or project if desired).

- *QA report*: A one-page stoplight (red/green/yellow) report showing variance, trends, and risk factors for the key project indicators for scope, cost, schedule, and quality.

- *Updated RTM* so that the business can see what features and use cases have been completed so far and compare with what they requested. The RTM contains traceability from a feature, with which they are familiar, to use cases to test cases and test results. The RTM also shows outstanding defects and approved CRs. (Sometimes I use a separate change request log with the people who requested the change, and when it was approved.)

BOX #	OWNER	INPUT	PROCESS	OUTPUT
15	APM	Updated RTM, Iteration test results, completed task tracking cards, defect stats	Prepare the iteration reports. (Review and Reporting)	QA and progress reports for management

Present the User Demo (Box 16)

The *user demo* is a stakeholder meeting to demonstrate the accumulation of product scope since the first iteration, with focus on the changes since the last user demo. The key purpose of the user demo is to collect feedback from the stakeholders, and improve the product going forward. The user demo also provides the opportunity to present various reports to the stakeholders, users, and other attendees about product progress. It strengthens business team and technical team relationships and trust. The APM talks with the stakeholders and explains the state of the project. The demo itself can be presented by anyone on the team.

User demos should be scheduled well in advance; they represent mini-releases and milestones to work toward. Every one-to-three iterations, the results of the previous iterations are packaged and presented to the stakeholders and users for their review. Although only a partial product, the build should be of final production quality at the end of each iteration.

Changes identified from the user demo meeting are recorded in the meeting minutes. If so, the build is returned to the team for repair, or for impact analysis for a requested CR; flow continues, as from Box 13. If there were no changes to the product, the build is staged for release (Box 17).

The user demo should include attendees besides the team and business stakeholders. It should include, if they wish, the people who must use it in the field: the helpdesk, maintenance programmers, staff and line managers, and possibly the public. They may not always attend, but they should be invited each time.

BOX #	OWNER	INPUT	PROCESS	OUTPUT
16	APM	Approved build, questions for stakeholders	Polish the build for a user demo, prepare the demo agenda. (Review and Reporting)	Reviewed user demo, answers to questions; changes, action plan, and meeting minutes

Stage or Release the Build (Box 17)

If the stakeholders have approved the user demo, then the build can be moved to *staging*. Staging is where the build is stored; it should no longer be modified (except to update with future builds). Depending on the organization, it may need to go through a formal alpha and beta test, an independent QA inspection, or wait until the operations staff can install it and the users have been trained to use it. The decision to release the product is a business decision, and outside the scope of the technical team. See also the section below *Prepare the Release*.

BOX #	OWNER	INPUT	PROCESS	OUTPUT
17	Developer	Approved build	Move the build to staging. (Release prep)	Production-quality build

Implicit Change Management Flow Within an Iteration

Agile change management *within an iteration* is not nearly as formal or explicit as with traditional projects. Like most agile concepts, agile change management is harder to explain than it is to do. Figure 8-3 recaps the change management process that is inside an agile iteration.

Describing the flow from left to right, everything starts with the requirements, at the arrow marked START.

- The BA completes a detailed use case with UX artifacts. When it is completed and approved, its summary (*use case* entry) is entered into the RTM (bottom arrow).

- The testers convert GUI and integration test cases from the use case. When the test cases are completed, the test IDs are entered into the RTM (*test case* entry). One use case maps to many GUI test cases and many integration test cases.

- The developers implement the use case with unit tests and code, uploading it into the development build each day. When the use case code is done, the developer enters the use case (*code complete entry*) into the RTM with the date of completion. The *code complete entry* date maps to a single use case.

- When the RTM contains entries for use cases, tests, and code, the testers download the test build and run all tests against the use case: GUI, integration, regression, and QA compliance. The testers record the pass date in the RTM only for tests that passed, and collect failed tests in the defect log (not shown). Only after *all* the test cases for the use case pass is the code entry marked complete with a second date. The use case is not complete until there are no unrepaired defects.

- All failed tests are taken into the defects and changes meeting. Each failed test results in one of four things.

  - *Requirements defect*: There is a problem with the use case so it is given to the BA to repair. Flow returns to the "use cases" step via connector A.

  - *Coding defect*: There is a problem with the code, so it is given to the developer to repair, including writing a unit test so it doesn't happen again. Flow returns to the "code and unit test" step via connector B.

  - *Test defect:* There is a problem with the test, so it is given to the tester to repair. Flow returns to the "test cases" step via connector C.

  - *Change request (CR)*: A change may be needed, either suggested by the team or the business. The CR form is filled out, and a developer provides the impact estimate. The PM gets stakeholder approval for the CR and its impact. If it is approved, flow returns to the "use cases" step via connector A. If it is not approved, the CR is recorded as denied. No further action is taken.

The change management flow recycles until there are no more defects or CRs. Eventually, every use case will have an entry in the RTM that indicates it has been implemented and passed all tests. When the build is fully complete, all use cases for the iteration will be associated with test pass dates, code complete dates, and code passed dates. Due to time constraints, the team or APM may defer some repairs and CRs to later iterations.

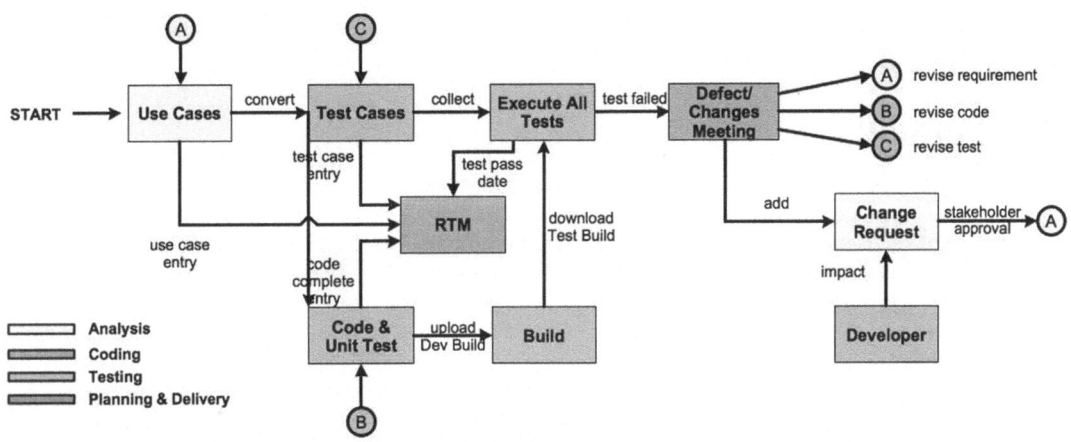

Figure 8-3. *Implicit change management flow within an iteration*

Prepare the Release

Preparing the release is not part of the iteration flow *per se* because it happens after many iterations are completed. In traditional projects, the product release will come near the conclusion of the project, or at year's end. For agile projects, the product (or partial product) may be released at the end of any iteration.

The technical team decides when an *iteration ends*—it is a technical decision. The business decides when a *product is released*—it is a business decision. Product release depends on coordinating a much larger group of people than the development team. There are also business decisions related to market timing and being support-ready.

Product release requires scheduling and coordinating with groups of people who must use it in the field: the helpdesk, maintenance programmers, staff and line managers, training department, and possibly the public. In many cases, training sessions are established to show users how to use the product at a different level than the user manual might explain. (These are the people who should attend the user demos so they can see what is coming, and possibly offer suggestions. At least, the user demo will help build user buy-in and adoption.)

The release will contain all the updated deliverables shown at each demo for the entirety of the product. There are product level reports that may be required for release: number of tests and pass rate for all tests, technical documentation to explain the product internally, and so forth. All the supporting technical documents, training schedules, and any other release-related documents are collected into a *release package*.

How much time and effort for a release depends on how much documentation is wanted, and how frequently the product is being released. Often, a week is scheduled for this last step. The more frequent the release, the smaller the release package—another reason to have frequent releases. Some software is released frequently enough that no special actions are taken except for the user to download the new product from an online repository.

Release deployment, a business responsibility, is the responsibility of the product owner or sponsor, but sometimes it is executed by the APM.

BOX #	OWNER	INPUT	PROCESS	OUTPUT
N/A	Team	Final staged build, team documents	Configure the build for Release; collect all technical, user, and operational documents. (Release)	Product release, all technical, user, and operational documents, project reports (release package)

PMI Parallels

Traditionally, the project plan is built before any requirements work or construction begins, and then it would progress through large function-based phases for analysis, design, construction, and testing. In the agile world, the team starts with a bare minimum of requirements—what can be collected in the first two weeks or so—analysis, design, construction, and testing begin concurrently with further requirements discovery. The scope is culled into iterations in which the processes are repeated, every two-to-four weeks. Business value can be delivered after a few iterations or so; whatever amount of scope makes sense for the business to deploy.

The PMI teaches that a work breakdown structure (a hierarchically structured scope document) is created, and then the activities that support that scope are defined and sequenced with a precedence network diagram (PND). The PND is not permitted to have any loops in it—it is a straight sequence of each task in the scope.

Agile differs strongly from the traditional approach when defining scope and task sequences. Agile uses loops for feedback as often as possible. There are feedback loops for iterations to adjust the project schedule and scope, feedback loops for tasks within an iteration for reviewing and improving task results, and even individual tasks are reviewed with others in *pairing* activities (e.g., pair programming) and the four-hour rule. (The four-hour rule says that if a person cannot solve a particular problem within four hours, then it is that person's duty to bring it to at least one other person to ask for help.) For clarity, I omitted many of the actual loops in Figure 8-1 and 8-2, but every task involves the whole team in constant feedback communication when discussing development progress.

Although traditional and agile projects have the same duration, agile projects get more business value out sooner. The product "feels" quicker to the stakeholders, a basic premise of agile, and is structured to ensure that fact (Rico 2009). Agile project schedules are broken into iterations, which are smaller than most traditional project phases or quality gates, so direction changes are easier, adaptive, and more fluid.

When agile practices coincide with cultural and organizational practices, agile practices work well; when agile teams conflict with managers who force traditional development practices, agile projects can fail. This is one of the characteristics of PM-2 over PM-1 theory described in Chapter 1.

In summary, Table 8-2 shows the major contrast points between traditional and agile. Of course, there are many variations on both practices, so only key principles can be shown.

Table 8-2. *Traditional vs. Agile by PMI Knowledge Areas*

Knowledge Area	Traditional	Agile
Integration	Large-scale predictability needed (full project work plans)	Short-term, history based predictability (iterations)
Scope	Detailed WBS before work starts	Small chunks taken a few a time by business-value priority
Time	Detailed and long-term project schedule is tightly coupled so that changes cause lock-step ripples and delays	Time-boxed iterations are loosely coupled; changes are absorbed within an iteration's time box, or the schedule is adjusted in iteration-sized chunks.
Cost	More costly because defects are repaired later, causing more rework.	Defects are repaired quickly, reducing rework and cost exponentially.
Quality	Infrequent business involvement, easier to get misaligned with expectations	Stays close to the business to maintain alignment and ensure business goals.
Human Resources	Siloed team members, especially in matrix organizations; frequent "multitasking" wastes time, decreases quality	Single projectized, multifunctional, empowered team working together on shared goals
Communications	Written reports, infrequent face-to-face, no or rare demos	Continual within team, frequently with business; frequent product demos to stakeholders
Risk	Business value delivered less frequently (annually); higher product risk in market; project risk depends on monitoring	Business value delivered as soon as its ready; reducing risk in losing market opportunities; less project risk because of closer monitoring
Procurement	About the same, time-to-obtain-window is wider because resources were planned further ahead.	About the same; time-to-obtain-window narrower for needed resources
Stakeholder Management	Periodic reporting, less frequent sponsor and stakeholder interaction; easier to misjudge expectations; order-taker relationship with project team	Continual stakeholder interaction is key, and stronger expectation management; partnering relationship with project team

Conclusion

This chapter described a set of conservative agile practices and processes within a single iteration. It is intended to enable the reader to understand agile more quickly and cause minimal adjustments when using agile in a traditional organization. It should help as a good guideline for a project manager and team members new to agile.

It is important to understand that these are principles of action, and the flow is not intended to be a prescriptive process. Agile teams may perform differently than that described in Figures 8-1 and 8-2, but these are the iteration procedures I would recommend, and that I have used quite successfully over the last 20 years.[6] Depending on how the team modifies it, the process flow can be tuned toward more extreme agile practices (like XP) or toward more traditional practices.

The agile approach is incremental and iterative, in that increments of scope are built on newer increments of scope, and the process of augmenting the product repeats, improving with each cycle.

Agile teams work more concurrently, and many of the tasks are worked out with the team at the same time. In the following chapters, which focus on the threads for requirements, development, testing, and project management, I attempt to show these concurrencies more clearly and in more detail.

Table 8-1 shows a Responsibility Assignment Matrix (RAM) that I call a CORA chart. CORA means Contributes, Owns, Reviews, and Approves. This is similar to the better-known RACI (Responsible, Accountable, Contributor, and Informs), but I think the meanings of the acronym CORA are more informative than those of RACI. The CORA chart shows how the different roles are involved with the different steps (tasks) of the iteration flow described.

✂ **Metaphor**   The "Additional Tools" section gives a summary of the agile process flow using a Kanban board for tracking. A few agile board terms and special cases are introduced that have occurred during some projects.

Software Development as Puzzle Building

We have come to the crux of the issue between different agile practices. Some agile teams code from use cases, some from user stories. There are more extreme approaches, such as the emergent design approach that does no upfront work at all. (Emergent design was discussed in Chapter 5.)

I believe that *some* upfront work is needed to maintain a context for the user stories: validated use cases instead of one-line statements of behavior. These differences can be illustrated using a jigsaw puzzle building metaphor.

Some people like to build a jigsaw puzzle by laying out the frame, which requires searching through the puzzle pieces to find those with straight edges, particularly the four pieces with corners. After they build the frame, they use the internal pieces to fit against the frame, working their way inward.

The user story teams build their puzzle differently. They pick a piece from the box and lay it down. They continue pulling one piece at a time and placing it at the bottom of the puzzle space. As they find a piece that connects to another, they connect it. If they find a straight edge, they move it to the left, right, top, or bottom of the puzzle space. As the team pulls more pieces from the box, they move the piece relative to the rest of the known puzzle pieces. Each time they find a new piece that fits somewhere, they attach it.

Those using emergent design principles are more extreme yet. They would not have the picture on the puzzle box as a guide. Eventually, the puzzle may get built, but only after moving pieces from here to there many, many times (refactoring and re-architecting).

Building puzzles frame-first or piece-first may be a personal preference, perhaps even a philosophical difference. However, unlike puzzle building, projects need to meet certain business objectives. Projects that go beyond their return on investment parameters become failed projects. The time it takes to complete a project by guess-and-check development is much greater than preparing a little bit up front. Progressive elaboration, a proven principle, allows subsequent steps to be derived from the previous ones: the puzzle frame, being easier to build, guides the remaining pieces into place.

---

[6]Agile formally launched 14 years ago with the *Agile Manifesto*, but it is based on the principles of *Concurrent Engineering* and *Kaizen*, which I began using in the mid-1990s.

Which is the best approach? Agile projects, whether the teams employ use cases or user stories, are successful, as measured by stakeholders' needs met and defect rates; much more successful than traditional projects. However, the studies show (see Chapter 1) that agile gets much of its success from small teams, team dynamics, and short feedback cycles, and not whether they use cases or user stories. Perhaps whether one is a frame-builder or a piece-builder *is* only a philosophical difference.

As a side note for comparison, I include traditional teams into this puzzle-building metaphor. Traditional management insists that the team defines the puzzle frame first. The team finds the framing pieces first, then the pieces for the top of the puzzle, then the middle pieces, then the bottom pieces—all before laying a single piece! In too many cases, the sponsors or stakeholders change before the puzzle is complete, and the new stakeholders switch the remaining puzzle pieces with a different puzzle, and insist that the team merge the new puzzle with the old.

Additional Tools

Agile Iteration Development and Terminology Summary

The following summary is for an agile software engineering project. Starting with the prioritized capability list from stakeholder capabilities, and assuming the system architecture is defined, each iteration is tracked on the online Kanban board (Anderson 2010).

Planning

- *Feature catalog:* Prioritize features from the stakeholders. Add any support tasks or other dependencies that are identified as necessary. Size each feature roughly, as small (5), medium (8), large (13), or very large (21). These sizes inform the number of iterations in the release plan.

- *Release plan:* Build the release plan by distributing features across all iterations based on the team's velocity. It usually takes at least three iterations to measure the team's velocity. The team can take a first pass guess at 15 points per iteration. The release plan will have an Iteration 0, Iterations 1 to N, and a cleanup or *hardening iteration*, just before each release. Give each iteration a topic, or a theme based on the features to be implemented in that iteration, to distinguish the work done in that iteration.

- *Use case catalog:*. Transform the features, in priority order, into use cases and system dependencies. Add any support tasks or other dependencies that are identified as necessary.

- *Iteration 0*: Set aside the first iteration period to install the infrastructure, finalize release preparations, and distribute the info needed for the iterations. Prepare as many use cases as time allows in Iteration 0 for Iteration 1: analyzed to produce a detailed use case, validating object model (sequence diagram, class diagram), and proposed UX artifacts.

Iteration Cadence (tracked on Kanban board)

- *Iteration planning:* The team sizes each use case in the use case catalog for what they are willing to commit to implement by the end of the iteration. Use story points with Fibonacci numbers: 1, 2, 3, 5, 8, and 13. Use cases larger than 13 points must be decomposed into smaller chunks of work.

- *Iteration backlog*: The PM places all committed cards onto the Kanban board's TODO column in priority order. (That column shows the iteration backlog.) Each person selects what he or she wants to work on. Each person works on no more than two cards at a time—a primary and a backup in case their primary is stalled.

- *Walk the board daily*: Each day the team walks the board from right (DONE) to left (TODO) to move their card toward completion, passing it off to another team member when necessary.

- *Team reviews*. The team holds reviews of *stage gate packages* for approval. No card is allowed to move pass the team review lane unless all agree. Team reviews are held on the following packages when the constituent artifacts are completed:

  - *Analysis and design package* (per use case): Detailed use case, wireframe(s), domain-only class and sequence diagram (optional), and UX artifacts for the use case.

  - *Test package* (per use case): The testers' perspective of the requirements, as reflected in the GUI and integration tests, aligns with the developers' interpretation of requirements.

  - *Defects and change meeting*: All defects on the failed tests log are resolved into a defect type of be repaired, or a change request. Defects must not stagnate.

  - *Build package*: Code and unit tests for all features in iteration, all defects repaired, GUI and integration testing reports completed, regression testing passed 100%.

- *Iteration closure:* At the end of the iteration (by date), the PM adds each point from cards that have reached the DONE column and builds the burn-up charts for the iteration, and for the product so far. The PM also collects data from the team to build the Defect report and the QA stoplight report.

- *User demo*: Each iteration will produce a build (product enhancement) that is of release quality, regardless of when a release is scheduled. Each one to three iterations the product is shown to the stakeholders, highlighting the new functionality since the last demo.

Special Cases

- *High priority items*: If an urgent task comes to light, it is marked as high-priority and someone agrees to take it; their task is then marked as Blocked until they can get back to it. Normally, the PM assigns urgency to a card, but anyone on the team can do that if necessary.

- *Impediments*: Some factor that causes a card to stop flowing. Impediments cause the card to be marked as Blocked. Impediments must be escalated after 24 hours as a risk to the iteration release. Impediments cause blockers.

- *Lingering:* A card that remains in the same lane for more than two days is said to be lingering, usually because the estimate was too low, and not because of an impediment. If that is the case, then the team "swarms" (described in this list) to get that card off the lane and moving forward.

- *Blockers:* Cards that have stopped because of an impediment or higher priority assignment, such as a team member being pulled off-task.

- *Defects and points:* Defects are also features but without points, and slows down the team's velocity. A use case is not completed until it is implemented and tested without defects, and no points for the use case can be tallied until is it completed.

- *Swarming:* When an unblocked card is stopped for more than two days (lingers), the card owner requires some help. The entire team drops what they are doing to help the card owner, and move the card out of its lane. This team action is called swarming.

- *Carryovers* (CYOs)*:* If a card is not completed by the end of the iteration, it is placed back in the iteration backlog (TODO lane) for the next iteration, or if deferred, into the product backlog for a later iteration. No points are tallied for the iteration in which it was not completed, even if *almost complete.* The points will be tallied in full when it is completed (hopefully in the next iteration).

- *New items*: Sometime a use case or task is discovered while an iteration is in progress (in flight). It is added to the product backlog for the next appropriate iteration. If the new item is urgent, it is added to the TODO column of the current iteration, and a card(s) of equal size is removed into the product backlog. Defects are added to the TODO list as they are found.

- *MMR* (*Marginally Marketable Release*): Each use case must be done completely—no outstanding defects or missing features. When the set of features are completed and added to the build, the build is considered ready for user demo, and possible production release (a business decision of the product owner or higher management).

- *Moving backward:* (a) A card may move backward if it fails team review. It is placed in the proper lane for the revisions to be made. (b) If a card lingers, the team may decide to move it back to the TODO lane for later (not to the Product Backlog because only the PM can add to that from the release plan). (c) Sometimes a team member moves a task prematurely and skips an associated task (e.g., team review), the card is moved back to the proper lane until that action is performed, and then can skip the lane in which the task is already completed. This kind of "lane-jumping" is poor behavior, and adds risk to the iteration and project.

- *Resizing in flight:* If a card is sized incorrectly, do not resize it, even though it probably decreases team velocity. These discrepancies are necessary to highlight the estimation error, and show where improvement is necessary. The next iteration planning session will adjust for the poor estimate and team velocity.

■ ■ ■

CHAPTER 9

Requirements Thread

Chapter 8 gave an overview of the iteration process, tasks, and artifacts for the team as a whole. This chapter contains a detailed look at the work of a Business Analyst (BA). It shows how the BA uses inputs from other team members and produces outputs for them. This chapter compares use cases and user stories, and describes a guideline for how agile BAs may do their job. It should help other team members understand the BA on their team, and possibly allow novice BAs working in an agile team to perform the business analysis and requirements function better. If the team does not have a BA, then this chapter may help others complete the requirements-centric tasks normally performed by the BA.

Is There Such as Thing as an Agile Business Analyst?

The three most popular forms of agile in use throughout the world today are Scrum, Extreme Programming (XP), and a hybrid of the two. What do these two methodologies say about the BA role?

Does Scrum Use a Business Analyst?

Scrum (Schwaber & Beetle, 2001) defines three roles: *Product Owner, Scrum Master*, and *Project Team*. Although Scrum says the project team is comprised of cross-functional roles, it does not define specifically what skill sets the project team uses. All requirements are given by the Product Owner, who is responsible for eliciting requirements from any other stakeholder in the business. Those requirements are loaded into the product backlog as *backlog items*—no further definition except that each item has a larger scope than a user story. The Product Owner does not have to be a business analyst trained in technical requirements, and will likely not be because the Product Owner is a business SME or stakeholder. In the description below, the BA helps the Product Owner with requirements skills that he or she often lacks.

For Scrum Teams, the Product Owner will do most of these tasks, and the BA will assist the PO with analytical details. In some teams, the BA acts as a Scrum Product Owner by serving as the central point of requirements reconciliation and liaison with the business team for product details. (The agile project manager liaises with the business team for *project* details.)

Does Extreme Programming Use a Business Analyst?

Extreme Programming (XP) (Beck, 200) defines two standard roles and two extended roles: *Customer, Developer, Agile Coach, and Tracker.* XP defines a "developer" as anyone on the project development team, so a developer may be a tester, technical documenter, or a business analyst. The customer provides requirements directly to the developer and the developer acts as the BA. No requirements specifications are created or written down. Without the use of written specifications, the XP team probably does not have a person skilled in business analysis; all requirements work is verified and validated in conversation with the customer and code. Requirements errors can be hidden in the mass of code refactoring that likely follows non-analyzed requirements. Considering that requirements defects are the greatest source of product defect, a skilled BA is needed.

Can the developer do these BA tasks? Perhaps, but even if they could, developers are on the critical path; they are usually the bottleneck of the team, and their time is better spent writing code and unit tests. So even if they could, they shouldn't. If developers could do the work of the BA, would they want to? He or she chose the developer profession, and not the BA profession, for a reason.

Does an Agile Team Need a Business Analyst?

As shown in Chapter 7, the same requirements problems occur today as they have decades ago, whether used for traditional or agile projects. Either approach must result in the codification of the stakeholder's requirements as a business value deliverable. Agile has not mitigated that problem although it has reduced the upfront planning, and reduced the time and cost of defect repair. For either kind of project, good requirements are critical to product quality. Developers, product owners, and business SMEs usually do not have the skills of the business analyst.

In many of our universities, business analysis is taught in the business school, and is given short shrift in the computer science department. From the day the new computer science graduate enters the work force, he or she brings with them the idea that requirements are not as important as development, because they were not taught requirements elicitation, validation, and management.

If the most popular agile methodologies in use today do not explicitly call out for a business analyst, do we need BAs in software development? Are the thousands of BAs obsolete before they graduate? Does the nation need Certified Business Analysts Professionals, as certified by the IIBA (International Institute of Business Analysis)? I emphatically think that we do. Without more learning up front in "getting to ready", we waste more time in the refactoring activities. It is easy to say "let's get coding and refactor as we need," without realizing that that kind of (guess-and-check) coding wastes time and reduces quality, which requires more refactoring, defect repair, and more testing.

Larry Putnam Jr. (2014) of QSM, an independent project-research company, has spent years researching these ideas.

> *More interesting, perhaps, is what we see when plotting productivity against the proportion of time spent on design and story writing. Agile projects, it seems, become noticeably more productive as they spend a larger proportion of their time on requirements and design versus coding, testing, and packaging for delivery. This is consonant with findings in the agile community in general that taking extra time "getting to ready" and ensuring user stories are well thought out and communicated is critical to the success of agile methods. (p3)*

For more on this topic, with an emphatic demand that we need more BAs on our teams, see George Pitagorsky (2014).

If an agile team has no designated BA, the APM is often the better choice over the developers and testers to fill the role because the APM and BA have similar roles regarding stakeholder management and scope control. Having the APM fill the BA role also frees up the developers and testers, who need as much time as they can get, but only if the APM has the needed BA skills.

Although other roles on the agile team may be able to pick up the slack and do some of the BA work, some responsibilities and tasks will not get done without a BA. For example, the PM can manage scope control at the high level, but unless the APM gets deeply involved in the details of the project, scope creep and gold plating will occur at the detailed level. Developers certainly will not catch subtle scope creep because they do not distinguish between authorized and unauthorized scope increases or changes; if they did, they wouldn't be the largest source of gold plating! Acceptance criteria (Definition of Done) can limit some of this, but the BA is the greatest ally to finding what these criteria are from the stakeholders and customer SMEs.

The Role of an Agile Business Analyst

Before we launch into what the BA role does within an iteration, let's discuss the BA role tasks in general. The BA is a key player on agile teams. He or she is essential to an agile team in eliciting, communicating, and managing requirements, and helping the PM manage stakeholder expectations and product scope control.

Stakeholder Expectation Management

The BA must manage expectations with the business almost as much, and sometimes more, than the project manager. There is a difference in focus: the BA focuses on the product at the level of the customer SMEs, and the PM focuses on the project at the level of the higher stakeholders. Usually, the PM works with executive management, and the BA spends more time with the business SMEs (or Product Owner in the case of Scrum).

Although the stakeholder provides needs, features, and desires, the BA must convert these into requirements. The BA is the requirements gatekeeper to the agile team during the iterations—no requirements get to the team without going through the BA. A clear understanding of what will actually be in the product, as resolved for all stakeholders, helps manage the stakeholders' expectations of the product.

Stakeholder expectations management is essential to a successful project: "Success is political, not technical." The team may build a perfect product, but the project will be deemed a failure if the key stakeholders do not like it; and they will not like it if their expectations are not met. It is critical to manage the stakeholders' expectations, and the BA helps the PM do that.

Product Scope Control

The BA is the gatekeeper for the product scope, to ensure that the product contains **all and only** what the sponsor is willing to pay for, before or after product release. The BA must prevent *gold plating* and *scope creep*, both of which add scope to the project without authorization, funding, or time allotted. Both push the project off-schedule or off-budget.

Gold plating has been called "theft" by one customer because good-intentioned developers add features to the product, thinking it will make a better product. They see it as adding a free feature because it didn't take much time to add it. Unfortunately, the stakeholders did not ask for those features and are charged for them anyway, charged through the team's salaries or contractor's invoices. Gold plating also adds time and cost for testing and debugging; there are *no free changes* in a software product. All changes, documented or not, have an impact.

Scope creep, another unauthorized scope increase, is a more subtle problem because features are often requested by one stakeholder but without knowledge or permission of the other stakeholders, or without the sponsor's authorization and subsequent funding. Scope creep is subtle because although it seems like the request is a stakeholder requirement, without proper authorization it has the same effect as gold plating.

Scope control also means the BA must capture a requirement at the right scope. For agile projects, should the BA employ use cases or user stories? The team decides how to code and test the requirements, but the BA plays a major part in choosing how to document and communicate those requirements.

Requirements Verification and Validation

Requirements verification means that the BA wrote the requirements correctly and the business SMEs and customers must agree that the requirement reflects what they said they wanted. *Requirements validation* is ensuring that the content and meaning of the requirements are correct, that they contain no defects—no missing data or logic and the requirement has what the business *implied*, much harder than mere verification. The worst thing a business SME can say about requirements to the BA (or to a developer) is, "You did what I said, but not what I meant."

If functional requirements are captured specifically as use cases, the BA has the ability to validate those requirements rigorously, and prevent requirements defects before design and coding are started. The BA can validate use cases using an object model, which is necessary for many kinds of software products. Object model validation, discussed below, can prevent at least half of the product defects from ever seeing the light of day; or better, from having the developer include them into the code. Formal requirements validation can reduce defects by more than half, and is highly recommended for complex and quality-driven products.

Requirements Communication

Requirements drive coding and testing, but even more importantly, they comprise a *document of communication* for use after the product is released. The development team relies on the requirements to be clear, concise, complete, modifiable, buildable, testable, and maintainable. Having a written or documented requirements artifact is important for maintaining what the project team agreed to earlier.

The requirements are a critical part of the history that the team leaves behind when the product is in production and must be maintained. The requirements document is one of the most important documents that must move into operations with the product. That does not mean the requirements must be highly detailed and voluminous; it merely needs to be *barely sufficient*, that is, adequate, for the task at hand.

Requirements Traceability

The stakeholders define a list of features that they pass to the development team, and trust that the team is building the final product properly. Yes, there is continual conversation between the team and the business, but the conversations focus at a lower level. The stakeholders also need to see the final product for the features identified. The BA maintains a list of features, use cases, and *user experience (UX) artifacts* to show that a request was transformed into a working product.

The Requirements Traceability Matrix (RTM) is the basis of change control and helps developers and testers locate defects when they occur. It also ensures that all features have been implemented and tested. (The testers also update the RTM with test cases and results, and sometimes the developers add the code modules or classes that support the particular feature.)

Change Control and the Definition of Done

Requirements drive formal change requests, schedules, budget allocations, and revisions. The BA must keep a written record of the requirements as a baseline for change control. Change requests mostly occur after the use case is part of the Build, and requires rework to make a change. A change will always have schedule, scope, or cost impact, and usually more than one. Depending on the formality of the project, the current state of construction, and the stakeholders' *volatility* (tendency to change their mind), a change can occur by merely asking for it. Agile change management is informal, and can occur at least once a week.

The requirements establish an anchor for what the stakeholders want. There must be a *definition of Done for the each requirement*, which leads to a full definition of how the product will look and behave in its final form *as is currently known* at the time of requirements definition. Although agile allows the requirement to change without a lot of ceremony, it still must be defined. Without knowing when Done is Done, the demands on the team for what features go into the product can change, and change, and change, especially as one stakeholder overrides or changes what another stakeholder wants.

Agilists say that the "final" requirements are not completed until after the Build is completed, because at that point, there is no "discovery" remaining, and the Build is now part of history. The requirement as definition of Done is needed so that the Build can complete, otherwise the scope of the iteration can be redone forever.

⚒ **Implementation Anecdote**   I advised on a project that was lingering. The customers were not happy, and they were not paying the contractors, who were also not happy. The customers refused to sign off on requirements because they said that "requirements always change." In an attempt to be a good contractor, the developers went forward with writing code on these volatile unwritten requirements. Still, the customers would not sign off on the delivered product because they continued to want changes after the code was written, for no increase in cost. There was no definition of Done. This project was originally scheduled for 9 months but was entering its fourth year! My advice was to stop all coding until at least one iteration of requirements were resolved, then write code for only those requirements. I also advised putting in an agile change management process acceptable to both customer and contractor. For some reason, the contracting company did not accomplish that. A year later, the project was still in progress and people were still unhappy.

The Business Analyst Tasks

During each iteration, the BA elicits detailed requirements from the stakeholders to produce detailed use cases and user stories, validates them for logic correctness and data completeness, and works with the business SMEs and developers to define user interface designs. The BA also plays a key role in all team meetings.

The BA's tasks are illustrated in the agile context shown in Chapter 8, and enumerated below for clarity.

- Decompose the features and workflows into use cases with the business SMEs (requirements elicitation hopefully started in Iteration 0)

- Contribute to the team iteration planning meeting (scope clarification for estimation)

- Expand use cases into detailed use cases with the business SME (scope refinement)

- Validate use cases at the analysis level of the problem domain (scope analysis validation), if necessary

- Contribute to user interface design, screen shots, and augment the use case with implementation ideas (initial design)

- Approve, with the business SME, the final user interface and design as being consistent and meeting requirements (initial design)

- Review the GUI and integration test scripts as being consistent with the requirements (requirements clarification and validation)

- Review the GUI test results to ensure that the user interface behaves consistent with the requirements (requirements clarification and validation)

- Contribute to the defects and change meeting to help resolve failed test issues (change management)

- Approve the Build for user demo and release with the other team members (scope validation)

- Contribute data to the iteration and QA reports, and to the Build release package (delivery and reporting)

- Contribute to the user demo meeting as needed (typically tracking changes and defects for the team to incorporate ,into the Build later)

Use Cases and User Stories

Ivar Jacobsen first developed the term *use cases* in 1986 (Jacobsen et al, 1992); he was one of the founders of the Rational Unified Approach, a very popular software technique sometimes known as RUP. Kent Beck (2000), founder of Extreme Programming, developed *user stories* in 2000. Beck wanted to have something with less formality than a use case to use as a discussion focus with a stakeholder. He thought that frequent conversations and code refactoring would take care of the details missing from a written use case.

Table 9-1 shows a comparison between user stories and use cases. Both user stories and use cases serve the purpose to capture user requirements in terms of interactions between the user and the system, but there are several important differences between them. ("User Story", 2014)

Table 9-1. *User Stories vs. Use Cases Comparison (Wikipedia)*

	User Stories	Use Cases
Similarities	• Generally formulated in users' everyday language. They should help the reader understand what the software should accomplish. • Must be accompanied by acceptance testing procedures (acceptance criteria) for clarification of behavior where ambiguous.	• Written in users' everyday business language, to facilitate stakeholder communications. • Must be accompanied and verifiable by test cases.
Differences	• Stories (and similar things, often called features) break requirements into chunks for planning purposes. Stories are explicitly broken down until they can be estimated as part of release planning process. • Provide a small-scale and easy-to-use presentation of information, with little detail, thus remaining open to interpretation, through conversations with on-site customers. • Usually written on small note cards. • Stories are usually more fine-grained because they have to be entirely buildable within an iteration.	• Use cases organize requirements to form a narrative of how users relate to and use a system. Hence they focus on user goals and how interacting with a system satisfies the goals. • Use case flows describe sequences of interactions, and may be worded in terms of a formal model. A use case is intended to provide sufficient detail for it to be understood on its own. • Usually delivered in a stand-alone document, and visualized by UML[1] diagrams. • A small use case may correspond entirely to a story; however a story might be one or more scenarios in a use case, or one or more steps in a use case.

---

[1]UML refers to *Unified Modeling Language*, a modeling language for visualizing the design of a system, an ISO and OMG standard since 1997.

Use cases provide a few advantages over user stories.

- Use cases provide a direct link between the workflow identified by the stakeholders and a more detailed requirement.

- Use cases can be written rigorously as a functional specification. Consequently, use cases can be validated rigorously and proven correct.

- Use cases bundle user stories to provide a context for the simplistic way a user story identifies a requirement. The scope of the use case is the sum of the user story estimates.

- Validated use cases are closer to the design than user stories, and provide a better context in which the user stories apply.

User stories provide a few advantages over use cases.

- User stories are easier to estimate during iteration planning. The BA could prepare a list of user stories for each use case, but stories are easy enough to extract from the use case that the team can do that in the iteration planning meeting.

- User stories work better for detailed coding, and writing unit tests and GUI tests. Before testing or coding, each use case must be broken down into its constituent user stories anyway.

One may say that another disadvantage of use cases is the time it takes to write them up, and maintain them as code changes, but this is true of any artifact, even the code that must be changed when the requirements change. It takes longer to change the code than to change the use cases description, which are usually one or two pages in length. If a technical manual is part of the product release, then the use case and object model are invaluable. If the maintenance programmers have no need of that, they can peruse the code as needed.

Variant   Some agile developers write the user stories instead of a business analyst. Not only does this take much-needed time away from the developers, but also developers are not trained as analysts. Developers and business analysis represent two different professions and follow different standards. That is not to say that some developers cannot do a good job on requirements, but it is not the priority for a developer. Developer-written requirements are often design-centric (harder to change later), get glossed over so the developer can get to writing code (inadequate definition), and need to be revised late in the project (insufficient comprehensiveness or correctness). Although developer-written user stories are quick to write, they fall under the maxim of "you get what you pay for."

⬆ Variant   Some agile teams skip writing use cases and develop directly from user stories. I think this approach is problematic because a user story is a very small chunk of scope without a context, like trying to develop a new system from hundreds of maintenance requests. It results in frequent refactoring because the context is constantly being re-evaluated.

Bertrand Meyer (2014) compares developing a product with finding a square root function. A person cannot determine the mathematical square root function merely because they are given a set of square root numbers; the relationships must be known. User stories are like square root numbers: they have no relationship or context. User stories are similar, and will result in a fractured (non-unified) product. I have used both approaches and prefer use cases for requirements that are decomposed into user stories just before implementation and testing. I have also worked on enough complex systems that the use case validation effort is more than justified.

⚡ Recommendation   Write both use cases and user stories for large and complex systems because it provides transparency to another level of progressive elaboration between stakeholder features, and detailed coding and unit testing. The user story is merely a path within the use case. If use cases are used for these kinds of systems, then the XUML[2] validation techniques should be used with them. If the product is a simple web application, or uses a straightforward user interface with obvious behavior, then user stories work fine.

The User Story Template

The common template for a user story is

> *"As a <user> I want to <action> so that I can <goal>."*

The user is whoever will interact with the system, and the action is how they will achieve the goal. The goal is the business value from that one path of the use case, and therefore a sub-goal of the enclosing use case goal. The following are two examples, normal and error path, from a typical ATM use case Withdraw Cash from Account.

- *Normal*: "As an account owner, I want to take money from the bank so that I can have more cash on hand."

- *Error*: "As the bank manager, I want the user to see an error message if the cash box is out of money when they try to get cash."

---

[2]XUML refers to eXtended UML notation. It augments standard UML sequence diagrams with data flows, and uses a slightly more concise notation to put more on the page. A brief tutorial on XUML validation is given in *Additional Tools*.

Behavior-Driven Design (BDD)

⚑ Variant Another way of writing low-level requirements instead of the above user story template is a similar approach using Given-When-Then (GWT) statements, which originated from another agile style, *Behavior-Driven Design* (BDD). GWT statements are of the form:

"GIVEN a <certain situation (precondition)>, WHEN I <the user> do some <action> THEN the system does <some action (post-condition)>."

An example of GWT statements for the above ATM example could look like the following:

-- Normal: "GIVEN that I have money in my account, WHEN I ask to withdraw a certain amount, THEN the cash box provides that cash to me."

-- Error: "GIVEN that the cash box has insufficient money in it for a particular withdraw request, WHEN I request more than the cash box has, THEN I see an error message that tells me the ATM is out of cash."

Some people find these more useful than use cases or the standard user story template, and the form is closely related to the dialog recorded in a use case description (pre-condition, user action, system response).

User stories come in different styles, like everything else. There are various open source tools to support either kind of user story.

INVEST for Use Cases or User Stories

The product backlog records scope as a list of features, the iteration backlog records scope as a list of use cases. Each use case can be extracted into user stories. Each use case will have a normal case or "happy path" where everything proceeds as expected. Each use case will also have at least one error path, which explains what the system or user must do when everything doesn't proceed as expected. Often, an error message is displayed or an exception code is implemented to handle these situations.

Both user stories and use cases should follow the INVEST mnemonic (Wake, 2003) explained in Table 9-2.

Table 9-2. *INVEST Mnemonic for User Stories*

Letter	Meaning	Description
I	Independent	The user story should be self-contained, in a way that there is no (or minimal) inherent dependency on another user story.
N	Negotiable	User stories, up until they are part of an iteration, can always be changed and rewritten.
V	Valuable	A user story must deliver value to the end user.
E	Estimable	You must always be able to estimate the size of a user story.
S	Scalable (small sized)	User stories should not be so big as to become impossible to plan, prioritize, or break into tasks with a certain level of certainty.
T	Testable	The user story or its related description must provide the necessary information to make test development possible.

By following the INVEST mnemonic when writing stories or use cases, the requirements, code, and tests are decoupled, meaning that a change in one place will not cause breakage that ripples to other parts of the system or requirements.

Validating Requirements

After the BA produces a detailed use case, he or she has an artifact describing the behavior and goal of the use case, the data it needs, and the data it produces. The BA does not yet know if the detailed use case is correct; customer verification is superficial, and hidden pitfalls may exist in the use case's ramifications. From experience with validating use cases, I have found that, on average, one-third of each use case will change as a result of validation, so it is worth the effort to validate the detailed use case. Without validation, that one-third use case will still change, but at the later stages of coding and testing, requiring more effort by the team.

Figure 9-1 illustrates a use case from the perspective of the user and the system. From the user's (or actor's) point of view, each business workflow is comprised of one or more use cases. Each use case defines a transaction between actor and system. The actor passes data or control to the system, which processes the input, and produces output back to the same or different actor. The actor is not aware of the internals of the system, only the data that flows in and out.

From the system perspective, each use case triggers an execution path along a series of objects (small circles) as one object calls another. Each part of the path is a call to another object's method (or function) and defines an object message from one object to another. The *Additional Tools* section shows the XUML sequence diagram in Figure 9B-7, so you can see an example transaction flow for a chain of method calls from object to object.

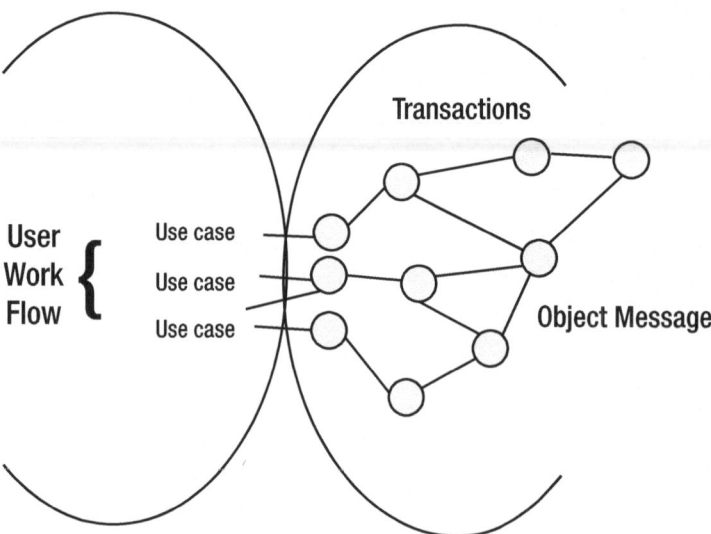

Figure 9-1. *User Perspective vs. System Perspective*

Leveraging Orthogonality for Validation

Use case requirements are produced by decomposing functional (procedural) logic from high-level workflows to use cases to much smaller detailed steps, the actor-system dialog. A use case transaction can be shown procedurally (by a flow chart, for example) that illustrates how one function calls another then another in sequence.

A use case's supporting entities (such as objects) can be characterized by an object model, which shows each object's jurisdiction and boundaries inside the system. Object models are produced by decomposing the use case's domain with scope-of-control logic (object decomposition). A use case's supporting objects can be shown by a static diagram, that is, a UML *class diagram*.

Both functional and object decomposition techniques are independent but consistent with each other. Mathematically speaking, they are *orthogonal*, in the same way that the independent x, y axes of a graph are orthogonal and define a single Cartesian point. We use the dual methods of functional decomposition and object decomposition to check for a match between the object methods that support a use case and the procedural logic that defines a use case to find inaccuracies.

Use case validation uses three artifacts: the detailed use case (procedural text description), a UML class diagram, and an XUML sequence diagram that ties the first two artifacts together. When all three artifacts are consistent, then the result is a *validated object model*, and the use case is *correct*. See *Additional Tools* for a brief tutorial on validating use cases.

- *Use Case*: The use case indicates the data input and output, and the detailed interaction between actor and system. The system is treated textually as a "black box:" the actor sees what happens, but doesn't know what goes on inside. (Design is hidden in a use case because a use case is a requirement, not a design artifact.)

- *UML Class Diagram*: A class diagram shows a static logical view of the supporting classes[3] of the problem domain, the same domain used by the Problem Domain Component (PDC) described in Chapter 5. The class diagram shows what classes contain and control which data, and the data relationships between the classes through a standard protocol: the methods of each class method. The other components of the MVP architecture are design-oriented and are not used during *requirements analysis*.

- *XUML Sequence Diagram*: The XUML sequence diagram shows the functional flow of the use case through its supporting scope-of-control objects. The XUML sequence diagram shows the transactional flow of the use case as a sequence of object messages with data. The methods are called in the order needed to execute the use case, receiving needed data, and returning data or status flags. At the analysis level, the sequence diagram is a "simulation" that focuses on the logical consistency and completeness of the actor-system dialogue.

All three artifacts together comprise an object model for the use case. Object models can be combined to make a cumulative object model for all the use cases, and object models can be expanded to derive designs for all components of the product.

Verify for Consistency

When the detailed use case, class diagram, and sequence diagram all agree, then the detailed use case is *correct*. Requirements correctness means that all data and functions are defined, as used in the use case, and there are no logic errors or data omissions.

---

[3]*Classes* are simple object specifications from which objects are constructed.

When the functionality illustrated in the sequence diagram simulates the use cases using the objects and data of the class diagram (and data input), many errors, data omissions, functions, and logical errors are found. By changing any of the three artifacts to make them all consistent, the business analyst thereby removes the requirements errors and omissions.

Validation of a use case is not a lengthy process. It takes only a couple hours, and is certainly worth the time. As an anonymous wit quipped, "Weeks of programming can save you hours of planning."

Formal object model validation does not guarantee *use case completeness*, because there may be an entire business flow missing. High-level workflows are shown on the project abstract's context diagram, so the BA has a major gap if these are missing. It is more likely that the missing workflows are out of scope. It is up to the business analyst to ensure that the scope boundaries are well-defined and all requirements are collected.

In summary, to validate the use case, the BA uses the detailed use case to draw a UML class diagram, showing the objects that enable the use case, and the methods and data used. The detailed use case is exercised, or simulated, on paper with an XUML sequence diagram, which shows the function calls and data passed to each object within the Problem Domain Component of the system. The use case's execution path enables the use case to produce the user-system dialog of the detailed use case. When all three artifacts match, the use case is considered correct.

To Validate or Not to Validate?

Recommendation   Validate all projects with XUML validation object models except for simple applications and web-based applications that consist primarily of "interactive screens." The IIBA[4] also requires requirements validation as an important project step, although they use UML sequence diagrams instead of XUML sequence diagrams (Heidt, 2012). I've also found that developers and testers that come onto the project team find the flow between architectural components and class files especially helpful for building onto the code.

Object model validation is an analysis step, and not a design step. Once the design is in place (which can be derived from the analysis object model), and the code is written, subsequent changes may occur. The object model has served its purpose, and it is not necessary that the object model be kept in sync with the code—unless the customer requires it. In that case, there are tools that will draw object models from the code.

Warning   Some teams prefer to code, unit test, and refactor instead of spending time on validation, accepting the extra work of refactoring because they think the upfront effort is wasted when the requirements change. Some agile developers perform some kind of requirements analysis, but they rarely do it as thoroughly or as well as professional business analysts who are trained for it. Developers focus on writing code, and requirements analysis is given short shrift. Defects tend to propagate from the requirements, and like a self-fulfilling prophecy, the developers are justified in thinking that validation is not worth the effort—until developers have no capacity for adding new features in an iteration, this becomes apparent when there is nothing new to demo!

[4]The International Institute for Business Analysis (IIBA), the standards body for Certified Business Analyst Professionals (CBAPs).

I propose a few counter-arguments to this idea of refactoring instead of requirements validation (see the Putnam quote above.) First, *refactoring* is often confused with *rework*. Refactoring is a code-cleaning task, and its effects will not be evident by the appearance or behavior of the product; rework is doing correctly what was done wrong in the first place. Rework takes more time than the validation effort, which takes about two hours per use case.

Secondly, skipping this step of *analyzing* the stated requirements is *why* there is so much rework to do later. It explains why the users are dissatisfied with typical results; or why defects show up in the production version, defects that affect the organization's reputation, especially if the users are public or corporate buyers of a commercial application.

Thirdly, constant code changes for any reason increase the entropy of the system code, and add to the refactoring load. (Refactoring was invented to reverse the entropy effects of frequent code changes, and thereby reduce *technical debt*). If TDD was used, then changing the corresponding unit tests add to the refactoring load.

⚒ **Implementation Note**   For projects in which use cases were validated, there were no requirements defects reported from QA. I have used this technique for over 70 projects in the last 20 years. Of those projects, 65% have had *zero product defects* when the products went into production, and even a higher percentage of those products had *zero requirements defects*. Imagine your cost and time savings of dropping the typical 55% defects due to requirements (per Alberts, Chapter 7) to zero!

Going Further

Although XUML and object model validation is intended for requirements analysis, it has benefits at the design and implementation levels as well. Object models can be expanded to design, and implementations can be "reverse engineered" to help refactoring and clean-up efforts.

Design and Design Validation

Peter Coad, who invented the original four-component model with Ed Yourdon, showed how the PDC of the analysis model could be expanded to a four-component design by showing implementation classes that supported the PDC. (Coad & Yourdon, 1990; Coad & Yourdon, 1991) These classes can be further designed and validated by augmenting the use case with design detail: a *design case*. The object model can be expanded by adding implementation and design-centric classes in a straightforward way. The MVP architecture of Chapter 5 is a generalization of the object model expansion to an architecture using these expansions principles.

⚒ **Implementation Note**   Although I have found design cases helpful in complex projects, agile designs change frequently while the developer rethinks and refactors. Keeping up with the design case documentation can become a burden. Our team got best results by creating the design case as best as possible at first, and then did not bother to maintain it. The design case's object model gave a good first-shot impetus to the developers, who then followed the normal agile practices of discussion and refactoring moving forward.

Implementation Analysis

Validation can also be done on the code to ensure that the architecture and design follows good coding practices, as defined by theory and the team coding standards. Some tools allow such reverse engineering practices.

✖ Implementation Anecdote   One of my teams finished about a year's worth of development on a somewhat complex, open source project. Although we started with coding standards and a solid architecture, we also experimented with emergent design. I began to suspect that we were suffering entropy effects as the program became harder and harder to grow or modify, despite frequent refactor-as-you-go efforts.

I decided to do a validation exercise on the implementation to find if and where we would need to refactor. I built class diagrams and XUML sequence diagrams against the finished code using the debugger–an exercise I don't recommend, by the way. The results were clear after perusing only a couple of use cases. The class diagrams showed that the class hierarchy was not as clean as it should be, and architectural principles and coding standards were violated. The five days I spent on this probing exercise would have been better spent on the upfront validation (which would have taken about one day) before coding. (Alternatively, Continual Integration (CI) tools may have prevented violations at check-in, but our team had not installed them yet.)

Perhaps the corruption in the program resulted from the result of many hands in the open-source pot, perhaps from emergent design, perhaps from the developers working very closely at the code level and not keeping the big picture in mind, or some other factor at work. Whatever the reason, the XUML validation technique allowed me to refactor the code relatively quickly along clean lines again, and emphasize to the team what went wrong so we could keep on track going forward. It also gave us impetus to install a CI tool.

The Business Analyst within the Agile Iteration

This section describes the work of the Business Analyst (BA) within the iteration process flow from a detailed perspective of the analyst. The iteration starts with the business analyst's role in the initial iteration planning meeting. The box numbers in each heading refer to the boxes in Figures 8-1 and 8-2 in Chapter 8.

Iteration Planning (Box 1)

At the beginning of the iteration, the APM facilitates a team *iteration planning* session. The iteration planning meeting allows the team to estimate the size of each use case relative to each other, and to determine how many use cases (or user stories) can be completed by the end of the iteration, as defined by the Definition of Done or the Acceptance Criteria.

Assuming the BA refined the work flows into use cases in Iteration 0 (as described in Chapter 7), the BA has a partial *use case catalog* to start the first iteration. The BA presents each detailed use case to the team, in priority order, and its constituent user stories for the team to estimate for size. Although the team should have read through the use case catalog before the meeting, questions always arise, and the BA has best knowledge at this point of how each use case should behave.

The BA leaves the meeting with a card which indicates his or her next task for the day: either (1) develop a User Experience (UX) artifact from the detailed use case; or (2) detail the next use case in the iteration backlog. If no cards apply, the BA further refines the next use case in the product backlog for the next iteration.

Develop the Detailed Use Case (Box 2)

Each use case in the use case catalog needs to be expanded into a detailed use case. Hopefully, this was finished before the iteration started, but sometimes not.

The detailed use case describes how the business value is achieved using a dialog between the actor[5] and the software system (product) being built. The business goal of the use case is stated, a description of the actor-system dialog, all input and output data needed, and pre- and post-conditions (when it applies). The SME tells what the business needs to do, and the BA elicits the data and business logic, checks for omissions, discrepancies, and needed clarifications, and puts the detailed use case into proper non-ambiguous wording.

If there are no User Experience (UX) artifacts to help design with the team, and no use cases to validate, then the BA details the next highest priority use case from the *product backlog* to keep ahead of the team for the next iteration, as discussed in Chapter 7. If the BA does not extract the user stories from the use case now, then testers and developers will need to do it later to write test scripts and code, respectively.

Validate the Use Case with an Object Model (Box 3)

The next step is optional, as indicated by the dotted line around Box 3 in Figure 8-1. Use case validation of this kind should be used on complex applications, and is probably not necessary for simpler products, like displaying a straightforward series of web pages. If the team has decided to validate use cases to remove defects at the requirements level, and to give the testers and developers a leg up on the Build, the BA performs the object model validation discussed in the sections earlier in this chapter.

The BA starts with the detailed use case and builds a UML class diagram for all those classes that probably support the use case. Earlier use cases have already provided some classes as starter material. The BA defines (or reuses) each class in the Problem Domain which object methods are needed, what data is contained in, or controlled by, which PDC class, and the relationships between the classes.

The BA then draws an XUML sequence diagram showing the transactional flow of the use case using the objects of the class diagram, making any changes needed for consistency and validation. The "final" detailed use case can be used to define the UX artifacts, enable better test cases, and start the internal design.

Develop the User Experience Artifact (Box 4)

The BA calls a team meeting to develop the user perspective and UX artifacts for a detailed use case. A UX artifact may define the screen layout, GUI widgets, report layout, or formats. A UX artifact is a communications tool to allow the parties involved to gain a visual understanding of the product's behavior of the use case. UX artifacts describe how the product will appear to and work with the user, and fall into the realm of design, and hence into the realm of the developer.

The BA works with the designer to define how it would look and behave on the computer screen, either in an application or in the browser. These two tasks, detailing the use case and defining the User Experience (UX) artifact, need to be done almost at the same time. The BA and SME can build a proposed UX artifact in Iteration 0, or wait until the developer gets involved during the iteration that the use case is being implemented.

---

[5]The *actor* may be a user (person) or an external system.

A general rule of requirements definition is that a use case as a *functional requirement* should not contain design information, which is usually contained in the Non-Functional Requirements (NFRs). However, there is arguably one exception to that rule. I have found it useful to the analyst, developer, and the user if the UX is referenced in the use case. It is helpful if the use case says something like, "Actor selects the book by clicking the drop-down selection list" instead of "Actor selects the book." The final use case will also contain design notes useful for implementing the use case. This design-augmented use case is dubbed a *design case* for convenience.

Be aware that the more design that is in the use case, the more maintenance it requires as implementation details change. As the use case changes, the tester must do more work to change the associated test cases, and there is more confusion with the team about how the use case should actually be described. The BA must walk the tightrope between too much design (increased maintenance costs) and development speed; the design case is closer to the design and implementation than a standard requirements abstraction, so it is less abstract and less flexible.

The UX artifact design meeting is a transitional meeting between requirements and design. These meetings last about 30 minutes.

■ **Warning** Some business SMEs provide what they think are "final" screen shots, with instructions to implement it "as is," thinking that there is nothing more to be said. *The screen shot is not sufficient as a requirement.* It contains no business rules, no field length restrictions, no default data, no behavior or navigational information, and cannot be implemented *as is.*

The BA (or developer) will continually need to return to the business SME for requirements questions, such as "What is the maximum length of this field? Is it required or optional? If field A is incorrect, should field B still be present?"

From the SME's point of view, he or she has already given the team all their requirements, and will begin to develop the attitude that the agile team isn't very good at their job. This "dump it over the development wall" is a mindset of traditional approaches, and only slows the development process.

The BA has the added burden of trying to convince the SME to spend more time on the project. It is important to set the business SME's expectations on their requirements role before actual product development begins. The PM should resolve the duration and frequency of SME engagements at the business kickoff meeting, and what each member's role needs to be on the project.

Start the RTM

The BA adds each approved use case and UX artifact to the Requirements Traceability Matrix (RTM). The RTM shows the stakeholder who wanted the feature, the use case associated with that feature, and now the UX artifact(s) associated with the use case. Use cases will map directly to user stories, test cases, and code, but features do not usually map cleanly to use cases. More detail on the RTM is given in *Chapter 7*. The *Additional Tools* section gives an example of an RTM for the ATM Project.

Repeat from Iteration Backlog

After the approved use case is recorded in the RTM, the use case is ready for development and testing. The use case cards are on the agile board, the developers begin writing code and unit tests, the testers begin identifying GUI and integration tests. The BA can return to the next use case in the iteration backlog; or if those use cases are detailed and approved, the BA can return to the product backlog to expand the features catalog further to add more use cases into the backlog for the next iteration.

Defects and Change Meeting (Box 13)

The Defects and Change meeting is part of agile's low-ceremony change control process. After the testers run their battery of tests against a use case of the current Build, the passed tests are recorded in the RTM, but the failed tests are recorded in the defect log and need to be discussed. Not every failed test is the result of a code defect. Other failed tests are the result of requirements defects, tests defects, or requirements interpretation. Sometimes the SME attends if a Change Request is needed or for an interpretation to be resolved.

The BA gets involved with the use case again when attending the Defects and Change meeting to discuss the results of testing the use case code. The tester and developer cull out the obvious code defects from the list of failed tests. If they both have the same interpretation of the requirement, code module, and test case, the developers quickly acknowledge the defect to be repaired. However, there are always those failed tests that the developers interpret differently, and do not think result from design or coding defects.

The BA, working from the business perspective, attends the meeting to clarify the requirement and kind of defect involved. If the failed test represents a coding or design defect, the BA should be able to point to the exact place in the requirement that went wrong. If the requirement is ambiguous or incomplete, the BA needs to repair the requirement. If the testers have the wrong interpretation of the requirement, or an invalid test, the testers need to repair their test. Sometimes tests are simply not appropriate to the use case.

In some cases, a Change Request (CR) is suggested. Someone must write up the change and a developer needs to find out how much time, money, or scope will be added by implementing the CR if it is approved by the customers. Often, the developer can quickly estimate the impact in the meeting, but the BA (or PM, depending on the impact) must take the CR to the business for approval. The BA usually has a good idea if the CR will be approved or not.

After the meeting, the team adds any tasks that need to be done as a result to the iteration backlog. The RTM is updated now if it was not updated earlier. See also the "Implicit Change Management Flow" section in Chapter 8.

Build Approved? (Box 14)

Before the Build gets packaged for user demo and staged, the APM polls the team to ensure that each member agrees that the Build is ready to go. Each team member is responsible for the Build's success, including the BA.

Any tasks needed to prepare the final Build must be completed as a high-priority card on the task board, but incomplete Builds at this point should be the exception rather than the rule.

The User Demo (Box 16)

The *user demo* is a stakeholder meeting to demonstrate the accumulation of product scope since the first iteration, with focus on the changes since the last user demo. The key purpose of the user demo is to collect feedback from the stakeholders, on the features developed during the iterations since the last demo, and improve the product going forward. The user demo also provides the opportunity to present various reports to the stakeholders, users, and other attendees about product progress. It strengthens business team and technical team relationships and trust. The APM reviews with the stakeholders the state of the project. The demo itself can be presented by anyone on the team.

The user demo meeting is important for the BA. He or she records the changes suggested during the demo, and may present the demo to the stakeholders and users. Changes and discovered defects will be part of the meeting minutes, along with a subsequent action plan. If a stakeholder or upper manager requests a change, it should be treated as a high priority item until the impact analysis is complete and the business SME sets a clearer priority (or does not accept the impact and change).

Stage or Release the Build (Box 17)

Any information that comes from the business regarding the release goes through the BA or the APM. The BA usually has little contribution to this design-oriented task; but sometimes, he or she has key information, such as what platforms or configurations are needed for the Build, or information about the production environment into which the Build is being released. The BA has the product knowledge to train the support and operational staff (maintenance programmers, helpdesk, field supervisors, etc.) to bring them up to speed on the new product if no one else in the organization has been assigned to it.

PMI Parallels

All the PMI parallels mentioned in *Chapter 8* are still true, but the following highlights some specifics for the BA role.

Scope: Both traditional and agile methodologies use progressive elaboration to discover and refine the requirements, but traditional methods do the requirements work up front before any development begins. Instead of writing a requirements specification before coding starts, the agile approach shaves off a small chunk from the first feature or two of the product backlog in the first two weeks, and whittles it down to a few use cases that can be implemented in the next iteration.

Traditional projects usually build from features instead of use cases, but features cannot be mapped easily as scope is refined to smaller granularity. Consequently, traditional requirements are packaged into thick volumes of intertwining specifications, or hundreds of short phrases in a spreadsheet or an expensive requirements tool serving as the RTM. By contrast, agile BAs write up detailed use cases or user stories and can easily track requirements at that level in the RTM.

Cost: A trained BA keeps the cost down by eliciting requirements, freeing time from the developers' load, and reducing the amount of rework that comes with development. If the BA uses requirements validation, the requirements will have little or no defects, and will reduce the exponential cost of change even more.

Product Quality: Features cannot be validated using the XUML method, so they (or any set of unvalidated requirements) start with a base of undiscovered defects. If an agile BA validates the use cases, then the developers and testers can start with a zero-defect requirements set. The user demo allows requirements changes to be found faster (at each iteration instead of each release) by the business, and therefore, developers are not building on bad code that must be reworked later.

Process Quality: After one to three iterations, a retrospective is held so that the team can identify what techniques and tools they want to keep, to change, and to try. The retrospective is a process improvement meeting that improves all subsequent iterations. Traditionally, a lessons-learned meeting was held and recorded, but the project was typically over, so the project did not benefit from the "lessons learned."

Human Resources: Traditionally, BAs are temporarily assigned to a project and work multiple projects at the same time. The BA's primary responsibility is to their resource manager, and they must divvy up their time among various projects; the BA is merely an assigned worker. Agile BAs are assigned full-time to the team, and are accountable for the project success equally with all team members. This project ownership and team inclusion enables better morale and productivity of most workers in significant ways.

Communications: The BA ensures that the requirements are well understood by those on the team who use the requirements, providing a fourth perspective to that of business, developer, and tester. The clarity allows the team to work faster and with less rework.

Stakeholder management: The agile BA takes an active role, working with the APM to manage stakeholder expectations. In traditional projects, most of that responsibility is on the PM. When the APM and BA both present a consistent front to the stakeholders, they present a more powerful statement than the PM does alone. The user demo also gives full team transparency to the stakeholders, so a more trustful relationship is established with the team. Agile projects encourage business-development team partnerships instead of the traditional "order-taker" relationship.

Conclusion

This chapter focused on the need, activities, and skill sets needed for a Business Analyst in both Region 1 and Region 2. The BA elicits and analyzes the product requirements, and helps the APM manage stakeholder expectations, one of the criteria for success. The BA needs to stay at least one iteration ahead at detailing the use cases from the product backlog to make them ready for the developers and testers during the next iteration. The BA also helps with the UX design and ensures that all requirements are met, resolving potential defects in the Build.

The CORA table (Table 9-3) summarizes the inputs, processes, and outputs undertaken by the BA. It is indexed by the box number of the Process Overview Diagram (Figures 8-1 and 8-2 in Chapter 8). The box numbers in brackets represent contributions instead of ownership of the task. Compare it with the CORA Matrix of Chapter 8.

Table 9-3. *CORA Matrix for Business Analyst (Brackets indicate that the BA contributes or reviews the artifact.)*

BOX #	INPUT	PROCESS	OUTPUT
[1]	Selected prioritized detailed use cases (user stories if available)	Iteration planning (scope estimation)	Committed and prioritized list of use cases to complete
2	Highest priority use case from iteration backlog	Expand use case into detailed use case (scope refinement)	Un-validated detailed use case
3	Detailed use case	Validate use case at analysis level with UML (scope validation)	Valid (revised) use case and object model: UML class diagram and XUML sequence diagram
[4]	Detailed use case	Design user interface, screen shots, and augment use case with implementation ideas (initial design)	Design case, with UX artifacts
[5]	Design case (UX artifacts and detailed use case)	Identify all test cases and expected results for GUI testing (test identification)	GUI test scripts, updated RTM
[6]	Design use case, optional sequence diagrams	Identify all test cases for integration testing (test identification)	Integration test scripts, updated RTM
[10]	Test Build, GUI test scripts	Run GUI test scripts (UX validation)	Defect log; updated RTM; update GUI regression test suite
[13]	Test results, defects list, QA checklists, change requests, RTM	Decide which failed tests should be repaired immediately, deferred, or have a change request (change management)	(a) Return Build to developers or approve Build; (b) Revise test cases, requirements, and/or code; (c) Proposed changes with impact
14	Iteration backlog, regression test results, defect log, QA checklists, RTM	Decide if Build is completed at proper quality or more work is needed (quality gate)	Decision: amount of work needed yet on the Build, or ready for demo
[16]	Approved Build, questions for stakeholders	Polish the Build for a user demo, prepare the demo agenda (review and reporting)	Reviewed user demo, answers to questions; changes, action plan, and meeting minutes
[17]	Approved Build	Move the Build to Staging (release prep)	Production-quality Build

Additional Tools

ATM Project

Table 9-4. *ATM Project -- Sample RTM*

Stakeholder	FEATURE	UC #	Use Case	UX artifact	Classes	Test Case	Date Passed
Bank Manager	Insert money at beginning of day	1	Initialize ATM	UX10. Admin startup report			
Customer SME	Ensure only the correct customer gets access to his account	2	Authorize	N/A			
Customer SME	Allow customer to deposit, withdraw, or transfer money	3	Deposit Money	UX01. Transaction Receipt			
		4	Withdraw Cash	UX01. Transaction Receipt			
		5	Transfer Money	UX01. Transaction Receipt			
Customer SME	Get account balance	6	Check balance on account	UX02. Account Balance			
Customer SME	End customers transactions	7	Quit	N/A			
Bank Systems Manager	Reconcile transaction with cashbox balance remaining	8	Reconcile	UX03. Reconcilement Report			
Bank Manager	N/A	9	Shutdown ATM	UX11. Admin shutdown report			

Note several features of the RTM (Table 9-4).

1. The three stakeholders of the context diagram are shown, although in a real RTM names would be used.

2. Some use cases do not have UX artifacts, and some use the same. One of the use cases (Shutdown ATM) has no driving feature, but is a technical dependency. (It was later determined that the Reconcile use case would happen automatically when the ATM Admin shutdown the machine.)

3. The features are mapped from stakeholder to feature to use case, and later test cases will be added. The last column is the date that the test passed and the use case is considered complete. The RTM is not a test status sheet. Both GUI tests and integration tests, and their results, are tracked on a different test tracking sheet. The final pass date is listed here as a summary of completed use cases and features.

4. This RTM shows the classes resulting from XUML validation. Of course, this column is missing its validation and is not done. It also only applies to the analysis (problem domain) class. Keeping the RTM maintained with design classes is too burdensome.

I prefer to use a spreadsheet for this activity. It is sortable and more easily manipulated than a word processer.

Validating Use Cases with XUML[6]
Overview

Use case validation is required by the IIBA for all professional business analysts. This paper presents two simple extensions to the standard sequence diagram notation of the Unified Modeling Language (UML) for the purpose of use case validation and clarity. To support use case validation, data is added to the standard UML sequence diagram flows. To support clarity, the return data from an object's method call is shown on the called method's flow lines to save space.

This paper describes the notational changes needed when comparing the sequence diagrams with the use case text and UML class diagrams to provide more powerful support for use case validation. A simple example is given to illustrate how hidden classes or misplaced data can be found through this kind of validation.

These options are available to the analyst, and it is the opinion of the author that proper use case correctness cannot easily be accomplished otherwise. XUML is also helpful for design and design validation using similar principles.

Notational Extensions
Object Lifeline Boxes

The first and most obvious difference is that the square boxes showing the lifetimes of objects are omitted from XUML. The background line behind the box is used instead. The boxes are not useful except for cases of object creation and destruction (memory allocation and deallocation, an implementation action), which is irrelevant for analysis. This is especially true for languages such as Java that have automatic garbage collection, in which the lifeline is not known. It is sufficient to merely create the object with the keyword new(. . .), which always returns the object to which it was sent.[7]

---

[6]*Extended Unified Modelling Language (XUML)for Use Case Validation*, Al Cline, PMP, PMI-ACP.
[7]The ellipsis in the method call indicates that the parameters are not known, or perhaps no parameters are passed.

Message Passing (Called Methods)

Standard UML shows control flow (message passing) between two objects' public methods as an arrow from the caller to the called object, with the name of the method on it. If the object calls itself (private method), then the line is a square loop back to itself, with the method on it.

Figure 9-2 shows object A calling the public method msg1() of object B, and object B calling its own private method msg2(). Data needed by the methods (input parameters) and data from the methods (return values) are not shown.

Figure 9-3 shows the XUML version of this transaction, augmented with input parameters and return values. B.msg1() requires parameter x, and returns value z; B.msg2() takes parameter y and returns value z.

The return value is shown under the method call in angle brackets instead of showing only an unadorned line from the called object, as with UML. Both UML and XUML show that control flow is returned to the caller, but only XUML shows what data is returned. If no data is returned, then the return is shown with empty angle brackets (< >). More on how XUML uses data in the flows in the validation section below.

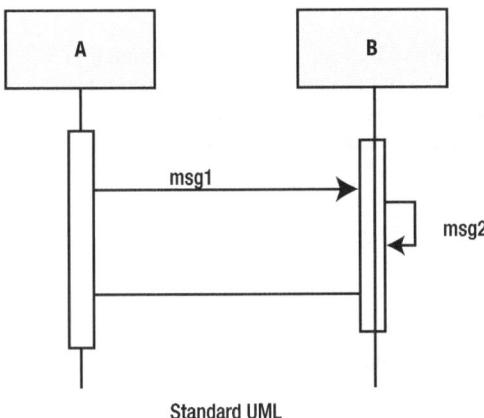

Figure 9-2. *Standard UML*

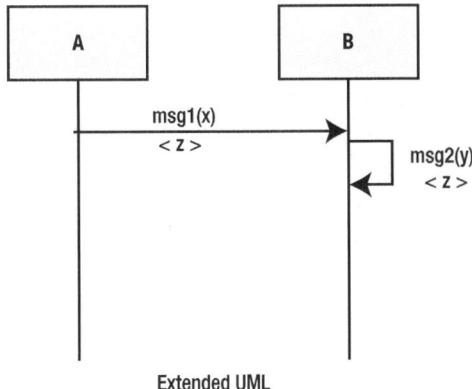

Figure 9-3. *Extended UML*

Objects are shown capitalized, but data is shown in lowerCamelCase. This is also illustrated in Figure 9-6.

Method Encapsulation

It is easy to see in Figure 9-3 that B.msg1(x) returns z because it was output from msg2(). However, object A does not need to know how object B implements its methods. For an entire use case, messages are chained from object to object by a sequence of method calls. During analysis, when only the problem domain objects are used (or known), calls can be made to implementation *objects* without caring about the implementation *methods*; each object's public interface is defined in terms of method signatures and return values. The implementation methods can be defined later during design, but the required problem domain interface (API) is defined during analysis, and assists with the design tasks.

Traversing the Sequence Flow

UML Sequence Diagrams

ULM sequence diagrams reflect time flow from left to right, and top to bottom: messages to the left and above others are invoked sooner. Putting the return value directly under the method call bothers some people because it is perceived as violating that flow rule. However, if one looks at the method call as a call to an object with encapsulated method calls, such as implementation methods, then the rule is upheld.

For example, Figure 9-2 shows B.msg1() being called, and a second line showing it returning later. When adding the private implementation method B.msg2(), it would be inserted between the incoming and outgoing control lines, as if it were added later.

Single-Stroke Rule

Usually understanding the flow between called and caller objects is clear enough from context, but in the rare case that it isn't, a simple rule can be used to show what is called (or returned) when. While traversing the method calls from top left to right, whenever an arrowhead is encountered vertically on the object lifeline, the control flow comes back; whenever a tail is encountered, the control follows that arrow. Of course, if there are no more method calls on the object lifeline, the control automatically returns. The ATM sequence diagram example in Figure 9-6- includes numbers to show how the control flows.

Internal Methods

Sometimes a private method may make a public method call to another object. In Figure 9B-4, a call is made to Q's public method msg1(y), which calls its private method Q.msg2(y), which needs to call the public method R.msg3(z). The public call-to-R arrow is drawn from within the private call arrow to the other object, and the loop return is extended to embrace the public call arrow.

Figure 9B-4 shows the private method msg2(y) returning w, but R.msg3(z) must be called to get w. Figure 9B-5 shows the corresponding class diagram for Figure 9B-4. The data z is assumed here to be an attribute of Q, but it may also have been passed to Q previously.

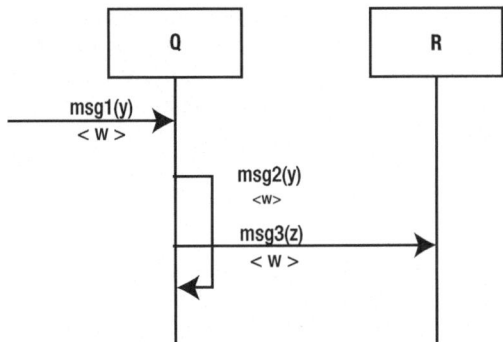

Figure 9-4. *Public method call from a private method call*

Q
z
+ msg1() - msg2()

R
w
+ msg3()

Figure 9-5. *Class Diagram for Figure 9B-2a*

Optional Methods

In general, optional flows are not shown in sequence diagrams. If it is needed once, it must still be validated, and shown. In cases where the analyst feels he or she must show flow bifurcation, then a small circle is placed on the tail of the call arrow, with the option condition to the left of the circle. The ATM sequence diagram example (Figure 9-7) includes several method calls with different kinds of return value options, including a method call with a Boolean result <T/F> from which the flow may go along the TRUE path, or along the FALSE path. Error conditions are frequently shown as <OK/ERR> return values; exception conditions and events are shown with dotted lines as in standard UML.

Granularity

How much detail needs to be shown in the sequence diagram? All data in the use case must be shown, unless that data flow is captured in another sequence diagram elsewhere. In that case, the subcase data flow can simply be referenced. The analyst must decide how much detail, but the encapsulated method approach means that the analyst may choose which implementation methods not to show. File I/O and internal GUI widget flows are frequently omitted from sequence diagrams unless they are particularly relevant.

Class Diagrams

XUML adds no extensions to UML for modeling classes. At the analysis levels, data types and method return types are not shown in the class diagram. (Of course, the analyst has the option to show that information, but usually that is left to the designer.)

Each piece of data is either passed between objects, calculated within an object, or is an attribute of an object. Sequence diagrams show them all (within the rules of granularity), but during analysis, calculated and passed data are not shown in the class; the class diagram shows only the attributes used. Class diagrams also do not show CRUD services (Create, Read, Update, Delete), which means constructors without parameters are not shown, and setters and getters are not shown.

Use Case Validation

Detailed (textual) use cases express functional decomposition, and class diagrams express scope-of-control decomposition (responsibility, behavior, and state). Both kinds of decomposition are orthogonal, which means that they have a mathematical basis for cross-checking each other, similar to the way a spreadsheet sums rows and columns to identify errors. The sequence diagram allows the analyst to execute the use case through the objects modeled by the class diagram, a kind of abstract desktop simulation of the use case through the system's problem domain. The objects of the sequence diagram must be consistent with the classes of the class diagram, and consistent with the transactional flow of the use case. Any discrepancies in methods or data indicate an error in one of those artifacts. In my experience, about 30% of a use case will undergo changes as a result of XUML validation.

Comparing Sequence and Class Diagrams

The following is an easy way to compare data and methods of the class diagram:

- Select a class for consideration, and its object in the sequence diagram.

- For each flow line tail on the object's lifeline: Any data that is passed or returned must be shown in the class diagram as an attribute, unless it is calculated or passed in. If it is missing and is definitely needed, either add it, find the missing calculation method, or find what object owns that data from which it was passed.

- For each flow line arrowhead on the object's lifeline: Any method that is called must be shown on the class diagram. Messages between objects are public methods; looped lines indicate private methods. Of course, CRUD services are not shown in the class diagram.

Use case correctness is achieved when the class diagram's methods and attributes match the sequence diagram's methods and data for each path of the use case.

A note of warning: Some people will develop the class model by building a sequence diagram reflecting the use case. This seems to work at first, but there is no validation between the class model and the functional use case because one is merely a reflection of the other. This class model will tend to contain a high number of function bags instead of proper classes, and more rework will be required to remove use case errors later.

Example: ATM Withdraw Transaction

An ATM problem example is so pervasive in object literature that it is almost obligatory. The following "Withdraw money from an ATM" example illustrates the ideas above plus a few others. (The numbers shown in Figure 9-7 are not part of XUML, but are entirely for clarification to show in what sequence the methods and their values are returned.)

ATM Withdraw Use Case

The customer withdraws a requested amount of money from her account, assuming that the cashbox and account have sufficient funds, and that the amount is in the correct denomination. (These days $20 bills often are the smallest denomination in the ATM.)

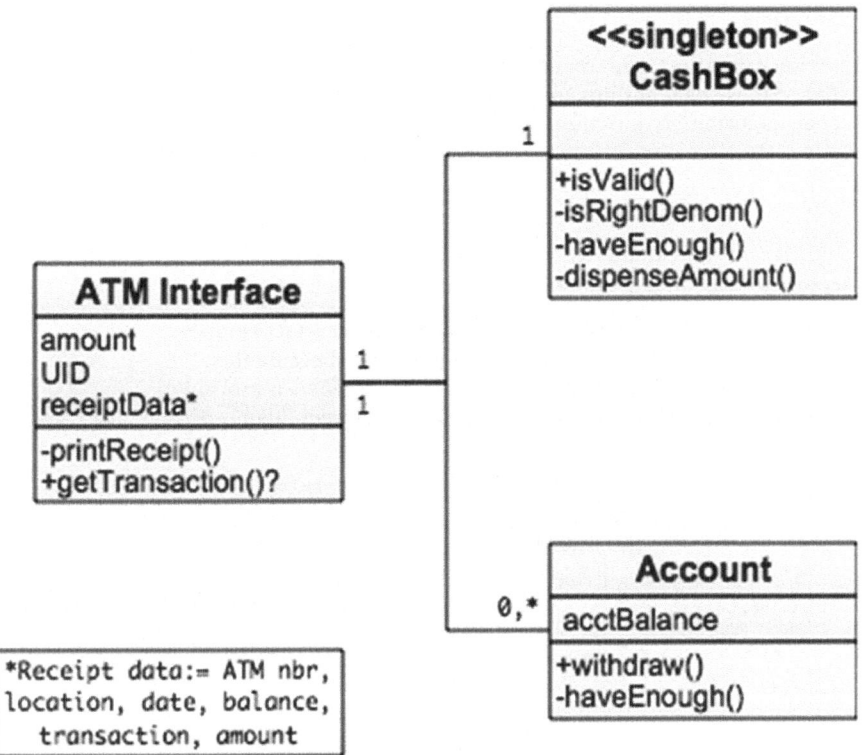

Figure 9-6. *First Pass: Class diagram supporting ATM Withdraw use case*

ATM Class Diagram

To develop the class diagram, we may think along these lines.

1. There is only one cashbox in an ATM, so a cashbox abstraction class will be a singleton across multiple sessions. We don't know what kinds of data it needs yet, but it should have methods to dispense money and validate withdrawal transactions.

2. Each customer may only take from their own account, so the customer's user ID (UID) and account balance must be maintained within this account. It must have methods to validate the request and deduct the money (withdraw). *NOTE: In this diagram, the UID is in the wrong place as reflected by our sequence diagram. The discrepancy says that we must adjust who owns that data.*

191

3. The ATM must coordinate the transaction and interact with the user. It is responsible for collecting the correct command and withdraw amount, and ensuring valid withdraw requests that result in providing the customer money and a receipt from the proper account. It will "own" the withdraw amount, the UID to get the right account, and the data for the receipt. Note that, as with UML, small notes can be placed outside the classes to represent passive data as is found on the receipt.

4. The ATM Interface uses the CashBox and the Account objects to fulfill its responsibility, so those relationships are shown. The ATM may interface to all accounts for all its customers, thus the 0,* relationship.

ATM Withdraw Sequence Diagram

Figure 9-7 shows the sequence diagram for this use case. This example is for illustrative purposes only; there is no need for the reader to evaluate whether the design is a good one or not.

> Step 1. The user enters the WITHDRAW command and the amount of money requested into the ATM Interface. No parentheses are shown because the Customer (person) cannot make method calls into objects. (There is probably a method called getTransaction() that collects the customer requests.)

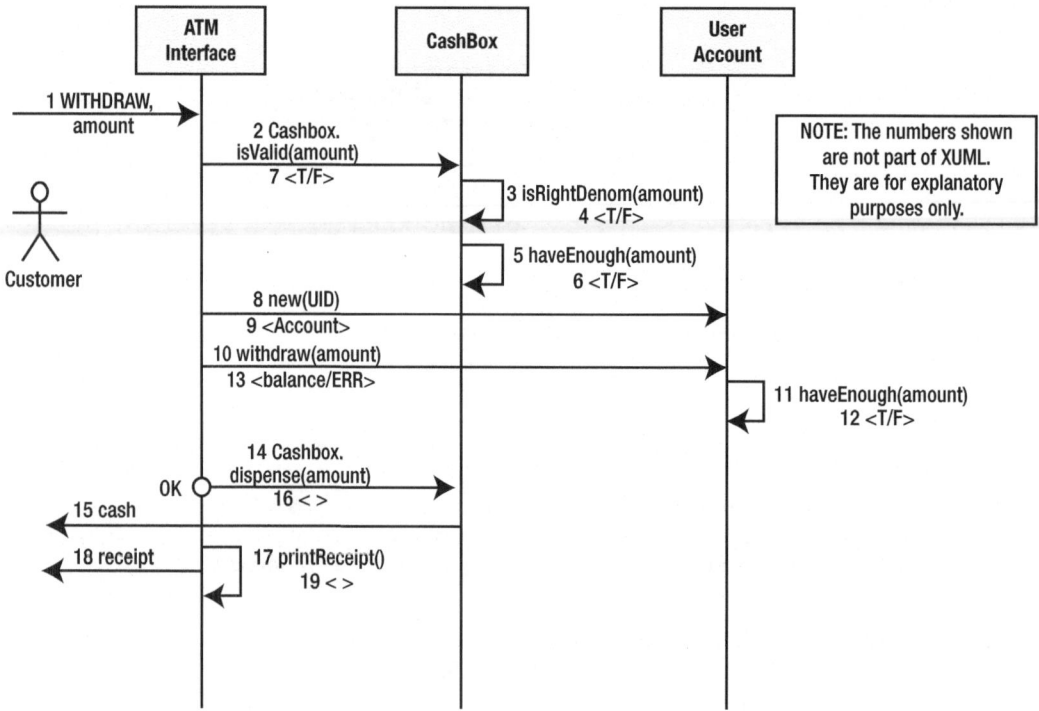

Figure 9-7. *ATM Withdraw sequence diagram in XUML*

Steps 2-6. The CashBox is a singleton, so the ATM makes a static method call (at least in Java) to check that the withdraw request is valid. The CashBox calls its own private methods isRightDenom(amount) to verify correct denominations are available, and haveEnough(amount) to verify enough money in the CashBox to dispense the requested amount.

Steps 7-9. The CashBox says the request is valid, so the ATM interface creates a new instance of the user's Account, passing the user ID (UID) with the constructor. The new keyword always calls an object's constructor and returns the called object.

Steps 10-13. Now that the ATM Interface has access to the right account, it asks the Account to withdraw the amount by the public call withdraw(amount). The Account first checks for sufficient funds with its private method haveEnough(amount). The withdraw() method returns either the balance after the deduction or an error.

Step 14. Up until now, error conditions were ignored, and the flow walked the use case's "happy path." The optional circle is shown on the next method call to emphasize that money will not be dispensed unless all verifications are true. On this path, the static call CashBox.dispense(amount) is called. It is static because ATM Interface does not have a reference to CashBox (that we know of); it never called CashBox's constructor. It is possible that an earlier use case (e.g. Initialize) got the reference to CashBox, and that would show in the pre-condition or invariant of the detailed use case.

Steps 15-16. CashBox dispenses cash to the customer, as shown by the arrow back to the customer. The single-stroke rule says that the flow continues from the tail of the arrow before returning back along the CashBox.dispense() method call.

Steps 17-19. After the CashBox method returns, the ATM Interface calls its private printReceipt() method. All data needed for the receipt is in the ATM Interface object, or was passed in, as in the case for the account balance. The receipt is printed, the method returns, and the use case ends.

But What About That Misplaced UID?

The sequence diagram shows that the UID was needed to instantiate the correct account. At first, many novices reasonably place the UID in the account, but the ATM Interface wouldn't know which account to create; it cannot get to a piece of data in an uninstantiated object. How does the ATM Interface get the UID? In all likelihood, the UID is best captured from a Security class that keeps the UID and account mappings. See Figure 9-8.

During the user's session login use case, the security agent authenticates the user login data and returns the proper UID. Since analysis rules dictate that only one class can own the same piece of data, it makes more sense for the Security class to own the UID instead of the ATM Interface, which is for coordinating. To create an instance of the user account, the ATM Interface would have saved the UID during the login use case and uses it now. The case of the misplaced UID shows how these two approaches force the analyst to rethink his or her analysis to get a consistent solution between the use case, sequence diagram, and class diagram.

Other Data

Notice that the CashBox's balance and the Account's balance were also missing in Figure 9-6, and are now shown; otherwise those class's methods would have nothing to calculate against.

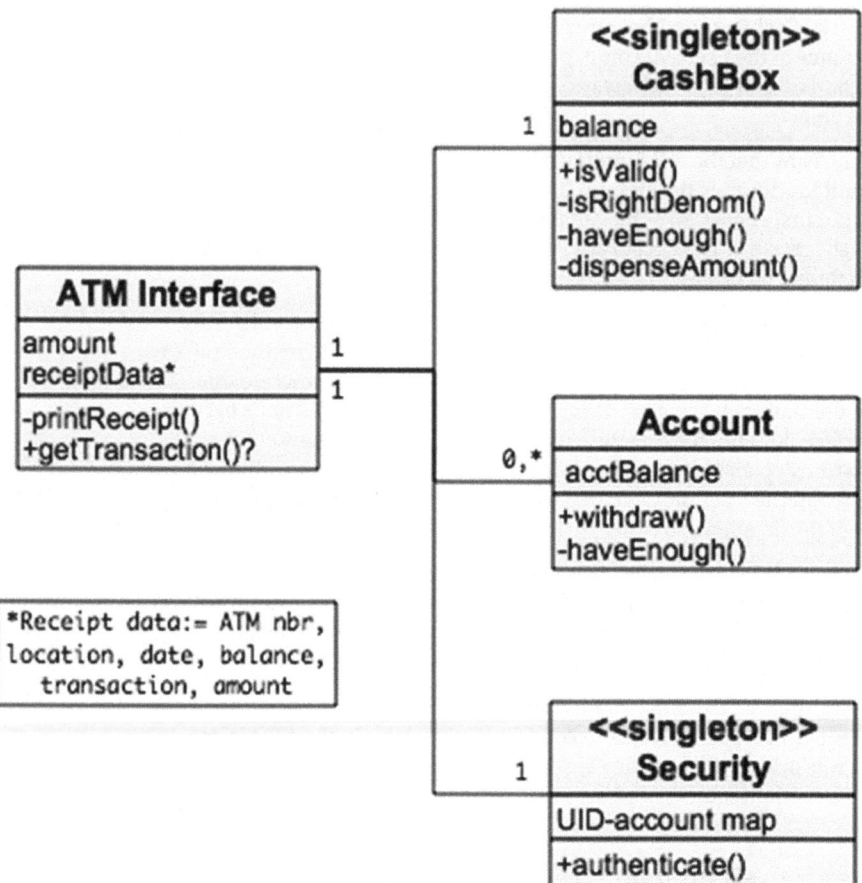

Figure 9-8. *Second Pass: Class diagram supporting ATM Withdraw use case*

Design Extensions

The above-described use case-to-object model validation can be performed at the design level too. The design level extends the analysis level by adding implementation classes, methods, and non-problem domain classes (e.g. persistence objects and GUI widgets). It also adds data types for parameters and return values. Due to the increased features in design, the design diagrams are about four times more complex (in my experience), although some have reported up to ten times more complexity. Design level validation is worth the time and effort if quality is a high priority.

Use Cases in Object Systems: A Deeper Look

Mathematically, one may think of each workflow of the system as the *composite function* of its constituent transactions: $W = T1 \circ T2 \circ T3 \circ \ldots$, where the transactions Tn are use cases. Similarly, a use case in an object-oriented system is a composite function comprised of individual object functions $Ti = f1 \circ f2 \circ f3 \circ \ldots$, where the constituent functions fn are the individual *method calls* to the objects on the use case path: the output of one is the input to the next on the path.

The use case T, which means the first method call $f1$, takes its inputs from outside the system, and delivers its outputs to outside the system.[8] Unless a complete execution of the input-process-output path (usually a circuit) is made, the use case is not complete; anything less is a *partial* use case.

An *object* is an entity that contains *identity, state*, and *unique behavior*, or responsibility. The object's responsibility is enabled by its functions, called *methods*. An object is not a procedural entity, but a scope-of-control entity. In objects, the functions are specially related.[9]

Intermixing object-oriented programming and procedural programming is not a good idea, as evidenced by the conflicts between the two paradigms in its earlier years. A programmer can write procedural code, or a programmer can write object-oriented code, but he or she should not try to mix the paradigms in the same program. Bjarne Stroustrup, inventor of the C++ language, evangelized C++ as a multi-purpose language. As he says in a 1995 talk to OOPSLA,[10]

> *C++ directly supports a variety of programming styles. In this, C++ deliberately differs from languages designed to support a single way of writing programs. This paper briefly presents key programming styles directly supported by C++ and argues that the support for multiple styles is one of its major strengths. The styles presented include traditional C-style, concrete classes, abstract classes, traditional class hierarchies, abstract classes and class hierarchies, and generic programming. To provide a context for this overview, I discuss criteria for a reasonable and useful definition of "object-oriented programming."*

However, it is exactly because of the orthogonal idea between procedural and object-oriented decomposition that BAs can validate their use cases.

Conclusion

XUML is another option for the analyst or designer, another tool to put into their belts. Standard UML is a fine tool, and all other rules of UML apply to what was said here, but validating use cases for correctness requires XUML at the analysis level because of the data flow checking. Over half of a software product's defects are in the requirements, so the quality of the product can be more than doubly improved simply by using this approach to build a consistent and unified object model.

---

[8]For each use case $F(x,y\ldots) \rightarrow z$, there may be zero or more input parameters $x, y \ldots$, and output data z can be void; in all cases, control is returned to an outside actor.

[9]Object methods are a special kind of function called *relation functions*, and dictate how they *should* interact with the objects' state and its other methods. For more on this topic, see *Conceptual Mathematics: A First Introduction to Categories "*, F. William Lawvere and Stephen Schanuel, Cambridge University Press, 1997.

[10]*Why C++ Is Not an Object-Oriented Language*, Bjarne Stroustrup, paper from talk given at OOPSLA95, Austin, TX, 1995.

CHAPTER 10

■ ■ ■

Development Thread

Chapter 8 gave an overview of the iteration process, tasks, and artifacts for the team as a whole. This chapter contains a detailed look at the work of a developer within an agile iteration. It shows how the developer uses inputs from other team members, and produces outputs to be used by them. This chapter can be considered a heuristic for how agile developers do their job. It should help other team members understand the developers on their team, and possibly enable non-trained developers to perform the design, construction, and unit testing functions better.

The Agile Software Developer

The role of "developer" is a high-level description for several technical specializations. An agile developer may be a programmer, a software designer, a database analyst, a web page designer, a network engineer, etc. This chapter is not going to delve into the technical differences and intricacies of their jobs. When a task is described as, "Developer designs the UI interface," it may refer to a user interface expert, a psychologist performing that duty, a web designer, or a programmer trying his or her best to get the web page to make sense. In general, the developer is someone who, at the individual workstation level, defines the design and UX artifacts for the requirements, writes the code and unit tests, and helps to resolve failed tests with the testers. The developer also plays a key role in all team meetings.

From Chapter 8, the tasks of the developer are to

- Contribute to estimating the use cases or user stories for the iteration planning meeting.

- Understand the use case clearly enough to implement and estimate the size of the work, including reviewing the use case validation model (if presented).

- Develop the UX artifact design, working with the BA, and possibly the business SME, to define web pages, screen layouts, and the like; and provide UX improvements from the design perspective if applicable.

- Approve the full use case and UX as sufficient for implementation.

- Review the GUI and integration tests as sufficient to test all use case paths.

- Write the final code for each use story and unit test, preferably with Test-Driven Development (TDD), the standard agile practice for minimizing coding effort and defects.

- Run the automated regression tests before delivering the Build to the shared codebase for the testers. Repair any defects found before submitting the code.

- Contribute to transferring the Development Build to the test environment (Test Build).

- Contribute to the Defect and Change meetings to resolve failed tests: cull out obvious defects, determine root cause of others, and perform impact analysis for any resulting Change Requests.

- Approve the Build as completely ready for the user demo, or make it so.

- Contribute to the iteration closing reports and update the RTM with use cases implemented.

- Contribute to the user demo meeting, perhaps facilitating some of them.

- Build deployment configurations for the necessary platforms and user profiles before the user demo and before release.

Variant Agile was invented by a developer for developers. Consequently, the project focus and iteration flow are strongly centered on developers. If they do have a person on the team with business analyst (BA) skills or requirements elicitations skills, then the BA's duty is to serve the developer by providing requirements so the evelopers can write code.

Some agile methodologies do not have a PM or BA role, and see that role as unnecessary. Scrum, for example, has a Product Owner who does the tasks of the BA and Business SME, as described in this book, except that requirements only originate from the Product Owner. This is fine if only one stakeholder provides the requirements, but usually that is not the case.

Agile Developer Characteristics and Idioms

Before we go into the specific developer tasks, there are aspects of agile life that are characteristic of agile teams, particularly for the developers. It is important to mention the various cultural and procedural idioms of an agile team that enables agile to make a difference.

1. Projectized Agile Teams vs. Developer Allocation

2. Iteration Planning (Poker Planning)

3. Sustainability

4. Agile Team Room

5. Pairing (Pair Programming)

6. Osmotic Communication

7. Information Radiators and Big Visible Charts

8. Daily "Standup" Meetings

9. Refactoring

10. Test-Driven Development for Unit Tests

Others are illustrated in the section "A Typical Day in the Life of an Agile Developer" at the end of this chapter.

Projectized Agile Teams vs. Developer Allocation

Projectized, or standing, agile teams, are the ideal teams for agile projects. They are already self-organized and self-empowered teams, so they will not need to go through the various group dynamic stages of forming, storming, norming, performing, and adjourning, famously called Tuckman's ladder (Tuckman, 1965). Wasted time is avoided. Standing teams already are high performing teams; projects are sent to them, like an assembly line takes car components and creates cars.

However, it is unlikely that an organization will have these projectized teams, especially for organizations new to agile. As an alternative, here are a few guidelines for how the team members can be allocated and organized. Although the description focuses on developers, the principle applies to any team member role.

Most traditional organizations are functional or matrix organizations, and teams are requested from a *resource manager* who is responsible for the professional performance and allocation of the team members. Each resource manager may be responsible for all people of a particular role within the corporation: project managers, developers, testers, etc. The project leader (PM) must usually negotiate with the resource manager to acquire the team members. If outsourcing is required, funding negotiations are added to the burden.

Assuming that all negotiations go well, there is still a policy of *how* team members are allocated. For example, there is a strong distinction between a programmer who develops a new product, a *developer*; and a programmer who maintains existing code in the production environment, a *maintenance programmer*. Historically, the former were generally considered more experienced and expert in their field, and the latter were assigned to make minor fixes and clean up the code once it was in production. It used to be thought that maintenance programming required lesser skills, so novice programmers were assigned maintenance tasks instead of new product development. The opposite seems to be true when one considers how complex legacy code can get.

The niche in which an organization places one kind of programmer or another determines what kind of projects they will be assigned to. Unfortunately, neither kind of programmer has a large influence on whether he or she is rotated between new projects or old ones, or permanently assigned to one kind of programming. The PM must negotiate with the resource managers to get the right developer for the job, and work with the organization to ensure that agile teams members are dedicated to the project team to focus better on the project .

Resource managers can place novice programmers in a new agile team instead of placing them initially in maintenance programming. Novice programmers will learn the standards and quality practices quicker during pair programming sessions for a new product, partly because they will be mentored by experienced developers. If a novice developer is placed into maintenance first, they will take longer to on-board, especially if they rely on the typically poor documentation associated with the product. In the worse case, the novice will write bad (or non-standard) code for a product already in production, and the users become the new and unwilling *de facto* QA department as they catch new errors created in the maintenance environment without regression testing.

Resource managers must be careful not to choose the best developers to rotate, and leave behind the lesser-skilled developers in maintenance. There are also those programmers who prefer maintenance work, and those preferences should be recognized and honored. On the other hand, sometime resource managers place the least expensive developers on a project to minimize funding sources instead of matching the skills required for the project.

☞ Recommendation If a static agile team cannot be set up, then as a second-best case, developers should rotate between new projects and maintenance duty. After a developer finishes a project, he or she serves for maintenance. When a new project comes along, the developer previously doing maintenance moves onto the new project. Developers rotate like the batting order of a baseball team. The frequency of rotation depends on how many new projects are moving through the agile development queue. In either case, the developer should be dedicated to the current product to which they are assigned until the project ends.

There may be another motivation for moving developers to maintenance with the product. If the newly released product is buggy and requires much cleanup, the developer will not be available for a new project until they get all their bugs repaired, and the product is clean. This incents developers to write their best code *before* release to minimize maintenance burdens *after* release, so they are free to move onto new development as soon as a new project is available.

Sustainability

Agile methods allow developers to work at a steady and sustainable pace. Traditional projects were famous for long bouts of overtime and stress, what Ed Yourdon called "Death March" projects. See *Chapter 3*.

If the APM made the project schedule using *adaptive planning* (estimating roughly on large targets far in the future and estimating in detail on small, closer targets), and the project is broken into iterations, then the developer need only be concerned with committing to what he or she will complete by the end of each iteration.

Teams that develop within time-boxed iterations at a sustainable pace will be less likely to fail (all other factors being equal), and achieve a better work-life balance by avoiding death march projects.

✖ Anecdote One project in a large company used a team of about 120 developers for a mission critical project. The developers worked overtime: 7am to 7pm, and a few hours on Saturday—for over a year! A death march project. Even during the customary Christmas break, many developers were working. One developer I was mentoring complained about not seeing his baby. She was learning to walk and talk, and he wasn't there.

Eventually, the project completed, and it went to market. The product was on the market for about one month when management redirected its mission and the product was cancelled. About 20 percent of the developers on the project quit the company. (Later, some returned with much increased salaries.) Death march projects kill morale and lowers productivity, and in this case, it damaged the company. Frequent releases and sustainability would have prevented this problem.

The Agile Team Room

Since the earliest days of Extreme Programming, agile teams have re-arranged the furniture to allow a large open area with shared table space for team members to work together. Developers work in the open without privacy and talk to each other in all the directions they can turn their head; no blocking walls, no scheduled appointments, no waiting for needed information. The open agile room enables *osmotic communications* and *pairing*, two concepts that are discussed in their own sections below.

People will communicate more frequently if they see each other and are in earshot of each other. They can spontaneously start a conversation and resolve a problem much sooner than if they need to get up and walk down the hall to a person's cubicle; or worse, if they must schedule an appointment.

The *agile room* concept grew from the earlier consultant's practice of a "war room," in which a consulting team was cloistered in a single large room for them to do their work, isolated from employee business. Consultants had nothing to do but complete the product. Progress charts, big visible charts, and diagrams adorned the walls. This arrangement is similar to how agile rooms work today.

The agile room contains all that is needed to build and test the code, with links to the development and test environments. Today, many of the repositories, like the shared codebase, reside in the cloud. A large TV screen to show online Kanban boards and burn-down charts of iteration progress may replace the 3x5 card wall. The TV screen works as a hybrid *information radiator* and projector, and costs are comparable.

Rearranging the furniture was controversial in the early days of agile, and one of the practices that made XP extreme. Kent Beck reports how his team clandestinely moved the furniture at night. I enjoy this example of Beck's "managerial courage."

> *All this screwing around with the furniture can get you in trouble. The facilities management people can get downright angry to find that someone has been moving desks around without their permission or involvement (never mind that a request for change can take weeks or months to fulfill). I say, "Too bad." I have software to write, and if getting rid of a partition helps me write that software better, I'm going to do it. If the organization can't stand that much initiative, then I don't want to work there, anyway." (Beck, 2000, p80)*

Cubicles arranged around the perimeter of the room provide privacy for design get-togethers, when the noise gets too distracting, or for personal communications; but the cubicles are still close to the team. In the worse case, the team member may move himself or herself to a private area for deep-think or other activity that requires no distractions. Agilists call this area the *cone of silence*[1] or *the cave*. Real privacy issues, such as performance reviews, are best done in small conference rooms outside the agile room.

Normally, the agile room is not used for meetings between the APM and upper management, or for the BA and the business SME. Upper management and the business stakeholders are always invited to see the team in action in the agile room, but it is not a common occurrence (it is distracting to the team). By extension, I have seen top executives, not involved with the project, visit the team to see what this weird new development technique called "agile" is all about. The big visible charts on the walls, or the Kanban board on the TV, or the strange room configuration of the agile room, attracts them.

Pairing (Pair Programming)

Pairing (originally called *pair programming*) is a coding style in which two developers, testers, or other people work at the keyboard at the same time, taking turns writing code, tests, or whatever the task at hand.

Pairing is natural for mentoring-mentored relationships, and works well to train a developer new to the project. It continues to be beneficial when two skilled developers work together. One keeps a mental focus at the high level on analysis and design, and the other works at the low level on the code. They switch off on the keyboard as ideas fly. They both work at getting the tests and code written. It is fun and it is productive. Pair programming has saved me (and others) hours in missed opportunities or coding errors I was *about to make* if it hadn't been for my partner.

---

[1]The *cone of silence* can refer to a physical location, or a mental state that one is in when they are in deep-think mode. Either way, it means to others, "Don't bother me. I'm busy."

Partners are not assigned to each other. The task is the focus, and two people decide to work that task together, usually because each has something to bring to the work. (I often work with a GUI expert, which I am not, and the GUI expert likes to see my Java coding idioms.) One developer may have several programming partners during the day.

There are also times when team members work on their own. This practice has become more commonplace as the vogue of pair-programming-as-dogma has diminished. The team members work separately or together as they need, and that flexibility is one of the values of agile.

Pairing sounds counter-intuitive at first, and certainly was not embraced by managers in the early days. Since pairing has become common, studies have been conducted to find if it is economically beneficial. After all, as early-day managers pointed out, "We are spending two salaries to get one piece of code." Rico, Sayani, and Sone (2009) report the results of 30 studies on pair programming.

> [30 studies] report an average of 34% cycle-time reductions, 76% productivity improvements, and 69% quality improvements. Eight of these studies had the detailed measurement data necessary to estimate return on investment, which averaged 2300%. That is, for every dollar invested, $23 was returned. This comes from a combination of high productivity and higher quality, which reduces the costs of software maintenance. Pair programming is far more efficient than traditional methods. (Rico, Sayani, Sone; p92)

✖ Anecdote   During one of my summer jobs when working my way through school, I liked working with a particular co-worker, Jay. We would take on tasks as frequently as we could get together. Jay and I challenged each other to get more work done, and we had fun, but management continued to break us up and put us on separate tasks. We were told, "If you and Jay are having fun, you can't have been working." Working individually, my other co-workers were surly, didn't seem to enjoy what they were doing, tried to slack off, and got a lot less done than what Jay and I) accomplished together. That job was my first example of the "pairing" dynamic, and of the wrong-headedness of management regarding productivity.

Osmotic Communication

Osmotic communication was an unexpected benefit of having an agile room. It enhances communication and saves time. Alistair Cockburn, one of the signatories of the Agile Manifesto, coined the phrase "osmotic communication" in his *Crystal Clear* book (Cockburn, 2004).

> Osmotic communication means that information flows into the background hearing of members of the team, so that they pick up relevant information as though by osmosis. This is normally accomplished by seating them in the same room. Then, when one person asks a question, others in the room can either tune in or tune out, contributing to the discussion or continuing with their work. Several people have related their experience of it much as this person did:

> "We had four people doing pair programming. The boss walked in and asked my partner a question. I started answering it, but gave the wrong name of a module. Nancy, programming with Neil, corrected me, without Neil ever noticing that she had spoken or that a question had been asked."

When osmotic communication is in place, questions and answers flow naturally and with surprisingly little disturbance among the team. Osmotic communication and frequent delivery facilitate such rapid and rich feedback that the project can operate with very little other structure.[2]

This effect is almost the opposite of the *cocktail party effect* of selective listening: A person has the ability to tune into one conversation and tune out others of little interest even when sound permeates a room.

The opposite effect is called a *draft:* unwanted information that flows across a team, usually unwanted because it does not affect the project or tasks at hand. In this case, the individuals holding off-topic conversations are better holding those discussions away from the team. Mutual respect and courtesy among team members make that happen. The net result is that the team stays centered on the project in the agile room, and only the work is discussed. Distractions are at a minimum.

Information Radiators and Big Visible Charts

Agile is known for having 3x5 cards, big visible charts (BVCs), and burn-up charts on the walls, on project web pages, and even in the hallways that allow the team and passers-by to provide self-evident data about the project. These devices are collectively known as *information radiators* because the observer gains information about the project quickly and easily, sometimes merely by walking by.

People want to be involved in a successful project, and displaying success helps people feel good about themselves. Using information radiators is one way to do that. It is a general rule of project management that the project must stay visible to the stakeholders (*transparency*), especially the sponsor. Projects that lose visibility often lose priority among the many other things stakeholders are doing, and eventually could lose support. As the wit says, "Out of sight, out of mind, out of budget."

Daily Standup Meetings

Agile has replaced the weekly one-hour status meetings with a 15-minute *daily standup meeting*. Daily standup meetings are not technically "status" meetings, but daily planning meetings. Each team member answers three questions each day:

- "What did I do yesterday?"

- "What will I complete today?"

- "What impediments are blocking my progress?"

Each team member learns what other team members are doing to better interact on their respective tasks. The meeting lasts about two minutes per person; no long rambling progress report of "what happened when." Daily meetings should be held as one of the earliest events of the day so that the team has the psychological context of getting the work done before they go home for the day.

Originally, the daily meetings were held standing up because each meeting was not supposed to be long enough for people to sit down, relax, and get off-target. The point is that the meetings should be very short, and standing up discourages a team from engaging in long discussions because they are relaxing, and treating the meeting as break-time. While standing, the "feeling" is to get back to work. It is not the standing up part that encourages brisk planning, but the daily pressure to move the product forward. Some agile

---

[2]Repeated on his blog at http://alistair.cockburn.us/Crystal+Clear+book, August 20, 2014.

teams do not literally stand during their daily meetings but they do use the short three-question format. The daily planning and pressure is more important than the standing.[3] The team stays focused and more gets done during the iteration.

Why bother with a special meeting every day? Why not gather all the information into one hour summaries at the end the week? There are several psychological principles that come into play related to task effort, timing, and progress. The daily meeting takes advantages of those principles' benefits, and minimizes their downsides.

- *90% Syndrome.* Developers report that they are 90% finished a task for 50% of the duration of the project (Boehm, 1981, p607). Daily meetings discuss *completed tasks,* so reporting work completed is an all-or-nothing situation. A task is not reported as being 90% done in a daily meeting because only completed tasks are reported.

- *Parkinson's Law and Deadline Effect.* Parkinson's Law states "Work expands to fill the available volume" (Parkinson, 1957; as reported in Boehm, p592); and its converse is the Deadline effect: *The amount of energy and effort devoted to an activity is strongly accelerated as one approaches the deadline for completing that activity.* (Boehm, p593). These two principles explain why many students cram for tests: they wait until the last minute then fill the remaining time with increased energy and effort—and usually stress—the foundation of procrastination.[4]

Parkinson's Law, in conjunction with the 90% Rule, yields an interesting effect: the time it takes to complete a task spills over into the time after the deadline by about 10%, and one late task accumulates on succeeding late tasks until the entire project is over 200% late. Schedule overages in traditional projects usually result in testing activities being unceremoniously truncated, which drastically affects quality: one deficiency on top of another. By setting a daily deadline for each task, the 10% spillover on a small task is much easier to recover from, and subsequently, the work progresses faster.

- *Increasing checkpoint frequency increases progress.* More frequent checkpoints reduce the resources needed, or when applied with the same number of resources, to shorten the time to complete the work (Boehm, 1981, pp45-46). By setting a daily deadline for each task in the daily meeting, the work progresses faster.

- *Psychological Lensing.* People estimate the effort and size of a task better for tasks that are nearer to the present time, and better for smaller tasks than larger tasks. The bigger the task and farther into the future the task is planned, the less accurate will be the estimated duration and size of that task. This principle accounts for the errors of long-range planning, even when unexpected changes *do not occur* to spoil the plan. Agile uses progressive elaboration and rolling wave planning to leverage this lensing affect. By shortening the estimate cycle for small daily tasks, estimates are more accurate. The daily meeting collects daily estimates of tasks that are imminent to keep the task completion the most accurate.

- *Completion pressure.* Daily meetings put psychological pressure on team members to finish a task each day, and the somewhat negative peer pressure of reporting an undone task helps enforce the completion of that task. The pressure of the deadline, applied well before the deadline, partially helps to counteract the Parkinsonian effect to assure that the task is completed on time.

---

[3] *Dilbert*, Scott Adam's satirical cartoon strip, illustrated a parody of the stand-up meeting: if making the attendees uncomfortable by standing worked, then it should work even better if someone throw office supplies at the attendees during the meeting to make it shorter.

[4] Music students are one of the groups that are exception to this rule because they must practice continually; they cannot wait until the last week to perform a one-year recital, for example.

Short daily meetings help synchronize communications between team members about interrelated tasks, and enable precise tracking of tasks completed during the iteration, and focuses on delivering one more piece of working software of value each day.

Refactoring

Refactoring means revising (improving) existing code without affecting its external appearance or behavior. Martin Fowler defines refactoring in his book on the mechanics of refactoring (Fowler, 2000):

> *Refactoring is the process of changing a software system in such as way that it does not alter the external behavior of the code yet improves its internal structure. It is a disciplined way to clean up code that minimizes the chances of introducing bugs. (preface, p xvi)*

Refactoring is not unique to agile, but agile cannot be accomplished without it. As code is changed over time, it gets less organized and veers from its original design. This is an *entropy*[5] effect and it gets progressively worse over time during product maintenance. Entropy is the root cause of why some code cannot be maintained after it gets too old; it must be rewritten. With agile coding practices of writing small chunks of code and revising them frequently, the code suffers from entropy more than traditional code. Refactoring is the answer to that: it is a direct effort of reversing the entropy of the code to improve its design, but the programmers must put in the energy to do so.

Refactoring is a continual process while writing code, not a scheduled event when the iteration development team stops and starts a multi-day refactoring effort. The agile cycle of development is (a) write a unit test, (b) write the code to make the test pass, then (c) refactor the code to clean it up and remove the interim code to improve its quality.

Refactoring is also used whenever the developer sees a place where it *can* be improved. If a developer is adding a method to an object, and sees where an improvement can be made, then the developer makes that improvement. Coding is a constant battle between the forces of entropy and the forces of clean coding. It is evident why regression testing is so important after each chunk of code is refactored. Fowler's book contains dozens of techniques for refactoring code for different situations and to improve the specific mechanics of coding. Smart Interactive Development Environments (IDEs) for developers have refactoring patterns built-in to make the entire process simpler and more likely for the developer to use it.

Test Driven Development for Unit Tests

The developers receive the approved requirements to implement at the same time the requirements are given to the testers to write test cases. The testers concurrently write integration and GUI test cases while the developers write the code and *unit tests*.

What Are Unit Tests?

Unit tests are critical to minimizing rework and writing clean code. Ottinger and Langr (2012) give a common definition for an agile unit test:

> *A unit test is a small automated test, coded by a programmer, that verifies whether or not a small piece of production code, a unit—works as expected in isolation.*

---

[5]Entropy is a measure of the amount of disorganization of a system, and energy is required to reverse entropy. Code gets disorganized as changes are made, and the energy of refactoring reverses that disorganization.

The unit being tested is usually one of the methods (functions) of an object. Michael Feathers (2005, p14) is often quoted as defining what a unit test is *not*.

Unit tests run fast. If they don't run fast, they aren't unit tests. Other kinds of tests often masquerade as unit tests. A test is not a unit test if:

- *It talks to a database.*

- *It communicates across a network.*

- *It touches the file system.*

- *You have to do special things to your environment (such as editing configuration files) to run it.*

To write a use case to avoid Feather's un-definition, then the developer would need to make mock databases, fake network connects, and other stub entities to make the test pass faster. This is exactly what must be done to support an integration test.

A unit test is distinguished from an integration test, regression test, system test, exploratory test, or other kind of test. Mike Hill (2009) coined the word *microtest* to refer to a small, automated unit test.

How Small Should a Unit Test Be?

Some say a unit test tests a single thing: there should only be one true/false assertion in the unit test. Others are comfortable packaging several short tests within the same test method, as long as each internal test is independent. I like to group my tests together if they have the same setup.

Feathers allows that the tests that violate his un-definition of a unit test (above quote) should also be run, but should be separated from calling them true unit tests. If they exercise less than a use case, then they are not integration tests either. We can take guidance from Mike Hill in defining true unit tests as *microtests*, and these other less-than-integration tests as, to coin a word, *macrotests*.

I feel comfortable having this other lower-level setup and teardown block of code *within* a test method for the microtest, but still requiring each microtest to be independent. That means a single test method may contain a series of independent microtests, each having their own `assert` statements. Some agilists would disagree, but I find it a convenient way of balancing large tests with many, many microtests repeating many, many identical setup and teardown blocks of code. Macrotests are more canonical and have their individual setups and teardowns within the test case. There are no semantic differences between microtests and macrotests, only a way of packaging sets of microtests in the same test method for convenience.

When to Define Unit Tests?

Unit tests are not pre-defined. They are built just before the developer writes the code. Unit tests are very design-centric, so until detailed design is done, unit tests cannot be written. TDD practice says that tests drive the code, so the test exhibits the behavior when the code enables the test to pass.

✗ Anecdote On one of my projects, part of a multimillion dollar, ten-project program, we had one week to define and deliver each unit test that we were going to build, but we had not yet collected requirements! The unit tests were due nine months before requirements, design, and coding were going to be started.

After discussions with management, they removed the mandate, but the team was astounded that they would ask for it in the first place. We argued that even in their traditional waterfall culture, we could give them integration tests after we had requirements, but not unit tests until design and coding were done. With an agile project, which they wanted us to do, we could give them the unit tests and integration tests at the end of each iteration, with possible updates afterwards.

By the first release date, we had produced tens of thousands of lines of code, and thousands of tests. Management had an outside independent QA group re-test the code (alpha test, as expected) but none of our tests were examined. I found out that the *number of tests* was used as a rivalry comparison between project managers in the program. "Who wrote the most tests" seemed to be more important than who had the lowest defect rate, or the most business value per unit of time. To add awe to amazement, the projects were not comparable: each project of the program was creating different sized products, with very different functionality, and was written in a different programming language!

Typical Agile Unit Test Cycle

When writing unit tests, there are several guidelines to follow for clean code.

   A.   How to define tests: Follow the F.I.R.S.T. rules.

   B.   How to write tests: Follow TDD practices.

   C.   What kind of test to write: Follow the NEBS method.

   D.   Comment the code and tests for those who must follow.

Each of these practices or guidelines is explained below.

A. Write Tests F.I.R.S.T.
When writing unit tests, keep in mind that they should comply with the F.I.R.S.T rules.[6]

- *Fast*: They must be fast so that the developer runs them frequently.

- *Isolated*: They must not rely on other tests to execute properly. They must do their own setup and teardown, and not rely on what order it and other tests are run.

- *Repeatable*: They not only should give the same results each time, but they should run the same regardless of platform or environment. The tests should isolate intermittent failures to guide the developer to repair the code or test; otherwise the test gets ignored.

---

[6]Bob Martin also discusses these rules in his book *Clean Code* (2009, pp132-132).

- *Self-Verifying.* The test should either pass or fail. They need to be objective, regardless of log files, text output, etc.

- *Timely:* Write the test just before the code is written. When the code needs to change, write the test for the end-state, which should fail, then write the code to make it pass, just as before with initial code.

B. Test-Driven Development (TDD)

The definition of TDD can be found on Wikipedia (TDD, 2014):

Test-driven development (TDD) is a software development process that relies on the repetition of a very short development cycle: first the developer writes an (initially failing) automated test case that defines a desired improvement or new function, then produces the minimum amount of code to pass that test, and finally refactors the new code to acceptable standards. Kent Beck, who is credited with having developed or "rediscovered" the technique, stated in 2003 that TDD encourages simple designs and inspires confidence.

There are several aspects to coding and unit testing using TDD. The typical construction procedure is as follows.[7]

1. Select a single action, a method within a class, that supports the user story under construction.

2. Write the unit test with no code implemented yet, thus the test will always fail the first time.

3. Write the simplest possible code to make the unit test pass.

4. Add another piece of the unit test to exercise another aspect of the code, and repeat. When all unit test are done, the method is completely tested, and the simplest code is written.

5. Submit the code and tests to the shared codebase and select another method to test for the user story. Repeat steps 1 to 5 until the entire user story is coded and unit tested.

The minimum code is written to pass the test. Agile uses the phrase YAGNI (You Aren't Going to Need It) to emphasize that only what is needed to pass the test should be written. Traditionally, developers have added features and data fields "just in case", and according to a Strandish Group study, 64% of the features written are never or rarely used (Johnson, 2002; Duong, 2009). Agile practices build only the Minimal Marketable Feature with which the developer can get to pass the test.

Tests are automated with *test frameworks or test runners* collectively named *xUnit*, such as JUnit for Java, CppUnit for C++, PyUnit for Python, and so on. Each test class is organized to correlate with a single (object) class, also stored in the *shared codebase.*

Running a test with xUnit tools produces a red bar for a failed test, and a green bar for a passed test, on the test runner interface. These tools are so common they have paved the way for another slogan: Red-Green-and-Clean.

---

[7]The procedure is typical for object-oriented languages because they are the most common development paradigms in use today. Functional languages are coming into vogue, including certain functional constructs being added to Java, an object-oriented language. Regardless of object-oriented or functional languages, TDD still seems to the testing paradigm of choice.

RED—the test fails first, then

GREEN—the code is written and the test passes, then

CLEAN—refactor the code to be more readable and "cleaner" by removing
interim statements and removing testing or logging artifacts.

The agile unit tester runs through the unit testing cycle of Red, Green, and Clean every few minutes. The green bar is so good to see after a series of red bars that the developer soon builds an emotional relation with the green bar. Sometimes a visitor to the agile room can see a developer shout, "Yes!" and pump his fist; the team knows the developer got a green bar after a long series of red bars.

One downside of TDD is that there are many tests, and the tests must be maintained. IBM and Microsoft (Nagappan, Maximilien, Bhat, and Williams, 2008) showed that for their TDD projects versus their control projects, the ratio of test code to source code was 0.51—about half the shared codebase contained test cases, but with 60% - 90% fewer defects. This research also showed that initial development time increased 15% -35% while the teams were ramping up on TDD technique. One of the early TDD reports said even with the overhead of writing test cases and refactoring them as needed, that they were able to speed their projects up by a factor of four!

The test cases *must* be maintained. If the tests are written initially, but not updated as the code is changed, then the developer gets the worst of two worlds: time spent on useless tests, and code that is not tested and may hide defects.

✖ **Anecdote**   For one of my complex projects, I measured that after about one year, almost 40% of the code base was comprised of test cases. Yes, it does take extra time to write and maintain those test cases, but without them, the product begins to fragment and situations get missed. I was concerned over this time burden of writing and maintaining the tests, so I measured it. I found that without the tests, it took several hours longer on average to implement and debug a use case than with them.

C. Follow the NEBS Method

When writing the unit tests, look for user paths that demonstrate the Normal situations (the "happy path"), Error situations, Boundary situations, and other Special cases that don't fall into the previous categories.

One of the critical Error cases is the *Null Parameter* test: passing null values into method parameters to see if the method handles the error gracefully, or crashes with a stack trace. The NEBS method is important in both unit testing and integration testing. The rule for whether you need a Null Parameter test or not is indicated by the rule: "If the code compiles with a null parameter, the null parameter test is required."

For a detailed description of the NEBS method, see *Chapter 10*.

D. Comment the Code

Most modern languages have the ability to self-document their public contract, or their Application Programming Interface (API).[8] Officially called documentation comments (Bloch, 2008; pp203-208), comments are inserted into the code for the developer or tester to understand what the public interfaces are, what they do, and what is needed for them to produce the desired effect. Javadoc is a Java tool that reads the code and creates well-formatted, browser-readable documentation automatically, based on the comments placed in the code by the developer.

---

[8]"Application Programming Interface" (API) is an unfortunate historical leftover. It does not apply only to "applications" but also to any public interface that another developer would need to know to work with that class, interface, object, method, or public data.

Document all public interfaces, classes, method calls, and data for use by other developers or technical readers. Not all agile developers think comments are necessary. Some think that comments should not be written within code. They claim that the code should "speak for itself," and that the comments are easy to get out of sync with the code itself, making the comments useless, or worse, misleading.

If the methods are small (less than 15 lines of code or so), like they should be, lack of comments works well enough. However, for longer methods that cannot be broken down (or take more work than the developer put in), complex methods, or methods that have a special circumstance or algorithm, comments are necessary.

Most modern IDEs like Eclipse will pop up Javadoc comments by merely hovering over the entity's name (method, class, interface, or field). If there is no Javadoc for the entity, no information is shown, and minutes are wasted searching for that method elsewhere; nor does Eclipse pop up the code to let it speak for itself.[9]

A second point about "letting the code speak for itself:" developers are not always the best at making their code (or comments) readable by others. Method names like `displayObjects()` and `calculateValue()` can be obscure. With comments, the reader has two chances of learning if they need the method or not, and how to make it work for them.

I do not like to examine someone else's code, or way of thinking, to figure out what that code is doing, especially if it is spread across multiple files because one method calls another method in a different class. It is easier to read a couple lines of comment text than to jump over to other files and read code. My mind is already focused on what I am trying to do, not what someone else tried to do, a distraction that slows me down.

Developers within the Iteration

This section describes the work of the team within the iteration process flow from a detailed perspective of the developer. The iteration starts with the developers' role in the iteration planning meeting. The box numbers in each heading refer to the boxes in Figures 8-1 and 8-2 of Chapter 8.

Iteration Planning (Box 1)

At the beginning of the iteration, the team holds an *iteration planning* session. The meeting allows the team to estimate the size of each use case relative to each other, and to determine how many use cases can be completed by the end of the iteration.

The APM or BA brings a list of prioritized detailed use cases from the product backlog to be estimated. The team must decide how many use cases can be completed by the end of the iteration. The developers have the primary responsibility of sizing each use case because the developers are responsible for implementing it. The testers contribute their estimates for testing, and the BA will ensure that the use case or story is understood.

When the developers leave the room, they will have an iteration backlog of prioritized use cases or user stories, and one specific card he or she will work on today. The developer can begin thinking about how the use case will be implemented, and be ready to design the UX artifacts. The developer may ask herself "What database schema is needed to support the screens?" or "What GUI widgets would work best for selection?"

Develop the User Experience Artifact (Box 4)

Soon after the iteration planning meeting, the BA facilitates a team meeting to develop the user perspective and UX artifacts for a detailed use case. A UX artifact is a communications tool to allow the parties involved to gain a visual understanding of the product's behavior and appearance of the use case. UX artifacts describe how the requirements will be presented to the user, and fall into the design realm of the developer. This UX artifact design meeting integrates requirements and design, and lasts about 30 minutes.

---

[9]To be fair, Eclipse has a shortcut to take the developer to the declaration of any method on which he or she hovers. However, the method must be in a known `class path` package for that to work.

The BA may provide a draft UX artifact developed with a business SME previously. The developer may have his or her own prototype artifact available for discussion too. The business SME may attend to help resolve and think through the many design options. Sometimes it matters to the business whether the users select from a drop-down box, enter text, or select radio buttons; these choices are resolved in the discussion.

There are many open source and commercial tools to help build screen shot artifacts, sometimes called *wireframes*. They can range from very low tech (low-fidelity), such as a drawing on a whiteboard captured with a cell phone camera, to a high-fidelity prototyping tool that makes the wireframe more formal, and writes some skeletal code.

The decision of low- or high-fidelity probably rests mostly on how long the wireframe will be used, and if it is going into the technical or user documentation. Agile usually relies on low-fidelity tools because they are quick to get the point across. Wireframes can be as simple as a snapshot from a mobile phone, or the result of an elaborate mockup application, like Balsalmiq.

At the end of the UX design meeting, the business SME, BA, and developer agree that the UX artifact establishes a *Definition of Done*, although it may change *by consensus* during implementation and testing. At the end of the iteration, after the UX artifact is implemented, tested, and approved during the user demo, further changes will require an informal Change Request (CR).

Implement Use Case and Unit Tests (Box 7)

At the same time that the testers are writing the test scripts, the developer will *implement* that use case, that is, write the code and unit test for it. Code is written one user story at a time because a use case is usually too large to code directly. A user story is short and has a single clear objective.

Code and unit tests are informed by the GUI and integration tests. The developer reviews the code and unit tests with the testers before writing the code.

Assumedly, the developer is using TDD, which means he or she writes a very small test, and then writes the code to get that test to pass. The whole process takes a couple of minutes. Next, the developer augments the unit test and code to make *that* test pass. After a series of such test-code-test cycles, the user story is complete. The developer submits the code and associated tests to the *shared code base*, the team-shared repository for all code, tests, and technical documents. The developer repeats the same cycle for other user stories in the use case until the entire use case is complete. It is easy to submit *something* to the shared code base daily.

For more detail, see *Refactoring* and *Test Drive Development Unit Tests* earlier in this chapter.

Run Regression Tests (Box 8)

Automated regression tests consist of all integration and unit tests that passed earlier for the Build. After each user story is completed, the developer runs the automated regression tests to ensure that old code was not "broken" by the new code (that is, it did not cause new defects). If something was broken, the developer repairs that code, old or new. The regression test will also cover all the other developers' code and unit tests that are downloaded each day.

If all the code has passed its unit tests, then it's time to run the automated regression suites. The regression suite contains all the unit tests and integration tests from all the developers that passed in earlier versions of the Build. If a *regression defect* appears from running a regression test, your code broke it, or it may have been caused by another developer's code being too fragile. Isolate the error, find the root cause, and pair with the other developer if necessary. Your code cannot be uploaded until there are *no defects* in the Build.

After the code is written, and all unit tests and regression tests pass, you can add the unit tests to the automated test suite for future regression testing. Merge your new code into the existing Build. Submit new code to the shared database frequently, at least once each day.

Daily Builds and the Shared Codebase

There is a maxim in agile that all code is community code, and no one developer "owns" it. All code and tests must be committed into a shared codebase at least once a day, where each developer's work is merged into a single Build. The frequent merge ensures that work is broken down into small parts, and potential integration conflicts are removed or kept to a minimum. Each day, all developers download a new copy of the updated codebase and new regression tests from the last Build. Open source tools, like Subversion (SVN) or Git, are available to manage this process well.

A shared codebase means there must be one *central point of authority*.[10] Anything that is not in the codebase is treated like it "doesn't exist" as a work product for the Build. The team stores documentation, requirements, procedures, public documentation, and other information in addition to code and tests. All these items go through revisions within the project duration, and need a central point of version control.

Update the RTM

The Build is available to the testers to run their tests against it after all the user stories for a use case are implemented, tested, and in the codebase. The developer updates the use case as "code complete" in the RTM by inserting the date all unit tests passed, to indicate to the test team that they can run their integration tests against it. The use case is not marked "complete" because a use case is not complete until all integration tests and regression tests pass too.

When the developer goes to update the RTM for use case code-complete, he or she may already see that the test case scripts have already been added to the RTM because it usually takes less time to define the test cases than to implement the use case. Also, the daily team meeting informs everyone which use cases are available for testing, which ones are waiting on coding, and which have been tested.

The developer will be involved with his code next after the testers test the use case, find defects, and call a Defects and Change Meeting.

Upload the Development Build for Testing (Box 9)

When the developers have completed implementing a use case in their Development Build, and it is uploaded to the codebase, it is now available so that the tester can download it to the test machine, at which time it becomes a Test Build. The testers can take the Build and run their battery of tests against it while the developers move onto the next use case and update the next version of the Development Build.

The developers no longer have control over the Test Build; they continue augmenting their Development Build. The Test Build is officially in QA (for the agile team) and code must not be changed in the test environment. A new Development Build will overwrite the Test Build later if changes are needed, or new use cases are ready for testing. A successful Test Build represents the latest Build to show the users at the upcoming user demo, and possibly staged for release.

When is the Development Build ready to become the Test Build? When the developers have (1) written all the code for the use case; (2) written all the unit tests for the use case code; (3) the Development Build passed all the regression tests 100%; and (4) the "code complete" date is recorded in the RTM for the use case.

---

[10]The version control tool *Git* allows each developer to have his or her own repository without requiring a central repository, and yet still keeps them in sync to establish a single Build.

Continual Improvement

Adding defective code to the code base from one developer "poisons the well" for everyone. Other developers must now clean the code before they can proceed to their own tasks. Automated Continual Improvement (CI) tools, like Jenkins, allow other tools to be run before allowing the uploaded code to merge. Full re-compilation, regression testing, style checking, compliance tests, and others can be run before the new code and tests are permitted to be merged into the code base. Errors can be caught and returned to the contributor without poisoning the well.

Anecdote At one company I visited, whenever someone tried to move a piece of code to the codebase with errors or failed regression tests, the CI tool triggered a bright blue flashing light and a klaxon to sound off. Since the developer had to sit in a particular chair to upload his code, everyone in the room could see who did it. The peer pressure (read: embarrassment) was humorously given and received, but was a powerful force to minimize defective code and encourage developers to check their code before uploading it to others.

Defects and Change Meeting (Box 13)

The Defects and Change meeting is part of agile's low-ceremony change control process. After the testers run their battery of tests against a use case of the current Build, the passed tests are recorded in the RTM, but the failed tests are recorded in the defect log and need to be discussed. Not every failed test is the result of a code defect. Some failed tests are the result of requirements defects, tests defects, or requirements interpretation. Sometimes the SME attends if a Change Request is needed or for an interpretation to be resolved.

The developers will immediately acknowledge some failed tests as code defects, and take responsibility to repair the code. For each failed test, the developer makes a card and puts it into the iteration backlog for repair; or, with team approval, defers it to a later iteration.[11] A defect card always has *zero points* and cannot extend the scope of a use case, although the *solution* to a defect repair may increase scope.

The team may defer the repairs until a later iteration, but the number of defects, and time to repair a defect, tend to *snowplow* by increasing exponentially the longer they are left in the backlog. Agilists have a phrase, *technical debt,* that they use to refer to the exponential cost of catching up, particularly with outstanding defects deferred too long.

It has long been known that defects cluster together. In general, they follow the Pareto rule: 80% of the defects are found in 20% of the code (Han, 2003; Ghahrai, 2008). This means that a defect not repaired can hide many more defects that will reveal themselves (with the proper tests) after the evident defect is fixed. This undoubtedly contributes to the snow plow effect. Therefore, what may seem like a repair of a few hours may reveal new defect repairs that could take days once found.

Complete repairs within the current iteration as quickly as possible to minimize technical debt and the impact they will have on the team's velocity. The snowplow effect is so onerous that defect repair frequently takes priority over any new code being written.

In addition to defect repairs of any variety, a few CRs may be triggered, all of which need estimates on how long the repair will take. Some impacts can be estimated in the meeting, others require a developer to analyze and will take longer.

When the meeting is over, the team will have a list of defects (of any kind) that must be repaired, and a list of CRs that must be evaluated for impact. The team adds any resulting tasks to the iteration backlog. The RTM is updated now if it was not updated earlier.

See also the "Implicit Change Management Flow" section of *Chapter 8*. For an example of a Defects and Change meeting, see the "A Typical Day in an Life of an Agile Developer" section below.

---

[11]Some teams work directly from the defects log, and do not add cards, but that approach cuts down on visibility.

Approve the Build (Box 14)

This step is the standard "Is it ready for release?" meeting. When all tests pass for the use cases designated for the iteration, and no CRs or repairs are needed for the current Test Build, then the Test Build can be approved as complete and ready to demo. If the use cases are not yet complete, but the iteration is ending, then the Build can still be approved, but with reduced scope.

All team members take accountability for the Build being ready. Each developer must be certain that there is no defective code in the Build, and all code fulfills the iteration requirements completely. All of the regression tests pass 100%. All defects in the defect log scheduled for this iteration are repaired.

After the team approves the Build to go in front of the stakeholders at the user demo, do not make any changes to it! Every Test Build that is approved is staged for the user demo, and should not be merged with subsequent Builds until that Build is approved by the stakeholders too. The team should continue to update the Dev Build if necessary, but keep the Test Build staged. I cannot recall the number of times that "just one little change" has caused the demo to fail, freeze, or crash because a last-minute change was not properly tested afterward. Although full regression testing may have succeeded, the user demo focuses on the GUI, and there is no quick and easy regression for that just before the user demo.

Build QA & Iteration Reports (Box 15)

The iteration reports are built from the cards the developers and other team members completed throughout the iteration. There is no special work the developer needs to do. See *Chapter 12* for more on the iteration reports.

The User Demo (Box 16)

The *user demo* is a stakeholder meeting to demonstrate the accumulation of product scope since the first iteration, with focus on the changes since the last user demo. The key purpose of the user demo is to collect feedback from the stakeholders, and improve the product going forward. The user demo also provides the opportunity to present various reports to the stakeholders, users, and other attendees about product progress. It strengthens business team and technical team relationships and trust. The PM talks with the stakeholders and explains the state of the project. The demo itself can be presented by anyone on the team.

The developer is responsible for preparing the Build for the user demo meeting, which means setting up whatever data or configuration files are needed, and network connections, so that the demo will go well. If the user demo is not going to be presented in the agile room, which sometimes is used for demonstrations, then the presenter must verify that the Build will work satisfactorily in whatever room is being used for the demo. Go to the room early and test it! Are the network connections working? Is Wi-Fi available and at sufficient speed? Are any stakeholders remote, and must be connected through some other tool like *TeamViewer* or *GoToMeeting*?

The presenter and the APM test out the demo in the presentation room as a matter of routine. If the presenter is a developer, then the developer walks through the demo quickly, to ensure that it will work properly for the customer. A demo that works only on the specialized machines in the development environment may not be a reliable demo because it may not reflect the actual performance of the product when it is in production.

Stage or Release the Build (Box 17)

The product configuration is set up for each user demo, so there is not a lot that needs to be done later when the product is released. Sometimes, the developer needs to set up platform-specific configurations, or package technical documents. A tester has a checklist of what needs to go with the Release into production, and the developer assists with that list.

PMI Parallels

All the PMI parallels of *Chapter 8* are still true, but the following highlights some specifics for the Developer role.

The greatest differences between traditional practices and agile occurs during iteration development. After Kent Beck began agile with the practices of Extreme Programming,[12] it continued to evolve, and more and better practices emerged. PMI does not actually prescribe how to run a software project because project management applies to a broad range of project types. Specific practices vary widely.

Fortunately, the Software Engineering Institute (SEI) and PMI have taken agile under its wing. They emphasize that the PM principles are still the same but the mechanics are different.

One large traditional corporation instituted an agile development group, and the SEI accredited them Level 3 of their CMMi capability maturity model. One of the assessors said that because of agile, the practice of pair programming complied with seven different quality methods of Level 3, which included peer reviews, code reviews, etc.

Scope: Traditional development often writes code at the component and subcomponent level, using bottom-up and top-down development. Agile developers write code using a thin-thread approach, a user story at a time. Consequently, agile development does not do *integration tests* (component interface interactions) in the same sense as traditionalists, thereby saving time and effort.

The number of tests between agile and traditional projects should be the same if we base it on the scope of code being the same. However, agile unit tests are automated, especially with TDD, and are quicker and easier to write. Therefore I think the developer writes many more unit tests than developers on traditional projects. Unlike traditional testing that verifies after coding, the agile developer relies on the unit tests to progress with new code. I have no formal data on this point, but it would make an interesting study to find the number of tests written per line of code between agile and traditional projects for the same type of product.

Time: Agile developers commit to building at a sustainable pace, avoiding the traditional death march projects that typically come in late anyway. Each iteration is time-boxed to two-to-four weeks. Even Kanban projects, which do not require iterations, make use of iteration timeboxes for reporting purposes and retrospectives

Cost: Agile does not decrease cost directly, but the synergy of all the other factors produces a higher productivity and better ROI. Cost reduction results from the smaller teams, and the lack of rework, for agile projects.

Quality: TDD developers write unit tests before they write the code for those tests, and TDD is characteristic of agile. TDD developers get better code coverage and fewer defects than with traditional development methods. All facets of the team—APM, analyst, testers, and developers—cross-check frequently with each other and their work products to reduce the risk of defects to almost zero. There is no need for a post-iteration QA group to further test the Build; it is ready for release.

Human Resources: The team works together holistically, self-organized and self-empowered to solve problems. Agile team members feel better about themselves, and feel that they are contributing, they are making a difference. Work-life balance and morale are maintained. There are no "death march" projects, in the words of Ed Yourdon (2004).

Communications: The team members communicate constantly within each other even if they are not always aware of it (osmotic communications). Stakeholders and other people outside the team have a frequent stream of communication with the team. Project progress is transparent and stakeholder expectations management is a key factor to success.

Risk: Risk is reduced to time-boxed iterations, so the scope, and therefore the impact of the risk, is greatly reduced and more easily managed. Most problems are resolved within the iteration.

[12]Ken Schwaber and Jeff Sutherland's SCRUM practices pre-dated XP, but SCRUM was not called an "agile method" until the Agile Manifesto was signed in 2001.

Procurement: Agile developers are more involved in vetting vendors than traditional developers. Developers are not involved in procurements *contracts*, but they are involved in defining tools that they need. If the project is an open-source project, developers can obtain open source tools by a simple and quick download from the Internet.

Stakeholder Management: Constant involvement with the stakeholders is important, but that involvement is better to have with the APM and BA. The developers are usually on the critical path, and so they should not be distracted by work others can do. Developers work with stakeholders at specified times: at the user demo, with the business SMEs at the requirements analysis meetings, and possibly at the Defects and Changes meeting.

Conclusion

This chapter focused on the activities for the developers on an agile team. Instead of a bulleted list of activities performed by an agile developer, I wrap it into a "typical day" scenario in the following section. Following the "typical day" is a CORA table (Table 10-1) that summarizes the inputs, processes, and outputs undertaken by the BA. It is indexed by the box number of the Process Overview Diagram (Figures 8-1 and 8-2) in *Chapter 8*. The box numbers in brackets represent contributions instead of ownership of the task. Compare it with the CORA Matrix of Chapter 8.

A Typical Day in the Life of an Agile Developer

Below is a description of a typical day in the life of an agile developer to illustrate how all the practices merge together on an agile team, based on several of my real-life projects in the last ten years. In this scenario, the detailed use cases are in progress, and Bob the developer is writing code.

The Agile Room: At the beginning of the day, Bob sets up his laptop on the community table in the agile room. He shares a large flat table with two testers and three other developers. The table is strewn with food: apples, candy, half-filled water bottles, and at this time of day, coffee cups galore. There is a small stuffed monkey on the table, the "code monkey," used to indicate whose turn it is to speak in the daily standup meetings. The table is also strewn with paper containing written thoughts, half-finished designs, and code snippets—a landfill of yesterday's discussions.

Unlike the old days, when wires were layered across the table like an electromagnetic tar pit to capture anything dropped on the table, the computers and centrally shared codebase server are all wirelessly connected. Unlike the old days with tons of colored 3x5 cards and sticky notes on the wall to record the tasks as they move across the "Agile Board," the tasks are now on an electronic Kanban web page that everyone can access with a flip of their browser page.

Bob downloads the current Build from the shared codebase. He tests that it is clean…and it is. The current Development Build contains all the integration tests (now acting as regression tests) that were uploaded previously by the testers, Tom and Mary. The Build also contains the work Bob has been doing, and new code and unit tests from the other developers.

Morning Coding: Bob selects a part of a user story to build. The full use case is too large to code directly; a user story is short with a clear objective. Bob writes a very small test, runs it against his code. JUnit pops up a bright RED bar—Fail. Bob is not perturbed. He then writes code to get that test to pass. JUnit pops up a bright GREEN bar--Pass! The whole process takes a couple of minutes. Bob then augments the test case for more scope of the user story, and writes the code to get that part to pass. After a series of such test-code-test cycles, the user story is complete (but not the use case). Bob removes some interim code statements he made while testing, cleans up a few comments, and changes a variable name. He runs the test again after refactoring, which passes. He then runs the regression test suite that came down with the Build earlier. After a few minutes, it also passes, and Bob uploads his new code and unit tests to the shared codebase, to be merged with the current development Build. Just in time…the daily standup meeting is going to start.

The Daily Standup Meeting: In the old days, each member of the team would stand up every morning and tell what they had done yesterday, what they were planning to finish today, and if they had any issue that was obstructing their progress. Team members would move sticky notes at the last minute from one place to another on the agile board to reflect that work's progress. On this new project, the team watches a Kanban board on a large shared TV. They do not stand. They talk about the electronic cards on the K-board, a simulation of an assembly line as the use case goes from analysis to code to testing to Done. Bob still uses the canonical three questions to spend a minute or two explaining his progress from yesterday, and his plans for today. He will finish use case 11 today. No problems are foreseen.

Fred the BA asks why one of cards is still in the same position as it was three days ago. Betty explains that she had to redo a database read function for use case 17. Dirk volunteers to help Betty to complete use case 17 by end of day. Betty says "Thanks!" and passes a donut to Dirk.

Impromptu UX Design meeting: After the 15-minute daily meeting, Fred asks Bob if he "has a minute" to work through a couple screen design issues for the current use case that Fred is working on. Fred and Bob move off to one of the more private side cubicles for the discussion. They work on a whiteboard sketching thoughts for a design. After 20 minutes, Fred captures the image on the whiteboard with his camera phone; the UX design is done and Bob returns to his coding.

Osmotic Communications: During the next hour, while in his Red-Green-Clean cycles, Bob overhears a conversation from Jim asking Dirk for the location of a special variable. Dirk doesn't know. Bob says, without breaking pace on his testing and coding, that the variable is in the common file at location so and so. "Great!" says Jim, and gets back to typing quickly on his laptop. Later, Dirk answers the same question when Betty asks it.

Defects and Changes Meeting: After lunch, Alphonse, the APM, asks the team to gather for a few minutes to talk about the defect list that Tom and Mary generated that morning. They pass out a report containing 33 test items. Most are labeled Pass, with a pass date. Several others items are labeled Fail, with a number beside it that indicates the impact of the failure on the system—critical, major, minor, or cosmetic. "Whew," thinks Bob, "no crucial show-stoppers on the list. We can handle this."

Within a few minutes, the developers acknowledge the failed tests that they think are definite defects. For one item, Mary had to pull out the use case and show what it was suppose to do.

Strong disagreement arises over item 22. Dirk says it works "as designed" but Mary says it doesn't match the use case. Betty suggests, "What if we did this..." and she explains an interpretation of the spec. Dirk says, "Sure, that wouldn't take me long to change—maybe 30 minutes." Fred the BA says, "I think I can get that past our SME with little trouble. Write it up on the CR form, and then I'll get the approval." All of them get back to work after this 45-minute meeting. Betty writes up the CR form in 5 minutes, containing the 30-minute time impact, plus another 15 minutes for testing, and gives the CR to Fred. Fred thinks that if the SME had been present at the meeting, the SME could have approved the change immediately. Now Fred has to email it and get it approved outside the meeting.

Pair Programming: Bob continues his testing and coding cycles for the rest of the afternoon, but he has moved into code that was mostly Dirk's area last week. He asks Dirk, who is working with Betty, if he can spend a few minutes with him. Dirk makes a few comments to Betty and rolls his chair over next to Bob. Dirk and Bob begin pair programming.

Bob explains what he is trying to do, and they start writing test cases and code. Bob begins to write a test for a much-used method, but Dirk explains that he wrote a helper class that would make it easier. Bob only needs to import the helper class and variable, and they should be all set. The helper method is faster too. Bob has it working with Dirk's help in a few minutes.

After an hour, Bob and Dirk have completed that part of the use case. Dirk returns to helping Betty. Bob continues with the use case on his own, and has no real problems; all test pass. He finished use case 11 early and runs the regression tests one last time for the day. The regression tests pass.

End of Day Uploads: Bob uploads his code for the day into the shared codebase. As the files are copied into the shared codebase, the QA compliance tools are triggered by the CI tool and run automatically. Bob figuratively holds his breath. Three minutes later all goes green and the code is merged. A new Build is ready for testers Tom and Mary whenever they are.

Next Task Card: Bob checks the Kanban board to see what's next. He sees that Jim or Mary have already moved the defective use cases they discussed today at the D&C meeting (that's what the team likes to call the Defects and Change meeting) from the testing column back to the development column. He sees a card he could probably get finished before he leaves for the day. He assigns himself to the card and moves it into the "Coding" column of the Kanban board. He reviews the use case, and 20 minutes later, he knows how he will approach its implementation tomorrow.

As he closes down his laptop, Betty and Mary see him and wander over with questions about various tests and a GUI artifact he helped with yesterday. He answers the questions, and leaves for the day, felling good about the work he and the team accomplished today.

Summary of Developer Roles

Table 10-1. ***CORA Matrix for Developer:*** *Summary of the Developer Role (Brackets Indicate that the BA Contributes or Reviews the Artifact.)*

BOX #	INPUT	PROCESS	OUTPUT
[1]	Top of use case catalog from iteration backlog	Contribute to iteration planning	List of prioritized use cases to be completed by iteration's end
[2]	Highest priority use case from iteration backlog	Expand use case into detailed use case (scope refinement)	Un-validated detailed use case
[3]	Use case with optional validation model	Review use case for buildability	Possible changes to use case to make it more buildable
4	Detailed use case	Design user interface, screen shots, and augment use case with implementation ideas (Initial design)	Design case, with UX artifacts
[5]	GUI test scripts	Review GUI tests to see if they are consistent with code and design	Approved GUI tests
[6]	Integration test scripts	Review integration tests to see if they are consistent with code and design	Approved integration tests
7	Detailed use cases; UX artifacts	Implement use cases and unit tests	Code and unit tests for code; regression suite updated by unit tests
8	Regression test suite	Run regression tests to see if Build broke	Confirmation of clean Build or regression defects to be repaired
[9]	Development Build	Contribute to moving the Development Build to the test machine	Test Build
[13]	List of failed tests	Contribute to resolving failed tests, and estimating CRs	Code defects, CRs for which to estimate impacts

(continued)

Table 10-1. (*continued*)

BOX #	INPUT	PROCESS	OUTPUT
14	Iteration backlog, regression test results, defect log, QA checklists, RTM	Approve Build for completeness at proper quality or more work is needed (Quality Gate)	Remaining work for the Build, or approved Build that is ready for user demo
[15]	Code complete, RTM updates	Contribute to progress reporting	Iteration and QA reports
[16]	Build ready for user demo	Contribute to the demo, including presenting, recording changes, or answering questions.	(BA prepares meeting minutes with proposed changes)
17	Final Build	Prepare final Release package	Build ready for production and operations

CHAPTER 11

■ ■ ■

Testing Thread

Chapter 8 gave an overview of the iteration process, tasks, and artifacts for the team as a whole. This chapter contains a detailed look at the work of an agile tester within an iteration. It shows how the tester uses input from other team members, and produces output to be used by them. This chapter can be considered a guideline for agile testers. It should help other team members understand the tester and QA efforts on their team, and possibly allow novice testers working in an agile team to perform the testing and QA functions better.

There is a mindset change between traditional testing groups and agile testing groups. Traditionally, a product was sent to an independent QA group for testing after coding was completed. With agile, testing occurs during the iteration, and acceptance testing occurs with the user demo, or while the Build is in release staging. No further functional testing is needed[1]: there is no QA group required afterward for any reason unless the organization requires it. Eventually, the management will realize that the QA group is redundant, especially since the QA group probably uses the same tests as the agile testers. For more about agile testing approaches, see Crispin & House (2003).

The Agile Tester

This chapter gives a detailed look at the work of the different kinds of tests and testers within an agile iteration. A tester is the team member who protects the quality of the code: nothing gets past them until they agree the product is ready. Although the developer does his or her best at the low level (with unit testing) to prevent defects from getting into the code, the tester double-checks the behavior of the product at the high level to ensure that the Build meets the requirements and complies with the agreed-upon quality standards. The testers' interpretations and the developers' interpretations provide yet another level of verification that the product behaves as the user requested.

The testers receive their input from the business analyst (requirements and UX artifacts) and from the developers (design, code, and unit tests), and produce output back to the team (defects for repair to the BA, developer, or tester), and the APM (test results for reporting).

There are two kinds of testers during the iteration: the GUI (Graphical User Interface) tester and the integration tester. One person may fill both these roles, but their tasks require slightly different skill sets. The distinction between GUI tests, the developers' unit tests, and integration tests are discussed below.

The GUI tester ensures that that user interface is correct, that the product has the right *look and feel*, which is a subjective term for the user's holistic experience when using the product. The GUI tester ensures that the user interface (screens, reports, and anything else that the user sees) behaves as expected, contains the right info at the right time, and navigates to the next screen page as expected.

---

[1]Sometimes system testing (non-functional) is performed while the Build is in staging awaiting its release date. System testing includes stress testing, capacity testing, and performance evaluation.

The integration tester ensures that the product works as a whole according to the requirements given. Integration tests exercise the entirety of a user story; programming skill is required to write the automated integration test cases. Integration testers are usually comfortable with the development environment because the automated testing tools, like JUnit, are often the same ones used for unit testing by the developers. From Figures 8-1 and 8-2 of *Chapter 8*, the tasks of the GUI tester or integration tester are as follows:

- Contribute to estimating the use cases or user stories for the iteration by factoring in the testing effort.

- Review and approve the use case, UX artifacts, and design considerations as something that is complete and testable.

- Write the GUI or integration test scripts for each user story, and review them with the other testers. Since GUI and integration tests inform each other, collaboration is necessary.

- Contribute tests to the regression suite that must run before final Build acceptance.

- Transfer the Build from the development environment to the test environment, and isolate it from the development environment. It is now the Test Build.

- (GUI tester) Execute the GUI test scripts for each user story against the Test Build. Record the passed tests in the RTM, and failed tests in the defect log.

- (Integration tester) Code and run the automated integration tests for each user story against the Test Build. Record the passed tests in the RTM, and failed tests in the defect log.

- Run all automated regression tests and QA compliance tests before approving the Build. Testers help define what is in the QA standards[2]. Record the passed tests in the RTM, and failed tests in the defect log.

- Contribute to the Defects and Change meetings to present the test results (RTM and defect log), help determine root cause of failed tests, and ensure that failed tests result in repairs or Change Requests. Maintain the RTM.

- Contribute to the Iteration and QA reports, particularly with test results and defect trends.

- Contribute to the user demo and Build release package as needed.

Test Cases

Before we talk about specific GUI and integration tests, let's talk about tests and testing in general. Agile products are built like an onion, layering newer functionality over previous functionality, always having a working product. Agile practices run automated integration tests frequently, often once each day. Agile integration tests are fast.

There are four kinds of tests run during the iteration:

- Unit tests, written and run by the developers;

- Integration tests, such as GUI and functional tests, written and run by the testers;

---

[2]QA standards address the development process, and are non-functional requirements or acceptance criteria (Definition of Done) with which the product must comply.

- Regression tests, the collection of all tests rerun each time the Build is updated;

- QA Compliance tests, the collection of tests that ensure compliance to QA standards (usually externally required) for coding, documentation, architecture, security, and other rule sets.

Some agile teams also use Acceptance Test-Driven Development (ATDD) in which the customers run tests on the product before accepting it into production. Sometimes they write the test cases down before testing.

System testing and performance evaluations are run outside the iteration, usually before a release. They are not covered in this chapter. Unit testing was covered in *Chapter 10*.

Integration Tests

An *integration test* applies to agile only for thin-thread testing, because agile uses only the thin-thread development approach.[3] A user story is a transaction with the user and the system, and the integration test confirms that the transaction behaves as expected. A *GUI test* is also a simulation of the product to confirm that it behaves and appears as it should at the visual level. Both kinds of tests simulate a thin-thread transaction, the thin thread executability defined by the user story.

An *integration test script* is a text file; the *test case summary* is a text entry in a spreadsheet; the actual *integration test* is a piece of code, typically written in the language of the product and run in a testing framework.[4]

The test coding language is usually the same as the programming language but simpler. Sometimes it is a test script of a commercial test application. Most languages have software tools to support test automation, such as Java's built-in support for JUnit. With the advent of automated testing tools that can be written in the programming language itself, there is little need for two languages and two skills sets.

Either a developer or a tester may write the integration test case. Some testers do not know how to program and cannot write test code. Strictly speaking, writing test code is a testing role because it is about writing and running gray box test cases. Therefore, if a developer is writing an integration test for a use case, the developer is filling the tester role.

Writing integration tests is simpler than writing product code. Often, a developer new to the project can get his or her feet wet by starting with integration tests. Alternatively, I have taught non-programming testers how to write JUnit tests, and that has worked sufficiently well.

Integration Tests and Software Architecture

The integration test (and tester) must be aware of the software architecture and its API to properly flow through the system. Figure 11-1 shows the software components for the MVP architectural model (4+1 Component model)[5] described in *Chapter 5*. It also shows how the JUnit testing framework integrates into the system for automated testing.

---

[3]Thin-thread development means that the product is developed and tested along input-process-output transactions at the user level. See the "Differences Between Agile and Traditional Integration Testing" section.

[4]Test scripts as used here are textural descriptions of tests that exercise the user story, as opposed to scripts that select and run suites of tests (like an Ant Build script). Scripts are still important for packaging and configuring Build issues and Continuous Improvement (CI) issues. Tools like Ant and Maven allow Builds to be written without the heavy-duty scripting that was once required.

[5]The four components are HIC (Human Interface Component), typically the GUI, but the HIC also includes report and printed outputs; the PDC (Problem Domain Component), which contains the business rules; the SIC (external Systems Interface Component), which handles external systems communications and networking; and the DMC (Data Management Component), which handles data persistence. See *Chapter 5*.

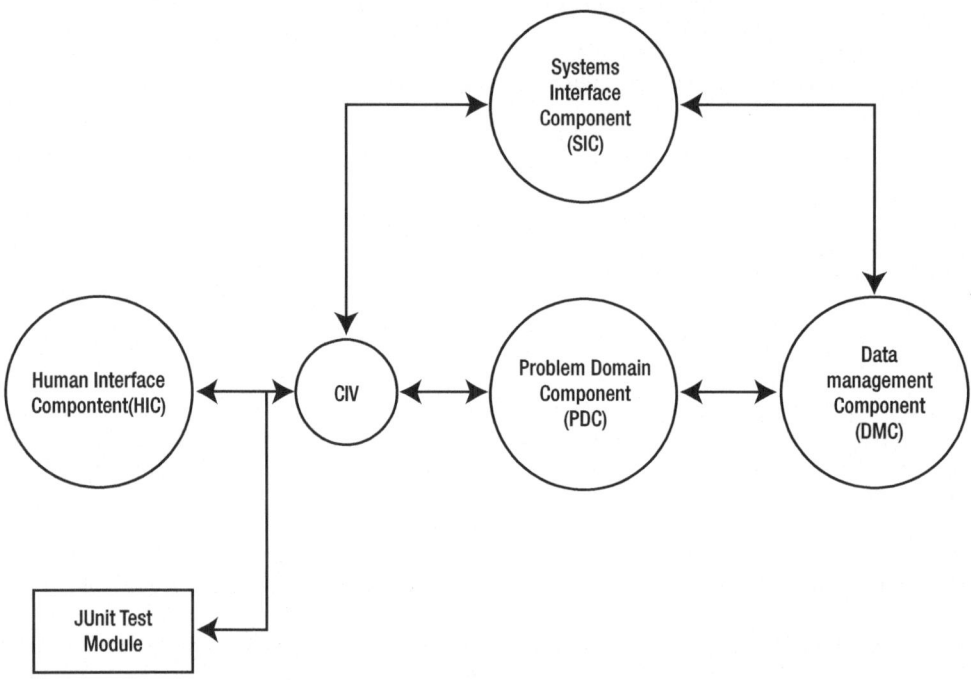

Figure 11-1. *The 4+1 software component architecture*

Integration tests are derived from the use case, a user story at a time. The GUI test cases and the design inform the integration test. Although the integration test simulates the GUI at the CIV, integration tests and GUI tests are usually not the same.

The MVP software architecture requires the following structural integrity (see Figure 11-1 and *Chapter 5*).

Production code passes input data from the HIC (usually GUI data from the user) to the PDC through the CIV, which validates the input data and formats it for efficient internal use. On the output side of the transaction, the CIV receives output data from the PDC, formats it as GUI strings, and passes it to the HIC.

For testing, the JUnit test driver plugs into the HIC socket of the CIV. It feeds simulated HIC data to the CIV, and receives output data from the CIV that normally is transmitted to, and displayed by, the GUI in the HIC. In short, it intervenes so that the HIC objects are not involved, and the results can be caught by the Test Module and confirmed.

✖ **Implementation**   Java makes the CIV socket very easy to use. The public methods in the CIV take an HIC object `Interface` type which can be easily implemented by the product code and the testing code both. The testing code implements the HIC Interface as a Proxy. For example, the HIC uses an input-output panel for user transactions called class `IOPanel`, which implements the `IOPanelInterface`. The test code implements `IOPanelInterface` with `IOPanelProxy`. Either implementations of `IOPanelInterface` can "plug into" the CIV object method that takes an `IOPanelInterface` parameter to provide inputs and make calls to the implementing object. Of course, `IOPanelProxy` outputs contain no GUI info, only logging data and assertions.

Differences Between Agile and Traditional Integration Testing

There are three major differences between traditional testing and agile testing: integration type, size, and frequency.

- **Integration type:** Traditionally, integration tests used several strategies: *top-down*, stubbing out the lower level units for the test; *bottom-up*, requiring a test harness at the higher levels to integrate the lower level units; and *thin-thread*, executing a transaction through the product from beginning to end. Agile testing, which is based on user stories, uses only thin-thread integration testing.

- **Integration size:** Traditional integration tests were run on subsystems, large modules, and sub-modules, and verified that these pieces ran together correctly. Unlike traditional integration testing that examines large pieces of the system, agile integration testing typically works at the lowest level scope: the object and its methods.[6]

- **Integration testing frequency:** Traditional integration tests were large and took a lot of time to run. Consequently, they were run late in the development cycle, usually just before release to QA or production. Agile integration testing is done at least once each time the Development Build is turned over to the testers. If integration test cases are not automated, they will not get run, and eventually, not built.

These differences allow automated agile testing to be run more often and earlier, removing defects earlier in the process, and thus more economically. However, the tests must be automated for them to have practical benefit.

Regression Tests

Regression testing involves running any test that previously passed to ensure that new code did not break old code, and that the passed test continues to pass as the product grows. Regression tests can contain any kind of test: integration tests, unit tests, GUI tests, or a combination. Automated regression tests contain all the automated tests that have passed once already.

Traditionally, regression testing took a long time to run, and so it was common practice to run a subset of the full set of tests. With Agile's thin-thread automated testing, all tests (the *test suite*) can be fully regression tested.

Regression testing is not restricted to agile; programmers have used it for decades. Any product built without regression testing will have quality problems.

Integration Regression Testing

The current integration tests are added to the last regression test suite and run again. Sometimes a new test that passed will fail within the regression test suite because the test is not as independent as the tester thought. The testing context has caused the problem; for example, a previous test has not reset the state properly. If the integration test fails in the regression suite, the tests before it give a clue as to the cause, and it can be repaired. The integration regression tests are automated, so running the entire suite should take not take long. Agile integration testing is usually not one of those run-it-overnight tasks because it takes too long to run during the day.

---

[6]Agile system testing, performed outside the iteration scope, works on the larger system pieces when needed, but the continual development paradigm rarely requires it. Performance evaluation is an exception in that it should always be done on the system in a real environment before being moved into production.

Graphical User Interface Regression Testing

The GUI must be regression tested, but I have not found an open-source tool that will perform complete and accurate *automated* GUI testing without a lot of overhead. Unfortunately, if the regression testing must be done manually, it is not performed every day like automated integration regression testing; time alone becomes prohibitive. At best, GUI regression is spot-checked when a use case is repaired, and at worst, once before a release.

☞ Recommendation for GUI Regression   When to perform manual GUI regression testing if you don't have an automated GUI test tool that you like? A good compromise allows selected stakeholders to examine the product as part of acceptance testing each iteration. This kind of acceptance testing is called *random* or *exploratory testing*. They may find unexpected defects and regression defects, but they will also think of changes they want to make. In any case, the continual communication will strengthen the bond with the stakeholders, contribute to their satisfaction with the project, and reduce the tedium on the GUI regression testers. If the stakeholders get ambitious, they might write automated test code before the product is written, and then the team is using ATDD.

Another alternative is to ask the help desk personnel to run GUI tests frequently. They must support the product after release, and I usually have not had a problem asking them to learn the product by testing. They often enjoy being released from the drudgery of repeated call-taking.

QA Compliance Tests

There is more to QA than integration testing. There are other checks: Did the developers follow the agreed-upon coding style? Were all Javadoc comments (or other developer-written documentation) completed for the technical documentation deliverable? Is the portion of the user manual completed and ready to go?

QA Compliance testing ensures that certain standards set by the team or organization have been met: test coverage, programming standards and metrics, and code documentation are key. It is up to the team to ensure that the standards have been followed, but unfortunately, that often falls to the testers. Fortunately, there are many automated tools available to assist with these checks. Below are listed a few that my project teams have used that you might consider.

- **Unit test coverage**: A couple of my project teams created custom Javadoc tags that went into the test code with the unit tests, tags that indicated which kind of NEBS tests were run. The Javadoc documentation generator checks for the existence of these tags for us. The tags also show up automatically in the HTML output describing the class's API. The QA tester can check that all unit tests are written, and which ones, for all object methods by reading the Javadoc.

- **Programming standards**: Some tools will check that the proper coding style was followed. The open source programming IDE *Eclipse* has features built in to warn of bad style. Eclipse also has a formatter so that code-format standards can be met with a simple reformat command. *Checkstyle* is an open-source tool that can run against the code, and can be customized to ensure that the code complies with standards. *Jenkins*, a continuous improvement tool, has a battery of compliance checkers that can be run when the code is uploaded into the shared codebase. These kinds of tools can be run by the developer, but the testers run them again to confirm that all standards are met.

- **Metrics:** Metric tools can ensure proper code structure and design. Many IDEs have plug-ins so that the developers can run them before submitting poor or fragile code. My favorite object-oriented metric is the Kemmerer metrics (Kemerer & Chidamber, 1994) which indicates various factors of good object-oriented design, and can be downloaded into Eclipse. The metric values are relative, and are used for comparison against the classes and methods in the product. If most code files have metric numbers in the 10-30 range, then if a code file with 800 appears, it is likely to be a chief source of defects. The developers determine if a problem truly exists and should be repaired; at the very least, the code file can be documented as to why its design generates a metric outlier.

- **Code Documentation:** There is a school of thought that says, "Write no comments; make your code readable instead." This idea, which a team may or may not adopt, does not apply for the Javadoc comments at the public class and public method level, which are used for technical documentation. Even the staunchest no-comment agilistas recognize that the API must be documented for others to use the code. The class comments are at a higher level than class methods, and are needed by people who are not looking at the code: maintenance programmers, new developers trying to get an idea of the larger picture, developers on the team who haven't worked in that area of the product before, and programmers who wrote the code but can no longer remember what certain methods do or in what order a method's parameters should be called.

The documentation comments standards for Java to which my teams have committed, and that I recommend, are the following:

- Document packages with an overview of why the package exists. We always use the MVP architecture; this document file is repeated as boilerplate.

- Document all public classes and methods so that those wanting to modify the code later will know what is happening and why.

- Inner classes and private methods comments are preferred but not required. (Default-scope or package-scope classes were prohibited in our standard.)

- Follow all standard Javadoc rules for documenting parameters, return values, and thrown exceptions.

- Each unit test method must have normal, error, and null test cases, with the associated `@Normal,` `@Error,` and `@Null` Javadoc tags. Boundary and special cases are optional, but if they are included, they must also have the `@Boundary` and `@Special` tags.

There are many other QA standards and metrics that could be validated, perhaps for multi-platform testing. Was each platform configuration test completed successfully? The point is that after the regression tests are run, other tests are run to ensure compliance. The developers may run them before the Test Build is delivered, but the testers must run them before they can approve the Build for user demo or delivery.

Concurrency

The approved requirements are given to the testers to convert into test cases at the same time the requirements are given to the developers to implement the code. The testers' path in the iteration workflow, running concurrently with the developers' path, complies with a few critical rules of development and testing. These rules apply to both unit tests and integration tests.

- **Rule #1.** *Tests are built from the requirements, not from the developers' code.* When the code is done, the test cases verify that the requirements are satisfied, not that the product "works as designed," a phrase often used as an escape for the developers not adhering to the users' needs as defined by the requirements.

- **Rule #2.** *The developer's code is independently tested.* It is important that the developer does not test his or her own code—another different perspective is required. The developer cannot see the blind spots that he or she built into the code. The developer can be successful enough at the unit test level, because only the developer is writing the unit, and the implementation at that level depends on the developer's perspective.

  At the use case level for integration testing, the use case is a text document that is unfortunately open to interpretation. The tester and developer provide two different perspectives (in addition to the BA) that cross-check each other so that any disagreement can be resolved. I cannot count the number of times a developer has told me that his code was error free before testing revealed a significant defect. "Oh," responds the developer, "I didn't think of it that way." Conversations with the tester and analyst prevent much of that effect, but verbal discussions are not as thorough as test cases.

- **Rule #3.** *All tests follow the NEBS technique.* Each use case can be viewed as a collection of paths that fall within one of four categories: *normal* paths (no errors), *error* paths, *boundary* paths (pairs of cases that are just outside and just inside the system boundary for the use case condition), and sometimes *special* cases that do not fall within the other three categories. Identifying test cases using NEBS will ensure that tests will cover all the functionality of the use case. These paths align with user stories.

Generally, the testers and developers play leapfrog on processing a use case. For each user story, the testers finish their test cases first and then "wait" for the code[7] so they can test it. The developer finishes the code and then "waits" for the tests to reveal defects for repair. The testers test again and then wait for the developers to finish defect repair.

Actually, testers begin writing test scripts for new uses cases while they "wait;" developers start coding the next use case while they "wait." Testers and developers often work two use cases in parallel as they leapfrog. Whoever is done first pulls the next use case from the iteration backlog to be implemented. If the developer has already pulled the next use case from the iteration backlog, then the tester needs to catch up, and write test cases for it. If the developer is still working on repairs or changes, then the tester pulls the next use case to start defining its tests.

Writing Test Cases

There are several aspects of an integration test case, and how they are written and recorded. The *test case summary*, the *test case script*, and *integration test code* are discussed below.

---

[7]Of course, on an agile team, no team member waits for another. Team members work on a different card while another card is being worked on by someone else. There is no down time on an agile team.

Defining Test Case Summaries

The *test case summary* contains a single goal and description for a test of a single user story. It is not a separate artifact but merely an entry in the spreadsheet, or a test tracking tool. The test entry is used to keep track of test status. The RTM serves as the final resting place for a passed test, but it is not the best place to keep track of the detailed test states, such as when it was tested, what defect resulted, test dates, repair dates, and the like; the RTM is a higher-level tracking tool. See Table 11-3 for a sample of test case summaries for the ATM Withdraw use case.

Why write test summaries before testing? The mindset is different when writing tests that when running tests. When the test cases are written, the tester can focus on all the logical possibilities without being bogged down by specific details about the test case—he or she is merely categorizing the kinds of tests that need to be written. The NEBS method is a good guideline for allowing the tester to be sure all the tests paths are identified.

This mindset difference is more pronounced when writing *automated* tests because when the tester writes test code, he or she must focus on the details mentioned above, but must also focus on setting up the test, defining expected results and error conditions, and resetting the system state, all in a rigorous non-natural (programming) language for testing. It is easy to forget some test cases while coding and running others.

When (and Why) to Write a Test Script

The *test script* [8] defines the details of preparing and executing the test case. The script contains descriptions of the inputs, expected outputs, procedure to set up the pre-conditions, procedure to verify the post-conditions, and results of the test. The script elaborates on the test case summary, and is a good communications document for developers and testers.

Scripts are more frequently built for GUI tests than for integration tests because the integration code serves as the script. If the XUML validation was performed on the use case, then each sequence diagram drives the test case, and can be used in lieu of a test script too. See Tables 11-4 and 11-6 for a test script form and example, respectively.

If the test case is required to find defects, and the RTM is required to track results, and the integration test code is required to execute automated tests, why write a test *script*?

All tests must eventually be used for regression: unit, GUI, and integration tests. The script describes what the test is doing long after the test author has forgotten about the test and its goals. *It is essential that the defect report form has a section explaining how to reproduce the failed test.* More traditional organizations keep an archive of all tests written for later production maintenance. Many agile teams will not write a test script but rely on the integration test code.

Developers do not write scripts for their unit tests because they write the code and that is sufficient for the small scope involved. The same argument can be made for integration tests—the test code is sufficient, unless the organization needs to keep the test forms for documentation and maintenance. Some agile teams may start with using the script form, then after a few iterations, work directly from the test case spreadsheet.

GUI tests are quick to write and run, but as GUI tests are run, there is an overwhelming desire to not check the results with pre-defined expected values. It is (erroneously) thought sufficient to see the behavior of the interface or return value and assume it is correct with only a "sanity check," if the result "seems reasonable." Sometimes the GUI tests returns something that is only close to correct. It is too easy to get caught up in the action of the moment and not think through all the test cases. This is another way that GUI scripts help catch defects.

---

[8]The term "test script" used here does not refer to the scripting language used in various automated testing tools. If an automated testing tool is being used, the tool's script can be used in lieu of the testing script discussed in this section.

⚷ Recommendation   In short, for GUI tests, I recommend that the tester writes test case summaries into the spreadsheet in one pass, and writes the GUI scripts and runs them in another pass. The script contains manual instructions on how to get to, and execute, the particular user story (path) in question.

For integration tests, the user summaries suffice, especially if XUML validation was performed on the use case; the sequence diagrams can be used in lieu of scripts to direct coding and testing. When I write integration tests, I put comments in my test code to remind me of the work I must accomplish in the tests.

GUI and integration tests must be entered into a spreadsheet for tracking passed and failed tests. Each test case name, GUI or integration, is also collected in the RTM for later tracking after it passes.

⚓ Variant   With my agile projects, many fewer defects were found than with traditional projects, so our teams wrote test scripts using that form *only when the test failed.* This approach worked for us well, with a minimum of documentation, despite the risk when new testers got involved and were not sure of what (or how) something was tested previously. Whether your team writes test scripts for all use cases, only for failed tests, or not at all, is left to the team.

Testers in the Iteration

This section describes the work of the team within the iteration process flow from a detailed perspective of the testers. The iteration starts with the tester's role in the iteration planning meeting. The box numbers in each heading refer to the boxes in Figures 8-1 and 8-2.

Iteration Planning (Box 1)

At the beginning of the iteration, the team holds an *iteration planning* session. The meeting allows the team to estimate the size of each use case relative to each other, and to determine how many use cases can be completed by the end of the iteration.

The testers contribute to the use case estimation meeting with everyone else to define the iteration backlog. Their efforts needed to test the use case are part of the use case sizing. For example, if the developers think a use case is three story points in size, the testers may up that to five because of some extra testing needed.

Any defects that must be repaired are added at this time too. Defects added during iteration planning are defects that escape repair in earlier iterations, and are coming back through the product backlog. The team must select and commit to fewer user stories in the iteration backlog because the time needed to repair defects must be considered. The team velocity will decrease as a result of the fewer user stories taken on in this current iteration.

Also, defects are automatically given *zero story point* value. The user story that had the defect already counted as done erroneously inflated team velocity. The zero point defect card resets the team velocity back to where it should have been.

The testers walk away from the meeting with the same list as everyone else: prioritized and sized use cases (or user stories) committed to be completed by the end of the iteration, written up on cards in the iteration backlog. Each tester will have one card from which they will start writing test cases today.

Develop GUI Test Cases (Box 5)

GUI testing ensures that the user experience is intuitive, compelling, efficient, and *as requested*. It focuses on the appearance of the user interface, including reports and other non-screen-oriented artifacts. GUI testing is called *black box testing* because the test case knows nothing about the product internals, but knows only about the inputs and outputs (behavior and appearance) of the product. Each test is treated as a stimulus into a black box which produces the desired outputs.

GUI tests are informed by integration tests and the code, so the GUI tester reviews the test scripts with the integration tester and developer as part of developing GUI test cases.

The GUI displays only string data and visual images, and contains only syntactical logic and widget control, and that is what GUI tests test. To maintain good separation of concerns, a primary design principle, and to enable the effective use of the testing framework with the MVP architecture (see Chapter 5), the majority of the input and output logic for validation and reformatting is in the CIV—the component between the GUI and the main application.

GUI tests send data from the GUI to the CIV, which validates the input data and reformats it for the main application. When the data returns from the main application at the end of the use case flow, the CIV reformats the output data it receives for the GUI.

In one project where this principle was diligently followed, 85% of the code was in the CIV or behind it, and could be tested automatically with integration tests. The GUI contained the other 15% of the code, and was manually tested as needed.

Can GUI tests be automated? Of course, any automation that saves time is desirable, but good GUI testing tools that don't require a large amount of overhead are rare. Many of the commercial tools we found had high startup time, high maintenance overhead, were expensive, or all of the above. Our team was not able to find an open source GUI testing tool that did not use up more time writing scripts and logging than the time needed to run the GUI tests manually. By keeping the majority of the logic out of the GUI and in the automated-test domain, we were able to minimize our GUI testing, and subsequently, reduce our risk of user interface defects.

Write Integration Test Cases (Box 6)

For agile, an *integration test* is a thin-thread test. It exercises all the objects and methods along a single path of a use case, and verifies the flow's expected responses. The integration test assumes that all the units (object methods) are working correctly, and runs them in sequence: the connections (API) between methods are being tested to ensure that they can pass off and receive data between them correctly.

Integration testing is called *gray box testing* because it knows more about the internals of the product than *black box testing,* but not as much as *white box testing* (unit testing). Integration tests have knowledge of each object's API in the CIV, but no further. They have some knowledge of the different paths that must be executed to identify the proper test inputs and outputs, but little else.

Integration tests do not test the GUI, but are informed by GUI test cases. Integration tests exercise the functionality of the use case throughout the system. They are coded and plugged into the system through the CIV component. See *Chapter 5.*

The testers write integration test scripts from the approved detailed use case, and record them in the RTM associated with the use case being tested. All integration tests become part of standard automated regression testing.

Developing an integration test script means three things:

- Design a set of inputs for known outputs that exercise a particular user story (normal, error, boundary, and special cases).

- Write test code to automate that test.

- Compare the expected results with the actual results automatically.

Although the test cases and scripts are developed now, they are not actually run until the testers have the Test Build, so they can only identify tests and record test information in the test scripts.

Integration tests are informed by GUI tests and the code, so the integration tester reviews the test scripts with the GUI tester and developer as part of developing integration test cases. If there are two different people writing GUI and integration tests, then the test review is even more important. GUI tests and integration tests inform each other, so both sets of test cases are improved in the comparison.

If the validating XUML sequence diagrams are available, the integration tests are much easier to write. The scripts are written together in preparation for when the Build is available for testing (Box 9).

⚷ Recommendation   If there is one person for both GUI and integration testing, then the GUI testing should be done first. GUI tests are easier, and less likely to change during coding. The interfaces used by testing will be more stable by the time the integration test scripts are written. GUI tests are also easier to change because they do not require changes to test code, like integration tests do.

Variant   It may not be necessary to write the actual iteration test *scripts* if iteration test code is written, except for complicated use cases and large systems. The test code is sufficient. However, it is essential that the test cases are identified, so that none are inadvertently omitted. The RTM ensures that all tests are identified and tracked.

Once the integration and GUI test cases are defined and recorded in a spreadsheet (for each use case or user story), the entire team reviews them. The team ensures that all user stories (paths) are covered. Knowing the tests also may bring out differing perspectives between tester and developer.

The sooner the developers and testers see what each other has in mind, the better. Developer/tester misunderstandings will show up in failed tests; better to remove them before they enter the code, or produce defective tests.

The test review step is not strictly a quality gate, so if the meeting is delayed or skipped, the testers can move forward and start running GUI tests and writing integration test code as soon as they have the Test Build. However, I have found that when this step is skipped, rework always follows, even if it is reconciling the testing and development perspectives later.

Agile teams encourage the test review to be done in short bursts of one or two cases at a time, which spawn many test cases. Still, the test review takes about 20 minutes.

Receive the Test Build (Box 9)

The tester moves the Development Build from the codebase, currently in the development environment, to the test environment, an isolated environment where the testers can exercise the current version. It is now the *Test Build*. Developers continue working on the Development Build and produce updated versions of it. They no longer have access to the Test Build, or its supporting structures and database files.

The test machine needs to be as close to the production environment as possible. Writing code for one platform will usually not run immediately on another platform; configuration changes will be needed at least. There are also links that need to be changed: production data files instead of development data files, web page links, etc. The test machine should be a clone of the production environment as much as possible, and not mirror the specialized development environment.

Some agilists may disagree with separating Test Builds from Development Builds because the "developers and testers work together to produce working software" as the pat answer suggests. However, the testers can not write reliable tests if the code is changing under their feet, and the developers don't have time to wait for the testing to be finished. They need to continue in parallel with the testers. I have been on teams that use the same Build for testers and developers–for a while. They stop when they realize they are on a hamster wheel of recurring defects, useless tests as code is changed, and regression defects galore. For a strong rebuttal against mixing Builds and for concurrency (or parallelism), see Gualtieri, 2011.

When is the Development Build ready to become the Test Build?

- When the developers have (1) written all the code for the use case; (2) written all the unit tests for the use case code; (3) the Development Build passed all the regression tests 100%; and (4) the "code complete" date is recorded in the RTM for the use case.

- When the testers have (1) written the GUI test scripts; (2) written the integration test scripts; and (3) both sets of test cases are recorded in the RTM for the use case.

- When the test machine is ready for testing.

Run the GUI Tests (Box 10)

GUI testing is fairly quick to do, but laborious and tedious to do multiple times for regression. GUI tests provide user inputs with expected outputs that reflects through-system functioning.

The following section offers words of warning regarding manual GUI testing, both its form and psychology.

Repetition is Grueling

GUI screen and web pages mostly deal with string data, or string-based GUI widgets. That means a lot of syntax checking must be performed for the GUI test to be complete, and once a tester has entered lots of syntax variations for one field, it is tedious to repeat that sequence for another input field. It is psychologically hard to do it again for another field, and even harder for the same screen later for regression testing. Manual GUI testing is not as productive as good automated testing. Consider GUI testing as a detailed check, and make sure that the users are running acceptance tests too: the more eyes-on the better.

✖ Anecdote   One company used two outsourced testers from Japan who came on-site. They had written a script for their GUI testing. One read the script, the other typed in the commands (and invalid commands). They did that for about 40 hours. After they had run through the use cases, they switched places and did it again for the same input data and product screens! The team lead couldn't believe how tedious a task they had set themselves. He couldn't even be in the room when they were doing it. I don't think most GUI testers will be as disciplined at the task as these two testers.

Unexpected Results Are Easy

Running a GUI command is fairly straightforward and tends to repeat earlier steps. For example, it is easy to think up test cases on the fly during the fifth step of the tenth iteration through a GUI procedure, and notice a new slant on the test. "I think I'll add that to the test set." This is done almost without thinking. Unfortunately, the expected result is critically important, and is very easy to skip, especially if a calculation is involved. Don't write any tests without including an expected value for the given input value.

⚒ **Anecdote** I once taught a sophomore level college programming course. Each student was tasked with writing a simple Celsius-to-Fahrenheit conversion program. One student announced he was finished after a short time. I asked if it worked. He said, "That's for the testers. It all compiles fine." I told him he had to make sure it worked, just because it compiled didn't mean he was done.

He complained and resisted, thinking it was someone else's job. I said, "OK, let's test it right now. Enter 100." He did, and the program returned 212. Correct. I asked him to enter 0, and the program returned 32. So far, so good. Then I asked him to enter -40. The program returned -40. I asked him, "Is that right? That looks like your input number. Perhaps your negative sign messed something up?"

For the next hour, he debugged, reviewed code, searched for a bug. Finally he returned back to me in chagrin, calculator finally in hand. "Hey!" he said, "-40 degrees Celsius *is* -40 degrees Fahrenheit!" I smiled and replied, "Yes, but now you know it." My friends who heard this story thought I played an evil prank. I hope he learned a valuable lesson: Know the result of your test case.

Record the failed tests in the defect log, and record the passed tests in the RTM with the date the tests passed. All tests are added to the regression test suite. If the GUI tests are not automated, the regression suite for GUI tests is probably a test binder containing GUI test forms.

Code and Run the Automated Integration Test Code (Box 11)

Agile development is very difficult, if not impossible, to do without automated testing for both the developers and the testers. Agile is based on the idea that the developer will run unit tests frequently, every few minutes, and the tests cannot take long to run. The same applies to integration tests.

All tests either pass or fail. The results are captured in the test tracking spreadsheet for later discussion with the developers, business analyst, and others (in the Defects and Change meeting, Box 13). The impact of a test failure may range from a cosmetic defect to a hard crash of the system. The impact of the failure is recorded with the failed test result and, *critically important*, with a procedure describing how to reproduce the failure. If the developer cannot work through the failed test, they cannot fix it; if the tester can not show the failure again, the defect will get ignored, and will likely propagate into the production environment to show up as a mysterious, intermittent problem.

Failed tests are recorded in the defect log, and passed tests are recorded in the RTM with the date the tests passed. All tests are added to the regression test suite.

Track the Passed Tests in the RTM

At the time of integration testing, the RTM contains, for each use case, a set of GUI test IDs and a set of integration test IDs (I use two different tabs on the same spreadsheet). They map 1:N (use case to test cases) in the RTM. For each integration test that passes, add the date that it passed to the RTM as test "completed." Add the test code to the regression suite too.

Eventually, all defects will be repaired, and each test case ID will have an associated pass date. Only then is the use case considered *done*.

Track the Failed Tests in the Test Results Form and the Defect Log

The *test results form* is a key artifact because of at least one feature: it provides a built-in procedure for reproducing the failed test, and is one of the biggest reasons to justify writing a test script for integration testing. The other information can be read directly from the defect log.

When tests fail, they can fail in different ways and with different levels of impact. The sample Test Results Form of Table 11-tk shows a scale from 0 (pass) to 6 (hard-crash). There are three levels within those six points: 1-2 for cosmetic (such as a misspelling in a message, or a wrong color widget); 3-4 for functional errors that have workarounds (such as a button missing but the same option available from the menu); and 5-6 for when the system is non-functional, or there are no workarounds for the failed functionality. The two values within each level allow the tester to be a little more discretionary. For example, the tester may feel that some cosmetic errors are more important than others, so assigns a 2 instead of a 1. (Grading scales other than 1-6 can be used.)

Originally, the purpose of grading the impact was for the testers to know when to stop spending time on a bad Build and return it to the developers. If the test points were too high, say 12 in our example scale, there was no reason to continue testing until the Build was repaired. The Build was *bounced* back to the developers as a way of saying, "This Build is not yet ready for testing." This was the case when the Build contained multiple use cases, or small- to medium-sized components, and were tested once every week or two.

Today with agile, tests are run a use case at a time, typically every day or two. The defects are returned to the developer for a single use case. The testing point system helps to prioritize the defect repair schedule more than to bounce the Build.

The *defect log* is a summary of the failed tests, as well as tracking the results. The test tracking spreadsheet contains the test ID, date tested, the failed impact grade, and the date the test passed. A partial sample defect log is shown in Table 11-1.

Table 11-1. Partial Sample Defect Log

Test ID	Test Date	Impact	Date Passed
TC03-N01	6/7/14	5	
	6/10/14	2	6/12/14
TC03-N03	6/7/14	3	
TC03-E02	6/7/14	2	
TC03-E05	6/7/14	5	
	6/8/14	2	6/12/14

When the test is run again later after defect repair, a new line is made for the date of the second test. If the test fails, another impact grade is put in the row; if the test passes, the pass date is added to the defect log (to close it out), and added to the RTM to acknowledge it as "Done."

From Table 11-1, you can infer from the tests numbered TC03-xnn that this set of tests were run for use case 03. Those that failed from the entire set were two Normal tests (N01 and N03), and two Error tests (E02 and E05). All the other numbered tests (N02, E01, E03, and E04) must have passed or were not run (need to check the RTM for passed tests). TC03-N01 failed twice, and passed on the third try 6/12/14, as did test E05. The tests without pass dates (N03 and E02) are still outstanding, and are pending retesting, either due to time or code repair.

What is important about this table is the impact grade is used to prioritize the defect repair.

Upload the Tests into the Regression Suite

After the testers have completed their most recent wave of GUI and integration testing for the Build, they add the latest integration tests that passed to the regression test suite, update the RTM, and upload the test suites to the shared codebase.

The uploaded test suite will contain the tests that passed *and* those that failed, so the developers can run them and repair them. The Test Build now has the new set of regression tests that the developers will download in the morning, and merge with the current Developer Build. Of course, this assumes that all the tests have been written. Using the NEBS method is a good way to ensure this.[9]

Run QA and Regression Tests (Box 12)

After all defects for the Test Build have been repaired (or deferred), the Build is ready for the user demo and possible Release. The tester runs the regression test suite one last time, and the QA compliance tests, before giving it the seal of approval. Any defects at this point are likely compliance issues, and those can quickly be repaired.

The tester should run each of the following kinds of tests:

- **Automated Regression tests** (unit tests and integration tests) are run to ensure that nothing has changed since the last time the Build was tested. Any "breakage" (new defects of old existing code) is recorded in the defect log as a regression defect, and the original pass date is removed (or annotated). Automated regression testing should take only a few minutes.

- **GUI testing** must be regression tested, but GUI tests are tedious and sometime laborious to run if they are not automated. Consequently, GUI regression testing is performed periodically, usually every third iteration. At the very least, the product must be GUI regression tested before Release, and given a quick sanity check before the next user demo.

- **RTM Update Verification**: A tester or the APM checks through the RTM to see if all committed use cases have been implemented and tested, with pass dates. A use case is not complete until all its tests pass. Of course, this assumes that all the tests have been written.

- **QA Compliance testing**: QA compliance testing includes other kinds of verifications: style checkers (ensuring code complies with team standards), automatic documenters (such as ensuring appropriate Javadoc comments were included), all defect log entries are closed as expected, and other tools are run (such as performance or profiler tools) to ensure that all standards have been followed. Some QA tests are automated, and others use manual checklists. If a compliance test fails, the tester writes an action item to bring the Build back into compliance, and mentions it as a "blocker" at the next daily meeting.

Each failed test—GUI, integration, regression, or QA compliance—is recorded in the defect log. The test script contains a place for an explanation to reproduce the failure; or, the developers talk with the tester who found the defect to learn how to reproduce it. More formal teams will have a written defect report that keeps

---

[9]My project team used NEBS for both unit tests and integration tests, customizing Javadoc tags and compiler flags to help us comply with the NEBS rules. The tests covered 99% of the code for the non-GUI components, 85% code coverage for the product. The only automated test code our tests didn't cover was in the GUI. The program manager said that our product set the QA bar for the other projects in his multi-million dollar program.

a history of the defect in case it happens again. The defect repair is expected in the next Build (not the next iteration) unless the team chooses to delay it for some reason. Passed tests are recorded in the RTM with the date they passed.

Defects and Change Meeting (Box 13)

The Defects and Change meeting is part of agile's low-ceremony change control process. After the testers run their battery of tests against a use case of the current Build, the passed tests are recorded in the RTM, but the failed tests are recorded in the defect log and need to be discussed. Not every failed test is the result of a code defect. Other failed tests are the result of requirements defects, tests defects, or requirements interpretation. If the customer SME is a daily part of the team, then the SME attends this meeting. Unfortunately, the SME works less frequently with the team in most organizations, so it is up to the BA to explain the requirement. The BA can confirm with the SME afterward, instead of waiting to schedule a change meeting, which can slow down the entire team.

The testers meet with the developers, analyst, and perhaps the business SME. The team walks though the list of test results to examine which ones passed or failed. This meeting is an informal discussion to resolve whether certain failed tests represent defects or not. Some may represent opportunities for change.

As discussed in *Chapter 8*, each failed tests can be resolved in one of several ways, summarized here:

- The failed test is recognized by the developers immediately as a coding defect, and can be scheduled immediately for repair. A few repairs may not be able to be repaired in the current iteration, so must be scheduled into a future iteration. The APM must be included in that discussion if rescheduling.

- The failed test indicates a difference in interpretation between the developer and tester and perhaps the analyst. There are several cases: (a) Sometimes a requirement is incomplete or ambiguous, and must be revised for clarity; (b) Sometimes the test is incorrect, must be revised, and tried again; (c) Sometimes the failed test, after discussion, does represent a code defect, and then must be repaired.

- The failed test may indicate a *small change*; perhaps someone on the team suggests an improvement. If the analyst thinks that the change would be acceptable to the business, then a Change Request (CR) can be written on a card, with its impact, knowing it is unlikely that the business will not agree with the analyst. The CR impact may be small enough to allow it to be implemented in the current iteration without affecting the schedule; otherwise, it must be scheduled into a later iteration. In any case, the stakeholder must approve the CR and impact before it is implemented.[10]

- The failed test may result in a *large change*; such as the business requests a requirements change because the failed test surfaced some information the business had not considered. A CR must be written and its impact estimated. The change must be estimated and added to the CR. The CR must be approved by the business. Often, these large CRs cause such a significant change in scope, cost, and schedule that the APM must discuss the CR with the stakeholders. Large changes from this D&C meeting are handled the same as an external CR initiated by a stakeholder and going through the APM.

---

[10]The change *can be implemented*, in a literal sense, before approval, and the team may take the risk that the change must be undone later if the business does not approve it. The bigger the change, the bigger the risk of rework; and whether the team decides to accept that risk and rework depends on the team's aversion or acceptance of the risk.

After the meeting, the team adds any tasks that need to be done as a result to the iteration backlog. The RTM is updated now if it was not updated earlier.

Build Approved? (Box 14)

After there are no more failed GUI and integration tests to repair, the regression tests have passed 100%, all compliance tests have passed, and the RTM is up-to-date, the team gathers to approve the Build. The APM will ask the question, "Is the Build ready to be shown to the users and stakeholders?" Sometimes a few defects still reside in the Build going to the user demo, but it is usually not a problem if the defects are noted and announced at the demo. The user demo is a more forgiving setting than the production environment. Each team member answers in turn that it is (or isn't) ready for the demo.

If the Test Build is approved, it is staged for the user demo. It must not be touched until after the demo. Experienced developers know that last minutes changes result in broken demos.

Build the Iteration and QA Reports (Box 15)

The iteration reports are built from the cards the testers and other team members completed throughout the iteration. See *Chapter 12* for more on the Iteration Reports.

The testers contribute to the iteration closing reports by submitting test statistics and the defect trend chart. The testers provide statistics for all tests unit tests, GUI tests, integration tests, regression tests, and compliance tests. Some metrics that can be collected are number of current defects, number of new defects found, number of defects repaired during the iteration, defect rates per category, mean time between repairs, and others. The testers can also provide the defect trend chart, which gives the average defect repair rate per day, and shows the repair trend visually. Figure 11-2 contains a sample Defect Trend chart, which indicates the defects found and repaired over the iteration.

The User Demo (Box 16)

The *user demo* is a stakeholder meeting to demonstrate the accumulation of product scope since the first iteration, with focus on the changes since the last user demo. The key purpose of the user demo is to collect feedback from the stakeholders, and improve the product going forward. The user demo also provides the opportunity to present various reports to the stakeholders, users, and other attendees about product progress. It strengthens the relationship and trust between the business team and the technical team. The PM talks with the stakeholders and explains the state of the project. The demo itself can be presented by anyone on the team.

Testers do not have a strong role in the demo meeting, but they should be on hand to discuss defects that might be found when the stakeholders run a few exploratory tests. Details of the user demo are discussed more in *Chapter 12*.

Stage or Release the Build (Box 17)

The testers do not usually play a strong role in the product release. However, applications that use multiple platforms need to be tested for each platform, so while one Build is being released for one platform, the testers often use the time to test other platforms.

PMI Parallels

All the PMI parallels of *Chapter 8* are still true, but the following highlights some specifics for the tester role.

The biggest differences between the roles of the testers for agile and traditional projects is (a) the testers work concurrently with the developers instead of waiting for the product to be nearly finished; and (b) the tests are run in small batches, a few at a time, instead of testing a huge batch of tests near the end of the cycle.

Unlike traditional projects, agile projects *require* automated testing, especially if Test-Driven Development (TDD) is used. (If TDD were used on traditional projects, automated testing would be equally required.) Automated regression testing is a requirement of regression testing. There are too many tests to rerun for almost any project. *Chapter 10* talked about the snowplow affect: how defects hide each other, and grow exponentially. This is especially true, and even more important to prevent, for voluminous testing like regression testing.

The following sections cover some PMI Bodies of Knowledge (BOK) that are different between traditional and agile testing.

Scope: There are several differences between traditional and agile testing scopes.

- Agile integration testing is actually thin-thread functional testing, and is not considered the same as component-interface testing performed after the components are built. Agile tests use the thin-thread approach that corresponds to executing use cases or user stories. Traditional projects may use top-down or bottom-up testing of components, which requires an explicit integration test phase between components. Agile products are built layer-on-layer so an explicit integration test is not needed.

- More agile integration tests are written because the testers have more time to write the tests than in traditional projects, when testing is left to the very end of the development process, and is frequently truncated; agile testing is done concurrently with development so it is not truncated.

- Testers are more actively involved in estimating the scope of the iteration in agile projects during iteration planning meetings.

Cost: Agile projects have quicker test feedback cycles than traditional projects, which catch defects sooner, and subsequently decrease the exponential cost of change.

Quality: Rico, Sayani, and Sone's (2009) studies have resolved quality issues of agile versus traditional methods:

> *Teams using agile methods produce higher quality products than those using traditional methods. Not only do agile teams, in a timely manner, make products that their customers ask for and need, but they produce few defects...agile methods have proven to result in software products at levels of quality beyond those of the best traditional methods and at a fraction of their cost...The benefits of agile methods range from 30 to 45% above those of the largest traditional methods. (Rico et al, 2009; p169)*

The Build, representing a ready-to-ship partial product, is at the highest quality after the demo is approved by the user.

Human Resources: Testers traditionally work outside the team, in QA groups. For agile, there are no external testing groups needed; the testers work daily with the developers, and sometimes they *are* the developers.

Communications: Agile teams have constant communications, meeting at least daily. The informality greases the tracks for getting the tests out faster and better.

Risk: The business value shown to the customer early in the user demo reduces the risk of releasing a poor product, and increases the chance of the stakeholders getting what they want.

Conclusion

This chapter discussed the iteration process view from the testers' perspective. It showed that the testers start concurrently with the developers, from estimating use case size to resolving defects and identifying potential changes as soon as possible. The artifacts developed in the early stages of the iteration are used by the testers in later stages of the iteration. Agile testing is integrated into the development process, instead of being tacked on at the end of coding.

Summary of Tester Roles

Table 11-2 contains a summary of the tasks of the GUI and integration testers, derived from the CORA matrix of Chapter 8.

Table 11-2. *Summary of the Tester Role. CORA Matrix for GUI and Integration Tester (Brackets Indicate That the BA Contributes or Reviews the Artifact)*

BOX #	INPUT	PROCESS	OUTPUT
[1]	Top of use case catalog from iteration backlog	Contribute to iteration planning.	List of prioritized use cases or user stories to be completed by iteration's end.
[2]	Detailed use case with optional validation model	Review use case and UX artifacts for testability.	Possible changes to use case or artifacts to make it more testable
[3]	Detailed use case	Validate use case at analysis level with UML (scope validation).	Valid (revised) use case and object model: UML class diagram and XUML sequence diagram
[4]	Detailed use case	Design user interface, screen shots, and augment use case with implementation ideas (initial design).	Design case, with UX artifacts
5	(GUI tester) Use case requirements	Write GUI test scripts; collaborate with integration tester, BA, and developer.	Final GUI tests
6	(Integration tester) Use case requirements	Write integration test scripts; collaborate with GUI tester, BA, and developers.	Final Integration tests

(*continued*)

Table 11-2. (*continued*)

BOX #	INPUT	PROCESS	OUTPUT
[8]	Use case code and regression test suite	Run automated regression tests until they pass (construction validation).	Regression test results; updated RTM; latest Build
9	Development Build	Transfer the Dev Build to the Test Build.	Test Build
10	(GUI Tester) GUI test scripts	Run the GUI tests.	Test results; updated RTM and defect log
11	(Integration Tester) Integration test scripts	Code and run integration tests.	Test results; updated RTM and defect log
12	QA standards; regression suite	Run the QA Compliance and full-Build regression tests.	Test results; updated RTM and defect log
13	List of failed and passed tests (defect log and RTM)	Contribute to resolving failed tests, and estimating CRs.	Defects (requirements, code, tests) to repair
14	Iteration backlog, regression test results, defect log, QA checklists, RTM	Approve Build for completeness at proper quality or more work is needed (quality gate).	Remaining work for the Build, or approved Build that is ready for user demo
[15]	Test statistics, defect log, RTM	Contribute to iteration closing reports.	Defect trend chart, QA report, iteration report
[16]	Build ready for User demo	Contribute to the user demo as needed.	[No outputs for testers]
[17]	Stage or Release Build	Contribute to final Release package.	[No outputs for testers]

Additional Tools

The NEBS Transform

Agile code is written one user story at a time, a thin-thread approach. The NEBS method is a technique to transform the stories (or a collection of stories, the use case) into test cases in accordance with thin-thread development, and achieve test coverage of the code as much as possible. Think of it as thin-thread testing.

The NEBS method is used for unit tests by the developers, and for integration tests by the QA testers. The test writers generate test cases for each user story using the NEBS method. NEBS stands for **N**ormal, **E**rror, **B**oundary, and **S**pecial.

- **Normal**: Create test cases that exercises the typical or normal ("happy path") through the use case with normal data that results in a successful output.

- **Error**. Create a test case that exercises the error path of the use case to produce the error message or internal system state. There are usually multiple error paths in a single use case, and therefore multiple error tests.

- **Boundary:** Create test cases that provide data just within the boundary of the applicability of the use case, and another just outside the boundary. Boundary tests are always produced in pairs. The first should work and the second should fail with a known error result. Boundary paths may not be specified in the use case, but the tester can find those boundary conditions in the context of the use case.

- **Special.** Create test cases for special situations that have not been tested before. All use cases have Normal, Error, and Boundary test cases, but not all will have Special test cases.

There is another rule about building NEBS cases. Some code paths would require an *infinite number* of test cases, which obviously is not fully testable. However, one can always define a *finite subset* of an infinite set for testing. For example, to exhaustively test the square root function, there are an infinite set of positive numbers that could be tried. No tester would attempt to do that. However, there are only a few subsets of all positive numbers: perfect squares, non-perfect square integers, non-integers, and perhaps the special cases of 0 and 1. There are also a few implementation-dependent boundary cases.

> **Simple Example:** Say you want to test the square root function that complies with NEBS. You would look for *normal* tests first, and write code to microtest perfect squares, such as 49, 25, and 5041. The test will fail until you write a square root method in some class.
>
> You write the code, and the test passes. Then you try non-perfect square integers, such as 48, 27, and 5040. If you wrote the code properly, it probably passes the first time. Next, you test non-integers: 24.6, 33.9, and 5111.21. In all cases, the test must compare against the expected values, which are built into the test.
>
> You then try *error* conditions. For a square root function returning only real numbers, inputting negative numbers, such as squareRoot(-99), should fail. Also, you could try the square root of the non-number "W" and would expect to get an error.
>
> One error condition that should *always* be tried (assuming it will compile) is the null input case. What is the squareRoot(null)? You would expect a NullPointerException to be thrown from the squareRoot method. If no other error condition is tried, the null input case should always be tried because null pointer problems are prevalent and often disastrous.
>
> You could then look at *boundary* cases. Boundary values always come in pairs near the boundary: one case barely inside the boundary that will pass, and another case barely outside the boundary that will fail. Very large and very small numbers at the limits of the computer hardware are obvious boundary cases. Variables of type Float and type Double in Java can cause intermittent problems because of the inexactness of these types. You should also try 0.9, 1.0, and 1.1 because the square root function changes character for values less than 1.0. The square root of these values (to four places) are .9487, 1.0000, and 1.0488, respectively.
>
> For one *special* case, you should try 1.0 because that is a number that is not exactly represented by a binary machine. Often it comes out to 0.9999999.... or 1.000000...1. It is important to what level of precision the requirements dictate.

For another special case, you could try the square root of zero. The square root of 0.0 is *defined* to be zero, so perhaps there is a special check in the square root algorithm for it. However, what would you get for the square root of negative 0? Interestingly, that depends on the implementation. If the code understands 0 = -0, then the squareRoot(-0) = 0. However, if the implementation checks polarity or syntax first, then squareRoot(-0) will produce an error because a negative number was input. The correct answer is, "What does the requirement need?"

The NEBS method is important enough that one of our large-project teams wrote Javadoc custom tags with which to annotate test cases to ensure @Normal, @Error, and @Null tests were written; and @Boundary and @Special cases could be counted. By forcing these tags onto our tests, it also encouraged tests to be good microtests. The tests covered 99% of our non-GUI product code. We had 85% code coverage because 15% of the product was GUI code without automated NEBS tests. The program manager said that our product set the QA bar for the other projects in his multi-million dollar program.

Naming Conventions

Integration tests are named after the use case, such as TC04 for use case 4. With NEBS, the name is suffixed by N, E, B, or S, and a counting number to further distinguish the test. So for UC04, the test tracker shows TC04-B01, TC04-N01, TC03-N02, etc. See the "Sample Integration Test Suite" section for an example of NEBS tests for the ATM Withdraw use case.

Sample Integration Test Suite

Table 11-3 shows the ATM Withdraw use case, called TC04. Withdraw Money, as per the naming convention explained in the last section.

Table 11-3. *ATM Withdraw Use Case, called TC04. Withdraw Money*

Goal	Give cash to customer from their account, deducting that amount. Provide a receipt of the transaction and an entry in the ATM log.				
Name	**Date Passed**	**Test Summary**	**Expected Result**	**Test Date**	**Actual Results**
NORMAL					
N01		Withdraw $100 from savings account with $100 in it.	Cashbox extends $100, receipt and log shows $100 deduction from savings account, and amount is deducted from the account (verify outside ATM). Verify that receipt and log have correct data fields.		
N01		Withdraw $100 from one ATM and *less than* 24 hours, withdraw $100 from another ATM.	Normal case, results same as N01 except receipt and log field will have different data.		

(continued)

Table 11-3. (continued)

N02	Withdraw $100 from checking account with more than $200 in it.	Cashbox extends $100, receipt and log shows $100 deduction from checking account, and amount is deducted from the account (verify outside ATM). Verify that receipt and log have correct data fields.
N03	Withdraw $100 from savings account with $100 in it.	Same as N01; savings account does not require a buffer.
N04	Withdraw $100 from one ATM and *after* 24 hours, withdraw $100 from another ATM.	Normal case, results same as N01 except receipt and log field will have different data.
ERROR		
E01	Withdraw $100 from checking account with only $80 in cashbox.	Get error message after amount is entered that the ATM does not have that amount, but customer can try another amount.
E02	Withdraw $105 from checking account.	Get error message that amount must be multiple of $20. (Note: Better to only allow multiples of 20 in the input field.)
E03	Withdraw $100 from checking account with $150 in it.	Error message of insufficient funds; checking account requires $100 buffer for withdrawal.
E04	Withdraw $100 from savings account with $80 in it.	Error message of insufficient funds.
E05	Withdraw $100 from checking account with $80 in it.	Error message of insufficient funds
E06	Withdraw $240 from checking account.	Error message of exceeded valid amount to withdraw, limit = $200.
E07	Attempt to withdraw $-20 from ATM.	Error for invalid amount (better: negative amounts should be blocked from attempting by GUI).

(*continued*)

Table 11-3. *(continued)*

E08	Withdraw $180 from one ATM and within 24 hours, withdraw $60 from another ATM.	Error message exceeded valid amount to withdraw, limit = $200 for *any* ATM for 24 hours.
BOUNDARY		
B01	Withdraw $100 from one ATM and within 24 hours, withdraw $40 from second, and $60 from a third ATM.	Normal case, results same as N01 except receipt and log field will have different data. Verify that there is not a two-ATM limit.
SPECIAL		
S01	Withdraw $100 from savings account with only $100 in it, then *transfer* $100 from checking account, and then withdraw a second $100.	Same as N01 if the withdraw is done on the same ATM.
S02	Withdraw $100 from savings account with only $100 in it. Then *transfer* $100 from checking account with $200 in it to savings. Then withdraw a second $100 from that checking account *from a second ATM.*	Error message for $200 limit; otherwise customers can take out more than they have in the bank by going to different ATMs. Depends on if the central banking system is keeping ATMs in sync or not.
15	**0**	**0**
# Tests	**# Passed**	**# Tested**

Notes:

1. The entries were originally entered in the order the tester thought of them: a mixture of normal and error cases, peppered with boundary and special cases after more thought. In this example, the spreadsheet sorted them into the sequence shown, but some testers prefer to keep them in the order of complexity so that they can write code from simplest to complex. The spreadsheet can also automatically number them.

2. The use case uses a numbering system named after the use case: UC04 becomes TC04. Each test *subcase* is numbered N, E, B, or S, and numbers restart within each category.

3. The test cases that deal with multiple ATMs (B01, E08, N01, N04, S01, S02) will be difficult to test as integrated code unless the ATMs are networked. Arguably, these are not integration tests, but system tests, and better left for later. However, it is better to record them now so that the test situation is not forgotten, and can be added to the system test suite later.

4. The dates of when the tests were run, and when they passed, are recorded at the bottom. This spreadsheet keeps a running record of success for the use case.

Test Script Form Instructions

Table 11-4 shows a test script form for the test authors to fill out.

Table 11-4. *Test Script Form for Test Authors to Fill Out*

Iteration		Test Case ID	
Created By		Date	
Test Case Objective			
Test Inputs			
Test Procedure			
Expected Results			
Special Instructions			
References and Use Cases	<Use case and UX IDs>		

The following sections explain the fields in the form in Table 11-4.

Iteration

Enter which iteration of the product this test is written for. Some tests are written for prior iterations as a result of late repairs or regression defects.

Test Case ID

Enter the designated identification number of this test case. It should follow the format
TC<UC#>-Xnn,
where

UC# is the use case number from which this test case originated;

X is one of N, E, B, or S;

nn is an sequential number counting the number of test cases within the N,E,B, or S categories.

Created By

Type in your name (author's name).

Date

Write in today's date, the date the script was written.

Test Case Objective

Describe a general high-level overview of this test case. What is the goal of the user story (path)? What is the goal of this specific test? Error tests should explain what and why the error expected will be triggered.

Test Inputs

Describe all data variables and their respective values to be input by the tester.

Test Procedure

List in order and without ambiguity commands to the tester on how to perform this test. Each of these commands needs to be precise and detailed, with special focus on the use try's pre-condition and post-condition. Test procedures almost always have the format of SETUP (establish pre-condition), DO (execute the test), VERIFY (establish the post-condition), and TEARDOWN (return the system to the pre-test state).

Expected Results

Describe all of the end results you expect the tester to observe.

Special Instructions

Define any specials observations or commands for the tester to adhere to. Also, list any notes on this specific test case here.

References and Use Cases

Identify any UX IDs or other documents that are relevant. The use case number is repeated here, even though it can be read from the Test Case ID.

Note that in the case of using JUnit to integration test, the Javadoc description of the JUnit test file can be attached or substituted after the test file has passed. If the test file does not pass, then a Defect Report should be filled out and returned to the lead developer (Table 11-5).

Table 11-5. *A Defect Report For Testers to Fill Out*

Iteration		Test Case ID	
Test Date		Tested By	

Result	☐ Pass (0 points)
	____ Points (Use any number from 1-6)
	For example:
	     Cosmetic = 1-2
	     Medium (error w/workarounds) = 3-4
	     Nonfunctional (crash) with no workarounds = 5-6		

If the test didn't meet the expected results, explain what you observed. Include enough information for the failure to be reproduced			
Tracking Number			

For testers to fill out:

Repeat the **iteration** and **Test Case ID** at the top to keep script and results together.

Test Date

Write in the day that this test case was executed (and passed or failed).

Tested By

Write in your name (person who ran the test).

Result

Check the appropriate box according to how the tester observed the result compared to the expected result. Check all that apply.

- **Pass:** The test matched the expected results completely and accurately. **Give a value of 0.**

- **High Incident/Defect:** The test didn't match the expected results at all. A system crash, wrong screen data, wrong data outputs, infinite waits, etc. fall under this definition. **Give an integer point value of 5 or 6, depending on severity.**

- **Medium Incident/Defect:** The observed results matched some of the expected results, but not all of them. **Give an integer point value of 3 or 4, depending on severity.**

- **Low Incident/Defect:** The observed results match almost all of the expected results. The only discrepancies are visual errors or are minor. **Give an integer point value of 1 or 2, depending on severity.**

If the test didn't meet the expected results, explain what you observed. List all observed results that didn't match the expected results.

Tracking Number

Write the tracking number(s) of this discrepancy in the current defect tracking system. There will be one tracking number per discrepancy. This is an internal number usually associated with the test's RTM entry line.

Test cases that passed retain their test cases numbering prefix of TC. For tests that fail, the Change Management Board (CMB) will later decide if these failed tests ("incidents") are Defects or should spawn change requests.

Now let's see a form that's filled in. See Table 11-6.

Table 11-6. *Example of a Test Case Form Filled Out*

Iteration	3	Test Case ID	TC04-N1
Created By	Darth Vader	**Date**	2/16/00
Test Case Objective	Successfully log on to the main system.		
Test Inputs			
1. User Name = "yoda" 2. Password = "c3po-r2d2"			
Test Procedure			
1. At login screen, enter the username and password listed in Test Inputs section. 2. Wait for message to appear "Welcome to Imperial Death Star Weapons Configuration Program." 3. Wait for a main menu screen to appear.			
Expected Results			
1. A welcome message as soon as you enter the username and password. 2. Expect a menu to appear with a list of system options.			
Special Instructions			
1. Make sure that when the menu appears that there isn't an "infinite wait" for a command prompt waiting for further input.			
References and Use Cases	Use Case 4. Logon. UX07. Logon screen UX01. Opening page		

For testers to fill out:

Iteration	3	**Test Case ID**	TC04N01-N03
Test Date	2/25/00	**Tested By**	Obi-Wan Kenobi
Result	☐ Pass (0 points) ____ Points (Use any number from 1-6) For example: Cosmetic = 1-2 Medium (error w/workarounds) = 3-4 Nonfunctional (crash) with no workarounds = 5-6		

If the test didn't meet the expected results, explain what you observed.

1. Upon entering the user name and password, a welcome message with the wrong message "Welcome to the Death Star Weapons Configuration Program of the Imperial Army" appeared. This is obviously a low discrepancy. **Give 2 points**

2. Then a little window appeared in the corner and gave me stock quotes. While stock quotes are helpful, they are not required. This is obviously gold plating and a medium discrepancy. **Give 4 points**

3. The system did bring up the main menu, but immediately after the menu was displayed, the Windows 95 "Blue Screen of Death" appeared. This is a high discrepancy. **Give 6 points**

Tracking Number	35, 37, 38

Note that in Table 11-6, the author put three related tests together, and gave the test three test IDs: TC04-N01 thru TC04-N03. Note also that there are three tracking numbers, each representing the number of three lines in the RTM where the test is registered. Figure 11-2 shows a sample defect trend chart from a QA report.

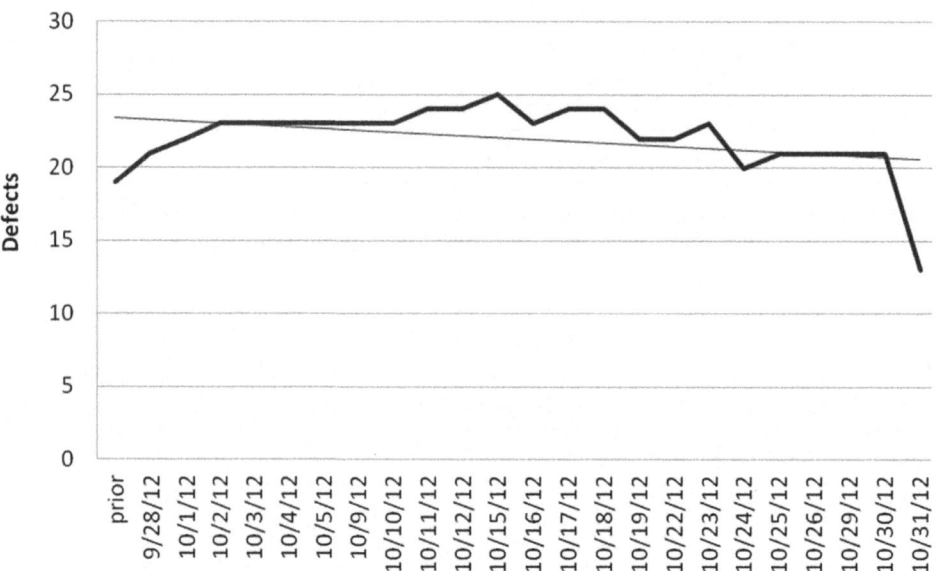

Figure 11-2. *Sample QA Report of Release2, Iteration 34*

■ ■ ■

CHAPTER 12

Project Management Thread

The Agile Project Manager

There are two aspects to the Agile Project Manager (APM): the work done outside the iterations, which I have been calling the PM and is similar to the traditional project manager; and the work done inside the iterations, which is sometimes called an *agile coach* and *servant leader*. The PM and the APM have a slightly different focus, and therefore involve slightly different skill sets between Region 2 (outside the iterations) and Region 1 (inside the iterations) of the project. (See *Chapter 1* for a discussion of how the regions differ, and how agile PM theory differs from traditional PM theory in this regard.) Usually the person filling the PM role is the same person who fills the APM role, but that does not necessarily have to be the case. The PM fills a more traditional role in Region 2 than does the APM in Region 1, so a PM that will work as an APM will need the same agile skills as the APM.

Chapter 8 contained agile process diagrams, Figures 8-1 and 8-2. Neither has a swim lane for the APM within the iteration because there is not a specific role that the APM plays alone. As an agile coach, the APM works with the team to guide, coordinate, and smooth the way from team results to stakeholder expectations. As a servant leader, the APM removes obstacles and distractions from the team, ensuring that the team is free to do their best work. Sometimes that includes helping them reach personal and career goals.

The APM writes reports for the stakeholders and upper management, but most of the data comes from the team. Sometimes the APM's hardest task is to convert the agile progress reports to a format that upper management expects and can understand, especially if management wants those reports to be consistent with their non-agile projects.

The duties of the APM in Region 2 have been discussed in earlier chapters: refining the charter and preliminary release plan, working with the BA and stakeholders to define the product backlog, acquiring the technical team, and managing stakeholder expectations and communications. This chapter will not discuss those responsibilities further, but will focus on the duties of the APM.

The APM continues the crucial task of managing stakeholder expectations throughout the iterations, in addition to the responsibilities of team coach and servant leader. In general, the APM is responsible for coaching and guiding the team in following agile practices, as they agreed in the team working agreement worked out in the technical team kickoff meeting, or one of the retrospectives. The APM monitors and reports the project schedule to the stakeholders, and oversees the QA and delivery of the Release to production. The team is responsible for getting the Build done right, but the APM is liaison to the stakeholders. After all, the APM will be the focal point of the stakeholders' *sturm und drang* if something goes wrong.

Agile Practices and Retrospectives

The APM set up a working team agreement during the technical team kickoff meeting in Iteration 0, so the APM monitors the team practices to ensure that they are following that agreement. Individual variances to the agreement are addressed informally by reminders, or during a team retrospective. Retrospectives are periodic forums (usually every 1 to 3 iterations) to allow the working agreement and agile practices to change.

Monitoring the Release Plan

The APM is responsible for informing the stakeholders of any changes that affect the project scope, cost, schedule, or quality in a significant way, and getting those changes approved by the sponsor and upper management before being implemented. The APM, like the PM, must monitor the progress of the project at the project level: ensuring the release plan is on track, or revising it as needed. The APM must know how to apply history to future iterations, and make course corrections when needed.

Daily Meetings

The team owns the daily 15-minute meetings but the APM is responsible that the meetings are not derailed by "rat holes:" problem-solving discussions, specific task details (too much "in the weeds"), off-topic discussions, overly long answers, and other distractions that take the meeting off the focus of the three questions: *(1) What did I complete yesterday?, (2) What will I complete today?,* and *(3) Do I have any impediments?* The best daily meetings are those that look like they are not facilitated, and the team members remind each other of the rules.

More specifically, the APM has the following duties within the iterations:

- Facilitate the iteration planning meeting, ensuring that the teams do not overcommit, and that defects and change requests are properly scheduled.

- Review the detailed use cases, UX artifacts, and design with the team to keep aware of the detailed requirements and scope.

- Facilitate the defects and changes meeting, resolving conflicts from failed tests, taking suggested changes back to the stakeholders for approval, or introducing changes from the stakeholders. This task is shared with the business analyst, but the BA works with the SME and the APM works with the higher level stakeholders.

- Facilitate the meeting in which all team members approve the Build as ready to go to product and the user demo. Expedite any changes to the Build that must be done near the end of the iteration, adjusting priorities accordingly (with team input).

- Build the iteration reports from team knowledge, and presentation to the stakeholders, which includes keeping the "living documents," such as the Requirements Traceability Matrix (RTM), and the iteration and project burn-up charts, current and correct.

- Facilitate the user demo to all attendees, or delegate to an appropriate person. Although others contribute through meeting minutes, the APM is responsible that it all goes well.

- Get the final Build and its associated artifacts approved by the stakeholders before it goes to production. This responsibility includes organizing operations and support personnel training, and that all transitions to the production environment go smoothly.

Agile Perspectives

Whether the project manager is working an agile project or not, there are certain perspectives that the PM must have when working with upper management and the team. There is also a perspective that the APM must engender between the agile team and the stakeholders. Without these perspectives, the PM receives unnecessary stress and conflict. The project community—sponsor, stakeholders, technical team, and other interested parties—need to know how the APM and agile team fit into the roles they are filling in the organization.

The APM Perspective with Management

Ironically, the APM gets the blame for failed projects, but they actually have little control over the project. One corporation calls it "influencing without authority," a good catch phrase for the entire project management profession. I include the stakeholders in this description with upper management because often the key stakeholders are high-level managers.

Regardless of the team's competency, commitment, or resource shortage, it is a truism that: "*If the project is successful, the kudos go to the team; if the project fails, the blame goes to the project manager.*" This is not said cynically, but in a way that reflects that the APM is responsible for making the project successful. The APM cannot do this by himself or herself, but the APM must ensure that the team works together well, overcomes obstacles, and meets their commitments.

Traditional PMs sometimes—and I'll use the worst case here—act as if the entire project was under their control: schedules, budgets, scope, quality, risk, and the rest. Actually, the PM is a facilitator, and has no real choice about key business decisions, such as excluding or including certain features of the project, extending project schedules, or risk tolerance factors. The PM should show the data and consequences of decisions that the stakeholders make. Traditional PMs add a lot of stress to themselves when they try to be a wall between the stakeholders and the project, when they should actually be a gate.

Managers must allow the team to make a commitment to do what they say, and hold them accountable to it. This is the essence of a *self-empowered team*, an agile staple. If management, or even the APM, tries to control tasks and set constraints without the buy-in of the team, there is no real internal or emotional commitment by the team to meet those goals. The best approach is to allow the team to define, frame, and commit to its own work, and then allow it to do it. Decisions are best made by the people doing the work.

One can see why the term *project manager* is not often applied to agile teams, and the word *agile coach* is used. "Manager" connotes a controlling force on the team, but *agile coach* connotes someone who focuses on the agile techniques, and does not have control for all aspects of the project. An APM is a servant leader of the team, a "first among equals" as Len Lagestee (2014) puts it, rather than a manager of people treated as mere "human resources."

The term *project coordinator* could also be used for an APM, but in the project management world, a project coordinator is usually an administrative person: a doer of checklists, without needing the skills for managing people, scope, budgets, etc. It is a lower level of responsibility than a project manager, who is responsible for success in all ten PMI Knowledge areas.

✗ Example   A Change Request (CR) is suggested by Bob, a business SME, but the schedule will be impacted by 15 days if it is implemented. With the schedule in mind, the traditional PM may say, "No, that's too long. We cannot afford the time to add that." It could become an argument between the SME and the PM, and eventually it gets escalated to the sponsor. Regardless of how the CR was resolved, the disagreement can lead to bad feelings that taint the relationship between the SME and PM from that point forward.

A better approach would be to assume that the business SME knows more about the business than the PM, and the business would be better off with the change. The PM brings the CR to the stakeholders and asks if they want the change. The PM takes himself or herself out of the mix, and it then becomes the SME's job to convince the stakeholders that the CR is needed and the delay is justified.

If the CR is approved, all stakeholders will be aware of, and have approved, the 15 day delay—which will also prevent stakeholder complaints later. The change can now go into the product backlog to be scheduled during an iteration.

If the CR is not approved, the PM will still have good relations with the SME. It may also improve the trust between the PM and the other stakeholders because they will understand that changes will not be "sneaked" into the project without them being aware.

The APM Perspective with the Agile Team

Some agilists would say that agile teams have no need for a project manager, thinking of the traditional kind of project manager, and the use of self-empowered teams. However, at the same time, most would agree that the team, empowered as it may be, still needs someone to coordinate the efforts and act as a liaison to upper management and the stakeholders.[1] If the team does not have a liaison, management will pick someone, because they don't want to meet with a different person each time they want to know what is going on in the project, nor do they want a gang of technical members reporting to them when one person will do.

This perception *no project manager* is changing as agile becomes more popular, and the term *agile project manager* is making more sense. Whatever the term used, that person's role must *value people over processes and tools*, ensure that the fifth and eleventh principles[2] of agile are enabled:

> *5. Build projects around motivated individuals. Give them the environment and support they need, and trust them to get the job done.*

> *11. The best architectures, requirements, and designs emerge from self-organizing teams.*

With agile project managers, the self-empowerment concept is much more evident than with traditional teams, even for the traditional PM who may follow a democratic or collaborative style. A micromanaging PM will not be successful with a truly empowered team, and a micromanaging PM will not be able to create an empowered team. As soon as team members do work *because the PM said so*, the team has lost its agility. The micromanager has lost his or her group of experts who can do the job; the team has become one person trying to build a product through remote hands. Team buy-in and shared problem solving will be missing, morale will fall, and the PM will create a failing agile project.

Key evidence of this difference is in assigning task cards during an iteration. Contrary to traditional methods, the PM *does not assign tasks* to the team; team members volunteer to do the tasks needed, an effect of a *self-organizing team*, another agile staple. Of course, in a team with specialty skills, everyone knows who is most likely to take on a particular task, and peer pressure will focus on the expected person. Sometimes, a team member may want to learn something new, or do a particular task for a change of pace,

---

[1]Scrum uses a Product Owner role on the business side to do that; XP would have the entire team meet with the stakeholders, *en masse* or individually, for requirements and daily discussions.
[2]*Principles Behind the Agile Manifesto,* Aug 1, 2014; http://agilemanifesto.org/ principles.html

or they will have some temporary "free time" and will volunteer to take a "stretch assignment" card. Stretch assignments help train the team, and the person will feel more likely to take the card because he or she knows there is a pairing safety net.

An APM will guide and coordinate, and the team will grow to make the commitment to build a successful product. In some cases, that means the APM must be hands off enough to allow a team member, or perhaps the iteration, to fail. Failing is an investment in better teamwork and strength of the team later, a result of the agile mantra to "Fail first and fail fast." An empowered team needs to know that *they* are building the product, and not merely taking orders.

The Agile Team and the Stakeholders

Too often the business people defining the product think they know how to build it. They *do* have the right to make changes in scope, cost, schedule, quality, and the other six project attributes, but they have also agreed (in the business team kickoff meeting) to use the product development process, which includes Change Management procedures; so the APM pushes them back into that process. (You, as APM, got their agreement to follow the Change Management process in the initial meetings, didn't you?)

The APM acts like a "flak jacket" to protect the agile team from interruptions, distractions, political fallout, and overly-eager business folk who wish to use them as their "personal programmers." More than once I had to gently escort a business SME from the desk of a developer because the SME was suggesting unofficial changes directly to the programmer.

Most team members think their duty is never tell a stakeholder "No" because "the customer is always right." They may think (perhaps rightly) that there is a political or career-affecting correlation of saying No to stakeholders or higher level managers. The technical term is CLM: *career-limiting move.*

I have had success by guiding team members from "Don't say 'No'" to saying "We will need to work it into the schedule. Talk to the APM." It is the APM's duty to smooth out those "quick and free" changes that are rarely quick, and never free. To be able to ride shotgun on the team and push back on a high-level manager is tough to do, and is described in XP as *managerial courage*, a required trait of any project manager.

Managerial courage is one of the skills of conflict resolution and is associated with good leadership. Chicago State University (2014) defines it as: *Tactfully dispenses direct and actionable feedback; is open and direct with others without being intimidating; deals head-on with people problems and prickly situations.*

Chrystel Martin (2012) explains several levels of expertise to managerial courage and its behavior indicators.

1. *Achieve results in a manner that is consistent with organizational expectations.*

2. *Provide corrective feedback to others.*

3. *Deal with people problems and situations head-on.*

4. *Swiftly administer action (negative or positive) if situation merits it.*

The main practical result of managerial courage is to make the project progress and problems *transparent*—the more opaque the project, the greater the distrust between team and management. With transparent projects, the stakeholders always know the current state of the project, and trust that the APM and technical team will not surprise them. Unless it is the unexpected paycheck, no one likes surprises. Although the stakeholders may not like learning that the project will be late, they will accept it much more readily that learning about it so late that it cannot be corrected. As one PM said, "Lying to the stakeholders never ends well."

Task Tracking: The Kanban Board

Agile is famous for its 3x5 or 4x6 cards-on-the-wall system of tracking tasks within an iteration: the *agile taskboard*. Tasks are written onto cards and put in a large visible space marked with columns, and moved from column to column as the card is completed. Cards start in an Iteration backlog column, move through other steps of the process, and are eventually moved to the Done column. Team members assign themselves to a card, and a card's owner may change as it moves.

My preferred method of task tracking is an online Kanban board, and it has been accepted by every team for which I suggested it; other methods met with mixed acceptance depending on the team. There are a few distinctions between the typical agile taskboard dynamics and the Kanban task board.

Kanban: A "Pull System"

The Kanban board is similar to other agile taskboard techniques. The Kanban board contains various columns that represent phases of the team's development process, an "assembly line" for working the cards. The actual columns can be as simple as ToDo, Doing, and Done; or more complicated, like Analysis, Construction, Testing, Review, and Done. There is always a Done column.

The Kanban board is a *pull system*, which means that a card cannot be pushed onto the board until there is an opening for it; in other words, when the card progresses to the next column, and someone is ready, another card is "pulled" onto the board; or someone takes a card in one column into the next to start working on it. In most cases, a person may finish their part of the card and move it to another column, and someone else will take over for that phase of the user story. This is common practice when skillsets are distributed across the team; that is, the team has an analyst, developer, tester, and APM role. If the team is made of generalists, then roles and cards switch around as they wish.

Work-in-Progress Limits

The point of a Kanban board is to track the work being done, but also to minimize the *Work in Progress* (WiP). Only one card per person should be on the board, and there is a limit, the *WiP limit*, as to how many story points can be in any column at a time. The WiP limit helps ensure that the "assembly line" does not get bloated by too many cards not being worked, which quickly identifies bottlenecks by a bunch of cards sitting in a particular column, waiting to move to the next column. When that symptom appears, the team knows to take a look at what might be bottlenecking the card flow. The team can react quicker to take corrective action. (This in no way negates the need to have a team retrospective every one-to-three iterations. The retrospective is used for changing the team process; the WiP limit bottleneck is a symptom of a product problem that can often be resolved by other team members pitching in to remove the load in the overloaded column.)

It is easy to see the visual difference between a Kanban board and other taskboards because Kanban boards look much sparser. Kanban boards will only have as many cards in progress as there are team members. Other agile task boards will have columns loaded with partially-completed cards. Agile processes use iterations for scope and risk control: changes can occur more frequently between iterations. With Kanban, changes are even more granular: changes can occur between cards.

No Iterations!

One interesting difference between a Kanban process and other agile processes is that Kanban does not require iterations. Since each member may have one card (or a second card as a backup for slack times), then there is no *functional need* to have two-week iterations. Why stack up cards in one column, when they are already in sorted order in the product backlog? Cards are pulled from the product backlog when needed, one at a time. Builds occur daily and user demos can occur whenever the team and stakeholder wish, as features are competed and demonstrable, or as two-to-four week events.

However, for purposes of stakeholder reporting, team commitment, and tracking the Release plan, iterations are recommended to keep the cadence of the team, and the user demos, on schedule. An iteration backlog is made so that the team will commit to that much scope, and they work on their build a card (or two) at a time. Team velocity is calculated at the end of an arbitrary (two-to-four week) pseudo-iteration instead of calculating it on some other time scale.

See the "Kanban Process Summary" section later in this chapter, and David Anderson's (2010) excellent book on Kanban.

Resizing Cards on the Fly

What happens if a new task is found during the iteration? What if a developer wants to upsize an existing card? As with any agile sizing, the commitment has been stated at the beginning of the iteration that N number of points will be delivered. If the size of the iteration must rise for one card, then another card of equal or lesser size must be removed. Place the card into the product backlog for the next iteration. It should be the first card moved into the iteration backlog at the next iteration.

If a card is downsized, do nothing. It adds margin to the iteration. If it looks like the team will finish all cards in the iteration backlog before the iteration is over, the APM puts the next card onto the iteration backlog from the product backlog.

The open-source (usually no-cost) online Kanban boards keep track of the story points within each column so that it is easy to see if the iteration scope is changing incorrectly.

Comparing Velocities Between Teams, Individuals, or Groups

Velocities is a subjective and arbitrary measure of scope, so cannot compared between teams, individuals, or groups. Each is discussed in turn in the following section.

Team Velocities

First rule of agile story points (or any agile sizing metric): *Do not use story points to compare against other project teams*. Second rule of agile story points: *Do not use story points to compare against other project teams*. The same goes for team velocity, which is based on agile sizing. Agile sizing is subjective and relative. Estimates are produced *relative* to the team member's perception of how much work they are doing. Team velocity depends on the team culture, *cadence* (sustained pace through the project, iteration by iteration), relative sizes of the other features in the product, experience the team has in the particular product domain, and even the tools used by the team.

Agile scope sizes are arbitrary and relative estimates, not objective measures like time worked, which is one reason why agile sizes of scope should not be converted to hours, a dimension of time. Story points (scope) cannot be mapped to elapsed hours (duration) or through hours worked (effort). A task has a particular size, and how long it takes to do that task correlates to relative size but is not the same. There is a powerful inclination to try to do that, especially by upper management, who do not understand this. They push on the APM to map tasks to hours worked. The simpler answer to upper management is the list of use cases that will be completed at the end of the iteration.

If one team has a velocity of 23.2 points over five iterations and another team has a velocity of 14.7 points over five iterations, which is the more productive team? *You can't tell!* Remember the first and second rules of agile sizing.

Individual Velocities

Some teams may have a member perceived by the rest of the team as not doing as much work as they should toward the team effort. Let's use the technical term *free rider,* or *slacker.* There is a powerful motivation to start tracking individual velocities so that it becomes evident there is a slacker on the team. Don't do it.

The cards are not individual assignments, and are moved from owner to owner. The card completion is a team goal, and breaking down team efforts into who-did-what-when-and-by-how-much erodes team cohesion. Also, it is not necessary. The team knows who the slacker is, and peer pressure works wonders against slackers. If the slacker is the rare case where even peer pressure does not work, then more formal measures need to be taken.

Another reason not to measure individual velocities is that is counter-productive. Agile teams are *empowered* teams. Adding a personal velocity metric can corrupt the much needed scoping metric. If people are measured on how many points they get done in an iteration, then there will be a conflicting goal on the team to bloat estimates. Scoping sizes are for team visibility, and relative reference; they are not performance metrics.

✗ Anecdote We had a team member who constantly came in late to our daily meetings. The team started a "late jar:" anyone later than two minutes to the meeting had to put $1 in the jar. All agreed (it passed by peer pressure). Of course, one member was almost always putting a dollar in the jar, but was late to meetings much less often. At the end of the project, we had a team party with the money, and the team members ironically thanked the slacker for the party.

✗ Anecdote Our team was a contentious group: constant bickering, interrupting each other, and generally not listening or responding to each other's comments. It was severe enough that our team was not getting anything done whenever they meet as a group.

I purchased a bright orange sports horn, one of those very loud pressure klaxons meant for drowning out crowd noises in large stadiums. At the next meeting, I apologized to the team members. I said I was sorry for interrupting people, which means that I didn't understand their point entirely since they didn't get to finish it. As a result, I would misunderstand what they were trying to say. I told them that I was sorry for being rude and discourteous and non-professional. I told them that the next time I did that (and I pulled out the sports horn), "Please blow it as a reminder to me. *And I will do the same.*"

One of the team members asked me to demonstrate it. I pushed the button for half a second, the least amount of time I could. It blew so loudly that the person not paying attention (typical) jerked and literally fell out of his seat onto the floor. A co-worker from outside the room, and a manager in the hallway, came in to see what was up. In the following 18 months, the horn was never needed once. It was the best $12 I ever spent on a project!

Group Velocities

Wouldn't it be nice to see how many points the testers are completing, and how many points the developers are completing, or the analysts? No, it is not useful, and can be counter-productive. The same reason for not comparing team velocities between project teams applies here, especially if the testers are a separate team or an isolated or outsourced subgroup of the team. An agile team is a holistic team working together on a common goal, and that powerful but fragile concept can be shattered by focusing on those things that splinter the team.

Agile and Earned Value Management

Project managers and upper management who like to use Earned Value Management (EVM) can easily get EVM metrics from the agile reports. EVM's power comes from comparing the metrics of scope, cost, and schedule using a common term, that of money. EVM uses Planned Value, Earned Value, Actual Cost, Cost Variance, Schedule Variance, Schedule Performance Index, and Cost Performance Index. These metrics compare actual versus planned status at a particular time in the project. Most of the EVM metrics show up visually on the burn-up chart and make EVM easier than for traditional projects.

The Components of Earned Value Management

Here is how one may convert the agile metrics to the EVM metrics. (All definitions *in italics* are from the PMI's fifth edition *Project Management Body of Knowledge* (PMBOK, 2013).

Planned Value (PV) is *the authorized budget assigned to scheduled work*; in other words, the amount of money to be spent on the project. This is no different for agile projects. For agile, we can break down the planned value into an average budget per iteration. Planned value shows up as story points per release (or iteration) on the burn-up chart.

> Example: To keep the numbers simple, say we have an approved budget of $500,000 for a 50-week project. That means 25 two-week iterations, assuming a two-week start-up and a two-week iteration 0, for $500,000. **PV = $500K** for the project, which is **PV = $20K per iteration**. Halfway through the project, **PV = $250K.**

Earned Value (EV) is *the measure of work performed expressed in terms of budget authorized for that work*. Earned value is merely the work completed, expressed in terms of money. Earned value shows up as story points completed per release (or iteration) on the burn-up chart.

The scope of projects is not known in detail at the beginning of the project, but EV is clear for an iteration. For budgets allocated quarterly, and assuming a cost spend per iteration, EV can be read as the number of iterations completed to the total number of iterations planned.

> Example: Halfway into our 50-week project, we should have an amount of work done equal to PV/2 = $250K. The EV will be what work was actually done. If the entire project was 1,000 story points, then halfway in, we should have 500 story points completed. However, if the team only completed 400 points, then EV = 400/500 = 80% of the expected $250K planned, or **EV = $200K**.

Actual Cost (AC) is *the realized cost incurred for the work performed on an activity during a specific time period*; in other words, what was spent so far. Actual cost does not show up on the burn-up chart, but it is easy to make a similar chart showing actual money accumulated per release.

> Example: Let's say for our example project that we actually spent $180K halfway through, therefore **AC = $180K**. It doesn't matter why; it is a measurement.

Cost Variance (CV) is the amount of budget deficient or surplus at a given point in time, expressed as the difference between the earned value and the actual cost. In other words, **CV = EV – AC.** Cost variance does not show on the burn-up chart, but it is easy to show the difference from cost planned on the actual cost per iteration chart.

> Example: If we had spent $250K halfway through the project, we would have no cost variance, and been on budget. However, we measured our actual cost of $180K at the halfway point, so we are under budget: CV = EV – AC = $250K - $180K, or **CV = $70K** under budget. We spent $70K less than expected for the work completed.

261

Schedule Variance (SV) is *a measure of schedule performance expressed as the difference between the earned value and the planned value.* In other works, **SV = EV − PV.** Schedule variance shows as the difference between story points planned minus actual, per release (or iteration) on the burn-up chart.

> Example: If we had completed half the work halfway through the project, we would have no schedule variance. However, we completed 400 points instead of 500 points, or 80% of the work instead of $250K, so SV = EV − PV = $200K - $250K, or **SV = -$50K** behind schedule. It seems strange expressing schedule in terms of dollars, but it gives us a common basis for comparison.

The Cost Performance Index and Schedule Performance Index indicate a team's efficiency,[3] so they can be used to forecast end points accurately.

Cost Performance Index (CPI) is *a measure of the cost efficiency of budgeted resources expressed as the ratio of earned value to actual cost;* in other words, **CPI = EV/AC.** If we got one dollar's worth of work for each dollar spent, then we would have a CPI = EV/AC = 1.00. The CPI does not show up on the burn-up chart, but it is the slope of the cost chart mentioned above. It is analogous to team velocity but for cost spent instead of scope completed.

> Example: For our project, we know that we spent **AC = $180K** for an **EV = $200K**, so **CPI = $200K/$180K = 1.11**. Therefore, we are getting more $1.11 amount of work for each dollar planned. The team is running at 111% efficiency over plan in terms of cost.

Schedule Performance Index (SPI), is *a measure of schedule efficiency expressed as the ratio of earned value to planned value;* in other words SPI = EV/PV. This is the team efficiency, which corresponds to the team velocity, in terms of dollars. If we got one dollar's worth of progress for each dollar spent on that progress, then we would have a SPI = EV/PV = 1.00. The SPI shows as the slope of the work done on the burn-up chart, and is the same as team velocity expressed in money.

> Example: For our project, we know that we have a planned value **PV = $250K**, but only earned 400 points for an earned value **EV = $200K**. Therefore, we have an **SPI = $200K/$250K = 0.80**. We are not getting the progress we expected for the money. We are running at 80% efficiency in terms of schedule, which explains the -$50K shortfall in SV.

> Team velocity is scope completed per iteration, so for halfway through the project, 12 iterations, team velocity = 400 points/12 iterations = 33.3 points per iterations. We can forecast that to complete 100 more points would take 100/33.3 = 3 iterations, or the team is 6 weeks behind, or $50K behind.

Figure 12-1 shows how the EVM components relate to each other. The PV is the budget, and extends to the end of the project, shown here as October 1. The EV and AC are reported at a particular point in time. For agile, that would be each iteration. The CV and SV are reflected by the difference between the two curves at reporting time: SV = PV − EV and CV = EV − AC, respectively. The slopes of the curve reflect the CPI and SPI, respectively.

---

[3] *Efficiency* in this case means actual/expected, and not input/output. Perhaps that is why PMI has defined it as an *index*—a nuanced difference of the technical definition.

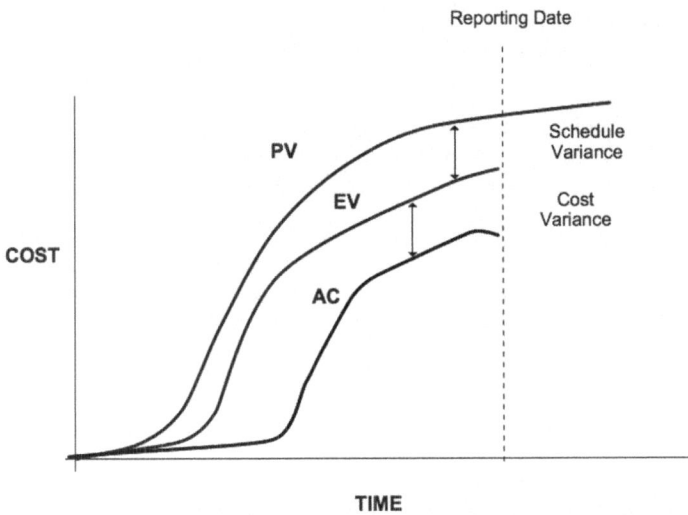

Figure 12-1. *EVM Components (Heldman, 2007)*

Figure 12-2 shows how to read the EVM values from the burn-up chart.

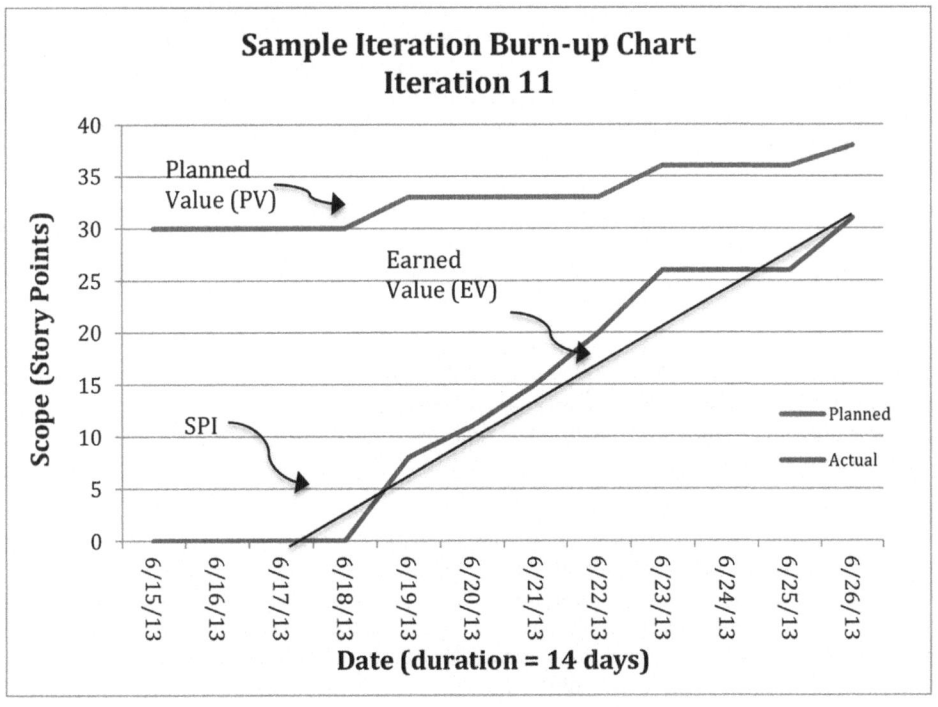

Figure 12-2. *Sample Burn-up Chart with EVM Components*

- *Planned Value* shows the planned number of story points for the iteration. In this case, 30 points were planned, but the team accepted an additional 8 points of work during the iteration.

- *Actual Value* is the number of story points completed. The first few days no work was completed, but the team rallied and completed 36 points, short of the commitment. At the next iteration planning meeting, the team cannot commit (or accept) more than 36 points.

- *Schedule Planning Index (SPI)* is the average story points per day completed for the iteration. Technically, SPI cannot be positive before actual points are done, but this SPI line reflects an average trend across the entire iteration. SPI is more useful when blending many iteration burn-up charts into a single project burn-up chart.

Putting It All Together

How are these metrics helpful? First, they allow the traditional or agile project manager to monitor the progress of the project in terms of cost and schedule. If the project seems to be trending away from its baselines, corrective action is needed. The sooner the PM knows to take corrective action, the smaller the action necessary—and the quicker it will come back in line. In extreme cases, the project may need to be stopped to prevent good money being spent on a bad investment.

If a project is running at 80% schedule efficiency (SPI =0.8), then it will take 20% longer to complete. Is the sponsor still happy with continuing the project if it won't get competed for 3 iterations (6 weeks) longer than originally planned, assuming the rate continues as it is? At the rate of spending, the cost efficiency CPI = 1.11 means that they will need 20% - 11% = 9% more money to extend the project, assuming the spend rate continues as it has. Is the sponsor willing to wait 6 more weeks and spend and extra $45K for the project? That is a question for the sponsor.

It is better to know the answer to that question now, at reporting time, than after the project has already consumed the time and money. Preparing the sponsor as early as possible is best for the APM-sponsor relationship. It is better to know three months ahead that the project is going to be late, than three weeks ahead. The sooner project variance is known, the sooner the project can be brought back on track with less disruption.

The full scope is not known at the beginning of a project. How can EV be calculated? Here are the traditional EVM components as they relate to agile projects:

- *Planned Value*: The planned value metric is the same for all projects, agile or not. It is the project budget. Many companies are now allocating funds each quarter so management can maintain better control over projects. This fits in well with agile, which delivers value an iteration at a time. See *Chapter 2* for a discussion of self-funding sustainable projects.

- *Actual Cost*: Normally, the actual cost metric is the same for all projects, agile or not. Sometimes the cost of the project team comes into play for team members who are "borrowed" or assigned from other departments, and especially if they are not full time. Their time can easily be counted back to dollars and a blended rate can be calculated to the team for each iteration. That means the cost can change for different iterations, but cost changes over time for traditional projects too. For extrapolating future cost, agile and traditional projects are the same. Agile products, unlike traditional products, may accumulate revenue during the project that offsets some or all of the cost.

- *Earned Value*: Agile projects count scope in terms of story points, ideal days, ideal hours, T-shirt sizes, or something else. However, at the beginning of the project, when the budget is defined (for the full or partial budget), the scope is no more accurate for agile projects than traditional ones, but agile project teams waste no time calculating it. The trend rates and performance indices (CPI, SPI) are even more important for measuring progress, and ultimately, ROI before the project is completed (see Figure 12-2).

- *Cost Variance*: The project cost variance is reported every iteration (agile), or for traditional projects, usually every month. Cost variance is the same for all projects, agile or not. Agile products, unlike traditional products, may accumulate revenue during the project that offsets some or all of the cost.

- *Schedule Variance*: During an iteration, each time the allocated number of story points are not completed, the carry-overs (unrepaired defects, accumulated technical debt, organization obligations, etc.) that push into future iterations may eventually cause the project to add another iteration. If the feature catalog is estimated in broad-strokes (say, T-shirt sizes), and the team's velocity is measured, then the number of iterations needed to be added or dropped can be extrapolated very well.

- Example: A feature catalog contains 400 remaining story points, give or take 80 (20%), for the next unknown number of iterations. The average team velocity is 20 points per iteration, as measured over the last three iterations. That means the project will take another 400/20 = 20 iterations to complete at the current rate. This estimate is based on the first 6 weeks into the project with a 20% confidence rate, which is better than most traditional projects experience. (I have found that feature catalog estimating is accurate to no better than 20%. One agile method, DSDM, recommends a 30% variance be worked into the backlog as a *feature buffer*.) Another benefit is that the team velocity tends to improve with time, so it is possible that number of planned iterations can decrease as the project progresses.

- *Cost Performance Index*: The rate at which projects spend money is not affected by whether a project is agile or not; but agile products, unlike traditional products, may accumulate revenue during the project that offsets some or all of the cost.

- *Schedule Performance Index*: The efficiency at which the team accomplishes work is slightly higher for projects that use daily meetings. Reporting commitment every day puts a psychological focus on the team members to get work done every day, and the productivity rate is higher; see *Chapter 10*. Figure 12-2 shows the iteration-average team velocity, which would be the SPI for the iteration, but SPI would be more valuable as a five-iteration average on a project burn-up chart.

The Agile Project Manager in the Iteration

This section describes the work of the team within the iteration process flow from a detailed perspective of the agile project manager (APM). The iteration starts with the APM's role in the iteration planning meeting. The box numbers in each heading refers to the boxes in Figures 8-1 and 8-2. There is no specific APM swimlane in the process flow (Figures 8-1 and 8-2) because the APM is more of a team facilitator and data tracker, and therefore is included in the Technical Team swimlane.

During the iteration, the APM ensures that the overall project schedule is not broken (scope creep) and tracks the team capacity, measured in units of scope completed per iteration. This metric is called *team velocity,* and helps the team set a limit of how many points they can commit to for the current iteration. Team velocity is a rolling average over typically five iterations and helps the APM predict when the product backlog will be finished.

Iteration Planning (Box 1)

At the beginning of the iteration, the team holds an *iteration planning* session. The meeting allows the team to estimate the size of each use case relative to each other, and to determine how many use cases can be completed by the end of the iteration. The stories are pulled from the already prioritized product backlog, to be implemented roughly in that order.

The APM facilitates the iteration planning meeting, in which all team members come together to estimate the amount of work to which they will commit for the iteration. The team members provide size estimates in some scope metric for each use case. If the use case catalog is sufficiently well along, the BA can walk the team through various detailed use cases and functionality.

At the initial iteration planning meeting (preferably during iteration 0), the APM must resolve with the team two things: what scope metric the team will use, and which tracking mechanism the team will use. It is not a definite and final decision because if it doesn't work out, the team can change their mind in a team retrospective after giving it a try, say, at the end of the third iteration. With that caveat said, an inexperienced team often will take my suggestion on how to start. I suggest story points for size estimating, and an online Kanban board for task tracking.

Normally, the APM announces the latest team velocity so that the team does not commit to more than they have accomplished in the past. Until three iterations are completed, the team has no experiential basis for team velocity, so the team must estimate as best they can on how much work they can get done within the iteration. As each iteration is completed, the team will have a better idea for each successive estimate. It is similar to Newton's method for calculating the square root: take a guess, check the result, and refine the guess.

The team leaves the meeting with a list of use cases (or user stories), their estimated size, the order in which they will be worked on, and a team commitment to have them all completed by the end of the iteration.

🌲 **Variant**   In some teams, instead of a single estimate for a user story, the team will fill out two cards for the same story. The developers record one size for coding and unit testing on one card, and the testers record a second size for testing. These two cards reflect the concurrency between the testers and the developers.

For example, if the developers think a use case is of size 5 story points, and the testers think it has testing effort of 2 story points, then the use case is considered to have a 7 story point scope. The sum of these two estimates often will not indicate Fibonacci numbers, but that is not important. This "shadow card" approach helps reduce the risk of increasing the story points on a card when the testers start to test it. Under the normal situation, the developer and testers would probably have estimated the single code-plus-test use case to have a scope of 8 story points (7 being disallowed under Fibonacci rules).

Design Approval Meeting (Box 5)

The APM does not need to attend the analysis and design meetings, but needs to be aware that they have been completed, and are on track. This result of this meeting should be announced in one of the daily meetings. The APM works with the team to start and maintain the Requirements Traceability Matric (RTM).

Defects and Change Meeting (Box 13)

The Defects and Change meeting is part of agile's low-ceremony change control process. After the testers run their battery of tests against a use case of the current Build, the passed tests are recorded in the RTM, but the failed tests are recorded in the defect log and need to be discussed. Not every failed test is the result of a code defect. Other failed tests are the result of requirements defects, tests defects, or requirements interpretation. Sometimes the SME attends if a change request is needed or for an interpretation to be resolved.

The APM should be involved in the meeting in which the testers show the defect list to the developers. If a significant Change Request (CR) arises from that meeting, the APM (or BA) needs to take the CR and the impact analysis back to the stakeholders for approval. If the CR is approved, then the APM must schedule it with the stakeholders into the backlog based on the stakeholders' priority; or in urgent situations, into the current iteration to replace one or more lower priority cards in the current commitment.

The stakeholders always have a right to insert a CR into the iteration by removing some other use case or CR that has already been scheduled. Scope changes are easily handled, like inserting a new card into a deck of cards, and removing an equal-sized card. These insertion CRs are so disruptive[4] that it often is easier for the stakeholder to place it at the top of the product backlog. Any increase in scope (or decrease) will be reflected in the burn-up chart.

In addition to defect repairs of any variety, a few CRs may be triggered, and all need estimates on how long they will take. Some impacts can be estimated in the meeting, but others require a developer to analyze and will take longer. The APM may also be involved, depending on the impact of the change. It could be something that can be worked into the schedule with relatively little effort (e.g., a use case that has not yet been started) or may require much effort (e.g., the code, tests, and requirements must be changed, resulting in significant schedule delay).

After the meeting, the team adds any tasks that need to be done as a result to the iteration backlog. The RTM is updated now if it was not updated earlier. See also *Chapter 8*.

Build Approved? (Box 14)

After all the committed use cases are done (or the iteration is out of time), the APM holds a meeting to evaluate the Build. Although this meeting sounds like a formality, many times what didn't want to be said before will, and must, be said now. The APM asks each team member in turn: "Do you approve this Build?" Each team member then responds "Yes" or "No" (and states the reason).

If the team agrees, when asked one by one, that there is nothing left to do on the latest use case—coding and testing are done, and all defects are repaired—the Build is ready for the user demo.

If anyone has a reason that it should not go to demo, then that part must be repaired as soon as possible. The APM often asks the question at this point, "Why is this issue coming up now?" The Build Approval meeting should have no surprises. If the Build needs some work—changes not yet in place, tests missing, defect not yet repaired, or some other standard not met—the needed work is identified and the whole team contributes to it.[5]

Sometimes when the iteration is close to ending, the APM may hold a Build Approval meeting to close out loose ends. Any new work will be stopped and defects will be repaired, so that the user demo works at production quality, even if it has less-than-expected scope.

---

[4]Insertion of requirements within an iteration is so disruptive that Scrum prohibits the practice; the iteration backlog is locked. New requirements may only be placed on the product backlog.

[5]This all-team-on-one-task is called *swarming* in agile, and can happen anytime in an iteration when the team contributes together to overcome some obstacle.

Build Iteration and QA Reports (Box 15)

The iteration reports are built from the cards the team members completed throughout the iteration. There is no special work the team needs to do other than provide their pertinent data.

There are many reports that can make project progress and status visible to those outside the team and inside the team. Team members need to see different things than upper management, but they also need to see what upper management sees.

The reports produced depend much on what upper management wants, and on what the APM uses to monitor the project. I have found the following reports valuable for end-of-iteration reporting; each is discussed in its section following.

1. *Iteration burn-up chart* showing the rate at which scope was completed through the iteration.

2. *Project burn-up chart* showing the rate at which scope was implemented throughout the project so far. It can be compared against the project schedule, and milestones of the project synopsis (or charter). For fixed-term projects, my burn-up chart also shows the ceiling constraint that limits the product in some way, usually by scope, sometimes by cost or schedule.

3. *Defect trend chart*, which is a line chart of the number of defects mapped against the days of the iteration. During the iteration, defects are found and repaired, so the line decreases from the defects at the start of the iteration to the number at the end of the iteration. A rising defect chart indicates a project in trouble.

4. *QA report*, which is a *stoplight report* showing each metric of scope, cost, time, and quality. Each metric is given a red/yellow/green icon[6] to visually show quickly and easily the quantitative variance of each metric. It also shows the variance trend. If EVM is desired for project status, the QA report can contain the key EVM indicators.

5. *Updated RTM* so that the business can see what features and use cases have been completed so far and compare with what they requested. The RTM contains traceability from a feature, with which they are familiar, to use cases to test cases and test results. The RTM also shows outstanding defects and approved CRs. Sometimes I use a separate Change Request log with the people who requested the change, and when a CR was approved. (Some people have short memories.)

The updated RTM, and keystones of iteration and progress, showing all features, associated use cases, associated test cases, associated code, and dates of passed tests, are used for internal tracking with the team, but also show the stakeholders a detailed progress list of user stories or features requested and completed. The RTM was discussed in *Chapter 8*.

Iteration Burn-up Chart

The iteration progress can be seen at a glance by a line graph showing the scope completed over time of the iteration to date. Scope units are usually measured in story points, but can also be ideal hours or some other metric. Time units are usually in days of the iteration, including weekends. The curve rises toward the expected value-to-be-completed by the end of the iteration. The average slope of the line indicates the average team velocity for the iteration at the reporting date. Extrapolating the average slope, the *trend line* indicates whether the current team velocity will complete the iteration on time. Most spreadsheets have a graphing feature that produces all these metrics at the press of a button.

---

[6]Some stoplight reports use *blue* to indicate that the metric exceeded expectations by the standard amount, usually 10-20%. I like to show the blue status indicator if the organization does not prohibit it; the military usually requires it.

Figure 12-3 shows a burn-up chart from a real project. Note the following:

- The planned scope increased during the duration,[7] perhaps due to many reasons: a better idea and estimate of the use case; urgent CRs; or re-estimating after seeing how much work a use case truly is. By Iteration 11, the team was better at estimating use cases. In this case, the team was getting a lot done fast, so it could take on the increased scope.

- The actual scope is flat for the first several days, which is typical when an iteration gets started. The developers and testers are working on their first use case for the iteration.

- The iteration started on a Thursday (6/13/2013) because of logistics with our team schedules. Therefore, the two flat points on the Actual curve (6/15-16/2013 and 6/21-22/2013) represent the weekends. (Weekends are including in the actual because calculating average team velocity is easier than extracting weekends and holidays, and correlates better with real time.)

- The stakeholders can see at a glance that the Actual work rose quickly to the Planned work, even when the Planned scope increased. Our team placed this chart on the website so that anyone with project access could see it. The Kanban board we used could display diagrams like this.

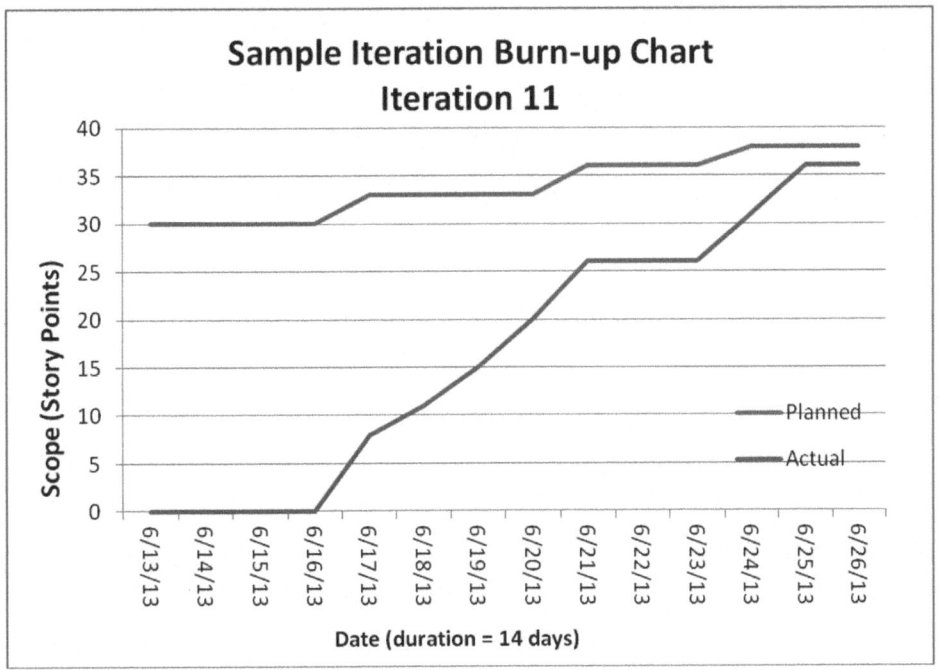

Figure 12-3. *Sample burn-up chart for iteration*

See the "Building a Burn-up Chart" section later in this chapter to see how card sizes and other statistics are updated into this chart, which takes less than five minutes each day.

---

[7]Iteration scope *should not increase*. This is such a key idea that SCRUM locks the iteration backlog so no changes are allowed. Other methods allow only replacement cards of lesser or equal scope.

Some people prefer to use burn-down charts. The same information is used, but instead of starting at 0 size and accumulating upward, the graph starts at the committed iteration scope and decreases as scope is completed. Choosing a burn-up or a burn-down chart is based on personal preference and what the stakeholders prefer to see.

Project Burn-up Chart

Each iteration's burn-up chart is combined into a single chart reflecting the progress made during the release, and shows progress against plan for the entire project. This level of breadth is usually the view the stakeholders would like to see, since they think in terms of project duration more than the day-to-day iteration progress. Figure 12-4 shows a product burn-up chart, with each time increment being two weeks, or one iteration.

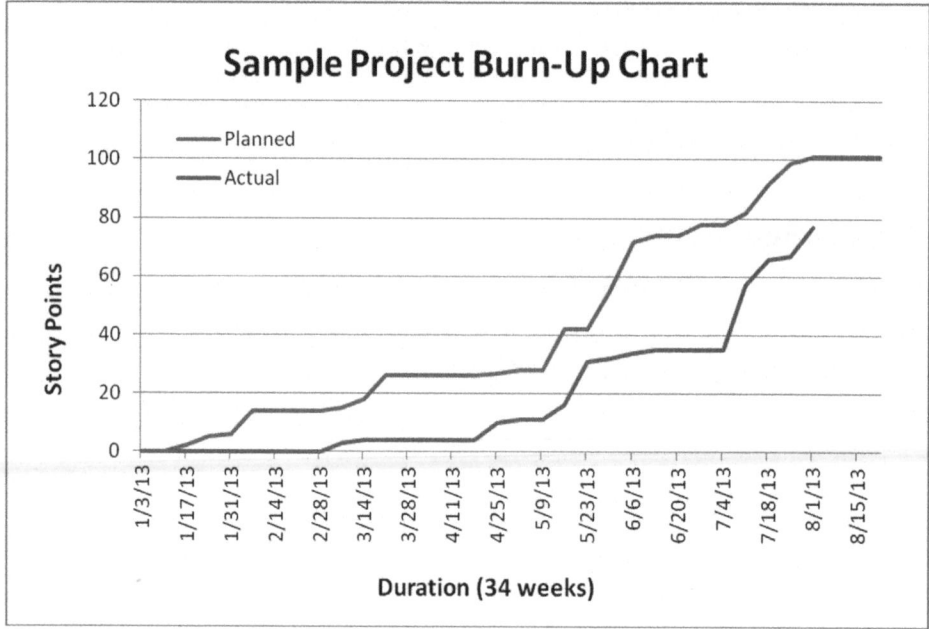

Figure 12-4. *Sample burn-up chart for project*

It is important to make the endpoints of the iteration burn-up charts continuous across the project; gaps and iteration lines that do not match indicate a problem. This indication has more than once caused me to go back and check my results, which revealed miscounted, duplicate, or missing cards.

For fixed-term projects, where the scope is pre-defined and cannot change, I add a horizontal black line across the top of the burn-up chart at the value of the project's fixed scope. The burn-up progress cannot go above that fixed black line, or our contract is in jeopardy. The trend line is important to show whether the team's progress is on track to reach that black line in time. In the best of cases, the trend line will intercept the scope ceiling right on the last day of the project, or for a little margin, during the last week of the project.

■ **Note**   The Actual curve mirrors the Planned curve but is always below it, for the following two reasons.

- This team went through three iterations of training at the start of the project, then iteration 0 took four weeks.

- Detailed requirements were not collected until the iteration started. A team retrospective later agreed that the BA needs to keep detailed requirements at least one iteration ahead so the team can start implementing when the iteration starts.

Both remedies were discussed in (and contribute to) *Chapter 3* and *Chapter 9*.

Defect Trend Report

While the burn-up chart is being updated, the testers can chart the recorded defects that have been found and repaired. The defect rate is a line graph that shows the defect repair rate per iteration. If the defect rate trend *increases* during the iteration, the project has a problem, or if the defect rate rises too swiftly across more than two iterations, the project is in jeopardy. Defects that are ignored tend to grow exponentially, the so-called *snow plow effect*. Repairing defects can sometimes reveal other defects that weren't previously known. It is a good rule (*strongly recommended!*) to repair defects as soon as possible, even if new use cases need to be delayed.

Figure 12-5 shows a sample defect report for the same project and iteration as Figure 12-2. Compare this chart with the data table below it (Table 12-1). The iteration started off with 21 defects, and 14 were repaired during the iteration, but 7 were added. The trend line shows that the average defect repair rate was 1.00 per day. However, with 7 more defects added, the product is only reducing the defect rate by 7 per iteration, or at a rate of .50 defects per day. Even with no more use cases being developed, it would take another week to clear all the defects. That load must be factored into the next iteration planning meeting.

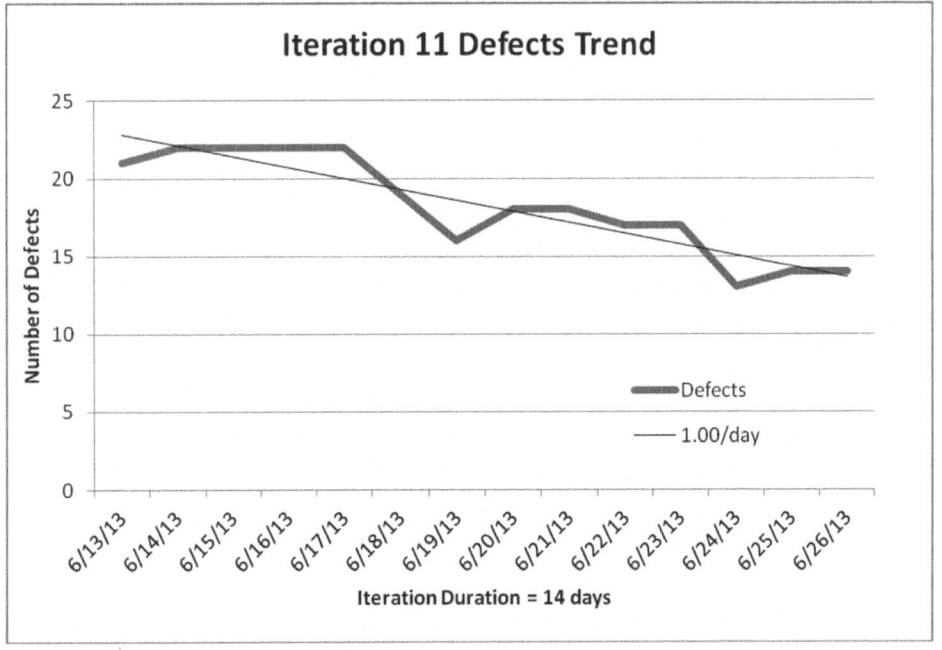

Figure 12-5. *Sample defect trend chart*

Table 12-1. *Data for Sample Defect Trend Chart*

DATE	Total Defects	Found	Closed
prior	**21**		
6/13/13	21	0	
6/14/13	22	2	1
6/15/13	22		
6/16/13	22		
6/17/13	22		
6/18/13	19		3
6/19/13	16		3
6/20/13	18	2	
6/21/13	18	1	1
6/22/13	17		1
6/23/13	17		
6/24/13	13		4
6/25/13	14	2	1
6/26/13	14		
Repair Rate	**1.00**	7	14
Net Defect Rate	**0.50**	7	14

In the burn-up chart, I like to use zeroes to indicate places where no cards were completed, and no scope was added. For the defect trends, however, I prefer to use space because this data table is sparser, and the defects found and defects repaired are easier to see.

Quality Assurance (QA) Report

The QA Report is an augmented stoplight dashboard, an optional report filled out by the APM to report quick status to the sponsor, portfolio team, and other upper managers. It is. Each metric of scope, cost, schedule, and quality is reported, and their trend from the previous iteration. Each metric is given a red, yellow, green, or blue indictor to reflect, respectively, significantly below expectations, marginally within expectations, met expectations, or significantly above expectations. The actual percent value of what is defined as *significant* is determined by the sponsor, but is set usually to a number between 10% and 20%, depending on the management's tolerance to variance.

The QA Report doesn't say a lot that the burn-up and defect charts don't say, but they summarize it in bright colors to catch the attention of a manager scanning over dozens of report statuses. A sample QA report with explanatory metrics is shown in Table 12-4. A summary of how those metrics are calculated follow. Each metric has a place to identify risk to the project from that metric's result, and perhaps a mitigation strategy.

- *Scope*: The number of story points implemented, and not implemented, with any scope changes recorded. The team velocity for the canonical five-iteration rolling average is given.

- *Schedule*: An iteration is time-boxed, so it is usually on schedule if the time-box is honored. However, it is possible that the iterations are not doing as much work as was expected up front, so the red or yellow indicator for the schedule metric means more iterations may need to be inserted in the Release Plan than originally planned.

- *Cost*: On a fixed-cost project, which this was, cost never changed. On a variable cost project, cost metric shows expected amount spent vs. actual amount spent, the cost's percent variance.

- *Quality*: The measure of defects found and repaired during the iteration. The defect repair rate is the ratio of repaired defects to known defects. However, as more defects are found, the found defects are added to the known defects, which reduces the net defect rate.

If EVM is used, the QA report is a great place to add on an EVM section to show the six EVM metrics.

The User Demo (Box 16)

The *user demo* is a stakeholder meeting to demonstrate the accumulation of product scope since the first iteration, with focus on the changes since the last user demo. The key purpose of the user demo is to collect feedback from the stakeholders, and improve the product going forward. The user demo also provides the opportunity to present various reports to the stakeholders, users, and other attendees about product progress. It strengthens the relationship and trust between the business team and the technical team. The APM reviews with the stakeholders the state of the project. The demo itself can be presented by anyone on the team.

The user demo unveils the work of the last iteration. The stakeholders find out if they got what they wanted. The APM owns the status reporting part of the meeting, but the entire team should be at the meeting. It is one of the few times the team gets to meet with the stakeholders. The developers want to show off their work, the analyst wants to make sure he or she did a good job in getting to what the user *needs* (not necessarily said), and the testers are on hand to discuss defects that might be found when the stakeholders run a few exploratory tests.

The frequency of user demos depends on the length of an iteration, a technical team decision. The frequency of when the product is released to operations is a business decision. Stakeholders typically decide how frequently they want to see a demo and hear project status, which depends on how much business value is in each iteration, and how much time they have available. The user demo meeting usually takes about one hour (15 minutes for status, 45 minutes for the demo).

Preparing the Demo

Each team member works on something to prepare for the user demo. The developers repair the last few defects and regression tests; the testers collect their test statistics for the QA report and build a defect repair report; the APM updates the burn-down charts. Drafts of these reports are taken to the user demo and presented with the current Build.

The user demo attendees should include others beside the business SMEs and the team. Invite people who must use it in the field: the help desk staff, maintenance programmers, staff and line managers, and possibly, even the public. They may not always come, but they should be invited each time. I am surprised sometimes at the number of people who show up out of curiosity about the product. Word-of-mouth from the user demos is good internal marketing and rains kudos on the sponsor, which is always good for her or his political capital, and eventually for the team.

If the iteration commitment was not achieved, the APM must be ready to discuss the shortfall with the stakeholders at the demo. He or she must explain why the shortfall occurred, which can be as simple as poor estimates. It could also be caused by pre-emptive tasks from the stakeholders (visible on the burn-up chart), or a technical blockage. The answer the APM needs to take into the demo is how the team (or stakeholder) is going to prevent another shortfall.

During the Meeting

The facilitator keeps the meeting on track, ensures that time is managed properly, and ensures that changes and defects are recorded. The APM presents the progress reports quickly and discusses any issues that the stakeholders need to know. A developer often facilitates for the demo portion of the meeting, while the BA takes minutes, recording defects and proposed changes.

Recommendation   Although the APM facilitates the meeting, I prefer to let the developer (or whoever was working on the particular user story being demonstrated) present that part of the demo, and the BA record the meeting minutes. It is the BA's role to record any changes and work them back into the requirements. By allowing the developer to present, the BA can focus on the meeting minutes, capturing the defects, changes, and action plan. It also allows the developer to shine in front of the business. To have one person presenting the demo and tracking changes at the same time often keeps that person too busy, and attendees waiting.

Most of the development issues are resolved within the iteration, so the user demo meeting is a good chance to talk about how successful the team was in overcoming obstacles. I prefer to show the demo last so that we can be sure of covering progress and issues first.

Warning   There is one danger with having the whole team there. It is easy for back-channels to get set up so that stakeholders start calling team members to ask questions, suggest changes, and generally by-pass the analyst or APM, the proper liaisons. These unofficial channels need to be stopped because the *whole team* is no longer aware of what is happening. If the stakeholders are making an end-run around the APM or analyst because they are dissatisfied, the APM has a serious problem and needs to resolve that as soon as possible.

After the Meeting

The meeting minutes are distributed to all participants and stakeholders, especially if they were not there. It is a good idea to include the managers of the participants as well. Defects and changes are brought back into the product backlog for repair. If there were no defects or changes that affected the current Build, then the Build is staged for Release.

Problems with the Build

What should the team do if not everything is according to plan? Here are a few problems you may encounter, and suggestions on what to try.

- *Skipping a demo* is not necessarily a problem. The most common reason for skipping a demo is because there is not enough business value in the Build to warrant the stakeholders reviewing it. The proper amount of scope may be completed, but the stakeholders may choose to wait. Not a problem.

  However, skipping a demo means that the feedback the team expected will not be given, so there is a risk that the product will need to be reworked after more code is added, making it more difficult and more time-consuming. It also means that the team is two weeks late in the mind of management (read: sponsor), who is still watching out for the bottom line and their ROI.

- *Slightly-incomplete Build:* If the Build is missing only a little functionality such that the demo can be given anyway, the stakeholders will need to know that the demo will not be as full as expected, and why that is the case. *No one likes surprises,* especially stakeholders! Either way, the APM talks with the stakeholders and explains the state of the demo. Usually they are satisfied to see a partial demo, or postpone it, and it is not an issue. Surprising the stakeholders *will* be an issue.

- *Greatly-incomplete Build*: If the Build has fallen far short of the functionality promised to the business, then the APM must be ready to explain why there is nothing to show. Was there a major obstacle? Is there too little difference between the last demo and this one to warrant the time to gather the stakeholders? The team will need to have a recovery plan, and it is probably a good idea for the APM to discuss it in private with the sponsor.

- *Sponsorship:* The sponsor must be there. He or she gets another chance to build political capital by producing a great product for the stakeholders. If the sponsor cannot make the meeting, schedule a special meeting for him or her. It is critical that the sponsor stay in the loop. As said before, *out of sight, out of mind, out of budget.*

  If the sponsor cannot attend, check if there is some reason that the sponsor cannot be—or doesn't want to be—at the meeting. If he or she (or any key stakeholder) is trying to disassociate from the project, you and the project may be in jeopardy. Perhaps the user demo needs to be shorter, making it easier for the sponsor to fit his or her schedule.

If the project is not going well, you may find that the sponsor doesn't show up, or many stakeholders do not show up to even routine meetings. Be sensitive to the reactions and interests of the stakeholders. If people are disappearing from the project, the project may be in jeopardy of being cancelled—the APM is usually the last to know.

Stage or Release the Build (Box 17)

Periodically, usually after each iteration, the APM steps back and views the Build and Product Backlog as a whole. Do the features completed match the Release Plan and expected items in the RTM? How much is completed out of what was promised? Box 17 is similar to Box 16 except that all items in the product backlog are considered instead of only the last iteration's set.

The Release will contain all the deliverables that each demo has, but it contains them for the accumulation of the project—all iterations that led up to the Release. There are usually Release deliverables that are not part of an iteration: the user manual, technical manuals for operations and maintenance programming, updating project files, etc. Release deliverables may also include contract deliverables.

The Release process requires scheduling and coordination with groups after the product moves into operations, the people who must use it in the field: the help desk staff, operations and maintenance programmers, staff and line managers, and possibly, the public.

It is normally not the responsibility of the APM, or anyone on the agile team, to facilitate the Release into production, perform training, or deal with the public. The team must produce a Build that is ready to be easily integrated and tested in the production environment, but the organizational aspects are left to staff and line managers.

Help desk personnel need to repair and answer questions from the many new users for the product. They will rely on the user manual but the APM may coordinate special training with the help desk manager for those personnel. After all, the team made the bed that the help desk must sleep in.

PMI Parallels

All the PMI parallels of *Chapter 8* are still true, but the following highlights some specifics for the APM role:

Scope: The APM manages the work and project constraints as a traditional PM would do, especially during Region 2 activities, but it is easier when the work is broken down into somewhat-independent iterations of scope, cost, quality, and time.

Time: The work is timeboxed, so the APM facilitates to ensure that the defined and committed work starts on time, proceeds smoothly, and ends on time. During Region 1 activities, the APM uses agile-specific practices and artifacts not found in traditional project management. The APM repeats this process with the team iteration after iteration.

Cost: The Cost project constraint is in smaller chunks, so is more manageable. Often, cost does not become a factor during iterations, but only at key milestones. If the APM uses EVM, the calculations and measurements are the same, but more clearly and easily reflected from the various iteration reports.

Quality: The product quality of agile has been shown to be higher than that of traditional projects due to shorter and more frequent feedback cycles, closer business involvement, and test-driven development, particularly by Rico et al (2009).

Human Resources: The APM must usually negotiate harder to work an agile team, which works best as a projectized team within the corporate organization. There are strong conflicts of interest when agile teams work in functional or weak matrix organizations. The APM must fight off multi-tasking (resource-splitting) by the resource manager, which makes coordinating an agile team more challenging. The APM must keep the agile team members empowered, and working closely as a value-driven team. It requires strong interpersonal communications skills and a collaborative leadership style.

Communications: Agile communications, particularly osmotic communications, is better done in agile rooms, and offers better communications than a team heavy-laden with documents and ceremony. The APM must walk the tightrope between enough specifications to communicate to the business and sponsor, and yet not too much to bog down the team.

Risk: The APM must still maintain risk triggers and responses, but is helped by the fact that risks will remain within a small iteration-sized window. Except at the very beginning of the project (Region 2), working agile iterations is like doing a series of small projects within the economies of scale of a program. Risks are minimized compared to traditional projects because agile methods force the APM to keep his or her "eye on the road" much more frequently, and make smaller course corrections sooner, if needed.

Stakeholder Management: The APM works closer with the stakeholders and sponsor than might happen with traditional PMs. The APM sets up a "business partnership" relationship, which engenders more communication, trust, and respect.

Conclusions

The APM needs to work differently with the business and the team than a traditional PM. The business and agile team work best as a business partnership, and the APM is the liaison to that partnership. Although the business analyst will work closely with the business SMEs for technical details of the product, the APM must keep the political aspects on track, and manage the expectations of all the stakeholders. The product burn-up chart and QA report show project progress to the stakeholders. For more financially focused organizations, the APM can augment the iteration reports with EVM aspects easily.

The APM holds a strong coordinating role for the team as a coach and agile mentor. He or she must empower the team members to take ownership and accountability of the product development. An iteration backlog, iteration and project burn-up charts, the defect list (and trend report), and an up-to-date RTM are minimal documents from which the team can work.

The APM coordinates the activities during the iteration, and has no specific role swimlane shown on the iteration process flow of Figure 8-1 and 8-2. The PMI parallels between a traditional PM and the APM reflect the key differences between agile work done during an iteration.

Additional Tools

Table 12-2 is a summary of the tasks of the APM, derived from the CORA matrix of Chapter 7.

Table 12-2. *Summary of the Agile Project Manager Role, CORA Matrix for <ROLE> (Brackets Indicate That the BA Contributes or Reviews the Artifact.)*

BOX #	INPUT	PROCESS	OUTPUT
1	Feature catalog and possibly use case catalog	Facilitate iteration planning meeting.	List of prioritized use cases to be completed by iteration's end
[2]	Detailed use cases	Review use case for proper priority, scope, testability, and implementability.	Possible changes to use case
[4]	Detailed use case; UX suggestions, design	Review the analysis and design.	Approved UX artifact, requirements, and design; attain better scope understanding
[9]	Development Build	Download last Build for testing purposes.	Test Build
[13]	List of failed and passed tests (defect log and RTM)	Facilitate or review resolving failed tests, and estimating CRs	Change requests to approve with stakeholders; defects needing repair
14	Iteration backlog, regression test results, defect log, QA checklists, RTM	Facilitate approval meeting for Build for each team member (quality gate).	Remaining work for the Build, or approved Build that is ready for user demo
15	Test statistics, defect log, RTM	Build QA and iteration closing reports.	Defect trend chart, QA report, burnup reports
16	Build ready for User demo	Facilitate or coordinate the use demo meeting.	Change lists and defect lists; possible project metric changes
[17]	Stage or Release Build contributions from team members	Approve Build release package.	Production-ready Build for staging or release

Kanban Process Summary

The following Kanban process summary was used on several project teams. However, each is modified slightly by the team and culture for the project, so this is only a representative sampling of the work done during a Kanban iteration. See Anderson (2010) for a fuller description.

Starting with the prioritized capability list from stakeholder capabilities, and assuming the system architecture is defined, each iteration is tracked on the online Kanban board.

Release Plan

Before any iterations get started (Iteration 0), the APM identifies the full expected functionality (features)[8] for the product with the stakeholders. The BA extracts the use cases for each feature with the stakeholders (progressive elaboration). All use cases are listed by theme, roughly equivalent to one or two iterations. Functional dependencies are included.

The following steps are repeated each iteration:

- The APM places a set of use cases in the Kanban Backlog area, proposed for one iteration. The team estimates each use case card, in priority order, until they reach the total amount of work they can accomplish for that iteration. Each use case card size is one of 1, 2, 3, 5, 8, or 13 story points, although little is known about each one yet. For relative sizing purposes, 5 can be arbitrarily set as the average size of a use case, with all other estimates relative to that anchor.

- During the iteration, each team member selects what they want to work on, and moves their desired card from one column to the next in progress. Typical actions are:

  - BAs from Iteration Backlog to Analysis where requirements are done

  - Developers from Analysis to Construction where coding and unit testing are done

  - Testers from Analysis to Testing where test scripts and testing are done

  - Testers from Testing to Team Review where use case and Build approval are done.

  - APM from Team Review to Done when the team says the use case is complete.

  - APM from Done to archives when the iteration reports are completed.

Each person works on no more than two cards at a time—a primary, and a backup in case their primary is stalled.

- Each day the team walks the Board from right (Done) to left (Backlog) to move their card toward completion. They tell the team the cards they moved yesterday, the cards they expect to move today, and if they have any blocking issues.

- The team holds reviews of Builds ready for user demo for approval. No card is allowed to move past the Team Review lane without the team's approval. Team reviews are held on the following packages when the constituent artifacts are completed:

---

[8]Kanban refers to each use case, task, or dependencies—anything that shows on the Board—as a feature, including defects. For clarity, this document will refer to "cards" instead of the word *feature* to avoid confusion.

- Analysis package (per use case): Detailed use case, wireframe(s), optional validation artifacts (domain sequence and class diagrams).

- Test package (per use case): GUI and integration test scripts.

- Build package: Code and unit testing completed, GUI and integration testing results report, regression testing passed 100%, public API documented.

- The APM adds each point from cards that reach the Done column to the Iteration burn-up chart. The burn-up chart visually shows actual progress against planned progress, scope change, and is easily converted to EV.

If the team needs more cards before the iteration is over, the APM can move the next few cards from the feature catalog to the Backlog lane; otherwise, a new set of cards are added to the Backlog each iteration. (The product backlog is continually rearranged for priority by the business, which has full control of that backlog.) The Backlog may also include CRs and defects that have been deferred from previous iterations.

Iteration Reports

The following reports are typical of agile iterations, but not specifically of Kanban, and are discussed in more detail elsewhere.

- *Iteration burn-up chart*: The accumulated size of each card completed is shown on a line graph of time vs. story points. The time is usually the days of the iteration, and the curve rises toward the expected value-to-be-completed by the end of the iteration. Extrapolating the average slope indicates whether the current team velocity will complete the iteration on time.

- *Release burn-up chart*: Each iteration's burn-up chart is combined into a single chart reflecting the progress made during the release, and shows progress vs. plan for the entire release.

- *Quality report*: Each metric of scope, cost, schedule, and quality are reported, and their trend from the previous iteration. Each metric is given a red, yellow, green, or blue indictor to reflect significantly below expectations, marginally within expectations, met expectations, or significantly above expectations, respectively. The percent below or above expectations is determined by the sponsor, and is typically about 10-20% variance before a color change is indicated.

User Demo and Releasable Build

- *MMR (Marginally Marketable Release)*: Each use case must be done completely—no outstanding defects or missing features. When the set of features are completed and added to the Build, the Build is considered ready for user demo, and possible production release (a business decision of the sponsor or higher management). The MMR will be attained when the Build comprises enough business value, offset by the transition overhead of Release and subsequent maintenance of the product, to be profitable.

Terminology and Special Cases

- *High priority items*: If an urgent task comes to light, one that cannot wait until the end of the iteration, the APM marks it as high priority, the team sizes it, and someone agrees to take it. The current card of the person who took on the urgent card is then marked as Blocked until they can get back to it. The Blocked card is not put into the Backlog because it needs to stay visible so stakeholders to show that the high priority task has pre-empted scheduled work. This is especially important if the team commitment for that iteration was not met.

- *Impediments*: Some factor that causes a card to stop flowing. Impediments cause the card to be marked as Blocked. An Impediment must be escalated after 24 hours if it is not resolved as a risk to the iteration release.

- *Blockers*: Cards that have stopped for some reason. Blockers can result from a dependency not yet completed, or a higher priority task preempting normal flow, or a team member being pulled off task.

- *Defects and points*: Defects are also cards but without points, which will reflect the lower team velocity due to incomplete scope. A use case is not completed until is has no defects, and no points can be tallied until is it completed.

- *Swarming*: When an unblocked card is stopped for more than 2 days, then the assignee requires some help. The entire team drops what they are doing to help the assignee, and move the card out of its lane. Everyone drops what they are doing to get that card moving again, even if it is the APM going for coffee.

- *Carry-Overs (CYOs)*: If a task is not completed by the end of the iteration, it is placed back in the Backlog for the next iteration. No points are tallied for the iteration in which it was not completed, regardless of how much of it was completed. Defects deferred from previous iterations are not considered CYOs because the (a) defect list is always re-evaluated at the beginning of each iteration, and (b) defects have no assigned point value.

- *New items*: Sometime a use case or task is discovered during the iteration. It is added to the Backlog to be moved onto the task board when someone is available. Defects are added to the Backlog as they are found (unless the team defers them during the Defects and Change meeting).

Building a Burn-Up Chart (Example)

A standard spreadsheet can be updated daily, or every couple of days, in a few minutes to graph to progress of the team. It can be used to calculated scope increase, competed scope, team velocities, and projected trends.

Each day, zero or more use case cards are moved to the Done column. There is also the possibility that a scope increase can occur, for one reason or another. Table 12-3 shows a sample spreadsheet that captured this data.

Table 12-3. Burn-up Data Sheet

Iteration 11: Project and Component Creation				
Date	**Planned**	**Actual**	**Added**	**Done**
Prior	**30**	**0**	**0**	**0**
6/13/13	30	0	0	0
6/14/13	30	0	0	0
6/15/13	30	0	0	0
6/16/13	30	0	0	0
6/17/13	33	8	3	8
6/18/13	33	11	0	3
6/19/13	33	15	0	4
6/20/13	33	20	0	5
6/21/13	36	26	3	6
6/22/13	36	26	0	0
6/23/13	36	26	0	0
6/24/13	38	31	2	5
6/25/13	38	36	0	5
6/26/13	38	36	0	0
		36	8	36
Cyo	2			
Duration	14			
Vel	2.57			

- The title line shows the goal of the iteration. The title is copied from the main project schedule in which each iteration has a goal listed. These titles may change, but this is the title at the time of the iteration.

- Each column represents the date of the iteration, the Planned scope committed (which should remain the same unless a scope change occurred), the Actual scope cumulative completed, any Add scope in case of change requests or undiscovered dependencies (which can go negative if scope decreases), and the Actual scope completed for the day.

- Each row represents the days of the iteration. In this case, the iteration is two weeks (14 days) with the weekends indicated by grey.

- The poker planning meeting determined that the team could accomplish 30 story points, and during the iteration, another 8 points were added (see last row). Although the team completed 36 points during the iteration, more than they had planned, the scope increased so that the net result was 2 points left over for the next release. That overage is indicated by the CYO cell. The next iteration will start with 2 story points planned, before the poker planning meeting adds more commitment.

- Each day the APM counts the scope on the Done column of the board. It takes only a couple minutes to add the Done cards into the Done column, and if any new scope was increased (there should be a card for it in the backlog). The graph is automatically plotted as the data is added, so the burn-up is updated in less than three minutes, from counting cards to Big Visible Chart.

- The team velocity (the Vel cell) is the Done total divided by the duration, or 36/14 = 2.57 story points per day. At the next poker planning meeting, the APM should not let the team commit to more than 36 points, possibly even fewer because the scope increased by 8 points.

- Despite the late productivity starts, the trend line shown of actual work completed in Figure 12-6 shows the team will get all the work done by 6/26/13.

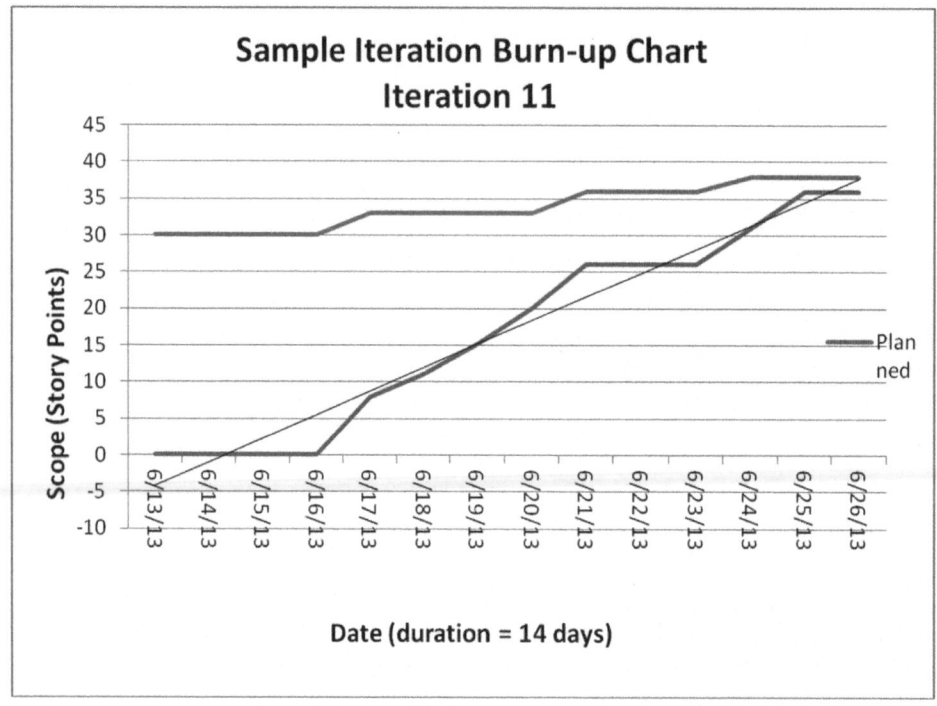

Figure 12-6. *Sample chart for data grid in Table 12-3*

Quality Report (Example)

Table 12-4 shows a sample QA report for Iteration 11. See the explanatory notes after the table. Table 12-5 shows the general legend.

Table 12-4. *Sample QA Report for Iteration 11*

Status	Milestone/ Target Metric	Notes & Comments	Risk
▬ ⇓ 95% completed	SCOPE: Implemented 36 points of work; 27% scope creep Average team velocity = 2.6 points per day	Work completed reflects what was originally committed plus new added scope.	Scope increase more than expected, causing net work rate to be less than 100%.
▬ ◊ No variance	SCHEDULE: On schedule! DURATION: 14 days	No significant delays.	None at this time.
▬ ◊ No variance	COST: Maintained budget	Cost is fixed.	None at this time.
⬡ ⇓ 50% repair rate	QUALITY: 21 existing defects, 7 new defects, 14 repaired. Defect repair rate = 1.00 per day; 50% of all defects repaired.	Metric indicates that the tests are catching more defects, or that the code contains more defects.	Investigate why defect repair rate is dropping.

Notes:

- The scope variance is based on the committed + added work in the iteration, instead of only the committed work. This helps focus estimates to foresee additional work that may be coming, and prevents the estimates from being low-balled. Although the scope variance may be lower, it improves the team's ability to estimate the iteration's work.

- The quality variance is based on the defects known + found during the iteration, for similar reasons the scope metric takes into account increased during the iteration.

Table 12-5. *General Legend*

Symbol	Meaning	Trend	Meaning
▬	Progress! Target metric is safe.	⇑	Progress/compliance in this area is better than last reporting period.
△	Caution! Target metric may be at risk	⇓	Progress/compliance in this area is worse than last reporting period.
⬡	Danger! Target metric is in jeopardy.	◊	Progress/compliance in this area is about the same as last reporting period.
!	Exceeded target metric		

■ **Note** The variance percentages in Tables 12-6 and 12-7 are sample numbers. The actual percentage variants are decided by upper management shortly after the business kick-off meeting. Some organizations have standard variance percentages for their projects predefined.

Table 12-6. *Metrics–Scope and Cost*

Symbol	SCOPE Metric	Symbol	COST Metric
▮	Over 80% of planned ideal days were completed and tested as expected.	▮	Budget is being maintained as planned within 10%.
△	Between 60% and 80% of planned ideal days were completed and tested.	△	Cost varies between 10% and 20%.
⬡	Fewer than 60% of planned ideal days were completed and tested.	⬡	Cost varies by 20% or more.

Table 12-7. *Metrics–Time and Quality*

Symbol	SCHEDULE Metric	Symbol	QUALITY Metric
▮	Iteration completed within 20% of schedule.	▮	Less than 20% of expected story points resulted in defects or change requests.
△	Iteration completed between 20% to 40% of plan date	△	Between 20% and 40% of expected story points resulted in defects or change requests.
⬡	Iteration late by 40% or more, or duration greater than 40% of planned.	⬡	More than 40% of expected story points resulted in defects or change requests.

References

Agile Principles. http://agilemanifesto.org/principles.html. 2001.

Agile Transformations Inc. "PMI Agile Certified Practioner (PMI-ACP) Prep Course." 2012.

Alberts, D. "The Economics of Software Quality Assurance." Proceedings of the 1976 National Computer Conference. New York, NY: AFIPS Press, 1976.

Anderson, D. *Kanban: Successful Evolutionary Change for Your Technology Business.* Sequim, QA: Blue Hole Press, 2010.

Armel, K. *Top Performing Projects Use Small Teams.* Quantitative Software Management (QSM). Jan 1, 2012. http://www.qsm.com/blog/2012/top-performing-projects-use-small-teams.

Bass, L., Clements, P., Kazman, R. *Software Architecture in Practice.* SEI Series in Software Engineering. Boston, MA: Addison-Wesley, 2003.

Beck, K. *Extreme Programming Explained.* Boston, MA: Addison-Welsey, 2000.

Bedell, C. *Solution architects' evolving role and Agile development methodology.* 2014. SearchSOAcom, http://searchsoa.techtarget.com/feature/Solution-architects-evolving-role-and-Agile-development-methodology.

Bedell, C. "Where Agile and enterprise architecture collide." 2014. SearchSOA.com. http://searchsoa.techtarget.com/feature/Where-Agile-and-enterprise-architecture-collide?

Bloch, J. *Effective Java, second edition.* Boston, MA: Addison-Wesley, Sun Microsystems, 2008.

Boehm, B. *Software Engineering Economics.* Upper Saddle River NJ: Prentice Hall PTR, 1981.

Booch, G. *Object-Oriented Analysis and Design with Applications, 2/e.* Santa Clara, CA: Benjamin/Cummings Publishing Company, 1994.

Bredemeyer, D. "Software Architecture and Related Concerns." The Architecture Discipline. Bredemeyer Consulting. July 9, 1999. http://www.bredemeyer.com.

Bregman, P. "How (and why) to Stop Multitasking." Boston, MA: Harvard Business Review, May 20, 2010.

Chicago State University, www.csu.edu/humanresources/empdev/documents/ManagerialCourage.pdf. August 4, 2014.

Cline, A. *Validating Use Cases with XUML.* Carolla Development, Inc, http://carolla.com/wp-delph.htm. 1999.

Cline, A. "Prioritization Process Using Delphi Technique." 2000. http://carolla.com/wp-delph.htm.

Cline, A. "Concurrent Engineering: Primary Principles." 2000. http://carolla.com/wp-delph.htm.

Craig-Hart, S. "Get the Facts: How Multitasking Is Hurting Your Business." August 21, 2014. http://smartsimplemarketing.com/get-the-facts-how-multitasking-is-hurting-your-business.

Coad, P., Yourdon, E. *Object-Oriented Analysis*. New York, NY: Prentice Hall, 1991.

Coad, P., Yourdon, E. *Object-Oriented Design*. New York, NY: Prentice Hall, 1991.

Cockburn, A. *Crystal Clear, A Human-Powered Methodology for Small Teams*. Boston, MA: Addison-Wesley Professional, 2004.

ConcEng. September 2014. http://en.wikipedia.org/wiki/Concurrent_engineering.

Cohn, M. *Agile Estimating and Planning*. Robert Martin series. Boston, MA: Prentice Hall PTR, 2006. pp187–190.

Cohn, M. *User Stories, Epics, and Themes*. Mountain Goat Software blog. October 24, 2011. http://www.mountaingoatsoftware.com/blog/stories-epics-and-themes.

Crispin, L, House, T. *Testing Extreme Programming*. Boston, MA: Addison-Wesley, 2003.

Crowe, A. *The PMI-ACP Exam: How to Pass on Your First Try*. published by Andy Crowe, PMI-ACP, CSM, PMP, PgMP. 2012.

Doran, G.T. "There's a S.M.A.R.T. way to write management's goals and objectives." Management Review. November 1981. Doran uses "objective" in the sense "milestone" is used above.

Dressler, Fritz, John Seybold. "People Productivity." *Modern Office Technology*, v 31, p12. June, 1986.

Duong, L. "Applying the '80-20' Rule with the Standish Group's Statistics on Software Usage." Luu Duong's Blog. March 4, 2009. http://luuduong.com/blog/archive/2009/03/04/applying-the-quot8020-rulequot-with-the-standish-groups-software-usage.aspx.

Feathers, M., *Working Effectively with Legacy Code*. Upper Saddle River NJ: Prentice Hall Professional Technical Reference, Pearson Education, 2005.

Fontdevila, D., Salias, S. "Software Architecture in the Agile Lifecycle." *The Architecture Journal*. March, 2010. http://msdn.microsoft.com/en-us/architecture/ff476940.aspx.

Friedman, D., Weinberg, G. *Handbook of Walkthroughs, Inspections, and Technical Reviews*. Dorset House, 1990. As Freedman once quipped, "The brain cannot absorb more than the butt can endure."

Foroughi, C., Werner N., Nelson E., Boehm-Davis, D. "Do Interruptions Affect Quality of Work?" Fairfax, VA: George Mason University, 2014.

Fowler, M. *Refactoring: Improving the Design of Existing Code*. Boston, MA: Addison-Wesley, 2000.

Fowler, M. "Is Design Dead?" XP 2000 keynote speech downloaded May 16, 2014. martinfowler.com/articles/designDead.html.

Gale, S.F. "Failure Rates Finally Drop." PM Network, PMI, August, 2011.

Ghahrai, A. "Seven Principles of Software Testing." Testing Excellence ISTQB site. November 30, 2008. http://www.testingexcellence.com/seven-principles-of-software-testing/.

Gallaugher, J., Ramanathan, S. "The Critical Choice of Client Server Architecture: A Comparison of Two and Three Tier Systems." Boston College. Accessed May 14, 2014. https://www2.bc.edu/~gallaugh/research/ism95/cccsa.html.

Goldratt, E., Cox, J. *The Goal, third edition*. Productivity and Quality Publishing, 2004.

Goncalves, M. "Modern Project Management." ASME course material. Spring 2014. Slide 88: "Managing and Reporting Information." `http://mgcgusa.com`.

Goodpasture, J.C. *Project Management the Agile Way: Making It Work in the Enterprise.* J. Ross Publishing, 2010.

Google. *Google Java Style.* Accessed September 13, 2014. `https://google-styleguide.googlecode.com/ svn/ trunk/javaguide.html`.

Griffiths, M. *PMI-ACP Exam Prep, Premier Edition: A Course in a Book for Passing the PMI Agile Certified Practitioner (PMI-ACP) Exam.* RMC Publications, Inc., 2012.

Gualtieri, M. "Agile Software is a Cop-Out; Here's What's Next." Forrester Blogs. October 12, 2011. `http:// blogs.forrester.com/mike_gualtieri/11-10-12-agile_software_is_ a_cop_ out_heres_whats_next`.

Hall, Nicholas, John Hershey, Larry Kessler, R. Craig Stotts. "A Model for Making Project Funding Decisions at the National Cancel Institute." *Operations Research*, v40, n6, 1992, pp1040–1052.

Han, S. *Metrics and Models in Software Quality Engineering.* Pearson Education, 2003.

Heidt, D. *10 Principles of Smart Requirements Gathering.* Enterprise Agility presentation. 2012.

Herodotus. *Herodotus: The Histories, Book Seven.* London, England: Penguin Books, translated 2002.

Highsmith, J. *Agile Project Management: Creating Innovative Products* (2nd Edition). Boston, MA: Addison-Wesley, 2009.

Hill, M. "They're Called Microtests." GeePawHill, May 29, 2009; July 10, 2014; Mike has a long list of qualifications that define a good automated unit test; `http://anarchycreek.com/ 2009/05/20/ theyre-called-microtests`.

Hyde, W.D. "How Small Groups Can Solve Problems." *Industrial Engineering*, 5986, v18, n2, pp42–49.

IEEE. *830 Standards, 830-1998* - IEEE Recommended Practice for Software Requirements Specifications, reaffirmed in 2009, C/S2ESC. Software & Systems Engineering Standards Committee, sponsored by IEEE Computer Society. Piscataway, NJ, 1998.

Jacobson I., Christerson M., Jonsson P., Övergaard G. *Object-Oriented Software Engineering - A Use Case Driven Approach.* Boston, MA: Addison-Wesley, 1992.

Johnson, J. Standish Group presentation XP2002, Sardinia conference; reported by Martin Fowler, July 2, 2002; `http//www.martinfowler.com/articles/xp2002.html`.

jc-Qualitystreet. "Agile Prototyping Tools: Paper, Whiteboard, and Balsamiq...." *Agile UX e-magazine.* Feb 2, 2012. `http://www.agile-ux.com/2011/02/22/agile-prototyping-tools-paper-whiteboard- and-balsamiq`.

Johansen T., Gilb T. "From Waterfall to Evolutionary Development (Evo): How we rapidly created faster, more user-friendly, and more productive software products for a competitive multi-national market." INCOSE (International Council on Systems Engineering). 2005.

Kano, N., Nobuhiku S., Fumio T., Shinichi T. "Attractive quality and must-be quality." Journal of the Japanese Society for Quality Control (in Japanese) 14 (2): 39–48. 1984.

Kano. "Kano Model." Accessed September 9, 2014. `http://en.wikipedia.org/wiki/Kano_model`.

Kemerer, C., Chidamber, S. "A Metrics Suite for Object-Oriented Design." *IEEE Transactions of Software Engineering*, Vol 20, No 6. June 1994.

Kernighan, B., Ritchie, D. *The C Programming Language, Second edition.* Upper Saddle River NJ: Prentice Hall, Inc., 1988. See also the usefulness and history of the Hello World program (going back to 1972) at http://en.wikipedia.org/wiki/Hello_world_program.

Knoernschild, K. *Java Application Architecture: Modularity Patterns with Examples Using OSGi.* Upper Saddle River, NJ: Prentice-Hall, 2012.

Kruchten, P. "Architectural Blueprints - The '4+1' View Model of Software Architecture." IEEE Software 12 (6). November, 1995.

Kuhn, T. *The Structure of Scientific Revolutions, second edition.* Foundations of the Unity of Science, series. Chicago, IL: University of Chicago Press, 1970.

Lagestee, L. "Servant Leadership Principles: Fostering a Culture of Agility." *Illustrated Agile.* August, 2014. http://www.illustratedagile.com.

Lalonde, P., Bourgalt, M., Findeli, A. "Building Pragmatist Theories of PM Practice: Theorizing the Act of Project Management." *Project Management Journal,* 2010.

Leffingwell, D. "Mastering the Iteration: An Agile White Paper." Rally Software Development Corp. This paper is an excerpt from Dean's latest book, *Scaling Software Agility: Best Practices for Large Enterprises,* Addison-Wesley, 2007.

Madu, Christian, Chu-Hua Kei, Assumpta Madu. "Setting Priorities for the IT Industry in Taiwan - A Delphi Study." *Long Range Planning,* 1991, v24, n5, pp105–118.

Manifesto. The Agile Manifesto. http://agilemanifesto.org/. 2010. Accessed August 15, 2014.

Martin, R. *Clean Code: A Handbook of Agile Software Craftmanship.* Upper Saddle River: Prentice-Hall, Pearson Education, 2009. pp132–132.

Martin, C. "What is Managerial Courage?" Excerpt from Managers' Synopsis 13b, Manageris blog. December 16, 2012. www.manageris.com/uk-blog-article-95-what-is-managerial-courage.html.

Meyer, B. *Agile!: The Good, the Hype and the Ugly.* Switzerland: Springer International Publishing, 2014.

Morris, P., Geraldi, J. "Managing the Institutional Context for Projects." *Project Management Journal,* December, 2011. pp20–32.

MoSCow. "MoSCoW Method." Accessed September 9, 2014. http://en.wikipedia.org/wiki/MoSCoW_method.

Nagappan, N., Maximilien E., Bhat, T., Williams, L. *Realizing Quality Improvement Through Test Driven Development: Results and Experiences of Four Industrial Teams.* Springer Science + Business Media, LLC, February 27, 2008.

Newman, James, editor. *The World of Mathematics, Volume II.* pp1069-1093. Simon & Schuster, 1956. Includes "The Constants of Nature" by Sir Arthur Stanley Eddington, quote from p1092.

Ottinger, T., Langr, J. "FIRST Properties of Unit Tests." 2012. Accessed July 9, 2014. http://pragprog.com/magazines/2012-01/unit-tests-are-first.

Parkinson, G. *Parkinson's Law and Other Studies in Administration,* Houghton-Mifflin, 1957.

Pitagorsky, G. *Everyone Needs Project Managers and Business Analysts. Project Managemt Times,* Nov 18, 2014. https://www.projecttimes.com/george-pitagorsky/everyone-needs-project-managers-and-business-analysts.html.

PMBOK. *A Guide to the Project Management Body of Knowledge (PMBOK), 5/e.* Pittsburg, PA: Project Management Institute, 2013.

PMI. Accessed June 18, 2014. `http://www.pmi.org/About-Us.aspx`.

Putnam, D. *Haste Makes Waste When You Over-Staff to Achieve Schedule Compression.* Quantitative Software Management. Dec 6, 2005. `http://www.qsm.com/risk_02.html`.

Putnam, L., Myers, W. *Measures for Excellence: Reliable Software On Time, Within Budget.* Upper Saddle River, NY: Yourdon Press, Prentice-Hall, 1992.

Putnam Jr., L. "Big Agile: Enterprise Savior or Oxymoron?" Agile Connection. March 25, 2014. `http://www.agileconnection.com/article/big-agile-enterprise-savior-or-oxymoron`;

Realization Corp. "The Effect of Multitasking on Organizations." Realization Corp, San Jose, CA; study report first published through PR Newswire, August 26, 2013.

Rico, D., Sayani, H., Sone, S. *The Business Value of Agile Software Methods: Maximizing ROI with Just-in-Time Processes and Documentation.* Fort Lauderdale, FL: J. Ross Publishing, 2009.

Rosen, C. "The Myth of Multitasking." *The New Atlantis: A Journal of Technology and Society*, No. 20, Spring 2008, pp105–110. Discusses the various uses and modes of multitasking and why people cannot do it well.

Satzinger, J., Jackson, R., Burd, S. *System Analysis & Design in a Changing World, Third edition.* Boston, MA: Thomson Course Technology, 2004.

Saynisch, M. "Mastering Complexity and Changes in Projects, Economy, and Society via Project Management Second Order (PM-2)." *Project Management Journal.* December, 2010. MSPM Foundation for PM and SPM Consult. Munich, Germany.

Schwaber, K., Beedle, M. *Agile Software Development with SCRUM.* Hoboken, NJ: John Wiley & Sons, 2001.

Schwaber, K., Sutherland, J. *Software in 30 Days.* Hoboken, NJ: John Wiley & Sons, 2012.

Scrum software development. Accessed April 30, 2013. `http://en.wikipedia.org/wiki/Scrum_(software_development)`.

SEI. "CMMI or Agile: Why Not Embrace Both?" Glazer, H., Dalton, J., Anderson, D., Konrad, M., Shrum, S. Technical Note CMU/SEI-2008-TN-003. Pittsurg, PA: Software Engineering Institute, November 2008.

SEI. Software Engineering Institute website. Accessed June 18, 2014. `http://www.sei.cmu.edu/about/`.

Shalloway, A., Beaver, G., Trott, J.R. Lean-Agile *Software Development: Achieving Enterprise Agility.* Pearson Education, 2010.

Sheldrick, Michael. "Automotive Electronics: the Oracle Speaks: Continued Strong Growth." *Electronic News*, April 20, 1992, v38, n1908, p17.

Silverman, D. *In Defense of Multitasking.* Harvard Business Review. June 9, 2010.

Singer, A. "How and Why to Reduce Meetings." *The Future Buzz,* September 23, 2010, `http://thefuturebuzz.com/2010/09/23/reduce-meetings/`.

Standish. "CHAOS Manifesto 2013." The Standish Group International, Inc. Accessed Sept 9, 2014. `http://www.versionone.com/assets/img/files/CHAOSManifesto2013.pdf`.

Symons, C., Peters, A., Cullen, A., Worthington, B. "The Five Essential Metrics for Managing IT." Forrester Research, April 4, 2008.

Taylor, Raymond, David Meinhardt. "Defining Computer Information Needs for Small Business: A Delphi Method." *Journal of Small Business Management.* April, 1985, v23, p3.

TDD. "Test-Driven Development." Accessed July 9, 2014. `http://en.wikipedia.org/wiki/Test-driven_development`.

Tuckman, B. "Developmental sequence in small groups." *Psychological Bulletin* 63 (6): 384–99. 1965. Retrieved August 11, 2015. doi:10.1037/h0022100. PMID 14314073.

User Story. Accessed June 25, 2014. http://en.wikipedia.org/wiki/User_story.

Venezia, P. "No interruptions! Technologist at Work." *InfoWorld*, August 4, 2014. http://www.infoworld.com/print/247487.

Wake, B. *INVEST in Good Stories, and SMART Tasks*. XP123. Exploring Extreme Programming blog, August 17, 2003.

Walker, D., Dart, C. "Frontinus—A Project Manager from the Roman Empire Era." *Project Management Journal*; September, 2011. pp4-16.

Wood, J., Silver, D. *Joint Application Development*. Hoboken, NY: John Wiley & Sons, 1995.

Yourdon, E. *Death March, second edition*. Englewood Cliffs, NJ: Yourdon Press, 2004.

Index

Get the eBook for only $5!

Why limit yourself?

Now you can take the weightless companion with you wherever you go and access your content on your PC, phone, tablet, or reader.

Since you've purchased this print book, we're happy to offer you the eBook in all 3 formats for just $5.

Convenient and fully searchable, the PDF version enables you to easily find and copy code—or perform examples by quickly toggling between instructions and applications. The MOBI format is ideal for your Kindle, while the ePUB can be utilized on a variety of mobile devices.

To learn more, go to www.apress.com/companion or contact support@apress.com.